ROYAL HISTORICAL SOCIETY

STUDIES IN HISTORY

New Series

PATTERNS OF PHILANTHROPY

PATTERNS OF PHILANTHROPY

CHARITY AND SOCIETY
IN NINETEENTH-CENTURY BRISTOL

Martin Gorsky

THE ROYAL HISTORICAL SOCIETY
THE BOYDELL PRESS

First published 1999

A Royal Historical Society publication
Published by The Boydell Press
an imprint of Boydell & Brewer Ltd
PO Box 9, Woodbridge, Suffolk IP12 3DF, UK
and of Boydell & Brewer Inc.
PO Box 41026, Rochester, NY 14604–4126, USA
website: http://www.boydell.co.uk

ISBN 0 86193 245 5

ISSN 0269–2244

A catalogue record for this book is available
from the British Library

Library of Congress Cataloging-in-Publication Data
Gorsky, Martin, 1956–
    Patterns of philanthropy : charity and society in nineteenth-
century Bristol / Martin Gorsky.
        p.   cm. – (Royal Historical Society studies in history. New
series, ISSN 0269–2244)
    Includes bibliographical references and index.
    ISBN 0–86193–245–5 (hardback : alk. paper)
    1. Charities – England – Bristol – History – 19th century.
    2. Voluntarism – England – Bristol – History – 19th century.
    I. Title. II. Series.
HV250.7G67   1999
361.7'09423'93'09034 – dc21   99–36469

This book is printed on acid-free paper

Printed in Great Britain by
St Edmundsbury Press, Bury St Edmunds, Suffolk

TO THE MEMORY OF DAVID GORSKY

Contents

List of Illustrations and Figures

List of Tables

Publication of this volume was aided by a grant from the Scouloudi Foundation, in association with the Institute of Historical Research.

Acknowledgements

I have accumulated many debts in the course of writing this book. The first is that which I owe to Bernard Harris, who first pointed me to the subject, supervised the early stages of the thesis on which the book is largely based and then continued, beyond the call of duty, to read and comment on subsequent drafts. Of equal importance to the project was David Feldman, who took over the supervision of the thesis; I thank him for his patience and his astute criticisms. I am grateful to Martin Daunton and to Pat Thane for encouraging me to develop the dissertation into a monograph and for their guidance on the form that it might take; I thank the latter in particular for her detailed comments. Many other scholars have offered advice and ideas. I was most fortunate to find in Jonathan Barry someone with overlapping interests in Bristol's history who was prepared to give extensive responses to earlier drafts. His influence will be clear from the various citations of his work, and I am most grateful to him for his generosity. Others were kind enough to read and comment on individual chapters or related papers, and of these I wish to thank in particular Bernard Alford, Peter Clark, Bob Humphreys, David Large and Rodney Lowe. Amanda Berry, Mary Fissell and Mary Clare Martin kindly allowed me to read work which at the time was unpublished. My colleague at the University of Portsmouth, John Mohan, has also been instrumental in the development of my ideas on voluntarism. In addition I have been helped by several archivists in the course of the research. John Williams and his team at the Bristol Record Office, along with the staff of the Bristol Reference Library provided an excellent service. For permitting me access to other sources I thank Miss E. Ralph, curator of the St Mary Redcliffe archive, and Mr Hawkins and Mrs Gammage of Bristol Municipal Charities. In addition to their hospitality the BMC trustees were kind enough to make a grant towards the cost of my research. In this respect I must also thank the Institute of Historical Research for electing me a Research Fellow during 1993–4; I am grateful to the Institute both for the material help and for offering me the opportunity to try out some of the ideas at its seminars. I suspect that my greatest debt is that which I owe to my immediate family, Gwen and Adam, for their unflagging love and support during the course of the writing. My chief inspiration though was my father, David Gorsky, who first showed me that history was the key to understanding ourselves in space and time. It is to his memory that I wish to dedicate this book.

Martin Gorsky
June 1999

Abbreviations

BABS	Bristol Auxiliary Bible Society
BCLASS	Bristol and Clifton Ladies Anti-Slavery Society
BI *State*	*The State of the Bristol Infirmary* (also at BRO 35893 21a–e)
BMC	Bristol Municipal Charities
BMC, MB	Bristol Municipal Charities, minute book
BMC, NC	Bristol Municipal Charities, newspaper cuttings
BRL	Bristol Reference Library
BRO	Bristol Record Office
BRO, FS	Bristol Record Office, quarter sessions, friendly society papers
DNB	*Dictionary of national biography*
EcHR	*Economic History Review*
EHR	*English Historical Review*
FFBJ	*Felix Farley's Bristol Journal*
GRB	*The great red book of Bristol*, ed. E. W. W. Veale, Bristol 1951
HJ	*Historical Journal*
LMDMS	Lewin's Mead Domestic Mission Society
LMCWVS	Lewin's Mead Chapel Working and Visiting Society
LRB	*The little red book of Bristol*, ed. F. Bickley, Bristol 1900
Manchee	*The Bristol charities, being the report of the commissioners for inquiring concerning charities in England and Wales so far as relates to the charitable institutions in Bristol*, ed. Thomas John Manchee, i, ii, Bristol 1831
OED	*Oxford English dictionary*
P&P	*Past & Present*
PMFS	Prudent Man's Friend Society
PRO	Public Record Office, Kew
SGFS	South Gloucestershire Friendly Society
Young	*Friendly and Benefit Building Societies Commission: reports of the assistant commissioners, southern and eastern counties, by Sir George Young, Bart*, PP 1874 xxiii, pt 2

Introduction
Philanthropy and Charity in the Nineteenth Century: Theories and Definitions

This book presents a study of voluntary provision in the city of Bristol between about 1800 and 1870. In employing the concept of 'voluntarism' to gather its various themes I follow the definition offered by William Beveridge in 1948: 'The term "Voluntary Action", as used here, means private action, that is to say not under the directions of any authority wielding the power of the State.' And, like Beveridge's, this study is limited to 'Voluntary Action outside each citizen's home for improving the condition of life for him and his fellows'.[1] The main areas under consideration are hierarchical forms of voluntarism, namely the city's old endowed charities and its philanthropic organisations; mutualist associations are largely excluded from the discussion though they have been treated elsewhere.[2] Although Beveridge's work was an attempt to claim an ongoing place for voluntarism within the 'social service state' by emphasising its past contribution, post-war historians of public policy were initially more concerned to explore the growth of statutory provision. However recent years have seen a renewed interest in the theme, partly as a result of critical reflection on earlier work and partly in response to changing political concerns. This chapter will survey the theoretical perspectives which have emerged from the literature, before setting out the themes and questions which the book will address.

Historians and voluntarism

Historians of British social policy writing since the 1980s have sought to 'deteleologise' accounts of the voluntarism before the welfare state.[3] Earlier narratives have been condemned for the assumption that the advance of state agency was an inexorable and desirable aspect of modernisation. Those held to be proponents of this linear, 'welfare state escalator' brand of history stand

---

[1] William Beveridge, *Voluntary action: a report on methods of social advance*, London 1948, 8.
[2] Martin Gorsky, 'Mutual aid and civil society: friendly societies in nineteenth-century Bristol', *Urban History* 25, 3 (1998), 302–22.
[3] Martin Daunton, 'Introduction', and Colin Jones, 'Some recent trends in the history of charity', in Martin Daunton (ed.), *Charity, self-interest and welfare in the English past*, London 1996, 1–22, 51–63, 52.

accused of a Whiggish penchant for seeing the origins of post-war institutions in much earlier statutory initiatives: for instance, the Poor Law Medical Service as antecedent to the NHS.[4] Instead attention is now focused on what Geoffrey Finlayson called the 'moving frontier' of welfare – the constantly changing roles of state, voluntarism, market and family in providing for social needs – and the goal of research has become the exploration of these different forms of provision and the interplay between them.[5] As others have observed, it is questionable whether this 'turn' has dealt justly with earlier welfare historians, who are rarely subjected to anything more systematic than a dismissive footnote and whose main error appears to be the use of Darwinian terminology of 'origins' and 'evolution'.[6] None the less, the 'moving frontier' has several strengths as an organising concept. It directs attention to the contingent role of political action in bringing about change, and it provides a standpoint from which to evaluate such issues as the disadvantaged position of women under the welfare state.[7] It also invites a critical perspective on the historiography of voluntarism.

The first narratives shaping the history of voluntary effort might be placed within the Whig/Liberal tradition in that they were structured by a sense of progress towards modernity. Kirkman Gray argued in 1905 that social provision proceeded through different phases, from an earlier era of endowed charity, to the age of the voluntary society in the eighteenth and nineteenth centuries, culminating in an increasing dominance of the state as the twentieth century approached.[8] The first study of provincial charity, Margaret Simey's work on Liverpool, regarded the Liberal social legislation as rooted in the sense of collective responsibility which voluntarism had fostered.[9] A framework of progress towards the present shaped W. K. Jordan's major text on English philanthropy in the early modern period, which saw benefactors

---

4   Critiques: Frank Prochaska, *The voluntary impulse*, London 1988, pp. xiii–xv; Geoffrey Finlayson, *Citizen, state and social welfare in Britain, 1830–1990*, Oxford 1994, 2–6; David Thomson, 'Welfare and the historians', in Lloyd Bonfield, Richard M. Smith and Keith Wrightson (eds), *The world we have gained: histories of population and social structure*, Oxford 1980, 355–78 at pp. 355–8. See also Derek Fraser, *The evolution of the British welfare state*, London 1973; Ursula Henriques, *Before the welfare state*, London 1979; Ruth G. Hodgkinson, *The origins of the National Health Service: the medical services of the new poor law, 1834–1871*, London 1967; Jeanne L. Brand, *Doctors and the state: the British medical profession and government action in public health, 1870–1912*, Baltimore 1965.
5   Geoffrey Finlayson, 'A moving frontier: voluntarism and the state in British social welfare, 1911–49', *Twentieth-Century British History* i (1990), 183–206; Daunton, 'Introduction', 17.
6   Pat Thane, *Foundations of the welfare state*, 2nd edn, Harlow 1996, 4.
7   Jane Lewis, 'Gender, the family and women's agency in the building of welfare states: the British case', *Social History* xix (1994), 37–55.
8   B. Kirkman Gray, *A history of English philanthropy*, London 1905.
9   Margaret Simey, *Charity rediscovered: a study of philanthropic effort in nineteenth-century Liverpool*, Liverpool 1992 (first publ. as *Charitable effort in Liverpool in the nineteenth century*, Liverpool 1951), ch. x.

as 'most effectively translating their ideals for society into a new philosophy of the state which we denominate liberalism'.[10] The argument pivoted around the origins and impact of the Elizabethan Statute of Charitable Uses, which enshrined the endowed charity as the principal form of redistribution. Endowments took the legal form of a trust, wherein money or land was given by deed or will and the annual income used to fund a scheme designated by the donor. Popular causes were schools, almshouses, hospitals, parish doles of food, money or clothing and loans to bind apprentices. Jordan characterised the new philanthropy as the secularisation of social policy following the dissolution of the monasteries and chantries and made large claims for the overall contribution of the private charitable sector, arguing that between 1560 and 1660 it provided 93 per cent of all national sums spent on the needy, as against a mere 7 per cent from the poor rates.[11] This work was shortly followed by David Owen's *English philanthropy, 1660–1960* which recounted the disillusion with the system of endowment that led to the founding of the Charity Commission in the early nineteenth century.[12] Voluntary charities, particularly hospitals, benevolent schools and poor relief institutions based on subscription, received a thorough, mainly empirical account. When the twentieth century was reached these heroic days were over and philanthropy had become the 'junior partner in the welfare firm'.[13] Both Jordan and Owen presented the motive for philanthropy in functional terms. Donors were simply reacting to changing social conditions, although this response might be influenced by such factors as the religious imperative, humanitarianism or personal example of the elite. Individual agency was in most cases simply unknowable, as Jordan famously put it, 'deep in the recesses of our nature, immune, perhaps happily from the fumbling probing of the historian, and, certainly happily, from the too arrogantly pitched enquiry of the psychoanalyst'.[14]

The new social history of the 1960s and 1970s was less reluctant to draw on social and anthropological theory to explain the motives of voluntary giving. With attention shifting to the concept of class formation and to the tensions associated with industrialisation, both Marxists and non-Marxists saw an active role for philanthropy in mediating social relations. For Thompson charity was one component of the 'theatre of the great' that secured plebeian consent for patrician rule in the eighteenth century.[15] Harold Perkin claimed a decisive shift in the nature of charity emanating from transformations in social structure in the early nineteenth century, which witnessed the disappearance of 'personal, face-to-face relationships of patronage' character-

---

10 W. K. Jordan, *Philanthropy in England, 1480–1660*, London 1959, 18, 321.
11 Ibid. 40–1.
12 David Owen, *English philanthropy, 1660–1960*, London 1964.
13 Ibid. ch. xix.
14 Jordan, *Philanthropy in England*, 44.
15 E. P. Thompson, *Customs in common*, London 1991, 46, 72, 74.

istic of the 'old society' in which alms were dispensed by 'the squire's wife and daughters'. The 'abdication of the governors' from paternalist commitment and the harsher attitudes to poverty associated with the aspiring middle class, gave rise to new forms of voluntary effort.[16] A similar identification of charitable initiative with changing class relationships informed Gareth Stedman Jones's study of mid-Victorian London, where 'old methods of social control based on the model of the squire, the parson, face-to-face relations, deference and paternalism, found less and less reflection in the urban reality'.[17] Themes of domination and authority were central to John Foster's reading of philanthropic agencies, such as the temperance movement, Sunday Schools and Mechanics Institutes, as weapons used by urban elites to assert hegemony over a potentially revolutionary workforce.[18] A similar case was made for the culture of 'respectability' promulgated to the Sheffield working class.[19] As the organising concept of social control gained favour in histories of policing and the suppression of popular leisure, so interpretation of philanthropy stressed its role as an instrument of class authority. For example Phillip McCann's work on education argued that where literacy was delivered through charity and Sunday Schools it tended to sustain the *status quo*, particularly if laced with heavy doses of evangelical religion.[20]

The most recent and schematic articulation of the relationship between voluntary charity and the 'birth of class' is set out in the works of R. J. Morris and Theodore Koditschek.[21] Class formation was defined by Morris as a fundamental shift in the way the middle class (a social structure of 'perceived regularities in social actions and relationships') experienced and thought about power relationships – political, ideological, cultural and economic. The transformation occurred between 1780 and 1850, with the 1830s the most intense phase of the project to assert 'group identity and authority'. Koditschek's formulation explicitly linked the new associational ethos with material concerns of the 'entrepreneurial bourgeoisie', whose identity was buttressed by the 'individualistic, salvation-centred brand of spirituality' of

[16] Harold Perkin, *Origins of modern English society*, London 1969, 50–1, 120–2, 183–95, 224–5. See also Mary E. Fissell, *Patients, power, and the poor in eighteenth-century Bristol*, Cambridge 1991.
[17] Gareth Stedman Jones, *Outcast London: a study in the relationship between classes in Victorian society*, Oxford 1971, 14.
[18] John Foster, *Class struggle in the industrial revolution: early industrial capitalism in three English towns*, London 1974.
[19] Caroline Reid, 'Middle-class values and working-class culture in nineteenth-century Sheffield: the pursuit of respectability', in S. Pollard and C. Holmes (eds), *Essays in the economic and social history of South Yorkshire*, Sheffield 1976, 275–95 at pp. 280–7.
[20] Phillip McCann, 'Popular education, socialisation and social control: Spitalfields 1812–1824', in Phillip McCann (ed.), *Popular education and socialisation in the nineteenth century*, London 1977, 1–40.
[21] R. J. Morris, 'Voluntary societies and British urban elites, 1780–1850: an analysis', *HJ* xxvi (1983), 95–118, and *Class, sect and party: the making of the British middle class: Leeds, 1820–1850*, Manchester 1990.

the nonconformist sects. Fortified by religious associationalism the middle class established 'spin-off' agencies, religious and secular, in which the liberal ideal of 'secular self-help' was promoted, and poverty viewed as moral failing.[22] Morris laid particular stress on the political and cultural dissatisfaction, along with the fear and conflict, which urban life in this period provoked, and suggested that the ideal medium for resolving these tensions and mobilising collective action was the voluntary society. Its form and conventions provided a 'neutral area of public life', in which the elite could lead all members of the middle class, regardless of status level, sect or party, and weld a coherent identity based on a 'common framework of assumptions'.[23] Power and authority could then be asserted in a dangerous, unpredictable and chaotic urban environment, and the consent of the working class for the new industrial order won. The 'British bourgeois ideology', achieved through voluntary action in this critical period, set the agenda for public life over the next century.[24]

Other historians of philanthropy drew from classical sociology the themes of the gift relationship and the principle of reciprocity. A comprehensive theory of the gift was first formulated by Marcel Mauss, based on observation of ritual prestation among traditional peoples, notably the 'potlatch' ceremony of the Kwakuitl Indians.[25] Salient features were the social obligation to give, as a register of status, and the obligation to repay: 'face is lost forever if it (repayment) is not made'. Mauss concluded that ritual gift exchange was a means of asserting status and establishing social structure, and he asked 'Are we certain that our own position is different and that wealth with us is not first and foremost a means of controlling others?'[26] The principle of reciprocity in the gift relationship was also suggested by Georg Simmel in his analysis of poverty. He defined 'the poor' as a social group characterised not by lack of material goods in an absolute sense, but by the assistance they receive (or should receive) because of this lack. Hence the purpose of giving to the poor is to 'mitigate certain extreme manifestations of social differentiation, so that the social structure may continue to be based on this differentiation'.[27] The means by which this is achieved is through gratitude: 'If every grateful action, which lingers on from good turns received in the past, were suddenly eliminated, society . . . would break apart.'[28] More recent applications have explored the gift within the family to assert its function as an

[22] Theodore Koditschek, Class formation and urban-industrial society: Bradford, 1750–1850, Cambridge 1990, chs ix, x, xi, esp. pp. 247–51, 287, 268–9.
[23] Morris, Class, sect and party, chs i, vii, x, xi, xiii, esp. pp. 1, 5, 323, 324.
[24] Ibid. 7.
[25] Marcel Mauss, The gift, Paris 1925, trans. I. Cunnison, repr. London 1967.
[26] Ibid. 37–41, 73.
[27] Georg Simmel, 'The poor', in K. Wolff (ed.), The sociology of Georg Simmel, first publ. 1950, trans. C. Jacobson, repr. New York 1964, 155.
[28] Idem, 'Faithfulness and gratitude', ibid. 259.

agency of socialisation, for example through its capacity to determine gender norms and establish reciprocal obligation between parent and child.[29]

Gift theory usefully augmented interpretations of philanthropy based upon class formation and interraction. If the purpose of the gift is to convey status then the function of public subscription lists can be understood as an announcement of membership of an elite, while the concept of reciprocity helped explain the role of charity in securing the worker's consent for the inequities of capitalist society. Thus Howard Newby saw charity as a vital aspect of the ingrained proletarian respect for hierarchy which he termed the 'deferential dialectic'.[30] Stedman Jones's application of the gift thesis dealt particularly with the Charity Organisation Society in late Victorian London, a group set up to co-ordinate charitable activity and ensure that recipients were only the genuinely needy. He argued that it arose from 'the deformation of the gift', the perception that the reciprocity of the charity relationship was being scorned by a feckless underclass who treated eleemosynary benevolence as a right, and made no effort to conform to the norms of respectability, self-help and temperance which the donors expected.[31]

Rethinking philanthropy

Thus far then it has been possible to place histories of voluntarism within a Whig/Liberal tradition or a model of nineteenth-century society premised upon class conflict. The latter, with its emphasis on philanthropy as a power relationship between different economic groups, continues to influence research.[32] However, recent revisionism has thrown the validity of both these models into question. In addition to the theoretical critique by Finlayson and others, the assumption of linear progress – from monastic to endowed charity to voluntary societies to welfare state – has been challenged by empirical work. We now have a more diverse notion of late medieval and early modern charity than that suggested by Jordan, embracing provisions made by the gilds, casual offering to beggars, hospitality, funeral alms, charity ales and

[29] B. Schwartz, 'The social psychology of the gift', *American Journal of Sociology* lxxiii (1967), 1–11; Claude Levi-Strauss, 'The principle of reciprocity', in L. Coser and B. Rosenberg (eds), *Sociological theory*, New York 1965, 61–9; James G. Carrier, 'The rituals of Christmas giving', in Daniel Miller (ed.), *Unwrapping Christmas*, Oxford 1993, 55–74.

[30] Howard Newby, 'The deferential dialectic', *Comparative Studies in Society and History* xvii (1975), 139–64.

[31] Stedman Jones, *Outcast London*, chs xiii, xiv, xv.

[32] M. J. D. Roberts, 'Reshaping the gift relationship: the London Mendicity Society and the suppression of begging in England, 1818–1869', *International Review of Social History* xxxvi (1991), 201–31; Neil Evans, 'Urbanisation, elite attitudes and philanthropy: Cardiff, 1850–1914', ibid. xxvii (1982), 292; Meg Whittle, 'Philanthropy in Preston: the changing face of charity in a nineteenth-century provincial town', unpubl. PhD diss. Lancaster 1990; Richard H. Trainor, *Black Country elites: the exercise of authority in an industrial area, 1830–1900*, Oxford 1993, ch. vii, esp. pp. 351–3.

paternalist price-fixing in times of dearth.[33] Investigation of the Old Poor Law has thoroughly overturned Jordan's more extravagant claims for private charity's supremacy over public provision, and his failure to adjust his calculation of the value of endowments for inflation has now been exhaustively discussed.[34] More controversially, work on care of the elderly and the Old Poor Law's medical services has suggested that the period between the Poor Law Amendment in 1834 and the Liberal welfare reforms is most notable for its meanness and restraint of public provision, rather than its place in the march of progress.[35] The emphasis is now on the diversity of systems of relief, the complex interplay between legislation and private effort and the importance of long-term continuities: 'attitudes we have inherited and must still largely adhere to since they could be as old as humanity itself'.[36]

The analysis of philanthropy in terms of class formation and class tension has also become more problematic, following fundamental reappraisals of social history's core assumptions. Orthodoxies of class formation have been attacked on two fronts, firstly by a reconsideration of how identity is constituted, and secondly by revised understanding of the material changes that underpinned both Marxist and liberal accounts. Historians of the linguistic turn have forcefully challenged correlations between a notional working-class identity arising from 'steam power and the cotton mill', and the ordinary person's subjective understanding of the social order.[37] Instead revisionists propose that we go 'beyond class' to understand social identities in terms of a

---

[33] Miri Rubin, *Charity and community in medieval Cambridge*, Cambridge 1987; N. P. Tanner, *The Church in late medieval Norwich*, Toronto 1984; J. J. Scarisbrick, *The Reformation and the English people*, Oxford 1984, ch. ii; Judith Bennett, 'Conviviality and charity in medieval and early modern England', *P&P* cxxxiv (1992), 19–41; Ben R. McRee, 'Charity and gild solidarity in late medieval England', *Journal of British Studies* xxxii (1993), 195–225; Felicity Heal, 'The idea of hospitality in early modern England', *P&P* cii (1984), 66–93; Susan Brigden, 'Religion and social obligation in early sixteenth-century London', ibid. ciii (1984), 67–112; Felicity Heal, *Hospitality in early modern England*, Oxford 1990, ch. vi; Barbara Harvey, *Living and dying in England, 1100–1540*, Oxford 1993, ch. i; John Walter, 'The social economy of dearth in early modern England', in John Walter and Roger Schofield (eds), *Famine, disease and the social order in early modern society*, Cambridge 1989, 75–128.

[34] Paul Slack, *Poverty and policy in Tudor and Stuart England*, London 1988, ch. viii; W. Bittle and R. Todd Lane, 'Inflation and philanthropy in England: a re-assessment of W. K. Jordan's data', *EcHR* 2nd ser. xxix (1976), 203–10; J. F. Hadwin, 'Deflating philanthropy', and comments by D. C. Coleman and J. D. Gould, ibid. xxxi (1978), 105–20.

[35] David Thomson, 'The decline of social welfare: falling state support for the elderly since early Victorian times', *Ageing and Society* iv (1984), 451–82, criticised by E. H. Hunt, 'Paupers and pensioners: past and present', ibid. ix (1990), 407–30; Irvine Loudon, *Medical care and the general practitioner, 1750–1850*, Oxford 1986, ch. xi.

[36] Marjorie K. McIntosh, 'Local responses to the poor in late medieval and Tudor England', *Continuity and Change* iii (1988), 209–45; Peter Laslett, 'Preface', in Margaret Pelling and Richard M. Smith (eds), *Life, death and the elderly: historical perspectives*, London 1991, p. xv.

[37] Adrian Wilson, 'A critical portrait of social history', in Adrian Wilson (ed.), *Rethinking social history: English society, 1570–1920, and its interpretation*, Manchester 1993, 9–58;

7

broadly based populism.[38] Meanwhile attempts at a synthetic treatment of the making of middle-class consciousness have failed to agree a chronology for the emergence of class identity or to establish its homegeneity.[39] For example, it is not clear that the new gender roles and domestic ideology that Leonore Davidoff and Catherine Hall discerned were really peculiar to the middle classes; it is also possible that there were two distinct middle-class identities, one metropolitan, the other provincial; or, it may be that 'making' was a constant process, punctuated by the cyclical 'rediscovery' of urban bourgeois values.[40] Old certainties about the ascendancy of a unitary 'entre-preneurial ideal' have also been undermined by economic historians. Work on tax and probate reveals that the wealth generated by revolutionised indus-tries was always less than old money, in land, finance and public office, while the 'gradualist' reappraisal of the chronology of industrialisation now high-lights regional diversity and the importance of the service sector.[41] What does all this mean for philanthropy? First, it raises doubts about the primacy of explanations of the growth of voluntarism couched in terms of changing class identities and of a rapid transition from gentle paternalism to hard-nosed social control. Instead it invites fuller consideration of the importance of longer-run continuities in urban associational life. Secondly, by emphasis-ing shared values cutting across class, it opens the way for interpretations of philanthropy as a manifestation of social consensus.

Indeed, the depiction of charity as an aspect of social harmony in the 'peacable kingdom' long predates the current revisionism. McCord dismissed the idea that the gift was inevitably laden with other concerns, and proffered a nominalist reading where philanthropy was just what it claimed to be –

Gareth Stedman Jones, 'Re-thinking Chartism', in his *Languages of class: studies in English working-class history, 1832–1982*, Cambridge 1983.

[38] Patrick Joyce, *Visions of the people: industrial England and the question of class, 1848–1914*, Cambridge 1991.

[39] Peter Earle, *The making of the English middle class: business, society and family life in London, 1660–1730*, London 1989; Leonore Davidoff and Catherine Hall, *Family fortunes: men and women of the English middle class, 1780–1850*, London 1987.

[40] Amanda Vickery, 'Golden age to separate spheres?: a review of the categories and chro-nology of English women's history', *HJ* xxxvi (1993), 393–401; Dror Wahrman, 'National society, communal culture: an argument about the recent historiography of eighteenth-century Britain', *Social History* xvii (1992), 43–72, and 'Virtual representation: parliamen-tary reporting and languages of class in the 1790s', *P&P* cxxxvi (1992), 83–113; Jonathan Barry, 'Bourgeois collectivism?: urban association and the middling sort', in Jonathan Barry and Christopher Brooks (eds), *The middling sort of people: culture, society and politics in England, 1550–1800*, London 1994, 84–112 at p. 112.

[41] W. D. Rubinstein (ed.), *Elites and the wealthy in modern British history*, Brighton 1987; P. J. Cain and A. G. Hopkins, *British imperialism: innovation and expansion 1688–1914*, London 1993, chs iii, iv; N. F. R. Crafts, *British economic growth during the industrial revolution*, Oxford 1985; E. A. Wrigley, *Continuity, chance and change: the character of the industrial revolution in England*, Cambridge 1988; C. H. Lee, *The British economy since 1700: a macro-economic per-spective*, Cambridge 1986.

open-hearted generosity.[42] Brian Harrison noted the extent of working-class involvement in charity, suggesting that the stabilisation of mid-Victorian Britain was founded less upon authority and submission, than on shared values generated from below as well as above.[43] The work of Frank Prochaska has reasserted these interpretations.[44] Prochaska acknowledges the use of philanthropy by the middle class to justify inequalities and elicit loyalty and accepts some degree of rejectionism on the part of recipients. However, this is set against the larger success of voluntarism in providing a forum for the working class to join 'together with the higher classes in a common cause'.[45] 'Charitable co-operation' is discerned in a range of activities and institutions, from collections for disasters, to mothers' meetings, to Bible societies, in which working-class members were present, as small subscribers, as enthusiastic recipients and as workers, such as Bible women, mission visitors and collectors. Inspiration for this involvement came from a yearning to improve social standing, and the result was social integration. Middle-class motives of social control were present but ineffective and insignificant given 'shared values', such as the belief that 'fitness, decency and independence were wholesome'.[46]

This more generous appraisal of voluntarism has attracted considerable interest, particularly in the context of late-twentieth century welfare debates. Indeed, Prochaska's work is couched in the rhetoric of rehabilitating a theme hitherto 'distorted by collectivist perspectives'.[47] The advance of state agency is not explained in terms of the limitations of voluntarism but rather as the outcome of political struggle between 'collectivists' and 'voluntarists', terms often deployed normatively rather than situated historically. And, in several respects, Prochaska views the eclipse of voluntarism as a cause for regret.[48] A more explicitly ideological literature has also emerged, largely from the Institute of Economic Affairs, which appraises the voluntary sector from the standpoint of New Right anti-statism.[49] The application of Friedmanite economics to philanthropy was pioneered by E. G. West, who argued that the human capital needs of industrialising Britain were successfully met by an elementary education system financed by parental fees and charitable

[42] N. McCord, 'Aspects of the relief of poverty in early nineteenth-century Britain', in R. M. Hartwell and others, *The long debate on poverty*, London 1972, 91–109 at p. 108.

[43] Brian Harrison, 'Philanthropy and the Victorians', *Victorian Studies* ix (1966), 353–74, rev. in his *Peacable kingdom: stability and change in modern Britain*, Oxford 1983, 217–59.

[44] Prochaska, *Voluntary impulse*, and 'Philanthropy', in F. M. L. Thompson (ed.), *The Cambridge social history of Britain, 1750–1950*, III: *Social agencies and institutions*, Cambridge 1990, 357–93.

[45] Ibid. 366, 369, 377, 379.

[46] Ibid. 366, 370–1.

[47] Ibid. 359; F. K. Prochaska, *Philanthropy and the hospitals of London: the King's Fund, 1897–1990*, Oxford 1992, p. vii.

[48] Ibid. ch. v, and *Voluntary impulse*, ch. v at pp. 87–8.

[49] Arthur Seldon (ed.), *Re-privatising welfare: after the lost century*, London 1996; D. G. Green, *Re-inventing civil society: the rediscovery of welfare without politics*, London 1993.

donations.[50] Revisionist surveys of health insurance, hospitals and education claim that private finance would have surged ahead like 'galloping horses' had it not been for the untimely intervention of a monolithic state bureaucracy.[51] The self-reliance and sterner moral fibre of Victorian Britons is contrasted unadmiringly with the dependency and 'contract culture' of the welfare state.[52]

British social histories of charity have therefore been heavily determined by the authors' underlying assumptions of class relations and the desirability of state welfare. Can economic theory offer a more dispassionate guide to research questions? Economic analysis of philanthropy is dominated by American scholars seeking to explain the existence of a large non-profit sector in such areas as health and treatment of the elderly. The starting point is Burton Weisbrod's thesis that the non-profit sector emerges to provide public goods in conditions of state and market failure. State failure occurs when government is unable to command sufficient electoral support to direct public funds towards a particular type of public good. Private markets are not a satisfactory alternative as the collective consumption goods they provide have fewer external benefits and are thus less socially efficient. The development of a voluntary sector is therefore the option pursued by 'dissatisfied customers' who demand collective goods which government cannot supply.[53] Weisbrod also predicts that voluntary rather than state provision is more likely to occur in societies with greater cultural heterogeneity, where the diversity of consumer demands will militate against a political consensus on state intervention.[54] Henry Hansmann has augmented the explanation of market performance with the notion of contract failure. Purchasers of public goods may be uncomfortable with market provision due to the asymmetry of information between consumer and producer. Unlike articles of individual consumption, the adequacy of services provided in such areas as health, childcare and nursing is hard to evaluate, particularly if the purchaser – parent or relative – is often not present. Managers of commercial institutions might exploit this situation and maximise their profits by reducing the quality of service. There is no such incentive in non-profits, which do not distribute excess earnings to reward individuals. The 'contract' between non-profit and consumer therefore offers greater assurance.[55] Both these

[50] E. G. West, 'Resource allocation and growth in early nineteenth-century British education', *EcHR* 2nd ser. xxxiii (1970), 68–95.

[51] Seldon, *Re-privatising welfare*, p. xiii.

[52] Gertrude Himmelfarb, *The demoralisation of society: from Victorian virtues to modern values*, London 1995; Robert Whelan, *The corrosion of charity: from moral renewal to contract culture*, London 1996.

[53] Burton A. Weisbrod, 'Toward a theory of the voluntary non-profit sector in a three-sector economy', in Edmund S. Phelps (ed.), *Altruism, morality and economic theory*, New York 1975, 171–95.

[54] Ibid. 190–1.

[55] Henry B. Hansmann, 'The role of nonprofit enterprise', *Yale Law Journal* lxxxix (1980), 835–901.

theories depict the non-profit organisation as a residual which emerges only in the event of state and market failure. Salamon rejects this, pointing to the long-standing 'partnership in public service' between state and non-profit sector. He suggests instead that voluntary institutions emerge first because they are the most desirable means of developing new forms of social provision. Their principal advantage is that they are localised and small-scale and therefore able to foster the sense of social obligation needed to inaugurate collective welfare projects. Government intervenes when the collective need is well established but where 'voluntary failure' prevents the non-profit sector from meeting it successfully.[56]

Economists have also examined the performance of non-profits, and work on hospitals in particular has demonstrated inherent difficulties of voluntarism. For example, because excess profits cannot be used to reward management there is a lack of incentive to manage effectively, hence the sector's failure to respond to changing patterns of demand as rapidly as private competitors.[57] Salamon's approach implies a series of both strengths and weaknesses.[58] Voluntary institutions, unlike statutory bodies, are not obliged to provide an even or equitable service and can target their provision to the needs of marginal or unpopular groups, while their smaller scale frees them from excessive bureaucracy and allows them to deliver a more personalised service. However, they are also vulnerable to 'philanthropic insufficiency' – the difficulty of generating adequate funding. This may arise from the tendency of potential donors to 'free ride' on the backs of the more generous, from a mismatch between local needs and local wealth, or merely from the whims of the benevolent in a given year. A second failure is 'philanthropic particularism', the likelihood that goods provided by non-profits will not be universally available but will go to specific groups, such as the 'deserving poor' or persons of a particular ethnicity or religion. Third, the demands of time and money required for voluntary sector involvement means that leadership often falls to those already holding wealth and power. Thus 'philanthropic paternalism' increases the dependence of the poor on the rich and may be resented by the needy as demeaning. A final 'voluntary failure' arises because workers may be attracted to the sector as a religious or moral calling; there is therefore a risk of 'philanthropic amateurism' where lack of training in areas such as management or social casework may lead to ineffectiveness. Thus government is likely to intervene to support or supersede non-profits when voluntary effort has won public acceptance for a given service, but compulsion is needed to secure financial support, universal provision and greater efficiency.

---

56 Lester M. Salamon, *Partners in public service: government-nonprofit relations in the modern welfare state*, London 1995.
57 Kenneth W. Clarkson, 'Some implications of property rights in hospital management', *Journal of Law and Economics* xv (1972), 363–84.
58 Salamon, *Partners in public service*, 45–7.

What can these theories of non-profits offer the historian? Thus far they have been presented either as static models of equilibrium adjustment or as responses to contemporary policy debates. Weisbrod has glanced back briefly to early modern England to characterise Jordan's upsurge of philanthropy as the work of undersatisfied consumers whose production of collective goods preceded state action; government provision came later as economic growth and changing 'population demand characteristics' permitted intervention.[59] His claims for the significance of cultural heterogeneity to the size of the voluntary sector also have temporal as well as spatial implications. Hansmann's insistence upon conscious consumer choice between market and non-profit limits the historical flexibility of his thesis to such areas as education where both types of provision coexisted.[60] None the less the core idea that voluntary institutions gained public support because they were regarded as trustworthy and accountable is one which might be tested more broadly. Salamon's conceptual framework is also promising, because it acknowledges the strengths of the voluntary sector without endorsing conservative critiques of state welfare, and it accepts the limitations of voluntarism without celebrating the superiority of statist solutions. These approaches are interested in questions of philanthropy's conflictual or consensual role in society only insofar as they bear on the larger issue of the effectiveness of voluntarism as a means of providing public goods. They also preclude a Whiggish reading of the rise of state agency because they assume the continuing coexistence of state and voluntary sector, in which responsibility shifts from one to the other in response to fresh social needs and the changing political consensus on which public goods government should supply.

Defining terms and subject matter

Before returning to the question of how the historiography informs the present work it is also worth discussing the way in which earlier writers drew the parameters of the subject. Jordan, bound by his methodology of quantifying charitable gifts in probate, equated early modern philanthropy with endowment. Owen, with the destination of the welfare state in mind, concentrated predominantly on health, education and poor relief, and was subsequently criticised for failing to place Victorian philanthropy in its broad context of religious endeavour and social reform movements.[61] Prochaska took this approach even further, also claiming for philanthropy familial care of relatives and dependants, and working-class neighbourhood sharing: 'It is suggestive to think of the history of philanthropy broadly as the history of

---

[59] Weisbrod, 'Non-profit sector', 185–6.
[60] Hansmann, 'Nonprofit enterprise', 896–7.
[61] Harrison, *Peacable kingdom*, 220–1.

kindness'.[62] However, despite this extensive subject area his work does not deal with the old endowed charities, and indeed, with few exceptions, the charitable endowment – ancient and modern – is absent from the post-Owen historiography.[63] Partly this is because accounts which privilege ideology as the dynamo of philanthropic effort cannot integrate discussion of the charitable trust in any obvious way, and partly because case studies of philanthropy have dwelt on cities which grew rapidly and thus were unusual in not having a significant number of endowments.[64] There is therefore an inconsistency and arbitrariness in the way the theme has been defined.

This makes it essential to pin down the meaning of the word 'philanthropy' more tightly. According to etymologists the earliest usage in Ancient Greece, in Plato for example, signified the love of the gods for humanity, so the notion of a relationship between powerful and powerless has been present from the outset.[65] As it diffused through classical civilisations to become a part of west European vocabulary, from about AD 500, it was possible to distinguish four meanings: 'first, a philosophical abstraction; second a political attribute; third, charity directed to the individual in want; fourth, philanthropy expressed in organised institutions'.[66] By the eighteenth century Dr Johnson's *Dictionary of the English language* offered 'love of mankind; good nature', while the French *Encyclopédie* coupled a recognition of philanthropy as a moral virtue, an imitation of divine love, with Enlightenment scepticism: 'The second kind is where one ingratiates oneself with others to please them, capture them and govern them. In this last practice, so common amongst polite society, it is not others who one loves, but oneself.'[67]

The word 'charity' has a rather different semantic history, although in contemporary usage it is almost interchangeable with 'philanthropy'.[68] It derives from the Latin *caritas*, whose root is *carus* meaning 'dear'.[69] The Bible established the word as a moral sentiment, love, in the sense of mutual caring, though the feeling was initially distinguished from the act: 'though I bestow all my goods to feed the poor . . . and have not charity, it profiteth me nothing' (Corinthians xiii). Common to both the Christian and Islamic traditions is the idea of charity as an exchange of wealth between have and have-not,

---

62 Prochaska, 'Philanthropy', 360.
63 R. Tompson, *The Charity Commission and the age of reform*, London 1979; Anne Digby, *British welfare policy*, London 1989, 87; P. Searby, 'The relief of the poor in Coventry, 1830–63', *HJ* xx (1977), 356–8.
64 Harrison, *Peacable kingdom*, 22; Morris, *Class, sect and party*, 169–70.
65 D. Constantelos, *Byzantine philanthropy and social welfare*, New Jersey 1968, chs i, ii; Greek root: φιλανθρωπια.
66 Ibid. 18.
67 Dr Johnson, *Dictionary of the English language*, London 1831, s.v 'philanthropy'; *Encyclopédie ou dictionnaire raisonné des sciences, des arts et des métiers: tome douzième*, Paris 1765, s.v. 'philanthropie'. I thank Tamizan Savill for her translation.
68 Prochaska, 'Philanthropy', 360.
69 Raymond Williams, *Keywords*, Glasgow 1976, 45–6.

whose importance was bound up with the chance of salvation it offered the donor.[70] In England the religious connotation gradually made way for an understanding which emphasised social obligation, as in Francis Bacon's injunction to free-riders in 1625: 'Defer not charities till death, for certainly he that doth so is rather liberal of another man's than his own.'[71] By the early nineteenth century 'charity' would have been understood variously as the virtue of Christian love, familial tenderness, 'liberality to the poor', and – in its precise legal sense – as an institution established by endowment.[72]

So, both philanthropy and charity are loose terms which have changed their meaning over time, and can bear a range of meanings at the same time. It is therefore helpful to begin by asking how contemporaries perceived the world of voluntary giving. Firstly, what of the old adage 'Charity begins at home', and its implication that inter-familial care was a type of philanthropy?[73] The difficulty here lies in disentangling philanthropy from custom, inter-generational life-cycle dependency, community norms and mutual obligation as motives for familial care. For example, the poor law regarded familial responsibility as obligation, not kindness, and the threat of prosecution for failure to support certain categories of relative remained up until the National Assistance Act of 1948.[74] Indeed, evidence that it was not the family but the community at large which shouldered the burden of care for the elderly may be discerned in the more distant past, for example in the contractual basis for 'retirement' operated by medieval manorial courts.[75] Secondly, what of the argument that philanthropy was a common feature of working-class life? There is no doubt that the working classes were proactively involved in such areas as the Sunday Schools and adult education, not to mention temperance; it must also be the case that many of the people who contributed to church collections for a charitable purpose, or joined a Band of Hope procession, were not especially well-off. It is less certain that 'philanthropy' should also embrace neighbourly activities like the sharing of food and clothing, the whip-round in the pub, or home-visiting needy acquaintances. The general verdict of historians studying working-class behaviour is that neighbourhood sharing was not benevolence but rather a reciprocal mechanism developed in close residential communities vulnerable to poverty

---

[70] References to charity in the *Koran* may be found at xxx. 38, 39; lxiv. 16.

[71] Francis Bacon, 'Of riches', in *Essays*, 1625.

[72] Johnson, *Dictionary*, *s.v* 'charity'.

[73] Harrison, *Peacable kingdom*, 220; Prochaska, 'Philanthropy', 360–2.

[74] M. A. Crowther 'Family responsibility and state responsibility in Britain before the welfare state', *HJ* xxv (1982), 131–45; David Thomson, ' "I am not my father's keeper": families and the elderly in nineteenth-century England', *Law and History Review* ii (1984), 267–86.

[75] Richard M. Smith, 'The manorial court and the elderly tenant in late medieval England', in Pelling and Smith, *Life, death and the elderly*, 39–61.

and urban disamenity.[76] Help for a neighbour was not simply an act of compassion, but motivated by the awareness that soon it might be the giver requiring help from the erstwhile recipient; this was mutual aid, not philanthropy, and its reprocity tangible, not spiritual.

A qualitative difference between vertical and hierarchical redistribution was well understood by contemporaries. Engels described it thus:

> As to the efficiency of this philanthropy . . . the poor are relieved much more by the poor than by the bourgeoisie; and such relief given by an honest proletarian who knows himself what it is to be hungry . . . such help has a wholly different ring to it from the carelessly tossed alms of the luxurious bourgeoisie.[77]

This differentiation was also accepted by the largest national friendly society, the Ancient Order of Foresters, whose teachings urged its members to practise 'benevolence'. This was defined as: 'a kind act, performed to one in necessity, without any accompanying feeling of selfishness' and distinct from 'kindness' where a man 'shared that which was not necessary for himself', and different again from 'charity' where a man gave 'out of his abundance what he could have well spared'.[78] These nuanced conceptions of the gift relationship are not easily captured by a capacious definition of philanthropy.

Figure 1 sets out the constituent parts of the voluntary arena which will be discussed in this book, dividing it into three categories bounded by the statutory and private sectors. Familial care of dependent relatives is placed in the private sector, and here too are the market choices which could act as alternatives to voluntary institutions. Rich and poor alike could pay for schooling, at least until the campaign against the dame schools removed alternatives to state and charity provision in the 1870s, while medical treatment was also available to suit the patient's pocket.[79] The middle-class solution to the insecurities of old age was to live on investment income, or, increasingly, to purchase life assurance.[80] The state's contribution was not limited to the poor

76 Ellen Ross, 'Survival networks: women's neighbourhood sharing in London before World War I', *History Workshop Journal* xv (1983), 4–27. See also Catharina Lis and Hugo Soly, 'Neighbourhood social change in West European cities, sixteenth to nineteenth centuries', *International Review of Social History* xxxviii (1993), 1–30; Bill Bramwell, 'Public space and local communities: the example of Birmingham, 1840–1880', in Gerry Kearns and Charles J. Withers (eds), *Urbanising Britain: essays on class and community in the nineteenth century*, Cambridge 1991, 31–54; Michael Anderson, *Family structure in nineteenth-century Lancashire*, Cambridge 1971.
77 F. Engels, *The condition of the working class in England*, London 1882, 304.
78 *Formularies and lectures of the Ancient Order of Foresters Friendly Society*, n.d., based on the 1857 Formularies; Trygve R. Tholfsen, *Working-class radicalism in mid-Victorian England*, London 1976, 295.
79 Philip W. Gardner *The lost elementary schools of Victorian England*, London 1984; Loudon, *Medical care*.
80 R. J. Morris, 'The middle class and the property cycle during the industrial revolution', in T. C. Smout (ed.), *The search for wealth and stability*, London 1979, 91–113.

Figure 1
Social provision in the nineteenth century

State	a) Charity	b) Voluntary societies/ Subscriber institutions	c) Mutual Aid	Private
Poor Law	Endowments: Almshouses Schools		Neighbourhood sharing	Family obligation
Friendly society	Loan monies Doles/gifts	Missions Visiting Hospitals		Market: Health
Registry	Sermons	Schools Homes	Friendly Societies	Education
Charity Commissions		Campaigns		Unearned/rentier income
Education Acts		Building societies Savings banks Annuitant societies Penny banks Patronised friendly societies		Life assurance

law, but also took in the Charity Commissions and a raft of legislation from 1793 to encourage the formation of friendly societies, savings banks and building societies. The education grant, which started in 1833, had only a tiny impact on the funding of schools initially, but from the 1850s a series of Youthful Offenders Acts instigated state funding for Ragged Schools and reformatories, then in 1870 came Forster's Act which established school boards, and triggered a final burst of charity spending on denominational schools.

Figure 1's Voluntary sector first embraces 'charity', which in the nineteenth century was understood to refer to institutions established by endowment. As observed, this theme has been neglected because in many cities the old charitable trusts did not make a great contribution to the relief of poverty. Table 1a gives some comparative figures drawn from the findings of the Brougham Commission, the first comprehensive charity commission, reporting between 1819 and 1837: comparison of income from Bradford's and Liverpool's endowments with those in Bristol illustrates the diversity of urban experience. Table 1b suggests that the contribution of voluntarism nationally cannot be properly comprehended without reference to endowed charity. It shows that in 1837, the last year of the Brougham Commission, the amount generated by endowments towards social spending was approximately 25 per cent of state welfare expenditure. This is an absolute minimum, because many of the charities investigated earlier on had reformed their management and vastly increased yield, to the extent that their income had almost doubled by the 1870s when the next commission reported. The relative value

Table 1
The extent of endowed charity in England and Wales, 1837.

1a: Annual income of endowed charities in selected cities, 1837.

London *	£ 120,846
Bristol	£ 19,874
Manchester	£ 12,513
Coventry	£ 10,367
Birmingham	£ 5,677
Bradford	£ 894
Liverpool	£ 509

1b: Endowed charity and public expenditure

Poor Law Expenditure	£ 4,045,000
Education Grant	£ 20,000
Total	£ 4,095,000

Brougham Commission, 1837	£ 1,199,223
Charity Commission, 1867-76	£ 2,198,464

* includes Westminster

Sources: *Analytical digest of the reports made by the Commissioners of Inquiry into Charities*, PP 1843 xvi. 544-8, 544-5, xvii. 488-91, 666-7; *General digest of endowed charities in England and Wales*, PP1877 lxvi. 34-5, Table III; B. R. Mitchell, *British historical statistics*, Cambridge 1988, 605; PP 1837-8 xxxviii. 325

of endowment income to public spending was therefore somewhere between a quarter and a half, significant enough to make it a central concern in the history of philanthropy.

The 'voluntary societies/subscriber institutions' category covers those themes most typically identified with histories of philanthropy. First the voluntary societies such as the domestic and foreign church missions, parochial home-visiting groups, Dorcas societies for pregnant and nursing mothers and campaigning groups such as abolitionists or temperance societies; secondly the subscription charities which supported institutions such as hospitals, dispensaries, schools and homes for orphans, prostitutes or the disabled. Some overtly political societies might be classified as philanthropic, on the grounds that they were identified with voluntary charities in trade directories, on the public platform and in their organisation and methods. Activists in societies concerned with anti-slavery and peace were also prominent in other philanthropic areas because they provided a focus for the same emotional and ideological concerns.[81] Philanthropy is distinguished from mutual aid in the manner discussed above, with the former understood as a transaction between have and have-not, and the latter as giving between those of similar income level. Although pressure of space precludes full consideration of mutual aid it will be argued that eighteenth-century charitable societies were coloured by mutualist sentiment. Also, as the diagram suggests, some institutions, such as building societies, savings banks and patronised friendly societies, could combine saving arrangements with hierarchical giving, thus straddling the two categories.

The voluntary sector was deeply embedded in the institutional structures of the provincial city. The role of the parish and the nonconformist chapel was crucial. Not only were they the locus of many voluntary societies and schools, but they were also responsible for trusteeship of the majority of endowments. As perpetual bodies the Anglican vestries controlled large numbers of small trusts, particularly those providing doles of food, money or clothing to parishioners. The Corporation itself managed most of the wealthiest endowments until the 1830s when its purported malfeasance and incompetence was used as ammunition by the Municipal Corporation reformers, and they were wrested away from it, to be managed by a new group of Charity Trustees. Gilds were another organisational precedent, with the decline of gild sociability in the eighteenth century opening the way for the voluntary charities of the middling sorts, which raised money for lying-in women and for apprenticeships, couching their appeals in the language of mutual solidarity, and adopting the familiar convivial pattern of gild celebrations. Pubs remained at the heart of friendly society life, but were dropped by all but a few old charities in the early nineteenth century, when philanthropic meetings transferred either to the institutions themselves, like schools, hospitals, or to respectable public rooms and halls.

This study addresses two aspects of change in the voluntary sector in the period. First the rejection by donors of the endowed trust as the favoured form of philanthropy, and second the proliferation of subscription charities. The decline of endowment is usually explained in the light of a loss of confidence in the management of charities by trustees, who were thought to be abusing the trusts for political or venal purposes. In effect then, this was 'contract failure', though not in the sense of a rejection of market solutions in favour of non-profits, but rather of a transition to a more satisfactory form of non-profit. Bristol's rich variety of ancient charities offers the opportunity for empirical investigation of the numbers and value of endowments made over the long term, and of the chronology of donor dissatisfaction. It will be argued that public opinion moved against endowment when it did, not because managerial failings were any more intense than hitherto, but because

[81] Clare Midgley, 'Anti-slavery and feminism in nineteenth-century Britain', *Gender and History* v (1993), 346, 351–2; Owen, *English philanthropy*, 129.

of the entangling of the charities question with reform politics. The explanation also focuses on the capacity of local government to respond to collective needs at a time of rapid urbanisation, relating the rejection of endowment to the decline of the parish as an administrative unit, eased aside by poor law union, borough police force and board of health.

Of course the displacement of endowed charity was not simply the result of the inadequacy of the old forms, but also of preference for the new. The Bristol evidence will suggest that the late eighteenth and early nineteenth centuries saw a marked increase in the number and character of voluntary charities. The argument here will stress the dual role of voluntary associations for the middle class, expressing the desire to exercise authority over the poor and at the same time representing a middle-class identity divided by religious and political allegiance. In this respect a bouyant voluntary sector was a product of heterogeneity of demand. Instead of mobilising opinion in support of public provision those concerned to provide new collective goods proceeded first by local initiative, often with church, chapel or diocese the primary site of action, but sometimes organised around other social groupings: doctors, or nonconformist women for instance. This allowed the delivery of welfare to be aligned closely with other objectives of voluntary actors, such as political or religious proselytising or the furtherance of professional goals. It also obviated the need for political consensus. Thus social action could proceed despite divisive issues of policy, such as the contest over denominational education, the question of how far poverty should be ameliorated by the ratepayer, or whether marginal groups like 'fallen women', debtors or the vulnerable young merited public support.

If the early nineteenth century saw the efflorescence of voluntarism, the remainder of the period was marked by its continuing vigour and its success in shifting the terms of public discourse in favour of more extensive provision of social welfare. In some cases this occurred relatively quickly, as in the financing of education which by the mid-century had developed as a partnership between charity, state and market. In medical charity the process was slower, although a shift away from active hierarchical charity began in the period, with increasing reliance on income from capital and the workmen's mutual insurance arrangements. Attention to the internal economic history of several Bristol charities points up certain characteristics of voluntarism which later opened the way to state involvement. Discussion will focus on the insufficiency and unpredictability of charity income, the free-rider problem, resentment against philanthropic paternalism, and on the nature of voluntarism's achievement in the fields of health and education.

The research questions of this study are therefore guided both by the perspectives developed by social historians, and by concepts drawn from work on the contemporary non-profit sector. It analyses the rejection of endowed charity as a form of contract failure mediated through political discourse and the changing structure of urban governance. The rise of subscriber voluntarism is viewed as the means by which a society of diverse interest groups initiated new forms of public provision in a situation where the state and market could not. The changing balance – the 'moving frontier' – between statutory and voluntary provision is interpreted in terms of the achievement of philanthropy in shaping popular attitudes to collective goods, and also in the light of the limitations of voluntarism. Before proceeding though it is necessary to say more of the urban case study selected to explore these themes. Charitable effort cannot be understood in isolation from the context of Bristol's economy and society in the period, which determined both the need for voluntary action and the capacity and desire to provide it. The next chapter therefore concentrates on those aspects of the urban experience which explicate the demand for a voluntary sector.

1

Bristol: The Context

Bristolians in the nineteenth century liked to claim that their town had 'long stood at the head of all other cities, for the number, magnitude and diversity of its benevolent institutions'.[1] There was substance behind this boast. In the period 1480 to 1660 the sums endowed to charity by Bristol merchants were second only to London amongst English towns.[2] Along with Cambridge and Winchester it was one of the earliest provincial towns to open an infirmary (1737).[3] Its name was linked to philanthropists whose reputation spread far beyond the city, such as Edward Colston, Richard Reynolds, Hannah More, Mary Carpenter and George Muller. As a large, long-established city, Bristol can illustrate the concentration of needs which provided demand for a voluntary sector and the emergence of the wealth which would finance the response to that demand. It offers the historian a case study with a plethora of institutions to examine, yet unlike London, not too many to forbid the possibility of a comprehensive picture.

Demography

Underpinning the social problems of the period was the rapid population growth which tested and strained existing institutions. Bristol was an old city, which from the late Middle Ages had ranked amongst the largest provincial towns: second in 1377, second in the 1520s, third in 1662, and second in 1700.[4] In the nineteenth century it slipped back to fourth in 1801, and sixth in 1861, dwarfed by Manchester, Liverpool and Birmingham. None the less its population expanded from around 55,000 in 1775, to 104,408 in 1831, to 182,696 by 1871.[5] This was slightly in excess of the rate for England and

---

1   *Matthews's annual Bristol directory and almanack*, Bristol 1841, 295.
2   W. K. Jordan, 'The forming of the charitable institutions of the west of England', *Transactions of the American Philosophical Society* i (1960), 8, 13.
3   G. Munro Smith, *A history of the Bristol Royal Infirmary*, Bristol 1917, 5–9.
4   W. G. Hoskins, *Local history in England*, London 1959, 3rd edn, London 1984, appendix 1; E. Anthony Wrigley, 'Urban growth and agricultural change: England and the continent in the early modern period', in P. Borsay (ed.), *The eighteenth-century town: a reader in English urban history*, London 1990, 39–82 at pp. 42–3, table 1.
5   C. M. Law, 'Some notes on the urban population of England and Wales in the eighteenth century', *The Local Historian* x (1972), 13–26; H. A. Shannon and E. Grebenick, *The population of Bristol*, Cambridge 1943, 6.

21

Table 2
Age structure of Bristol and national population, 1821-71

	1821	1841	1851	1861	1871
Bristol					
Dependency ratio	825	656	970	1024	1061
% population aged 0-15	38	33	42	43	44
% population aged 60+	8	7	7	7	7
England and Wales a)					
Dependency ratio	870*	748	741	756	773
% population aged 0-15	39*	36	35	36	36
% population aged 60+	7*	7	7	7	7
England b)					
Dependency ratio	848	758	744	755	771
% population aged 0-14	39	37	36	36	36
% population aged 60+	7	7	7	7	7

*=England only
Sources: *Census of Great Britain. Population (England and Wales)*
1821-71; b): E. A. Wrigley and R. S. Schofield, *The population history*
of England 1541-1871: a reconstruction, Cambridge 1981, 529.

Wales as a whole, though in the 1820s and 1860s it was substantially higher,
and in the 1840s lower.[6] Set against the average for the seventy-two largest
UK towns this growth was distinctly less impressive; it exceeded the average
urban growth rate only in the 1860s, and even in the expansive 1820s lagged
behind (Bristol, 23 per cent; seventy-two towns, 32 per cent).[7] Population in
the parishes of the old city centre grew until the mid-century, and from the
1860s experienced a net outflow as the inner city was given over to business.
Increase was initially more marked in the 'concentric ring' of surrounding
suburbs, like wealthy Clifton and Kingsdown, incorporated in 1835, and
working-class Bedminster. From the mid-century the areas of most dynamic
growth were eastern suburbs such as St George, Easton and Stapleton, finally
incorporated in 1897.[8]

How was the population constituted? Table 2 compares the age structure
of Bristol with that of England and Wales. Conclusions are tentative given
the unreliability of the early census returns, particularly for 1821 where only

6 Ibid. 8.
7 B. W. E. Alford, 'The economic development of Bristol in the nineteenth century: an
enigma?', in P. McGrath and J. Cannon (eds), *Essays in Bristol and Gloucestershire history*,
Bristol 1976, 252–83 at p. 257.
8 Shannon and Grebenick, *Population of Bristol*, 7–8.

a sample of the town's population was used. None the less, it appears that while initially there was nothing exceptional in the level of dependency, the city's experience then diverged. In the latter part of the sequence the proportion of persons aged fifteen or under was much greater than for the nation as a whole. A further distinguishing characteristic was that as a transport hub Bristol had a large migrant population. The 1851 census reported that 49 per cent of inhabitants were born outside the town itself, of which the majority (80 per cent) came from beyond Gloucestershire.[9] It was thought that a substantial number of migrants were transitory, working temporarily in the city, then moving on.[10] Of these the Irish were significant: Engels claimed 24,000 were settled in the city in 1845, though the 1851 census recorded only 4,761 out of a population of 137,328.[11] Whatever the true number, the port of Bristol annually funnelled Irish trampers to and from harvest, and its poor law authorities were saddled with the heavy expense of paying the passage of the destitute. In 1833, for example, 3,378 Irish vagrants were 'passed' through the city.[12]

Economy and society

The nature of the relationship between the city's economy and its voluntary sector is obscured by conflicting schools of thought on its economic performance. As its comparatively sluggish population growth attests, its economy expanded more slowly than similar urban centres. In part this reflects the lack of an industrialising hinterland, with output from the Gloucestershire coalfield far more modest than those in North and South Wales.[13] A further environmental disadvantage was the relative inaccessibility of the narrow, tidal Avon in comparison to the Mersey and Clyde; established industries such as sugar-refining and glass-making suffered.[14] Pessimists go beyond this to argue that entrepreneurship was also deficient. Cautious Atlantic mer-

---

9 *Census of Great Britain: population (England and Wales)*, 1851: birth-places of the inhabitants of the principal cities and towns, p. clxxxiii.

10 Anon., *Report of the Committee to Inquire into the Condition of the Bristol Poor* (cited hereinafter as *Condition of the poor*), Bristol 1884, 28–9; Alford, 'Economic development', 267–9.

11 Engels, *Condition of the working class*, 104.

12 E. E. Butcher, *Bristol Corporation of the Poor, 1696–1834*, Bristol 1932, 30–1, 81–2, 99, 107, 110, 117, 122, 129, 134, 139, 140, 154, 156; *Appendix to the first report from the Commissioners on the Poor Laws*, PP 1834 xxviii. 894–7.

13 W. E. Minchinton, 'Bristol: metropolis of the west in the eighteenth century', *Transactions of the Royal Historical Society* 5th ser. iv (1954), 69–89, and 'The port of Bristol in the eighteenth century', in P. McGrath (ed.), *Bristol in the eighteenth century*, Newton Abbot 1972, 128–60 at pp. 157–8; M. Flinn, *The history of the British coal industry*, iii, Oxford 1984, 27.

14 B. W. E. Alford, 'The flint and bottle glass industry in the early nineteenth century: a case study of a Bristol firm', *Business History* x (1968), 12–21.

chants dangerously narrowed their interests to the apparently sure returns of the sugar trade; where investment in industry did occur the short-termism of the mercantile mentality outweighed long-run needs.[15] Venality and self-interest on the part of the Corporation and the Merchant Venturers (the merchants' gild) kept port duties uncompetitive and inhibited the development of municipal services.[16] Even firms which were successful in the mid-century, such as soapmakers Christopher Thomas & Brothers, and chocolate manufacturers J. S. Fry and Son, lacked the aggressive promotional skills needed to retain their places as market leaders.[17] In contrast, the optimist's reading points to the diversity of the Bristol economy as a strength, arguing that decline in some areas was offset by strength in others, such as financial services, brewing, printing and packaging, boot- and shoe-making and tobacco.[18] Projects like the Great Western Cotton Factory, Railway and Steamship demonstrate that Bristol's business leadership did have a 'grand strategy' for the city's recovery.[19] Nor is the criticism of the Corporation and the later Docks Committee, some argue, altogether warranted.[20]

As far as local philanthropy is concerned, we need not assume that a comparatively weak economy led to increased need, nor that it inhibited relief. In 1845 the workhouse surgeon observed that:

> Bristol not being a manufacturing place, the labouring classes are not subject to fluctuations between high wages and total want of employment; therefore large masses of artisans, suddenly reduced to a state bordering on starvation, are fortunately unknown to us. Besides, Bristol, being an ancient city, possesses many charitable endowments, and . . . these . . . preserve many families from suffering.[21]

Indeed, slower population growth could indicate an improved quality of life in some respects, such as better access to schooling. Neither need we suppose that the city lacked wealth which could be diverted to charity. For instance, occupation indicators (table 3) suggest that Bristol had a larger wealth-

---

15 Kenneth Morgan, 'Bristol and the Atlantic trade in the eighteenth century', *EHR* cvii (1992), 626–50, and *Bristol and the Atlantic trade in the eighteenth century*, Cambridge 1993; Alford, 'Economic development', 263–4.

16 Ibid. 265–6.

17 S. J. Diaper, 'Christopher Thomas and Brothers Ltd: the last Bristol soapmakers: an aspect of Bristol's economic development in the nineteenth century', *Transactions of the Bristol and Gloucestershire Archaeological Society* cv (1987), 229–31, and 'J. S. Fry & Sons: growth and decline in the chocolate industry, 1753–1918', in Charles Harvey and Jon Press (eds), *Studies in the business history of Bristol*, Bristol 1988, 33–54 at p. 49.

18 Charles Harvey and Jon Press, 'Industrial change and the economic life of Bristol', ibid. 1–32.

19 B. J. Atkinson, 'An early example of the decline of the industrial spirit?: Bristol "enterprise" in the first half of the nineteenth century', *Southern History* ix (1987), 69–89.

20 Ibid. 81–5; *The port of Bristol, 1848–84*, ed. D. Large (Bristol Record Society xxxvi, 1984), pp. xxii–vi.

21 Sir H. T. De La Beche and Dr Lyon Playfair, *Report on the sanatory* [sic] *condition of Bristol*, Bristol 1845, 23.

Table 3
Wealth indicators per 1,000 population, Bristol, Sheffield, Leeds, 1841

	Leeds	Sheffield	Bristol
Persons of independent means	21	20	45
Select professions*	21	21	50
Domestic servants	37	39	69

* armed services, law, church, medicine, education, banking, accounting, per 1,000 occupied, less domestic servants.

Source: 1841 Census, occupations abstract, England and Wales, 46-51, 222-37

holding sector than northern industrial cities of a similar size.[22] Taxation records leave a similar impression. The amount of assessed taxes paid in the 1840s per head of population in Bristol was £0.30, compared to Liverpool, £0.11; Manchester, £0.05; Birmingham, £0.13; and Leeds £0.04.[23] The percentage of the Bristol population paying Schedule B, D and E income tax in 1859–60 was 19, compared to Liverpool, 17; Manchester, 15; Birmingham, 14; Leeds, 11; and Sheffield, 10.[24]

The wealth which sustained voluntary effort came principally from the middle class, despite the attraction of 'the Nobility and Gentry' to the Hotwells spa and the luxurious terraces of Clifton.[25] Bristol's merchant oligarchy had ousted the power of landed wealth in the late Middle Ages, and thereafter aristocrats had played little part in local philanthropy.[26] It will not be argued here that changes in the nature of voluntarism should be associated with a new breed of entrepreneur and in this respect Bristol is unlike, for example, Marland's West Yorkshire medical charities, so heavily supported by

[22] Methodology: Alan Armstrong, *Stability and change in an English county town: a social study of York, 1801–51*, Cambridge 1974, 30–1.
[23] Mean of assessed taxes 1845–7, population, 1841: *A return of the total amount of assessed taxes for each of the years ending 5th. April 1845, 1846, and 1847*, PP 1847–8 xxxix. 233.
[24] W. D. Rubinstein, 'The size and distribution of the English middle classes in 1860', *Historical Research* lxi (1988), 82–7, table 1.
[25] *FFBJ*, 12 Jan. 1811.
[26] C. Ross, 'Bristol in the Middle Ages', in C. Macinnes and W. Whittard (eds), *Bristol and its adjoining counties*, Bristol 1955, 179–92; David Harris Sacks, *The widening gate: Bristol and the Atlantic economy, 1450–1700*, London 1991, pt I; Jordan, 'Forming of the charitable institutions', 13.

textile manufacturers.[27] Certainly there were growth areas of the city's economy, in the professions, services and distributive trades, but the 'revolutionised' industries made only a small showing: less than 10 per cent of occupied males worked in metal or extractive industries, while mass production of cotton was limited to the one large factory financed by a consortium of Atlantic merchants.[28] The great fortunes of the nineteenth century, such as those of Thomas Daniel (sugar merchant), George Thomas (wholesale grocer), and the Wills and Fry families (tobacco, chocolate), were founded on the town's position as transport hub, importing and processing familiar commodities of its maritime trade.[29] Nor was there a dramatic handover of local political power to aspiring new men in 1835, and it was religious and political beliefs that separated Liberals and Tories in the reform era, rather than large differences in wealth or occupational background.[30]

Relative wealth and a diverse economy did not insulate Bristol from the harsh results of slumps in the trade cycle. Large sections of the working population were vulnerable to seasonal and cyclical downturns, as a brief consideration of the occupational structure will show. Of the 31,465 occupied males in 1841, the most numerous jobs were labourer (5,537), boot/shoe-maker (2,003), carpenter (1,232), mason (1,054), smith (1,036), tailor (952), domestic servant (924), and painter/plumber/glazier (752); of 15,715 females employed, the popular areas were domestic servant (7,568), dress-maker (1,648), laundry-keeper (1,115), boot-/shoe-maker (599) and cotton manufacturer (594).[31] Of these groups, builders, shoe-makers and labourers had frequent recourse to the poor rates.[32] Dock labour had a seasonal rhythm, with the arrival of the West Indies sugar fleet in the summer months, and a slack period in the winter, other than in the Irish and Canadian trades.[33] Not only was the building trade poor in bad winters, but the Bristol industry's speculative nature meant that it was vulnerable when investment con-

---

[27] Hilary Marland, *Medicine and society in Wakefield and Huddersfield, 1780–1870*, Cambridge 1987, 117–45.

[28] E. Baigent, 'Bristol society in the later eighteenth century with special reference to the handling by computer of fragmentary historical sources', unpubl. DPhil. diss. Oxford 1985, and 'Economy and society in eighteenth-century English towns: Bristol in the 1770s', in Dietrich Denecke and Gareth Shaw (eds), *Urban historical geography: recent progress in Britain and Germany*, Cambridge 1988, 109–24 at pp. 115–16; *Census of Great Britain: population (England and Wales)*, 1841, occupations abstract; Harvey and Press, 'Industrial change', 9–10.

[29] Alford, 'Economic development', 266.

[30] Graham Bush, *Bristol and its municipal government 1820–1851* (Bristol Record Society xxix, 1976), 212–13; Atkinson, 'Early example', 82–6.

[31] *1841 Census*, occupations.

[32] *Appendix to the first report from the Commissioners on the Poor Laws: answers to town queries*, 1832, Joseph Webb, Master of St Peter's Hospital, response to query 37.

[33] BRL, microfiche 97290/1, 3, 6, 8, 10, 12, Bristol presentments, 1801, 1811, 1821, 1831, 1841, 1851.

tracted.[34] Also at the mercy of the trade cycle were tailors, dress-makers and shoe-makers supplying warehouses for the colonial market.[35]

In order to establish when such cyclical fluctuations occurred table 4 presents a collection of serial indicators of the Bristol economy. None of these is helpful in isolation. First the changing level of the poor rate is shown to suggest variations in the scale of need for relief.[36] There are several drawbacks here: surviving sources do not permit consideration of rising property (and hence rateable) values over the period; a relatively stable level of rating (such as 1831–3) might disguise a sudden widespread incapacity to pay; and similarly we cannot assume that rates levied in a particular year necessarily reflected the need for social spending in that year.[37] The next set of indicators relate to the port. Following municipalisation of the docks in 1848 the Docks Committee records showed the number of vessels entering the port, their tonnage on entry, and the gross amount of customs duties received at Bristol. Earlier annual accounts of the Bristol Dock Company produce two further series dating back to 1818, showing the tonnage duties received and the total duties, though these are marred by reductions to the schedule of tonnage rates by the company in 1834, and again after municipalisation in the late 1840s.[38] The two final series are from individual industries, though the profits of the Wills tobacco firm were too idiosyncratic for use as a general indicator. Shipbuilding tonnage is more reliable, always allowing for the fact that the industry entered long-term decline from the mid-century due to the Avon's unsuitability for large ocean-going vessels.[39]

With these shortcomings in mind, what broad conclusions can be drawn? The surging poor rates mark out the second decade of the century as particularly difficult, with unemployment high and the volume of trade passing through the docks failing to accelerate, although shipbuilding's recovery demonstrates the importance of the cessation of the Napoleonic Wars.[40] By the late 1820s public spending was falling, the docks were busier, organised

[34] BRL, B7065, LMDMS, 2nd annual report, Bristol 1841, 3; J. Ward, 'Speculative building at Bristol and Clifton, 1783–1793', Business History xx (1978), 12–15.

[35] BRL, B7067, LMDMS, 18th annual report, Bristol 1858.

[36] 1801–20: J. B. Kington, 'A burgess's' letters, Bristol 1836, 311, here shown as year of collection, though Kington records the sum against the previous year; 1820–58: Bristol Gazette; 1859–70: Comparative statement of the amount of poor rates levied and expended during the year ended at Lady-day, 1859.....1870, PP 1859 xxiv; 1860 lviii; 1861 liii; 1862 xlviii; 1863 li; 1864 li; 1865 xlviii; 1866 lxii; 1867 lx; 1868 lx; 1869 liii; 1870 lviii.

[37] P. J. Waller, Town, city and nation: England, 1850–1914, Oxford 1983, 257–9.

[38] BRO, Bristol Dock Company accounts; Port of Bristol, introduction, pp. xiii, xx; total duties = tonnage + other duties such as lockage tolls and boat licences: Bush, Bristol and its municipal government, 166–73.

[39] B. W. E. Alford, W. D. and H. O. Wills and the development of the UK tobacco industry, 1786–1965, London 1973, 464–6, table v, and 'Economic development', 273–5; G. Farr, Shipbuilding in the port of Bristol, London 1977, appendix 4; Harvey and Press, 'Industrial change', 6.

[40] BRO 36097b, John Bennet, untitled manuscript, typescript copy, Portishead 1858, 12–15.

Table 4
Selected indicators showing fluctuations in Bristol's economy

Year	Poor rate	Vessels in no.	Tonnage in '000	Customs duties £'000	Tonnage duties £	Total duties	Wills profits £	Shipbuilding tonnage
1800								1,796
1801	13,812							2,679
1802	12,350							1,103
1803	11,700							1,349
1804	11,350						600	2,090
1805	11,250						1,700	1,062
1806	11,500						3,700	1,610
1807	11,750						2,262	1,620
1808	11,500						4,700	948
1809	10,500						1,200	1,214
1810	12,000							1,662
1811	14,000						1,200	1,638
1812	14,500						1,700	167
1813	15,500						2,400	2,896
1814	16,000						2,100	581
1815	16,000						2,000	1,153
1816	15,500						-169	1,224
1817	15,500							1,951
1818	20,500				10,373	23,093	-6231	1,546
1819	27,500				13,132	32,056	2,700	2,623
1820	27,500				11,091	31,444	600	2,872
1821	24,000				10,470	22,286		2,107
1822	23,000				10,531	30,690		1,879
1823	24,500				10,748	32,829		3,200
1824	34,146				12,395	36,451		3,917
1825	23,619				13,424	42,021		3,723
1826	19,425				14,863	43,096	-518	1,870
1827	21,263				13,934	43,152	1,600	2,800
1828	27,020				15,292	44,188	800	3,860
1829	31,577				15,833	43,670	300	3,079
1830	28,278				15,999	43,712	1,200	2,173
1831	24,771				16,708	45,388	1,200	1,997
1832	25,842				15,784	45,257	1,800	1,160
1833	25,526				13,511	40,093	2,300	1,989
1834	30,693				13,164	39,311		1,979
1835	29,957				14,620	40,152	4,200	3,391
1836	27,095				14,479	40,304	4,500	856
1837	29,516				14,827	40,076	5,100	2,090
1838	19,705				15,328	42,631	9,300	2,135
1839	16,161				14,907	41,940	19,000	2,529
1840	14,779				17,999	40,484		2,049
1841	16,279				18,416	46,767	6,600	3,233
1842	21,887				15,858	43,885	10,500	6,160
1843	21,287				16,292	40,012	5,100	4,587
1844	25,994				17,906	43,557		1,339
1845	23,555				18,552	48,786	2,100	2,145
1846	27,907				19,822	51,762	4,500	444
1847	23,963				19,768	47,914	3,000	1,661
1848	27,564	7,215	544	1,037	21,025	42,628	3,400	1,117

Year	Poor rate	Vessels in no.	Tonnage in '000	Customs duties £'000	Tonnage duties £	Total duties	Wills profits £	Shipbuilding tonnage
1849	28,090	7,260	559	1,042	19,145	36,757	4,000	5,545
1850	22,000	7,177	553	1,052	12,088	42,343	5,000	1,188
1851	26,594	6,758	529	1,101	12,794	45,695	8,400	4,218
1852	24,184	6,389	512	1,020	12,047	47,475	3,000	1,221
1853	27,889	5,680	526	1,194	12,822	43,262	4,000	714
1854	28,422	5,631	557	1,228	15,274	40,717	4,600	2,768
1855	31,779	5,771	531	1,112	13,288	36,890	4,000	4,020
1856	31,516	5,811	546	1,193	13,031	34,316	3,000	3,892
1857	32,573	5,684	557	1,211	17,291	39,206	8,000	2,343
1858	28,090	6,599	621	1,296	18,075	47,328	11,160	3,003
1859	25,047	7,435	693	1,284	18,840	58,808	10,440	439
1860	26,339	7,747	710	1,219	19,329	52,017	10,890	1,318
1861	27,668	7,618	753	1,336	22,721	59,230	11,520	1,079
1862	29,500	9,230	849	1,317	19,827	54,943	13,500	1,438
1863	34,376	7,449	738	1,151	20,160	48,206	13,950	1,199
1864	40,919	7,528	716	1,103	17,915	55,600	7,920	4,402
1865	31,828	7,358	739	1,106	18,642	58,545	8,370	3,400
1866	36,720	7,916	780	1,174	18,920	65,067	7,920	370
1867	39,356	7,885	798	1,110	19,760	69,405	11,052	138
1868	42,427	7,987	805	1,120	20,791	69,554	12,024	1,293
1869	36,966	8,031	853	1,184	21,034	66,176	12,024	692
1870	35,432	8,706	912	1,000	24,211	61,955	12,024	200

Sources: Rates 1801-20, Kington *"A burgess's" letters*, 311; 1820-58, annual accounts published in *Bristol Gazette*; 1859-70, Parliamentary Papers: 1859 xxiv, 1860 lviii, 1861 liii, 1862 xlviii, 1863 li, 1864 li, 1865 xlviii, 1866 lxii, 1867 lx, 1868 lx, 1869 liii, 1870 lviii; vessels, tonnage, duties: Large (ed.), *Port of Bristol*, pp. xiii, xx; Wills: Alford, *W.D. & H.O.Wills*, 464-6; ship-building: Farr, *Shipbuilding*, Appendix 4.

labour was more active, and shipbuilding was retaining the level of output it had achieved in the post-war period, though 1826 witnessed a slump in several sectors.[41] Most indicators point to a downturn in the early to mid-1830s, stabilised at the end of the decade and the early 1840s, then another difficult cycle in the late 1840s, with the rates leaping up again, the port failing to expand, and both tobacco and shipbuilding performing poorly (this was also a slow phase of population growth).[42] The 1850s were a more successful period, with the benefits of the changed management of the docks evident by the latter part of the decade, tobacco enjoying profit increases, and shipbuilding remaining fairly stable. This situation continued until the

41 *FFBJ*, 12 Feb., 5, 12 Mar., 16 Apr. 1825; M. Gorsky, 'James Tuckfield's ride: combination and social drama in early nineteenth-century Bristol', *Social History* xix (1994), 319–38; P. Ollerenshaw, 'The development of banking in the Bristol region', in Harvey and Press, *Business history of Bristol*, 55–82 at pp. 57–8.
42 Kington, 'A burgess's' letters, passim; John Latimer, *Annals of Bristol in the nineteenth century*, Bristol 1887, 194–5; *Bristol Mercury*, 12 Dec. 1846, appeal by the Revd J. H. Woodward.

mid-1860s when again all the serials show a slowing of growth, coupled with a dramatic hike in the poor rates.

Finer detail can be added to this by comparing Bristol's experience to the peaks and troughs of the British trade cycles identified by Rostow.[43] In most cases Bristol's indicators move in line with national trends, matching Rostow's troughs in 1811, 1829, 1842, 1848, 1855, 1862 and 1868, and peaks in 1825, 1831, 1836, 1839 and 1845. Again though, using the poor rates to discern a 'strong' match is not particularly reliable, since tax increases could lag behind years of need. For example in 1818 the rating increased from £15,500 to £20,500, and this may well have reflected the exigencies faced by the guardians in 1816.

Politics and religion

Bristol's political life was important to the development of the voluntary sector in two ways. First it provided an arena in which the desirability and means of provision of public goods was debated. The perception of contract failure, the crisis of confidence which lay behind the shift from endowed to subscriber charity, emerged when the accountability of corporate and parochial management of trusts became an issue in electoral contests. Second, political division and exclusion was an aspect of the heterogeneity of demand which stimulated voluntary initiative. In an era of restricted franchise in which urban governance remained in the hands of a small elite, control of charities provided an alternative sphere of power which carried with it a degree of patronage. Political affiliation was often overlayed with religious loyalty, with a clear divide in early Victorian elections between Liberal-voting dissenting ministers and Tory-supporting clergy.[44] Thus identity could also be an organising focus for voluntarism, with particular societies and institutions associated with one or other party. Philanthropic activists also figured prominently in groups whose activities combined charitable concern with political suasion: anti-slavery and opposition to the Contagious Diseases Acts for instance.

In national politics the city was a borough seat for which two members were returned; electors had two votes which could be cast for any combination of candidates, though they might also choose to 'plump' for one alone. The eighteenth-century ideal of the party machines was that one Whig and one Tory should be elected, theoretically representing the balance of interests in the town, but in practice this rarely held.[45] Uncontested elections were unusual: the pre-reform constituency had a large freeman electorate

43 W. W. Rostow, 'Cycles in the British economy: 1790–1914', in Derek Aldcroft and Peter Fearon (eds), British economic fluctuations, 1790–1939, London 1972, 74–96 at p. 77.
44 John Vincent, Pollbooks: how Victorians voted, Cambridge 1967, 67–9, 82–3, 84–5.
45 Nicholas Rogers, Whigs and cities: popular politics in the age of Walpole and Pitt, Oxford 1989, 299–301.

Table 5
Party standing in parliamentary elections, Bristol, 1800-70

	Elected		Defeated	
1801*	Tory			
1802	Tory	Whig		
1803*	Tory			
1806	Tory	Whig		
1807	Tory	Whig		
1812*	Tory		Radical	
1812	Tory	Whig	Reform Whig	Radical
1818	Tory	Whig	Reform Whig	
1820	Whig	Tory	Reform Whig	
1826	Tory	Whig	Reform Whig	
1830	Tory	Whig	Reform Whig	Radical
1831	Whig	Reform Whig		
1832	Tory	Whig	Reform Whig	Independent
1835	Conservative	Conservative	Liberal	Liberal
1837	Conservative	Liberal	Conservative	
1841	Conservative	Liberal	Conservative	
1847	Liberal	Conservative	Conservative	Radical
1852	Liberal	Liberal	Conservative	
1857	Liberal	Liberal		
1859	Liberal	Liberal	Conservative	
1865	Liberal	Liberal	Conservative	
1868*	Conservative		Liberal	
1868	Liberal	Liberal	Conservative	
1870*	Liberal		Conservative	

*= by-election

Source: Beaven, *Bristol lists*, 170-4, party names are listed as in
Beaven; they broadly conform to those current in the local press

high level of participation, a tradition of unusually intense partisan division
which sometimes engendered violence and corrupt practices, and a succes-
sion of candidates representing markedly different shades of opinion.[46]
General elections in nineteenth-century Bristol were rarely a straight fight
between Tory and Whig, and table 5 shows the pattern of party results, the

[46] Ibid.; J. A. Phillips, *Electoral behaviour in unreformed England, plumpers, splitters and
straights*, Princeton 1982, 28–30, and *The Great Reform Bill in the boroughs: English electoral
behaviour, 1818–41*, Oxford 1992, ch. ii; James Bradley, *Religion, revolution and English radicalism: nonconformity in eighteenth-century politics and society*, Cambridge 1990; Mark Harrison, *Crowds and history: mass phenomena in English towns, 1790–1835*, Cambridge 1988.

order in which the parties appear in each row representing their place in the poll of that year.

The first decade saw political consensus represented by uncontested elections, though this broke down in 1812 with the emergence of the Radical challenge of 'Orator' Hunt.[47] Henceforth the main focus of excitement lay with the infighting between the conservative and Reform Whigs, notably on the issue of slavery, spiced by the occasional challenge of a Radical or Independent candidate, such as James Acland in 1830.[48] Tory strength in the city is demonstrated by their topping the poll throughout the first four decades, with the exception of 1820 and the 1831 reform crisis. The 1840s saw Conservative divisions. 'Ordinary citizen' William Fripp fought 'gentleman' candidate Philip Miles, with the former presenting himself as a supporter of free trade, against the latter's protectionism.[49] The 1850s and 1860s were characterised by Liberal hegemony, marred only by a Conservative by-election success in 1868.

Bristol's closed Corporation was dominated by the Tories from 1812, although pre-reform Whig councillors eschewed radicalism.[50] The Municipal Corporations Act failed to deliver the change that local Liberals hoped for, as the distribution of seats favoured wealthier wards. The result was a hung council in which an 'Old Whig' defection ensured the Tory predominance in the election of the aldermen; a Conservative majority then prevailed throughout the period.[51] In the course of the century more and more tasks were transferred from the parish to the city. The process had in fact begun as far back as 1696, with Bristol's pioneering Corporation of the Poor, a body that centrally administered parish poor relief and managed the town's workhouse, St Peter's Hospital.[52] Other public bodies included the Dock Company, the Paving Commissioners and the Turnpike Trustees; after municipal reform a regular police force was established in 1836, and in 1851 a local board of health.[53]

The city's vigorous religious culture was another stimulus to its voluntary sector. Church and chapel provided organisational foci and again heterogeneity of demand is suggested by the efforts of different sects to address distinct social needs or identify particular groups with which to work. Bristol had a long tradition of dissent, embracing Lollardy in the fifteenth century and

[47] Peter Brett, 'The Liberal middle classes and politics in three provincial towns – Newcastle, Bristol and York – c. 1812–1841', unpubl. PhD diss. Durham 1991, 86–95; Harrison, *Crowds and history*, 209–19.

[48] Brett, 'Liberal middle classes', 220–1; Peter Marshall, *Bristol and the abolition of slavery: the politics of emancipation*, Bristol 1975, 24–6.

[49] *FFBJ*, 10 July 1841; A. B. Beaven, *Bristol lists municipal and miscellaneous*, Bristol 1899, 172.

[50] Bush, *Bristol and its municipal government*, ch. ii.

[51] Ibid. ch. vii; H. E. Meller, *Leisure and the changing city, 1870–1914*, London 1976, 85–90.

[52] Slack, *Poverty and policy*, 196–7; Butcher, *Bristol Corporation of the Poor*.

[53] Bush, *Bristol and its municipal government*, chs i, ix; Roderick Walters, *The establishment of the Bristol police force*, Bristol 1975.

Table 6
Number of sittings per 1,000 population in Bristol, selected towns and England and Wales, 1851

	Church of England	Independent	Baptist	Quaker	Unitarian
Bristol	232	81	43	4	7
Bath	379	26	42	5	5
Birmingham	132	28	31	3	13
Cheltenham	309	58	65	3	8
Leeds	148	48	33	6	7
Liverpool	161	21	17	2	5
Manchester	125	43	15	4	9
Sheffield	144	3	16	6	7
England & Wales	274	56	39	5	4

Source: *Census of Great Britain: religious worship (England and Wales)*, 1851, PP 1852-3, lxxxix. pp. clxxviii-ix, cclii-v, cclx-xi, cclxiii, cclxviii

Quakerism in the seventeenth and eighteenth; the number of registered non-conformist places of worship had grown dramatically by the 1810s.[54] 1820 trade directory listings showed twenty-two Anglican churches and chapels (including the cathedral), and twenty-five dissenting: three Baptist chapels, two Friends' meeting houses, a synagogue, a Unitarian chapel, four Independent chapels, a Roman Catholic church, eight Methodist chapels (including one Whitfieldite), as well as chapels for French Protestants, 'Christians', Seceders, the Countess of Huntingdon's Connexion and the Welsh.[55] By 1850 the growing city boasted thirty-eight Anglican and forty-six dissenting places of worship.[56]

Evidence from the 1851 Religious Census revealed Bristol to be a comparatively devout city. Table 6 demonstrates this from the perspective of 'sittings' – the available seats in places of worship – focusing only on Anglicanism and old dissent. Though slightly below the national average in Anglican sittings, Bristol was unusually strong in its Independent congregations, while the popularity of old dissent is also shown by comparing numbers of Baptists with other large towns. The Church of England in Bristol was not as powerful as it was in smaller, less industrialised towns like Bath and

[54] Sacks, *Widening gate*, 154–6, chs ix, x; BRO, EP/A/43/4; Jonathan Barry, 'The parish in civic life: Bristol and its churches, 1640–1750', in S. J.Wright (ed.), *Parish, church and people*, London 1988, 153–78 at pp. 157–64.
[55] *Matthews's directory 1820*, 8–12.
[56] *Matthews's directory 1850*, 28–37.

Cheltenham, but set against the fast-growing major cities it held up well. In terms of overall attendance the percentage actually worshipping in Bristol was 57, just below the mean for England and Wales, and well in excess of Liverpool's 45, Birmingham's 36, and Manchester's 32; in this respect it ranked twenty-third among English towns. The vitality of dissent was a major factor, with nonconformity accounting for 56 per cent of both sittings and worshippers.[57] Nor was secularisation advancing: a religious census in 1881 counted total attendances (morning and evening service) of 109,452 worshippers out of a population of 206,874.[58] None the less the progress of religious liberalism in the city was slow. Establishment unease over the extension of freedoms to dissenters lingered long after the repeal of the Test and Corporation Acts, and hostility to Jews and Catholics remained firmly entrenched.[59]

The Church was crucial to the development of voluntarism in Bristol, with the 'religious subculture' discerned by Kent in the late Victorian city equally active in the earlier period.[60] First, the network of churches provided the locus of many associations, which arose sometimes from individual congregations or sects, sometimes from the diocese, sometimes from evangelical groupings and sometimes from ecumenical initiatives. Sectarian competition was a recurrent theme and was held to be important in sustaining support.[61] Second, although the motives for individual philanthropy were multi-faceted it was not unusual for them to be articulated in the changing language of personal religious commitment. Thus an early nineteenth-century evangelical could savour 'the pleasure of doing good', which brought 'a glow and warmth around his heart', while a Quaker domestic missionary of the 1860s could interpret success in rescue work as God's reward for 'spiritual labour', intended to 'refresh the souls of his children'.[62] Third, the desire to evangelise was the *raison d'être* for many associations, and central to the appeal of others. The motif of the Church beset by apathy and infidelity in the growing city was pervasive, and the desire to extend 'the benignant influence of Pastoral superintendence' not only fired campaigns for church building but also the educational charity of National School proponents and the sabbatarian-

[57] *Census of Great Britain: religious worship (England and Wales)*, 1851, PP 1852–3 lxxxix; K. S. Inglis, 'Patterns of religious worship in 1851', *Journal of Ecclesiastical History* xi (1960), 74–86.

[58] J. F. Nicholls and John Taylor, *Bristol past and present*, II: *Ecclesiastical history*, Bristol 1881, 305–8.

[59] Madge Dresser, 'Protestants, Catholics and Jews: religious difference and political status in Bristol, 1750–1850', in Madge Dresser and Philip Ollerenshaw (eds), *The making of modern Bristol*, Tiverton 1996, 96–123; *Bristol Gazette*, 19 May 1836.

[60] Meller, *Leisure and the changing city*; John Kent, 'The role of religion in the cultural structure of the later Victorian city', *Transactions of the Royal Historical Society* 5th ser. xxiii (1972), 153–73

[61] *FFBJ*, 3 Dec. 1814; 16 May 1846; *Bristol Gazette*, 15 Sept. 1836.

[62] *FFBJ*, 19 Nov. 1814; BRO, SF/A9/4a, *First report of the mission to the navvies*, Bristol 1861.

ism of domestic missionaries.[63] Bible and tract societies proselytised through home-visiting, while a group of predominantly Anglican associations dating from the Evangelical revival were geared towards the conversion of Jews and Catholics, a task often emotively characterised as a 'battle . . . between light and darkness'.[64] More broadly the Churches' campaign to reform popular manners exerted a varying degree of influence on cultural life throughout the period, and philanthropic effort was variously directed against blasphemy, vice and the evils of drink. Though in some respects a minority position, religious reformism was an influential element in the urban government of the 1830s, for example in the suppression of the city's 'pleasure fairs' and the establishment of the police force, whose brief extended to apprehending prostitutes and beggars and enforcing the closure of alehouses during divine service.[65]

This chapter has deployed social and economic statistics to highlight some of the city's distinctive features. Though hardly an industrial or commercial backwater, nineteenth-century Bristol did not share the experience of towns in the Midlands, South Wales and the North that benefited from the classic sectors of the industrial revolution – textiles, coal and metals. None the less, its role as an entrepôt and its diverse industries and services ensured that it remained one of the nation's major centres, with a wealthy middle class. The city's rapid growth, the structure of its labour market and the tendency of the port to attract migrant workers all gave rise to need and poverty which voluntary bodies attempted to meet. Local politics had a tradition of hard fought elections in which issues mattered; conservatism dominated through much of the period, though this did not prevent an eventual Liberal triumph in the parliamentary seats. Bristol's churches appear to have exerted a greater influence than in cities of comparable size and the strength of dissent was particularly notable. If the economy called forth the need for voluntary effort and the wherewithal to address it, it was the political and religious identities of Bristolians which were to animate the process.

63 *Bristol Gazette*, 15 Dec. 1836; *FFBJ*, 28 Jan., 12 Feb., 16 July 1814; 10 Jan. 1846; *Bristol Mirror*, 10 Feb. 1814.
64 *FFBJ*, 26 Mar. 1814; 30 May, 1 Aug. 1846; *Bristol Gazette*, 27 Jan. 1836; *Bristol Mercury*, 18 Dec. 1858; 16 May 1868.
65 BRO, Common Council proceedings, 16 July 1838, 377–89; BRO 34908 16a, *Bristol police instruction book*, Bristol 1836, 42–8.

PART I

ENDOWED CHARITY
IN NINETEENTH-CENTURY BRISTOL

2

The 'Pattern of Philanthropy'

In 1826 the *Bristol Mirror* reported Edward Philips's speech at a subscription appeal for 'distressed manufacturers' in the neighbouring counties: 'From the well-known character of Bristol and the illustrious names to be found in its history, including Burton, Canynge, Colston, and Reynolds, he anticipated great results.'[1] The charitable reputation alluded to in Philips's exhortation was not an abstraction but a reference to the multiplicity of endowed trusts which operated in the city. Indeed, when the term 'charity' was employed in public discussion in this period, its meaning was understood by Bristolians to denote the endowments rather than the benevolent voluntary societies which were comparatively new arrivals in the philanthropic arena. Trade directories throughout the century offer a similar representation, with separate entries under the 'Benevolent Institutions' section for the municipal endowments and almshouses.[2]

Despite looming so large in public awareness, endowed charity has been largely ignored in the historiography of philanthropy. The critiques of Jordan's claims for 'prodigal outpourings' of charitable giving perhaps discouraged later researchers from exploring the subsequent role of the endowments. Owen's survey recounted the parliamentary reform of endowed charity, but the absence of statistical analysis left the reader, as one reviewer noted, with no real sense of the 'pattern or scale of philanthropy'.[3] A later scholar of the Charity Commission was also daunted by the potential pitfalls of quantifying endowments.[4] In the absence of such discussion historians explaining the supersession of the endowed trust by subscriber charities have tended to proceed by general inference or ahistorical assertion. This ranges from the simple observation that 'Charity Bequests had fallen out of fashion', to speculation that the steady rise in poor rates made testators less inclined to public beneficence when they wrote their wills.[5] Most typically writers have accepted that the accusations preceding the establishment of the nineteenth-century Charity Commissions prove corrupt administration to have been the decisive factor. Georgian hospitals were funded by subscription because 'the lump-sum bequest . . . almost inevitably fell prey . . . to

---

1 *Bristol Mirror*, 20 May 1826.
2 *Matthews's directory 1841*; *Wright's directory 1900*.
3 Harrison, 'Philanthropy and the Victorians', 354, 373.
4 Tompson, *Charity Commission*, 198–201.
5 Bush, *Bristol and its municipal government*, 67; Earle, *Making of the English middle class*, 319.

misappropriation, malversation, or embezzlement'.[6] Langford has summarised the standard viewpoint:

> There was much awareness of the deficiencies of the old paternalism. The terms of ancient benefactions were easily ignored or abused, and trustees in perpetuity had a way of giving in to unbusinesslike habits, political manipulations, even downright corruption. It was believed that large sums of money had either been misused or forgotten: in 1786 Parliament initiated a great inquiry into parochial endowments in an attempt to arrest such neglect.[7]

This chapter provides an empirical survey of endowed charity in Bristol, as a basis for subsequent analysis of the causes of its decline. It begins with a discussion of the nature of endowment and the sources available for its study. The central section uses parliamentary returns to reconstruct the pattern of giving in the city over the long term. It asks how the numbers and value of endowments made changed over time, and also whether change was discernible in terms of the category of recipient, the nature of the charity or the trustees chosen to administer it. It will conclude with some preliminary remarks on the implications of these findings for a reassessment of the causes of decline.

The nature of endowed charity and its sources

Endowed charities were those which operated through the establishment of trusts, either in deed or will, by which some form of capital was bequeathed, yielding an annual return to be directed at the donor's chosen target. Precedents of the form may be traced to the Middle Ages, in the urban hospital foundations of the late thirteenth century and the testamentary requirement of alms distribution by parish fraternities.[8] Legal codification of endowed charity was provided by the Elizabethan Statute of Charitable Uses (1601), which formed one aspect of the late Tudor poor law legislation.[9] This act encouraged the habit of endowment by specifying the meaning of a charitable gift and establishing Charity Commissioners to review disputed trusts; subsequent equity rulings tended to favour the charity rather than the

---

[6] Roy Porter, 'The gift relation: philanthropy and provincial hospitals in eighteenth-century England', in Lindsay Granshaw and Roy Porter (eds), *The hospital in history*, London 1989, 149–78 at pp. 156–7.

[7] Paul Langford, *A polite and commercial people, England, 1727–1783*, Oxford 1989, 482–3; Kirkman Gray, *History of English philanthropy*, 225–7.

[8] Miri Rubin, 'Development and change in English hospitals, 1100–1500', in Granshaw and Porter, *Hospital in history*, 41–59 at pp. 46–56; *Parish fraternity registers*, ed. Patricia Basing, London 1982, entries 63, 62, 69, 82, 113, 125; Gareth Jones, *History of the law of charity, 1532–1827*, Cambridge 1969, ch. i.

[9] 43 Elizabeth I c.4 1601; Jordan, *Philanthropy in England*, 114; Jones, *Law of charity*, 23, 52.

aggrieved heir-at-law.[10] Eighteenth-century courts tipped the balance back in favour of the testator's family, with the Mortmain Act (1736) forbidding deathbed gifts of land to charity, *cy-pres* rulings becoming less generous, and the appeals process in Chancery becoming prohibitively expensive and slow.[11]

How did endowment work in Bristol? To assure perpetuity the group of trustees had to be a permanent body, typically a parish vestry, the town corporation, a gild or dissenting chapel. Capital initially took the form of property which engendered rents and leasing fees, but with the rise of the securities market in the eighteenth century it became more common either to leave consols or a lump sum for the purchase of stock. Income was targeted at the alleviation of poverty and sickness through the provision of doles, orphan-schools and almshouses, and also met broader social needs such as education, civil works, business loans and apprenticeship fees. Four main parliamentary sources hold details of Bristol's endowments: the Gilbert Returns of 1786–7, the first Charity Commission of enquiry reporting 1819–37 (the Brougham Commission), and two updated digests of the commission's findings, appearing in 1868–76 and 1891–2.[12] Use has also been made of gift and charity books from individual parishes, where extant, and records of the Bristol Municipal Charity Trustees.

Government first strove to survey the nation's charitable spending on its poor and needy in the 1770s and 1780s, driven by the efforts of Thomas Gilbert to promote poor law reform.[13] Having included almshouses in the 1776 Commons Committee investigation into workhouse provision, Gilbert then established the 'Committee on certain returns relative to the state of the poor and to charitable donations and co.'.[14] Its report of 1787 was based on a questionnaire submitted to every parish in the land, though doubts were expressed as to the veracity and comprehensiveness of the responses, prompting Gilbert to write again urging vestries to 'reconsider' their returns. The abstract of returns for Bristol details names of donors, date, charitable head, form of investment (land or money), total amount given and annual income generated. A fundamental limitation of the source is that it is concerned with endowments vested in the parish for the benefit of the poor, hence omitting those under the aegis of the Corporation and the gilds; these were substantial,

10 Ibid. chs iv, v.
11 Ibid. chs vi–xi; *cy-pres* rulings occurred when the terms of the trust could not be fulfilled, and had to be reformulated as 'near' as possible to the original objective.
12 Bristol: Gilbert: *Abstract of returns of charitable donations for benefit of poor persons: – 26 Geo. III, 1786*, PP 1816 xvia, 434–52; Charity Commissions: 1819–37: *Analytical digest*, PP 1843 xvi. 40–1; xvii. 226–55; 1868–76: *Copies of the general digest of endowed charities for the counties and cities mentioned in the fourteenth report of the Charity Commissioners, &c.*, PP 1873 li. 416–53; *Return of the digest of endowed charities in the county of Gloucester including Bristol*, PP 1893–4 lxvii. 574–89.
13 Tompson, *Charity Commission*, 83–4; Owen, *English philanthropy*, 85–7.
14 26 Geo. III 1786.

particularly those for educational purposes. As to reliability, the absence of visiting commissioners undoubtedly invited laxity: when the Brougham Commissioners reported on St Stephen's in 1822 they prefaced their remarks by observing that insufficient effort had been made to respond to Gilbert with the 'particularity required'.[15] The real problem seems to have been the *ad hoc* administrative and accounting procedures of the vestries rather than deliberate obstruction. In 1819 St James's parish pre-empted the commissioners' visit by ordering a full review of their endowments, on the grounds that the recent deaths of several vestry officers left the remainder 'in complete ignorance of their trust funds'.[16] The less conscientious Temple parish was told to employ an accountant so that the the churchwardens' accounts might be 'kept by such a method as may appear more explicit'; it duly handed its charity records to attornies, who produced a long list of incorrect distributions.[17] Such examples cast doubt on the reliability of the Gilbert returns and their use here is confined to cross-checking dates of endowment missing from the abstract of the Brougham Commission, and as a source for Quaker and Methodist charities, which fell outside the latter's ambit.

The Brougham Commission developed from the select committee investigating 'The education of the lower orders in the metropolis', appointed in 1816.[18] Two years later Brougham had succeeded in expanding its field of research country-wide, and was promoting a bill to widen the range to all charities. This was enacted in an emasculated form, exempting universities, public schools and Jewish and Quaker charities from investigation, along with all institutions or societies predominantly funded by voluntary contributions or subscription.[19] The commissioners visited Bristol in 1821 and 1822 and the results were published in their sixth and tenth reports.[20] These were later reprinted by a local newsman, Thomas Manchee (one-time editor of the Liberal *Bristol Mercury*) with a 300-guinea contribution raised from various worthies. A full nation-wide digest was finally prepared in 1843, and this, along with the reports, has been the main source for the analysis below. In addition to the information offered by the Gilbert returns, these have fuller accounts of each endowment, often transcribing the precise wording of wills still held in the parish chest, or, in the case of more ancient charities, the details in benefaction tables and on boards or tablets in the church. Non-parochial charities are dealt with at length, while appendices detail rentals and leases of trust property. With some reservations, the Brougham Commission can be said to have achieved a reliable record of the trusts. As already

---

[15] Manchee, i. 301.

[16] Ibid. i. 467.

[17] BRO, P/Tm/E 1 46; P/Tm/V, 4 Dec. 1821.

[18] Owen, *English philanthropy*, 183; Chester New, *The life of Henry Brougham to 1830*, Oxford 1961, ch. xii; A. Aspinall, *Lord Brougham and the Whig party*, Manchester 1927, 236.

[19] 59 Geo. III, PP 1818 i. 502, 1819 i A 455; Kevin Grady, 'The records of the Charity Commissions as a source for urban history', *Urban History Yearbook* (1982), 31–7.

[20] *6th Report 30 June 1821*, PP 1821 xii; *10th Report, 28th June 1823*, PP 1824 xiii.

noted, the presence of visiting commissioners does appear to have prompted a genuine desire by the vestries to account fully for their gifts and correct prior malversation; more will be said of this below when the degree of pre-reform corruption is evaluated. The Merchant Venturers also found themselves criticised for their operation of one of the Colston legacies and after a long battle in Chancery were compelled to refund monies to the charity. It is in the case of the Corporation's activities that the accuracy of the commission's findings are most dubious. There were criticisms, for instance of the Grammar School over-charging, and of the Corporation illegally calculating excessive interest on a debt owed to them by Queen Elizabeth's Hospital. Overall though the Corporation escaped censure, and it is notable that its charity administration was not a feature of the later Municipal Corporation Commissioners' report. Subsequent to this, in his evidence to the House of Lords in petitioning against the Municipal Corporations Bill, Daniel Burges, the Corporation's solicitor, cited the approval of the Brougham Commissioners for the conscientious administration of the monies.[21] Doubts only began to surface when an independent body of Municipal Charity Trustees was established after the reform of the Corporation. In the extensive litigation accompanying the trustees' efforts to wrest control of charitable assets from the Council further malpractices came to light. None the less, these do not seriously call into question those findings of the 1821/2 investigation which have been used for the quantitative survey here, since the disputes relate mostly to pre-1680 endowments and to the question of favouritism in the choice of recipients, neither of which distort the data employed.

The appointment in 1860 of a permanent Charity Commission with clearly delegated legal powers, led to the next phase of inquiry.[22] Bristol was surveyed again in 1869–70, and as before a summary was published locally, detailing the endowments made since 1822. Where a parish had kept a clear record of nineteenth-century endowments, St Paul's for example, it has been possible to cross-reference and confirm the thoroughness of the latter survey. The later Commission reports broadened the range of charities surveyed to include those institutions primarily funded by subscription, such as the Infirmary and the Orphan Asylum.

These sources are analysed through the collation of quantitative information on endowed charity in Bristol between 1680 and 1890 with a statistical presentation of the numbers and values of gifts at decadal intervals, under the various charitable heads. In pushing the starting date back to 1680 the object has been not only to catch all the potential fluctuations of the eighteenth century, the putative time of decline, but to view the situation before the establishment of Bristol's workhouse (1696) and infirmary (1737), and so to judge whether the existence of union poor rates or subscription charity might have restrained endowments.

---

[21] *House of Lords Journal*, 5 Aug. 1835, 405.
[22] Tompson, *Charity Commission*, ch. ix.

Numbers and values of endowments

Figure 2 presents the numbers of new endowments made by decade, specifying the different categories of trustee. 'Parish' bequests were those administered by the churchwarden or vestry of the older city parishes, while 'new parish' refers to those established from the late eighteenth century. These Anglican charities are distinguished from those of 'dissenters', primarily Baptists, Quakers and Unitarians. Of the non-parochial gifts, 'others' are those under the supervision of the Corporation, the Municipal Charity Trustees, the Merchant Venturers, or some other specified body of feoffees, such as charities that were predominantly funded by subscription or non-trust donations.

Long-term numerical decline began in the latter part of the eighteenth century, despite a brief rally between 1800 and 1820. The most striking component of this decline was the reduced role of charities in the trust of parish vestries, a trend which was not offset by the few endowments to newly created parishes. Parochial charities were by far the most numerous form of endowment, amounting to 650 of the 737 which the Brougham Commissioners surveyed. The fact that the majority of these were targeted at poor relief underlines the dual function of the parish in tackling poverty. On the one hand parishes were integral to the Corporation of the Poor as the bureaucracies which assessed and collected the rates, on the other they had the resources to offer doles of money, bread, coal and clothing to their local needy. However, by the mid eighteenth century the number of beneficent testators prepared to establish such dole funds had begun a long-term decline, which despite occasional revivals was to continue throughout the nineteenth century.

A similar pattern was followed by the non-parochial charities. Dissenting charities were concerned with the maintenance of ministers and sectarian education, and these too did not thrive in the nineteenth century. Bequests to 'others' were usually geared to a city-wide clientele, with almshouses, education and health figuring strongly in the category. The 1790s and 1810s saw these flourishing. However, although the municipal corporations reform of 1835 removed the administration of many of these from the city corporation to the Municipal Charity Trustees there was no dramatic increase in endowment of these gifts as a result; in fact the mid nineteenth century was a particularly low point. At the end of the sequence only endowments to voluntary institutions, notably the hospitals, were clear growth areas.[23]

If the values of new endowments are considered (figure 3) it is extremely difficult to discern any clear pattern over the period, though there are some points of comparison with figure 2. The graph is calculated on annual income

---

[23] *Return of the digest*, PP 1893–4 lxvii. 574–89.

Figure 2

Number of new endowments made by decade, showing category of trustee, Bristol, 1680–1869

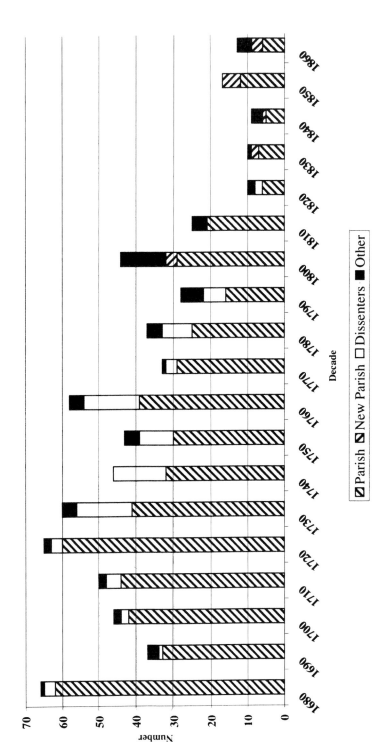

Sources: Gilbert: *Abstract of returns*, PP 1816 xvia. 434–52; Charity Commissions: 1819–37: *Analytical digest*, PP 1843 xvi. 40–1; xvii. 226–55; 1868–76: *Copies of the general digest*, PP 1873 li. 416–53; *Return of the digest*, PP 1893–4 lxviii. 574–89; Manchee; BRO, P/St J/Ch/92, St James's vestry, list of charities, 1915; BMC, YB, Year book and notes 1987.

Figure 3

Annual income per decade from new endowments, shown at constant prices (1820s), Bristol, 1680–1869

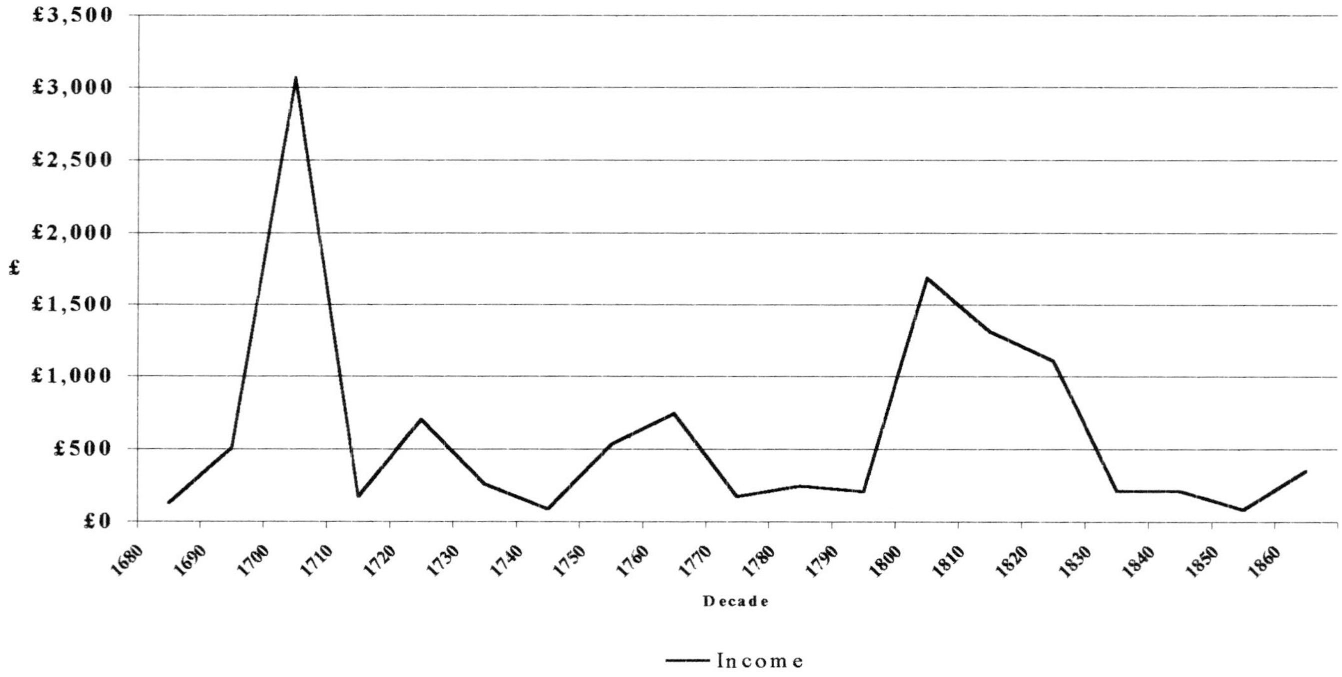

Source: As fig. 2.

generated by all new endowments made over the period, by decade. This represents the amount of new money coming available to the spending authorities, rather than the actual capital sums bequeathed. Since earlier endowments took the form of property it is impossible to measure financial worth in terms of capital value, hence the use of annual income of new trusts as the indicator (see appendix 1). The values recorded by the Brougham Commission, which visited Bristol in 1821–2, have been used and the subsequent endowments adjusted to 1820s prices by means of the Rousseaux price index.

While retaining some of the fluctuations of figure 2, such as the upturn of 1800–20 and the downturn of 1830–59, there was otherwise no necessary correspondence between the volume and value of new trusts. There is no clear evidence of a gradual decline in size of endowments throughout the two centuries. The lowest value decades, the 1740s and 1850s, occur at apparently random points in the survey, nor are any trends maintained for more than three decades, as demonstrated by the contrast between 1770–1800 and the preceding and successive decades. The irregularity of the results can be explained partly in terms of the impact of individual donors. Without Edward Colston's foundation gift for his school the years 1700–9 would have mustered a mere £149 7s. 0d., and the same could be said of 1820–9, when Bonville's gift of shares in the Dock Company, made for almshouse and benevolent school purposes, accounted for 96 per cent of the decadal total. So while the practice of endowment was continuous, the scale of new gifts was uneven and apparently owed more to individual inclination than social need.

This evidence also points to a disjuncture between the actual sequence of decline and that which might be expected if anxiety about corruption had indeed been widespread. At national level the political concern over charity administration which led to the various commissions of enquiry gathered pace at the start of the nineteenth century. However, in money terms the mid to late eighteenth century was poorly endowed, with a marked revival in the post-Gilbert era when Brougham and others were forcing the issue of venal management of charities onto the political agenda. A new nadir was reached in the mid nineteenth century, with 1830–59 a notably low value tri-decadal cycle, yet this period saw the most significant reforms to charitable trusts in over two hundred years, with the investigative work of the Commission, the establishment of Municipal Charity Trustees, and the Charitable Trusts Act of 1853. Figure 2 shows the same pattern, with a rise in number of gifts between 1800 and 1819, and a slump between 1820 and 1869. This throws into question any simplistic causal link between corruption and the establishment of government enquiries into charity. It is almost the reverse of what might be expected.

The charitable heads

Table 7 records the number of endowments made, grouping them into various categories. At the bottom of each column a percentage figure shows the proportion of the whole which each charitable head accounted for in financial terms at the time of the second Charity Commission report of 1868–9. The exercise amply demonstrates that the numerical demise of endowed charity was due to a decisive drop in gifts to the church and to the poor, with the decade commencing 1770 representing the pivotal point. This trend is directly related to the falling off in gifts to parish trusteeship noted in figure 2. However, in terms of overall financial contribution the parish trusts for church and poor did not amount to more than 24 per cent. Bequests for the elderly and education were sustained through this period and beyond, while the increase in gifts for health purposes reflects the growing tendency to bequeath to subscription institutions. The remainder of this section will concentrate on a development of this process, breaking down the charitable heads into their constituent parts and illustrating their operation.

The Church

This category covers endowments providing for sermons and payment for the minister, though occasionally bell-ringing and upkeep of the building feature. Often these gifts would be closely linked with the establishment of a poor dole: an example from the peak years of the early eighteenth century is that of John and George Hudson of Temple parish, a father and son, who in 1710 established a fund that combined several of the characteristic donor aspirations. A rent charge produced £5 5s. annually, of which £1 13s. 4d. went to the minister, 4s. to the clerk, 2s. 8d. to the sexton, 5s. to the churchwardens and the remainder to four poor widows and the poor of the parish. These payments were made on Ash Wednesday and on the feast of St John the Evangelist, on which days the minister was enjoined in the will to preach a sermon.[24] Only rarely does the motive of this kind of donor appear explicitly, as in the case of Ezekiel Nash, who in 1800 left money for a sermon and bread dole to St James's parish to mark 'the donor's thankfulness to Almighty God, for his wonderful preservation in an engagement with a French frigate, March 8th 1762'.[25] In both these cases the sermon was the condition of the gift, and it may be that the testator sought to cheat death's finality through regular commemoration in these sermons; perhaps also this practice was the heir to the medieval chantries, which ensured the welfare of the soul in the afterlife.[26]

---

[24] Manchee, i. 392–3.

[25] Ibid. i. 464.

[26] Clive Burgess, ' "A fond thing vainly invented": an essay on purgatory and pious motive in later medieval England', in S. J. Wright (ed.), *Parish, church and people*, London 1988, 56–83.

Table 7
Number of new endowments by type, Bristol, 1680-1889

Decade	Church	Poor	Elderly	Economic	Health	Education	Misc.
1680s	2	58	5				
1690s	5	24	8				
1700s	10	29	3	1		3	
1710s	11	29	4	2		5	
1720s	10	45	7			3	
1730s	6	30	14	1		9	
1740s	9	22	3	1		11	
1750s	4	27	3		2	6	1
1760s	11	30	9		1	7	
1770s	5	17	6		1	5	
1780s	3	16	13		1	3	1
1790s	6	9	9			4	
1800s	7	16	11	4	3	6	2
1810s	5	12	5			2	1
1820s	4	2	3			1	
1830s	2	4	4		1	1	
1840s	1	7	3		2		
1850s	1	10	3			2	
1860s	2	4	3		2	3	1
1870s	4	5	2		9	4	
1880s	2	6	2		4	4	
% Income, 1868-9:	14.0%	9.4%	25.3%	1.7%	7.9%	41.5%	0.3%

Church: sermons, repairs, maintenance of clergy; Poor: doles of clothing,
money, bread, coal; Elderly: almshouses, pensions; Economic: loans,
apprenticeship fees; Misc.: aid for prisoners, debtors; public works;
Education: schools, scholarships; Health: aid to blind; pregnancy; hospitals

Source: As for fig. 2

There is a long-term slide in church-based endowments throughout the sequence, with the numbers in the mid eighteenth century sustained by funds established by the Baptists to train and provide livings for their ministers. Anglican enthusiasm for this type of gift waned from the 1730s, while Quakers and Unitarians preferred to bequeath money for the poor and for education. The commemorative sermon did endure into the nineteenth century, but by this time donors were also beginning to specify church repairs or maintenance: only one such gift was made before 1790, eight were made in the next sixty years. Mrs Chetham Strode's bestowal of £30 government stock to pay for the cleaning and upkeep of her husband's monument in St Paul's church typefies the newer form, which, though circumventing the minister, still sought some permanence in the face of death.

The poor
This category consists of doles of clothing, bread, coal and money. These form the bulk of the parish charities, and along with the church funds, it was their decline which contributed most noticeably to the numerical fall-off of parochial endowment. Bread and money doles were the most popular type: for example, the 1710s saw twelve money gifts, fourteen of bread, one of clothing and two of coal, and the 1810s six of money, four bread, one clothing and one coal. Like the church gifts a sustained decline began from the 1770s, becoming particularly marked by the 1820s, though some fresh endowments continued to be made throughout the nineteenth century.

In addition to specifying the type of relief they wished to provide donors would most usually indicate which section of the poor were to receive their benevolence, upon what date the gift would be made, and to whom the administration was entrusted. In 1755, for instance, Robert Sandford left £1,000 to the minister and churchwardens, the interest of which was to be paid to thirty poor housekeepers not in receipt of alms, annually on St Thomas's Day.[27] Daniel Lane's bequest of 1802 produced 10s. to go to widowed housekeepers not receiving alms every 7 November.[28] The choice of distribution dates which were neither saints' days nor public holidays was made clear by Elizabeth Nicklus, whose will in 1731 specified 1 February, 'being the day of her birth'. Nicklus's target group was six poor sailors' widows or six poor housekeepers not in receipt of alms; she would no doubt have been doubly chagrined to discover that by 1821 the churchwardens had merged her £1 10s. interest in with the general Christmas gifts.[29] Others were far less precise in their intentions, though this could simply be a function of the perfunctory form in which the wills were recorded in the church tables, such as that of

[27] Manchee, ii. 85.
[28] Ibid. ii 358.
[29] Ibid. ii. 394.

Samuel Hale, who in 1666 'gave £10, the profit thereof to the poor weekly, in bread, forever'.[30]

Viewed collectively then, there is much common ground between these gifts to the poor. The trustees were almost always minister and churchwardens, the vestry, or the feoffees of the church lands, rather than nominated individuals. Days when the benefaction was distributed were either Sundays, Christmas, a saint's day or a specified date of particular significance to the testator. The 'poor' were conceptualised either as a carefully circumscribed subgroup of the needy, such as housekeepers, widows or regular churchgoers, or as a group which, though not identified precisely, would be recognisable to the trustees. One of the most common qualifications was that the 'poor' should not be in receipt of 'alms'; in other words, charity should not be used as a supplement to the poor rate.

The elderly/widows

Bequests to the elderly and to widows are treated separately here, though this is an ambiguous aspect of the taxonomy since such recipients were not always clearly distinguished from the 'poor'.[31] Three types of gift have been grouped under this head, doles geared to the elderly and to widows, and bequests to almshouses. Doles aimed at the elderly as a general group were most infrequent, there being only six made since 1680. Most almshouses examined by the Brougham Commissioners were recorded as housing the elderly, in phrases such as 'poor old maids', or 'old poor decayed bachelors', though age was only rarely specified, as in the case of Fry's Mercy House, which insisted its almswomen 'should not be under the age of fifty years at the time of election'.[32] Whether doles aimed at widows were intended for the elderly is more questionable, the most typical wording of a parish gift being simply 'poor widows'.[33] A rare designation of age is found in Mary Partridge's gift, whose recipients were required to be '40 years or upwards'.[34] Bequests to the elderly and widows followed a different pattern from those for the poor. Almshouse endowments continued into the mid nineteenth century, and indeed this was one area where donors were prepared to endow funds to the charge of the new Municipal Charity Trustees.[35] It is unclear whether the desert of the 'widow' recipient hinged principally on age or the condition of widowhood, but donors retained their level of concern for this group, at least until the 1830s.

Why did the provision of gifts to widows fall away so decisively? This was most probably an aspect of the decline in parochial endowments, the last

[30] Ibid. ii. 277.
[31] Ibid. i. 123; ii. 56–7.
[32] Ibid. i. 79, 89, 192, 199, 217, 405; ii. 61.
[33] Ibid. i. 433, 445–6, 457–9, 462–3, 449–50, 456, 460–2.
[34] Ibid. i. 463.
[35] Copies of the general digest, PP 1873 li. 418–19.

parish gifts to widows being recorded in the 1830s. Another factor was the changing nature of women's philanthropy. Endowments made to widows were particularly favoured by female testators, perhaps in response to their personal experience of widowhood.[36] It may be that the new forms of voluntarism that developed in the nineteenth century, such as lying-in (childbirth) and visiting charities, offered a greater range of possibilities to the benevolent woman. Interestingly, such gifts continued to be made to the Bristol Municipal Charity Trustees well into the twentieth century, now sometimes specifying widows and sometimes women of a particular age.[37] Philanthropic concern for the elderly was an enduring sentiment, even after the introduction of state pension schemes, possibly because the travails of old age were also shared by benevolent testators contemplating the imminence of their own deaths.

The persistence of almshouse bequests is to be explained partly in terms of trusteeship, and partly by the nature of the institutions. Non-parochial trustees were consistently chosen to administer such endowments, as some of these were intended to be city-wide institutions, or to cater to a particular clientele, such as retired seamen. Of the twenty-five almshouses listed in the city directory of 1841 only six appear to be specifically parochial in name or funding, while four were for dissenters, and two received funding from the poor rates.[38] This type of gift was therefore less sensitive to the decline in the role of the parish as the administrator of charity. It may also be that the material presence of almshouses and their manifest use as old peoples' homes/hospices rendered them more impervious to changing attitudes to the poor. Lastly, demographic pressure for almshouse provision intensified as the national proportion of over-60s in the population rose from one in fifteen in 1826, to one in thirteen by 1911.[39] Despite this there was no very significant increase in provision. Table 8 samples trade directories between 1793 and 1884 to demonstrate the modest growth of almshouse places in the city. This is particularly strange given the impressive increase in income from Bristol almshouse endowments between the Brougham Commission report and the Commission of 1869–70 – a rise from £3,706 to £12,177; as a proportion of total endowed income the almshouse share rose from 18% to 25%.[40]

Economic aid

This category of endowment covers gifts designed to create employment, either through loans to enable a prospective business to be established, or

36 Manchee, i. 433, 445–6, 456, 460–3.
37 BMC, 'Year book and notes on Bristol municipal charities and endowed schools 1987'.
38 *Matthews's directory 1841*, 311–12.
39 Michael Anderson, 'The social implications of demographic change', in Thompson, *Cambridge social history of Britain*, ii. 1–70 at p. 46.
40 1819–37: *Analytical digest*, PP 1843 xvi. 40–1; xvii. 226–55.

Table 8

Number of almshouse places in Bristol, 1793-4, 1852, 1884

	Men	Women	Either	Total
1793-4	52	177	77	306
1852	43	199	82	324
1884	66	210	73	349

Sources: *Matthews's directory,* 1793-4, 1852; *Wright's directory,* 1884

money to pay for apprenticing. This was not a popular charitable head, and was almost entirely restricted to the earlier part of the period under consideration. Of those recorded in the eighteenth century, only one was a loan fund, set up in 1735 for Quaker tradesmen.[41]

All the rest were sums for apprenticing the young, though only one such fund was set up after the 1740s. By the nineteenth century parish involvement in apprenticeships persisted, for example in St Mary Redcliffe, where pupils of the Pile Street School had the benefit of a fund to pay a few premiums.[42] The Municipal Charity Trustees also made occasional agreements for the school pupils in their charge: in 1837 Henry Newman was apprenticed to sea with a Captain Newman, as was William Edwards to Samuel Butler, chemist, for a premium of £10.[43] The practice endured, but the funds were old ones.

The continued existence of interest-free loan monies also owed much to gifts from an earlier age, although three such endowments were set up at the start of the nineteenth century. These were all made by Paul Orchard, and the Charity Commission's observations on them explain the rarity of this kind of gift. Of the several parishes left money by Orchard only St Philip and St Jacob's had made successful use of it. St James's had yet to make a loan twenty years after receipt of the gift, perhaps due to the difficulty of finding trustworthy applicants who could provide the necessary securities. St Nicholas's had made several loans, one of which had not been returned in the agreed time-span, and the commissioners observed that 'there seems reason to apprehend that some, if not all of them, are in a precarious situation'.[44] Municipal loan funds were fraught with similar problems. In the case of default the trustees would have to initiate legal proceeding against those who had put up bonds as surety for the loan.[45] The scarcity of this type of gift can

[41] *Abstract of returns,* PP 1816 xvia. 436.
[42] Manchee, ii. 54–5.
[43] BMC, MB i, 27 Oct., 10 Nov. 1837.
[44] Manchee, i. 465; ii. 197, 298.
[45] BMC, MB i, 8 Jan. 1837.

therefore be understood in terms of its risk factor; default would either lead to court costs and inconvenience, or would wipe out the fund. There was also a strong incentive for trustees to plead difficulties, while watching interest accrue to the general parish account which they were not legally obliged to remit to the trust, since the terms establishing loan funds presupposed they would be interest-free. By the nineteenth century the trustee savings bank emerged as a more suitable vehicle for this kind of philanthropy, with the Bristol Loan Fund offering interest-free loans 'for the promotion of economy and prudence among the labouring classes'. Applications were made at the Savings Bank, and repayments were made on the basis of 1s. in the pound per week.[46]

Health

Charities concerned with health were not numerous. The category includes gifts to lying-in women and doles for the blind, along with the various endowments made to the voluntary hospitals in the later nineteenth century. Funds for women in childbirth set up by Ann Thurston (1756) and Mary Ann Peloquin (1768) were in the gift of the mayor's wife and confined to wives of freemen of the city.[47] Charity for the relief of the blind was the result of a particular enthusiasm of three individuals, Alderman Merlott, his wife Elizabeth and Richard Reynolds, who, between 1784 and 1806 established and augmented a fund which, by 1822, was generating £454 *per annum*, to be administered by the Corporation. There is a notable overlap with charity to the elderly here, for preference in the distribution of the £10 doles was given to blind applicants over seventy years old, and in any case the charity catered only to those over fifty.[48]

Education

Endowments to schools are fairly consistent from the start of the eighteenth century, but as the city grew both private- and subscriber-funded education superseded the evolving system of parish charity schools financed through trusts.[49] Three types of school were involved with endowments. First the large city schools, such as the Red Maids School and the Grammar School, mostly founded in an earlier period, and under the supervision of either the Corporation or the Merchant Venturers.[50] Apart from the huge Colston benefaction of 1708 the trend in these schools was for occasional gifts to be made to augment existing funds, such as the money left by Samuel Gist in 1808, which allowed a further three boys and three girls to join Queen

---

46 *Matthews's directory 1841*, 309.
47 Manchee, i. 103–4, 106–10; Fissell, *Patients, power, and the poor*, 91–2.
48 Manchee, i. 104–5.
49 Jonathan Barry, 'The cultural life of Bristol, 1640–1775', unpubl. PhD diss. Oxford 1985, ch. ii.
50 C. Hill, *The history of the Bristol Grammar School*, Bath 1951; J. Vanes, *Apparelled in red*, Gloucester 1984; F. W. E. Bowen, *Queen Elizabeth's Hospital, Bristol*, Clevedon 1971.

Elizabeth Hospital and Red Maids School respectively, or the exhibition fund set up for the Grammar School in 1866 by John Naish Sanders.[51]

A second category was schools endowed by a congregation.[52] For example, many of the gifts made in the second half of the eighteenth century were small donations made to fund the school in Stokes Croft for Protestant dissenters. This had actually been started by voluntary subscription and a trust had been created after the erection of the building, to which relatively minor capital sums, usually £50 or £100 were added.[53] Lastly there were the parish schools. One such was established for St Nicholas's in 1785, following the same pattern as that of the Protestant dissenters, in that it was launched by subscription under the aegis of the vestry. Three endowments were made to augment income from subscriptions, and the school seems to have functioned successfully until 1813. At this point, according to the Charity Commissioners, a National School was set up, and 'a decided preference was given by the parishioners to the instruction which was to be obtained there; so that by degrees the parish school above-mentioned was deserted, and fell into total disuse'.[54]

Miscellaneous charities

There were so few of these that no general trends may be discerned, although two of them dated from the early nineteenth century and therefore contributed to the revival of endowed charity in this period. These were both sums to support prisoners, one supplying them with bread, meat and coals, the other set up for the release of small debtors. William Vick's 1753 donation to the Merchant Venturers is the only example of a trust established for civic works in the period surveyed.[55] The purpose was to start a fund which would eventually be sufficient to pay for a bridge over the Avon, linking Clifton to Leigh Woods; over 100 years later Vick's objective was realised, with the opening of the Clifton Suspension Bridge, designed by Brunel.[56] Why the lack of interest in civic works? Following the Mortmain Act of 1736 the courts were more reluctant to classify them as a form of charity, thus perhaps deterring donors.[57] Otherwise, testators' reluctance probably arose from the

---

[51] Manchee, i. 19, 55, 174–6.
[52] See M. G. Jones, *The charity school movement in the XVIII century*, Cambridge 1938; Derek Robson, *Some aspects of education in Cheshire in the eighteenth century* (Chetham Society 3rd ser. xiii, 1966); Joan Simon, 'Was there a charity school movement?: the Leicestershire evidence', in Brian Simon (ed.), *Education in Leicestershire, 1640–1940*, Leicester 1968, 55–100.
[53] Manchee, i. 202–5.
[54] Ibid. ii. 197–9.
[55] Ibid. i. 267–70; John Latimer, *Annals of Bristol in the eighteenth century*, Bristol 1893, 308–9.
[56] Latimer, *Annals . . . nineteenth century*, 131–4.
[57] Jones, *Law of charity*, 122–7.

Corporation's growing involvement in public building schemes and the use of subscription to fund such works as the Assembly Room and the Theatre Royal.[58]

The pattern of philanthropy

The principal trend revealed in this survey has been the relative decline of endowed charity in the nineteenth century. This was not necessarily a financial decline, as some very large sums were endowed at the end of the sequence. However, the habit of making this type of charitable bequest was diminishing, nowhere more so than in gifts in the trust of the parish to support the church and provide doles to the poor. The full extent of the failure of endowment becomes obvious when set in the broader context of public spending in the city. Unfortunately it is impossible to compare the overall contributions of public and private support mechanisms in the town, since it is is only possible to guess at the amounts generated through subscription and donation. Previous estimates of such income are: in the 1770s £1,489 *per annum*, rising to £10,107 in 1830, £60,000 in 1851, and £91,000 in 1894.[59] The former two are probably not comprehensive, and the latter probably inaccurate, nor do they break down the sums into the various target groups in a way that would facilitate comparison. The only source which does so is the 1884 *Report of the Committee to Inquire into the Condition of the Bristol Poor*, and Robert Humphreys has made use of this, and the Charity Commission report of 1873, to offer a comparison for the late Victorian period.[60] His concern is limited to the question of whether the poor law outweighed charity in the amount spent on direct relief of the poor, and he determines that by this period it did, setting £41,072 (out-relief) against £20,701 (endowments) and £12,100 (voluntary charities). Unrecorded philanthropy to beggars and personal applicants is ignored in this calculation, despite the unsubstantiated allusion in the report to a possible sum of £50,000 *per annum* dispensed informally.[61]

Figure 4 is a speculative comparison of the sums raised from Bristol's poor rates with an estimate of income from analogous endowments (those directed at the elderly, health and poor relief). It shows the annual income averaged over the decade with inflation adjustment to 1820s prices, and also includes the income of the Infirmary, as the pre-eminent representative of the newer

---

58 Latimer, *Annals . . . eighteenth century*, 59–60, 118, 180, 218, 226, 334–6; Walter Ison, *The Georgian buildings of Bristol*, London 1952, 90–1, 95–105, 109, 114–23, 124.
59 1770's: Barry, 'Cultural life', table xiv; 1830: BRO 36771/73, Livock papers; 1851: Matthews's directory 1851; 1894: S. A. Barnett, *Canon Barnett, his life, work and friends*, ii, London 1918, 220.
60 Robert Humphreys, *Bygone charity: myths and realities* (LSE Working Paper no. 23/94, 1994), 7–10.
61 *Condition of the poor*, 179–80.

Figure 4

Private and public spending on the poor at constant prices (1820s), Bristol, 1700–1869: poor law, endowed charity and Bristol Infirmary

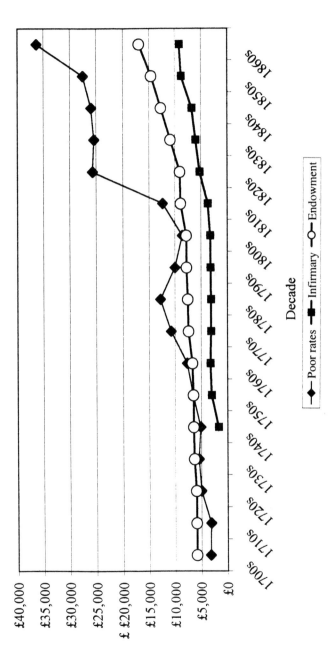

Sources: Charities: as fig. 2; Poor rates: as table 4; Infirmary: BI *State.*

subscription charities.[62] Given the absence of a reliable total for endowment income before the Brougham Commission this must be treated only as a general indicator of comparative growth (see appendix 1). It suggests that while at the start of the eighteenth century the trusts played a major role in the relief of poverty, it was taxation that was more able to meet the needs which demographic expansion and cyclical slumps produced over the long term. Only in the 1750s did rating begin to outstrip the older civic charities, and the trend did not become decisive until the Napoleonic Wars. While both indices show a marked response to the stresses which war and its after-math placed on relief agencies from 1800 to 1820 public taxation could respond more flexibly to changing need. The increase in trust income between 1820 and 1869 does not reflect a surge of new bequests, but demonstrates instead the success of reforms of existing trusts set in motion by the Charity Commission. Therefore, although the trend shown in this graph indicates the continuity of the trusts as a provider of poor relief, it also confirms their decline relative to other forms. Since endowment was by its nature perpetual and cumulative it could never be superseded completely by alternatives, but if a linear model of the evolution of poor relief were to be sought, then for Bristol the mid eighteenth century was the time when the diminution of the trust income as a proportion of total provision became irreversible.

Is it possible that enthusiasm for endowment waned because of the rise in the poor rate? Although the greater responsiveness of the rates to the rising scale of need is suggested in figure 4, it seems that contemporaries viewed the two systems as complementary and exclusive of each other. Jordan showed that Bristol had an unusually high level of giving, second only to London in the range and value of urban charity provided. Yet by the late seventeenth century it also had a comparatively high level of poor law activity, exceeding most other provincial towns in both the size of the rates, and the amount spent on out-relief.[63] Many of the wills establishing gifts for the poor acknowledge the existence of the rates and squarely address the question of how the two types of relief should co-exist. The merchant William Colston, for example, in setting up a parish dole in 1681, specified that it 'be equally divided among six poor housekeepers, not receiving alms of the parish', and this qualification featured regularly throughout the eighteenth century.[64] Rather than the rates undermining the tendency to endow it appears that they enforced two distinct categories of 'poor' – deserving and undeserving of charity. This was not a distinction drawn between regular claimants and the urgent cases or transients, both of whom were aided by the Old Poor Law, but reflected instead the judgement of the churchwardens, who not only wielded

62 See appendix 1.
63 Slack, *Poverty and policy*, 178, 181.
64 Manchee, i. 332. See also pp. 354–7, 359–61, 363–5, 367, 371–2, 376, 378, 381, 441, 444, 455–6, 459, 464.

the power of vestry distribution of doles but also held some responsibility for public relief.[65] Although Bristol parishes had long been united in the Corporation of the Poor for rating purposes, the churchwardens still participated in setting the rate and also received a proportion of the money levied for giving as parish out-relief.[66] Parish charity doles supplemented the income of those who were not in the greatest need, but who were known to the trustees and who, most probably, were Anglicans, since choice of recipient was often 'as the minister and churchwardens should think fit'.[67]

Also, if the rising rate burden was crowding out private philanthropy then gifts to the poor could be expected to disappear from wills and deeds. This was not the case. Although endowed trusts declined in number, testators did not abandon the habit of philanthropic giving, they simply chose a different form. The gifts of three Bristol donors will illustrate the point. Richard Reynolds has already been mentioned as a member of the pantheon of Bristol philanthropists whose name was regularly invoked in speeches and sermons as an inspiration to the wealthy.[68] By deed in 1809 he set up an endowment funded by several properties in Wales to generate money in support of several subscription charities such as the Bristol Infirmary, the Bristol Samaritan Society, the Stranger's Friend Society and the Bristol Female Misericordia.[69] Reynolds was closely involved with the benevolent associations that flourished at the time, and chose to adapt the older style endowments to the new medium. The 1836 will of Thomas Whippie, a 'liberal benefactor' of Clifton Wood, provides further evidence of how new voluntary institutions, reflecting the personal concerns of the benevolent, now inclined them against endowment. Recipients included the Wesleyan Missionary Society for the West Indies, the Clifton Dispensary, the Moravian Mission Society, the General Hospital and the Superannuated Wesleyan Preachers Society.[70] The will of George Thomas suggests that even after reform had removed the municipal charities from the 'corrupt' hands of the Corporation the beneficent testator now preferred voluntary organisations. Thomas, a member of both the Corporation and Bristol Municipal Charity Trustees, and one of the town's richest men, might at first sight appear to have been likely to establish a trust when he died in 1869. But again, rather than a generalised gift to the poor, Thomas, like Whippie and Reynolds, chose immediate and specific targets which suited his own enthusiasms, including the Bristol Infirmary, the

---

65 Karel Williams, *From pauperism to poverty*, London 1981.
66 Kington, 'An analysis of the report of the commissioners of corporate enquiry for the city and county of Bristol', in *A burgess's letters*, 19–20; Barry, 'The parish in civic life', 153–78 at pp. 168–9; Martin Gorsky, 'Experiments in poor relief: Bristol, 1816–1817', *The Local Historian* xxv (1995), 17–30 at pp. 17–18, 28–9.
67 Manchee, i. 360.
68 *Bristol Mercury*, 9 Dec. 1816.
69 Manchee, i. 105, 227–31; Tompson, *Charity Commission*, 72; Owen, *English philanthropy*, 79–80.
70 *Bristol Gazette*, 1 Sept. 1836.

General Hospital, the Bristol Guardian House and the various Friends' Day Schools.[71]

All this suggests that the rise of voluntarism, rather than the rate burden was central to the decline of endowment, and that the trust gave way to a new form of legacy. Indeed, it was common for the major institutions such as Bristol Infirmary to include a *pro forma* bequest in their annual reports to encourage potential benefactors.[72] There was no trust established, no designated recipients, no delegated day of distribution, no perpetuation of the donor's memory. A lump sum bequest simply went to the hospital governors to apply 'to the charitable use of the said Infirmary'. It would be strange if this new flow of testamentary charity had not diverted giving away from the more traditional trusts. Contemporary evidence that the Infirmary was viewed more favourably than the older charities comes from a publication of 1775, which described it in these terms:

> It is founded on a plan the least liable of any to be abused and perverted, viz. that of yearly subscriptions, and has accordingly been so well conducted as to meet with the assistance of most of the opulent inhabitants of Bristol and its environs.[73]

Reference to the taint of corruption surrounding other charities prompted donors to favour hospitals and other subscriber institutions for the transparency of their accounting and management – a characteristic noted by other hospital historians.[74] The positive appeal of the new voluntary charities was broadly based, rooted in their role as instruments of sociability, their religious and political identifications, and their greater freedom of action under the law in comparison to the more tightly restricted trusts.[75]

So, while there is no clear evidence that the escalating burden of the poor rates deterred givers, the rejection of endowed charity appears to have resulted from a growing disenchantment with maladministration of trusts, coinciding with the emergent counter-attraction of new subscriber charities. Will this explanation suffice? For all their virtues, it is by no means clear that the benefits of the new charities outweighed the costs of the old. First, the great strength of endowed charity was its self-perpetuating nature; once a gift of this sort was made it produced a return, year in, year out. By contrast, those which were funded by subscription could not be certain of their future income and were frequently faced with a loss of momentum as the originators

71 J. Nicholls, *Bristol biographies: life of George Thomas*, Bristol 1870.
72 *BI State.*
73 Anon, *An account of hospitals, alms-houses and public schools in Bristol*, Bristol 1775.
74 Anne Borsay, ' "Persons of honour and reputation" : the voluntary hospital in an age of corruption', *Medical History* xxv (1991), 281–94; Kathleen Wilson, 'Urban culture and political activism in Hanoverian England: an example of voluntary hospitals', in Eckhart Hellmuth (ed.), *The transformation of political culture: England and Germany in the late eighteenth century*, Oxford 1990, 165–84 at pp. 172–3, 180–1.
75 Tompson, *Charity Commission*, 68–72.

moved on or died and new causes came to the fore. Second, although this greater reliability of trusts was offset in the early nineteenth century by a certain amount of dishonest and incompetent trusteeship, this began to be rectified with the establishment of the Commission in 1819. Open accounting and the correction of past abuses was the *raison d'être* of this body, whose eighteen-year investigation entailed the scrutiny of all original deeds and bequests to assess subsequent trustee performance.[76] It clearly showed the endowments most vulnerable to distortion of donors' original intentions to be those based on property. There were various potential pitfalls: the costs of fabric deterioration, the alienation of parcels of land by rapacious trustees, and leasing on over-generous terms to cronies which failed to take full advantage of rising land values. However, once the Commission had brought the trusts into the public domain their honest management was more assured and there were striking increases in profitability, as in Bristol, where between the enquiries of 1819–37 and 1867–76 income generated increased by £ 18,587 *per annum*.[77] Yet despite this improvement the seventy years following the establishment of the Commission witnessed the lowest number of new endowed trusts established. A related development which should have enhanced the attraction of the charitable trust was the growth of the securities market. Before the mid eighteenth century income from endowment was typically generated by property, with all its attendant problems. However the 'financial revolution' and the restructuring of the national debt in the wake of the South Sea Bubble witnessed the arrival, between 1720 and 1750, of charitable trusts with investment accounts in government stock.[78] Henceforth the growing market in securities offered donors a predictable return with none of the pitfalls of endowing property. Further encouragement for this trend towards leaving personal rather than real estate came from the Mortmain Act, which weighted the courts' judgements in favour of aggrieved relatives appealing against the terms of a trust.[79]

The rejection of endowed charity presents a paradox. Why did it occur at just the time when state supervision and improved investment opportunities should have stimulated it? Reliability, predictability and permanence were the hallmarks of endowment after the Charity Commission. Here was a form of charity with manifest benefits, and yet if the timetable of reform is set against trends in figures 2 and 3 there is no congruence. Decline began in the mid eighteenth century, yet this pre-dated the calls for reform and investigation In the early 1800s, when concern about corruption was supposedly prompting parliamentary enquiry there was a brief recovery in number and value of endowments. In the 1830s endowment fell to a new low, just when

---

[76] Ibid. 186–98.
[77] *General digest*, PP 1877 lxvi. 34–5.
[78] P. Dickson, *The financial revolution in England*, London 1967, 283–4, 299–300.
[79] Jones, *Law of charity*, chs vi, ix; Whittle, 'Philanthropy in Preston', 5.

open accounting revealed that the most glaring examples of Corporation property mismanagement had occurred not recently but two centuries before, and when the benefits of reform were becoming clear. It is the reverse of what might be expected if concern with corruption was the key determinant. There is therefore a problem with a *post hoc* explanation which presents the decline of endowed charity as the inevitable supersession of the old and inefficient by the new and improved. As an effective means of delivering charity the trust was actually becoming more viable at the time of its demise – there was no functional imperative undermining it. If the changing attitudes of donors are to be understood, then enquiry must focus not on rational calculations of the trusts' effectiveness but on the specific meanings that different kinds of charities held for the citizen. In particular it must ask why the argument that charity administration had become corrupt held such sway in early nineteenth-century Bristol.

3

The Politics of Charity

The argument advanced thus far has identified a chronology of rejection of endowed charity and attributed this to a perception of 'contract failure' – a sense that the bond of trust between the giver and those charged with the administration of the gift was vulnerable to severance. The newer forms of voluntary charity with their financial openness and public meetings seemed to offer a more accountable channel of philanthropy. However the disjuncture between the patterns of endowment and the chronology of charity reform make it unlikely that the decline of the trust resulted from a widespread failure of the system. There had always been divergences from the strict letter of charitable trusts.[1] The historical problem is not so much to explain the existence of abuses, but rather to ask why endowment came under attack, and why there was a receptive audience for these attacks. The answer to this lies with electoral politics, in particular the agenda of Radical reform agitation, where the charities question became an important weapon for promoting change. Charity corruption emerged as a prominent issue in local politics not because it was an issue of pressing popular concern, but because of its metaphorical power: its use was primarily symbolic of social and political change. In the case of Bristol the political debate over charity corruption did not so much reflect the reality of decline and disenchantment, as help to shape it. Two inter-related arguments will support this claim. First, endowed charity's place in public discourse is traced, to demonstrate that its presence was closely linked to the quest for advantage in electoral politics. Secondly, the Liberal trustees who took control of the Corporation's charities after municipal reform are compared to their Tory predecessors. They emerge as a rival political elite, whose interest in the charities was driven not by a yearning to benefit needy recipients, but rather by the urge to grasp a vital lever of local government power.

Charity administration and party politics: before 1835

The entangling of endowed charity with local electoral politics was always likely. Benefactors needed to leave their wealth to a permanent body, a vestry or corporation, yet in so doing they added to the power of closed political

---

[1] Jones, *Law of charity*, 18–19, 52.

institutions. In the eighteenth century accusations by vanquished candidates that the other side had bribed voters with the Corporation charities were a recurrent feature of national elections in Bristol, the charge being made by the Whigs John Scrope in 1734 and Henry Cruger in 1781.[2] The use of charity enquiries as a political weapon also had a long history, dating back at least to the threat of a Commission of Charitable Uses made by the bishop of Bristol to the Corporation in 1676.[3] A century later *An account of the hospitals, almshouses and public schools in Bristol* (1775) also used the charities to make barely concealed digs at Corporation management.[4] This pamphlet purported to be an informative document detailing several charities, mostly in the gift of the Corporation, and though superficially apolitical there were heavy hints of a hidden agenda.[5] For example, the probity of the Infirmary's management was stressed, the workhouse was praised for averting 'any design of misapplications . . . a case that too often occurs in handling the public's money', and the rights of dissenters to claim on particular funds were emphasised.[6] Bristol Grammar School also attracted comment.[7] Dubious administration was highly visible: in 1766 the Corporation had exchanged the Grammar School's premises for those of the superior site of Queen Elizabeth's Hospital, to the detriment of the pauper children in the latter school.[8] In 1803 a group of Grammar School old boys petitioned the Corporation to reverse the actions of headmaster Richard Lee who had not only virtually eradicated free scholars from the institution, but was preparing to shed the fee-paying boarders and convert his position to a sinecure. The Corporation was unwilling to take action and the fortunes of the school languished until the era of the Charity Trustees.[9]

These nagging concerns were transformed into a major electoral issue in Henry 'Orator' Hunt's 1812 election campaigns in Bristol.[10] Hunt's platform was the Radical critique of 'Old Corruption', an attack on the Westminster patronage system which contended that policy was determined by self-interest, not the public good. Hence the evil of the large national debt to

[2] BRO, Common council proceedings, 1722–38, 376–9; Rogers, *Whigs and cities*, 279–80; *Bristol poll books, 1781–1832*, election petition, 12 Mar. 1781.
[3] J. F. Nicholls and John Taylor, *Bristol: past and present*, III: *Civil and modern history*, Bristol 1882, 68–9.
[4] Anon., *An account of hospitals*.
[5] Latimer, *Annals . . . eighteenth century*, 409–11.
[6] Anon., *An account of hospitals*.
[7] Tompson, *Charity Commission*, 79, 246; Hill, *Bristol Grammar School*, 29–31; Manchee, i. 35.
[8] J. W. Arrowsmith, *Dictionary of Bristol*, Bristol 1906, 169; Bush, *Bristol and its municipal government*, 65.
[9] Hill, *Bristol Grammar School*, 61–3.
[10] Henry Hunt, *Memoirs of Henry Hunt*, London 1821, repr. New York 1970, ii. 495–568; iii. 1–136; Harrison, *Crowds and history*, 209–19; John Belchem, *'Orator' Hunt: Henry Hunt and English working-class radicalism*, Oxford 1985, 34–41; Brett, 'Liberal middle classes', 86–96.

fund the placemen, and the burden of taxes on the poor required to service it. The association of charity administration with a conspiracy of vested interests provided Hunt with an ideal means of dramatising these themes to the Bristol electorate. The 'Orator's' strategy was to characterise the local charities as the fund for the corrupt life-style of the Bristol Corporation, an example in microcosm of his main theme, the public purse abused for individual gain. A pre-election pamphlet contained a list of local charities, mostly those entrusted to the Corporation, detailing capital sums and target applicants.[11] The premise was that charity funds represented common rights that had been quietly suppressed in the interest of the ruling elite. Hunt hoped the campaign for electoral reform had stimulated in his supporters 'a resolution to look into your own concerns; to trace back your rights to their origin; and to act as becomes men who entertain a just sense of those rights'.[12] Two defeats, first in the July by-election, then in the general election, only flamed Hunt's ardour.[13] Unwilling to concede his failure he launched an election petition which accused both the Whig, Protheroe, and the Tory, Davis, of bribery, intimidation and treating.

The furore surrounding the petition prompted a more explicit account of the vulnerability of endowed charity to political chicanery. Hunt characterised the party system as little more than a confidence trick perpetrated on the voters by the elite: 'All the corporation, all the merchants, all the tradesmen, all the clergy and priests, whether of the church of England or of the numberless sects of dissenters . . . were volunteers to uphold the most corrupt and profligate system of election that ever disgraced the rottenest of rotten boroughs.'[14] Central to the argument was the belief that a vast tide of popular support was restrained from a free vote: 'Hundreds upon hundreds came to say that they were anxious to vote for me, but if they did so they would lose their bread and their families would be ruined.'[15] Whether 'bread' is interpreted strictly or as a general reference to parish doles, Hunt's inference is clear: the Corporation and vestries were using the threat of witholding charities in their gift in order to buy votes. He explained how trust property was also prey to venal interest:

> In the first place, the original property is in most instances granted out upon long leases, or upon lives, for a mere nominal premium and nominal rent, to the tools and dependants of the Corporation. In truth almost all the Corporation, all their dirty instruments, and the major part of their parsons and lawyers, are tenants. Large sums of money are lent by the Corporation, to the members of the Corporation, at mere nominal interest. Almost all the

---

11 Henry Hunt, A letter from Mr Hunt to the freemen of Bristol, London 1812.
12 Ibid. 3.
13 Beaven, Bristol lists, 171.
14 Hunt, Memoirs, ii. 528, 530.
15 Ibid. ii. 544.

merchants and tradesmen of the city hold something under the Corporation, and at the time of the elections are their abject tools.[16]

Hunt's petition failed, but his efforts did yield a more permanent legacy of the attempt to politicise charity. This was a book written by a member of his election committee, John Cranidge, entitled A *mirror for the burgesses and commonalty of the city of Bristol* (1818).[17] Though prefaced by a poem darkly admonishing the trustees against witholding 'thy neighbour's due', Cranidge failed to provide any damning evidence of malversation. However, he carefully aligned the charities issue with the interest of the middle classes by stressing its relationship to the poor rates. The survey of the charities was prefaced with the hope that: 'should it in any wise lead to a Reduction of the Parochial Rates and Public Taxes, the end for which it is designed will be obtained'.[18] To drive the point emphatically home Cranidge ended each section on parish charities with a note of how much that parish had paid in the most recent poor rate assessment, inviting the reader to contrast the escalating rates with the abundance of the trusts, if only they were conscientiously applied.[19]

Early nineteenth-century Radicalism therefore placed charity on Bristol's political agenda as an issue which concerned all citizens outside the elite of power. Hunt's popular backing is indicated by a surviving list of his 235 voters in the 1812 by-election; it seems that the small artisans and builders were the source of his support, with cordwainers, carpenters, tailors and masons forming the largest sub-groups.[20] He was also aiming at the vote-less, to whom corrupt electioneering was academic, but depriving them of their rightful dues was not.[21] Hunt told them that a more honest charity policy would mean 'there would not be a citizen of Bristol that would not be handsomely provided for out of these funds'.[22] In this populist rhetoric used in 1812, and again in Hunt's campaign of 1816, 'the people' were pitted against the merchants, tradesmen, parsons and lawyers, who wielded political power through an unjust franchise and a corrupt electoral system.[23] Hunt and Cranidge aimed to link the question of charity administration to municipal reform in the public mind, so that endowed charity, once a symbol of reciprocal obligation between rich and poor, began to represent the gulf between rulers and ruled.

---

[16] Ibid. iii. 131–2.

[17] J. Cranidge, A *mirror for the burgesses and commonalty of the city of Bristol*, Bristol 1818.

[18] Ibid. preamble.

[19] Ibid. 13–14.

[20] Hunt, *Memoirs*, iii. 7–12; Belchem, '*Orator*' *Hunt*, 49.

[21] Frank O'Gorman, 'Campaign rituals and ceremonies: the social meaning of elections in England, 1780–1860', *P&P* cxxxv (1992), 79–105 esp. p. 81.

[22] Hunt, *Memoirs*, iii. 135.

[23] Gorsky, 'Experiments in poor relief', 17–30; Harrison, *Crowds and history*, 119, 125, 150, 155; David Large, *Radicalism in Bristol in the nineteenth century*, Bristol 1981, 8–9.

In the interval between Hunt's campaigns and the Municipal Corporations Act charity slipped from view as an electoral issue, no doubt because the investigations of the Brougham Commission could be easily evoked to quell any public doubts. However, its lingering potential as a weapon in reform politics remained. In 1827, for instance, a London publishing firm produced *Rights of the poor*, a digest of the Charity Commission report on the Bristol trusts, which was more critical than Cranidge of the Corporation's handling of educational endowments and loan charities.[24] Here again endowed charities were viewed as a customary right, now 'grossly perverted' and requiring the 'talisman of publicity' so they might resume their place in relieving poverty.[25] In national politics the Whigs made use of charity malversation in their campaign for the reform of local government. The 1830 Select Committee held as the precursor to Hobhouse's Select Vestries Act concerned itself in part with parochial charities, and called for evidence from Bristol in the course of proceedings.[26] The questioning of Lionel Bigg, vestry clerk to All Saints, and William Fripp, alderman for the ward of St Mary Redcliffe, was pointedly geared to establishing the involvement of the vestries in the electoral process.[27] Asked about charity distribution to loyal voters Bigg frankly acknowledged that since 'vestries are composed of, persons of all tempers, some having more party spirit than others . . . it may be possible that just after the conclusion of an election there may be some little distinction'.[28] Here then was the issue articulated at the heart of Reform politics, in the measure which Hobhouse later described as 'not a bad pilot balloon for the great act of 1832'.[29]

It was therefore natural that the matter should arise in the debate preceding the Municipal Corporations Act. Though initially ignored in the Bristol report of the Commissioners of Corporate Enquiry, charity was debated when the Corporation presented its petition against the bill before the House of Lords, to be met with a counter petition in favour from the 'Burgesses and Commonalty'.[30] The Corporation and its solicitors stressed the approval they had received from the Brougham Commissioners, the regular audit of charity accounts, and the cost implications of moving administration to a trustee

---

[24] Anon, *Rights of the poor, charities of Bristol*, London 1827, collected in BRO, Bristol pamphlets, volume iv. 76, 91–2, 106–7, 110–11.

[25] Ibid. 'Address'.

[26] Robert E. Zegger, *John Cam Hobhouse, a political life, 1819–1852*, Columbia 1973; W. Tate, *The parish chest*, Cambridge 1946, 22–3; Sidney Webb and Beatrice Webb, *English local government: statutory authorities for special purposes*, London 1922, 449.

[27] *Minutes of evidence before Select Committee on Select and Other Vestries*, PP 1830 iv. 662–4, 11 Mar. 1830.

[28] Ibid. 665.

[29] John Cam Hobhouse, *Recollections of a long life*, i. 131, cited in Zegger, *Hobhouse*, 154.

[30] *English Municipal Commission: report on the city and council of Bristol*, PP 1835 xxiv. 482–579; Bush, *Bristol and its municipal government*, ch. vi; Kington, 'An analysis', in 'A burgess's' *letters*.

body.[31] The counter-petitioners pointed out that the Corporation charities were largely distributed on the recommendation of churchwardens, whom they characterised as *ex officio* Tory election agents, with the result that 'poor electors generally look upon their political subserviency as the best title which they can prefer to these gifts'.[32] While it is unlikely that this debate influenced the pro- or anti-reform camps, it clearly revealed the extent to which Hunt's argument had been absorbed by the city's Liberals. In the twenty-five years since he had seized on the theme, charity had been transformed from a marginal matter to a central concern of Bristol party politics. And yet this had occurred at a time when new endowments were made with more frequency and generosity than they had been in the late eighteenth century.

Charity administration and party politics: after 1835

In the fifteen years following the passage of the Municipal Corporations Act the issue of charity administration was prominent in national and local elections in Bristol. Why was this, and what caused its disappearance? It did not arise from a distinct approach to social policy associated with the Liberals. Instead it should be understood in the context of the extreme party animosity of the 1830s and 1840s, when the 'reform' section of Bristol's elite sought to seize the reins of power in the wake of local government changes, while the Tories strove to retain their position.[33] Reform allowed the true picture of charity mismanagement to emerge, but the potency of the issue in dramatising the fissure within the elite rapidly obscured the actual and heightened the symbolic.

The signal for a bitter party dispute was the section of the Municipal Corporations Act which provided that after August 1836 the Lord Chancellor should appoint new trustees for charities previously under the administration of the Corporation, on the basis of a local petition. An angry debate ensued on the composition of the trustee body, followed by a tussle between the predominantly Liberal trustees and the predominantly Tory Council over the recovery of the charity funds.[34] The Liberals put forward a petition to the Lord Chancellor, suggesting a board of Charity Trustees eighteen-strong, half Tory, half Liberal, but the consensus approach was upset by a Chancery decision, which recommended an uneven number of members, thus opening the

---

31 'Petition from the Corporation', 'Municipal Corporation Reform Bill', 'Proceedings having especial reference to Bristol', ibid. 2–3; *House of Lords Journal*, 5 Aug. 1835.
32 Kington, 'A *burgess's' letters*, 34–40.
33 G. B. A. M. Finlayson, 'The politics of municipal reform, 1835', *EHR* lxxxi (1966), 673–92; Derek Fraser, *Urban politics in Victorian England: the structure of politics in Victorian cities*, Leicester 1976.
34 Bush, *Bristol and its municipal government*, 148–9, 155–6; Latimer, *Annals . . . nineteenth century*, 230–6; Brett, 'Liberal middle classes', 299–300.

question to partisan concerns; the Liberals then responded by claiming the additional trustee for themselves. Piqued that they, as the majority party in the Council were not to dominate the body, the Tories declined to participate further in the selection process, presumably in the hope that this would stall it. They had miscalculated. A further petition resulted in the nomination of the Bristol Municipal Charity Trustees, consisting of eighteen Liberals and a mere three Tories, an outcome probably determined by the close links between local Liberals and the Westminster leadership.[35]

Bristol's Liberals were not motivated primarily by the desire to cleanse charity administration. Consideration of the developing political landscape suggests instead that their capture of the board was part of a broader electoral strategy. Liberal optimism at the prospect of increased influence ushered in by the Municipal Corporations Act had rapidly dissipated, primarily as a result of the decisions of the boundary commissioners who visited Bristol to redraw the wards in the now expanded electoral district (Bristol Council was henceforth to represent Clifton and Bedminster too). The forty-eight seats were allocated amongst the wards, which conformed to parish boundaries, on the basis of the number of rated houses they contained. This gave a dispro- portionately large number of seats to Clifton, St Augustine's and St Michael's, where the Tories were stronger, against the populous wards of St James's, Bedminster and St Philip's where the Liberals were dominant.[36] The result of the first election gave ample ammunition to those who viewed this as a naked gerrymander. While the Liberals had won a majority of the total vote, the parties each held twenty-four seats.[37] The balance of power tilted further in the aldermanic elections when the defection of one of the old Whigs, Christopher George, ensured that twelve Tories were chosen against only three Liberals.[38] There was therefore a compelling reason to fight for representation on all possible committees to ensure that Liberal influence was exerted. The Charity Trustees could be of political significance within this context, as the patronage attached to the funds and property was sub- stantial. The association of Liberal councillors with the city's celebrated insti- tutions could provide an electorally beneficial image, while honest Liberal stewardship could be publicised to highlight the defects of Tory adminis- tration under the old system.

That the new Charity Trustees had every intention of exploiting their position for political gain became abundantly clear in the general election of 1837. The *Bristol Mercury* was the chief mouthpiece of the Liberal campaign, and made charity corruption central to a vigorous editorial attack on the Tories that crowed over their loss of lying-in gifts, doles and school places:

[35] Ibid. 177, 288, 299.
[36] Ibid. 297–8; Latimer, *Annals . . . nineteenth century*, 208–11; Bush, *Bristol and its munici- pal government*, 116–21.
[37] Ibid. 121.
[38] Ibid. 122–3; Latimer, *Annals . . . nineteenth century*, 211–12.

'All this immense patronage they have lost.'[39] As the campaign intensified the newspaper became more intemperate: 'We leave the admitted facts that eighteen out of twenty-one of the Charity Trustees are good, straight-forward Liberals; and that in the distribution of their vast funds, they will be sure NOT to reward a single Tory vote.'[40] The ambiguity of the statement was no doubt intentional, but the Conservative *Journal* was quick to interpret it as an unblushing attempt to intimidate voters.[41] The *Mercury* was unrepentant in its last edition before the poll, printing a poem which savagely lampooned Corporation charity administration:

> And from Peloquin's gifts the means shall be found,
> To keep a full stock in our vaults underground,
> At the corner of Broad Street of wine of each sort –
> Champaign and Madeira, Hock, Sherry and Port.
> . . . But we, my good sir, never feel any qualms
> To take from the poor what is left them in alms.[42]

Now the association of the charities with corruption, which had begun with Hunt and the Radicals as a means of attacking the town's elite, and had then been co-opted by the Liberals as a means of attacking the Tories, was to become a weapon of the Conservatives for attacking the Liberals. After the Liberal victory the Tory *Journal* had been quick to explain the loss of the second Conservative seat in terms of the 'shameful prostitution of the charities of Bristol' by the new trustees, who were using the funds for bribery.[43] Meanwhile the *Mercury* was quick to crow at the 'destructive crush of Tory influence' that had resulted from their loss of the 'power of misappropriating the Charity trusts'.[44] Was this mere bluster? Investigation of the distribution of the Peloquin and Whitson gifts in 1833, 1834 and 1835 showed that out of 232 gifts made, 184 went to freemen who had split their votes between the two Tories.[45] The margin separating Berkeley from Fripp was a mere fifty-six votes, so the newspaper's assertion is perfectly possible, though not verifiable at this distance. More significant was the fact that both parties now saw charity as symbolic of democratic virtue in a changed political landscape.

Why did charity remain an issue after 1837? After all, the national election had seen the return of bi-partisan representation in the two borough seats, and it was clear that the Tory majority on the Council was firmly ensconced. However the Liberal Charity Trustees soon discovered there was

---

39 *Bristol Mercury*, 8 July 1837.
40 Ibid. 15 July 1837.
41 *FFBJ*, 22 July 1837.
42 *Bristol Mercury*, 22 July 1837.
43 *FFBJ*, 29 July 1837.
44 Ibid. 5 July 1837; Beaven, *Bristol lists*, 172.
45 *Bristol Mercury*, 29 July 1837; Brett, 'Liberal middle classes', 299–300; *Minutes of evidence taken before the Select Committee on Bribery at Elections*, 1835, questions 6308–464, 6544–744, 6745–920, 6921–7186.

more ammunition on hand with which to attack their Tory rivals. The separation of charities from the Council necessitated a transfer of the funds, stock, accounts and property deeds to the trustees. This the Council had been very loath to do. At first it refused to even acknowledge, let alone respond to, the trustees' applications for the monies, while the new Board grew increasingly suspicious of the interminable delays.[46] This obstructionism was to some extent party political, but primarily economic. Reform of the Municipal Corporations had been borne along by the expectation that more representative councils would be better able to meet the demands of the mushrooming cities for improved policing, sanitation and so on.[47] Yet in Bristol the new council was faced with a heavy burden from the public spending of its predecessor, occasioned by such items as the building of the New Gaol, and more recently the compensation owing to victims of the 1831 'Reform Riots'.[48] In this context it needed to maximise all available assets.

As the deeds were reluctantly yielded to the trustees it became clear that the Liberals were being presented with another opportunity to make political capital from the endowed charities. Their secretary, Manchee, solicitor, Brittain, and accountant, Joshua Jones, subjected the records to a tougher scrutiny than the Charity Commissioners had managed.[49] Claims were advanced on behalf of four of the charities, Queen Elizabeth Hospital and Owen's lands (Grammar School) for misappropriation of income, and Bartholomew Lands (Grammar School) and Carr's Lands (Trinity Hospital) for illegal title to their property. The amount owing to the trustees was, and is, a matter of debate, since it hinges on the theoretical scale of interest calculated on the misappropriated capital sums or properties; Latimer suggested it 'certainly exceeded a quarter of a million pounds' while Bush repeated the trustees' own estimate of £344,000.[50] The Conservatives sought to deflect the trustees with a counter-attack. In November 1837 they launched an election petition claiming that two Liberal trustees, Cunningham and Harwood, had used charity funds to bribe electors.[51] The petition collapsed amidst claims of perjury, and the Council was left with no other tactic but to delay the inevitable.[52] With suits of £86,000 outstanding the Council finally agreed, in 1842, to pay compensation of £11,000 for its past misdeeds, and make good all income accrued on the charities since 1836.

---

46 BMC, MB i, Oct. 1836–Feb. 1842, 14 July 1837, 27 Oct. 1837; Brittain to Council, BRO 00568, folder 3, correspondence concerning transference and miscellaneous charity deeds and papers.
47 Derek Fraser, *Power and authority in the Victorian city*, Oxford 1979, 17–21.
48 Bush, *Bristol and its municipal government*, 74–9, 153–4.
49 BMC, MB i, 11 Nov. 1836.
50 Latimer, *Annals . . . nineteenth century*, 235; Bush, *Bristol and its municipal government*, 155–6.
51 *FFBJ*, 14 Oct., 25 Nov. 1837.
52 *FFBJ, Bristol Mercury*, 24 Feb. 1838; Latimer, *Annals . . . nineteenth century*, 239–40. On petitioning see Norman Gash, *Politics in the age of Peel*, London 1952, 133–6.

Previous historians have downplayed the party political aspect of the charity dispute. Latimer, himself a nineteenth-century Liberal, described the episode in terms of a struggle between enlightened reform and corrupt self-interest. Bush viewed it as 'the last chapter in the practical transition from the old form of municipal government in Bristol to the new'.[53] Neither makes it clear that the trustees were also the core group of Liberal activists in the Council, nor that the party was already exploiting their position for electioneering purposes when the dispute first arose. As one of the trustees admitted when the claim was debated: 'Neither did they for a moment contemplate any such arrears of interest being called for, as appeared to have accumulated; this monstrous amount only represented as in a mirror the injustice done by the counter-claim against the Charity.'[54] In other words, the money itself was not the issue since most trustees were also councillors, with no intention of bankrupting the city treasury. The real aim was to make political capital. Bristol's governing elite was divided and the charities were one of the battlegrounds on which it fought.

A final confirmation that it was the exigencies of electoral politics which forced charity administration into public discourse can be obtained by asking why it eventually disappeared from view. There were several elements which undermined its potency, and all point to its redundancy as an electoral tactic. First, the Conservatives recognised that the ploy of besmirching the Liberal trustees' reputation was unlikely to succeed and could rebound on them. The 1841 election was the last in which the Tory press mounted a sustained campaign on the charities question, but the manner in which it was presented was seen as unproductive. Things started well enough, with hints at the impropriety of the links between prominent trustees and the Liberal candidate's electoral committee.[55] Further capital was made out of the contradictions of dissenting trustees having control of Anglican charities, a matter recently under consideration in the House of Lords.[56] However, as the campaign neared its close the Tory *Journal* dropped injudicious hints about vestry generosity: 'The freemen must remember that while Conservatives have six hundred and thirty-one gifts at their disposal, the number in the hands of the Charity Trustees amounts only to one hundred and twenty-nine.'[57] This proved to be a double-edged sword for Conservatism as it reminded the public of the past malversation of the Tory-controlled Corporation; no one seriously challenged this now and the Tory hierarchy hoped that their zealous

---

[53] Bush, *Bristol and its municipal government*, 156; Latimer, *Annals . . . nineteenth century*, 233–6.
[54] BRO, Common Council proceedings, Oct. 1837.
[55] *FFBJ*, 5 June 1841.
[56] Ibid. 24 Apr. 1841; BRL 10103, Collection of broadsides, addresses, notices etc., relating to the election of 1841: 'A few words to the electors of Bristol'.
[57] *FFBJ*, 26 June 1841.

campaigners and pugnacious editors would abandon the issue.[58] The Liberals could point out that they had been exonerated in the election petition of 1837, while that of 1835 had inculpated the Tories, and to crown their argument, there was tangible evidence of improvement under the trustees, for instance an increase in boys attending Queen Elizabeth Hospital.

However, the Liberals had their own motives for dropping charity from their electoral platform. The issues which it symbolised – venal interest versus public spirit, corruption versus open administration – were rendered increasingly redundant by the realignment within party politics. Crucially, it risked opening up the thorny question of poor relief, which increasingly divided the Liberal leadership from Radical activists, at a time when working-class politics in the city were diverging from the main party programmes. Poverty had been an issue of great moment in the 1830s, yet the political debate which surrounded the endowed charity question in Bristol did not engage with it. Instead, the problem was posed as one of management style: which group within the town's middle class could be best entrusted to administer the funds honestly? In their enthusiasm to advance charity malversation as a metaphor for 'Old Corruption' Bristol's Liberals failed to address the question of how their control of the endowments might improve the delivery of poor relief in the town. Of course the fruits of charity would no longer be the sole preserve of Tory voters, and there are glancing references to restoring property rights.[59] Yet the language of practical care or benevolent compassion for the needy was wholly absent.

This should come as no surprise, given the argument advanced here that the debate over endowed charity related to electoral advantage and had little to do with the question of need. Middle-class Liberal and working-class Chartist could comfortably unite against graft within an effete, unaccountable elite, but the New Poor Law was more divisive. For example the speeches and literature of the 'journeymen of the trades' of Bristol in support of Berkeley in 1837 were a good deal further from the Whig ministry than their superiors in the local party.[60] True, the familiar antipathy between 'the productive classes' and the 'palaced paupers' (idle landowners), was central to the analysis.[61] However the political programme of the Liberal journeymen included repeal of the corn laws ('the Tory machine for destroying by starvation a surplus poor population'), reform of the poor laws, secret ballot and extension of the suffrage.[62] A few months later the division between Chartists and Liberals became more explicit. At the first meeting of the new Working Men's Association the mood flowed strongly against the Liberals:

---

[58] Bristol Mercury, 13 Mar., 26 June 1841; Latimer, Annals . . . nineteenth century, 240.
[59] George Thomas's address to voters, Bristol Mercury, FFBJ, Bristol Gazette, 4 Nov. 1837.
[60] Bristol Mercury, 15, 22 July 1837; FFBJ, 29 July 1837.
[61] Bristol Mercury, 15 July 1837; Stedman Jones, 'Re-thinking Chartism'.
[62] Bristol Mercury, 22 July 1837.

Where were they when that infernal Whig poor law was passed? (hear) Did they stand up and defend the rights of the working classes? No, they left them in the lurch. In the reign of Elizabeth laws were enacted for the purpose of assisting the poor – these laws provided that, when a man was destitute or unable to work, he should be provided for; but the Whigs said 'that was too much – it was too good – the working man must not be allowed to press so much upon the property of the rate payers'. Why did they forget that the whole of that property was derived from the industry of the working men (hear)?[63]

The gulf which opened within the Liberal constituency on this issue helps explain why charity was discussed within different parameters. Radicals claimed parish poor relief as a property right of the worker, given in compensation after the confiscation of monastic lands, and as noted, a language of property rights was sometimes employed in discussing charity administration.[64] However this sat awkwardly with the arguments supporting the New Poor Law. As mouthpiece of the party leadership the *Bristol Mercury* defended government policy against Chartist attacks. Not only had 'the idle and vicious paupers – the surplus population . . . been driven to habits of sobriety and industry', but in addition 'the insolence . . . which used to distinguish the old poor law is exchanged for that respectful behaviour which is due from the relative station in which the labourer is placed'.[65] What did the *Mercury*'s working-class readership make of this? Two weeks earlier the paper had urged them to vote out the Tories who 'take from the poor what is left them in alms', yet now it seemed that the 'Rads' regarded welfare not as a right but as a paternal arrangement which enforced subordination.

Discussion of endowed charity within the frame of reference of Whig thought on poverty therefore risked alienating a portion of the Liberal electorate. This is not to say that the Malthusian attack on indiscriminate out-relief could not be applied equally to charity, as Henry Brougham's later writing testifies. In 1834 the progenitor of the Charity Commission argued that the only acceptable charities were those catering to 'the sick, the aged and the impotent', though even almshouses were suspect, since 'all prudent men of independent spirit, will, in the vigour of their days, lay by sufficient to maintain them'. Educational endowments should no longer board poor children, as this promoted dependence, while money doles should be reserved 'rigorously for periods of extraordinary distress, and then bestowing them upon persons above the lowest classes'.[66]

---

63 Ibid. 28 Oct. 1837.
64 William Cobbett, *History of the Protestant Reformation in England and Ireland*, London 1824–7, repr. London 1896, chs v, vi, vii, xvi; *Political Register*, 9, 30 Nov. 1816; 10 Oct. 1818. See also José Harris, *Private lives, public spirit: Britain, 1870–1914*, Oxford 1993, repr. Harmondsworth 1994, 111–12.
65 *Bristol Mercury*, 12 Aug. 1837.
66 Henry Brougham, *Lord Brougham's speeches*, iii, Edinburgh 1838, 64–5, 486–7.

Such sentiments may have arisen from the logic of Whig social philosophy, but they were electorally dangerous, given the Chartist critique of the poor law, and the shifting political sociology it brought in its train. Bristol Chartists now proposed a three-tier model for society, 'the upper, or aristocratic, the middle, or trading, and the lower, or working classes: the first is chiefly composed of Tories, the second of Whigs, the last of Radicals'.[67] The poor law was portrayed as a conspiracy against the 'industrious mechanic and labourer, upon whom the two above-named classes fatten like drones in a hive', and the true motive of the Malthusians was the cheap manipulation of the labour market.[68] Tories pitching to 'fellow labourers in the True Blue cause – the working classes' also seized upon the issue of 'the cursed poor law bastilles which these reformers have built for them . . . for the "enormous" crime of POVERTY'.[69] Pushed to articulate a party stance on charity and poor relief the Liberal position was at last clarified: 'Where cases of real hardship occur, the remedy must be applied by individual charity – a virtue for which no system of compulsory relief can or ought to be a substitute.'[70] The contradictions of Liberal administration of the charities were thus exposed. Was the aim to resurrect long-held rights of the poor through honest management? Or was it to provide a salve for those caught between the attenuation of welfare benefits and the cyclical trade depressions, with the 'individual' or face-to-face nature of charity ensuring that relief went only to the genuinely deserving? Thus as Chartism grew increasingly vociferous, and as Liberal voters divided on their opinions of poor relief, the charity issue became less suitable as a rallying cause.

In the end though, it was the tension within the Tory camp which rendered the Liberal recourse to charity as a campaign theme unnecessary. William Fripp had been nominated by local Tories in 1841 to run with Miles against Berkeley in the hope of capturing both Bristol seats for the Conservatives. This scheme had not pleased Miles, who was conscious of the 'impropriety of his endeavouring to monopolise the franchise of a voter'.[71] The hapless Fripp was also attacked by the Tory MP for Somerset, James Adam Gordon, whose priority was to promote the new Portbury Dock in parliament, and who urged voters to back the Miles/Berkeley ticket as both had firmly supported his bill.[72] In 1847 William Fripp made a further unsuccessful bid for a seat, this time as the free-trade candidate against Miles's protectionism. Election literature was dominated by questions of free trade, dock ownership and character assassination, to which the Miles camp brought

67 *Bristol Mercury*, 25 Nov. 1837, 11–23 Nov. 1837 passim for a correspondence between the Chartist Moses Clements and two Liberals, 'Yorick' and 'Cosmopolite' debating the Poor Law Amendment Act.
68 *Bristol Mercury*, 9 Dec. 1837.
69 'Advertisement from W. Bulphin', *FFBJ*, 3 Mar. 1838.
70 *Bristol Mercury*, 16 Dec. 1837.
71 *FFBJ*, 10 July 1841.
72 BRL, Collection . . . 1841, passim; Beaven, *Bristol lists*, 172.

considerably more aplomb and venom in their attack on Fripp than the Liberals had ever managed.[73] A reference to charity appears in one such poster:

> Who was the Leader of the old Charity Trust System?   William Fripp.
> Who stated, ON OATH, before the House of Lords, that the Charity
> Trusts had been 'honestly, piously and discreetly administered'?
> William Fripp.
> Who is the most Stingy, Mean and Tyrannical Man in Bristol?
> William Fripp.
> WE'LL NEVER HAVE HIM![74]

The symbolic elasticity of charity administration in Bristol electoral politics had therefore taken it on a long journey, beginning with the radical challenge to 'Old Corruption' and ending as a weapon brandished in Conservative internecine warfare.

In 1851 the depoliticisation of charity was made manifest in the constitution of the Board of Trustees. The deaths of several members prompted the Conservatives to petition the Lord Chancellor to establish a new (Tory) board. A Liberal counter-proposal followed, and the upshot was the appointment of a genuinely bi-partisan group.[75] Charity was to become prominent in political debate again when the Taunton Commission (1864) and the Endowed Schools Act (1869) prompted proposals for the merger of the endowments into a single fund to support new day schools and more accommodation for girls, with a reduced number of free places.[76] Although the Conservative press milked the protests at this to castigate Gladstone's government the overwhelming impression given by the Charity Trustees' responses is that local opinion was united against what was seen as unwarranted interference from the centre.[77] The administration of endowed charitable trusts was no longer the potent issue in local party politics that it had been in the Reform era.

The debate about corrupt administration of endowed charity in Bristol was closely entwined with the concerns of electoral politics. It did not arise in response to public unease about the probity of trustees, and indeed made its first appearance at a time when endowment was enjoying renewed popularity. Nor did it properly engage the broader question of poor relief, and the role of charity within a local strategy for social provision. Instead its rise and fall was linked firmly to the short term party considerations of its proponents, be they Radicals or Reform Whigs, for whom charity corruption aptly symbolised the

---

[73] *Port of Bristol*, pp. vii–ix.
[74] BRL, Collection . . . 1847, unpaginated.
[75] Latimer, *Annals . . . nineteenth century*, 236; Bush, *Bristol and its municipal government*, 148–9.
[76] Hill, *Bristol Grammar School*, 96–103; Bowen, *Queen Elizabeth's Hospital*, ch. xv; Vanes, *Apparrelled in red*, 88–96.
[77] BMC, NC.

graft and lack of accountability of the *ancien régime*, or Tory and Liberal party managers, both seeking to tarnish the reputation of the other by casting aspersions on their trusteeship. There was no unilinear relationship between corruption, decline and reform of endowed trusts.

Liberals and Tories: a 'circulation of the elite'?

Is it none the less possible to describe the Liberal Charity Trustees as reformers? The historiography lacks consensus. Traditionally the social implications of the Municipal Corporations Act are understood as a transfer of power to the newly enfranchised middle classes: the replacement of old Tory 'co-optive oligarchies' by 'Dissenters and shop-keepers'.[78] Alternatively, the new men might be seen not so much as representatives of a new class, but of a new ethic – embodying a more professional approach to local government, and the 'administrative purity and competence' which the Municipal Commissioners and Radical supporters claimed greater democracy would bring?[79] Or, most pessimistically, should the whole episode be regarded merely as a 'circulation of the elite', where socio-economic divisions were irrelevant, and the key motivation was the desire of 'ambitious and frustrated outsiders' to oust 'traditional insiders'?[80] To some social theorists the constant friction of elite and counter-elite in politics suggested that issues of democracy and accountability have no immanent significance, but are 'means commonly used, especially today, to get rid of one aristocracy and replace it with another'.[81] Given the enthusiasm with which all sides within Bristol's elite adopted the charities issue when it suited them, is this last position the most appropriate?

As a prelude to comparison of the Charity Trustees with the Tory 'insiders' table 9 shows party, religious affiliation, occupation and wealth at time of death of the twenty-one members. This was in no sense a non-partisan body purely concerned with charity. Liberal predominance has already been noted, and the membership included Bristol's leading party activists. William Herapath had gained a reputation as a Radical through his presidency of Bristol's pre-reform Political Union and subsequent role in the riots of 1831, where he intervened in the closing stages to help calm the situation.[82] Harman Visger

---

78 G. M. Trevelyan, *English social history*, Cambridge 1942, rev. edn, Harmondsworth 1949, 539; G. D. H. Cole and Raymond Postgate, *The common people, 1746–1938*, London 1938, 267.

79 Perkin, *Origins*, 123; E. L. Woodward, *The age of reform, 1815–1870*, Oxford 1938, 442; Fraser, *Urban politics*, 119–21.

80 Ibid. 115–18.

81 V. Pareto, *Manual of political economy*, Glencoe, Ill. 1927, repr. New York 1971, 93, cited in D. Taylor and F. Moghaddam, *Theories of inter-group relations: international social psychological perspectives*, New York 1987, 136; V. Pareto, *The mind and society: a treatise on general sociology*, trans. Andrea Bongiorno and Arthur Livingstone, London 1935.

82 Susan Thomas, *The Bristol riots*, Bristol 1974.

Table 9
Bristol Municipal Charity Trustees, 1836-52

	Party	Religion	Occupation	Wealth*
Richard Ash	L	Independent	attorney	£ 90,000
George Bengough	L	Unitarian	attorney	£ 35,000
Samuel Brown	L	Anglican	manufacturer	£ 35,000
Thomas Carlisle	L	Anglican	wholesaler	£ 14,000
Michael Castle	L	Unitarian	manufacturer	£ 35,000
James Cunningham	L	Anglican	merchant	£ 5,000
Thomas Davies	L	n/k	merchant	n/k
Robert Fiske	L	Anglican	wholesaler	£ 6,000
Charles Bowles Fripp	L	Anglican	manufacturer	£ 30,000
John Kerle Haberfield	T	Anglican	attorney	£ 40,000
William Harwood	L	Baptist	wholesaler	£ 3,000
William Herepath	L	Unitarian	chemist	£ 600
Thomas Powell	L	Anglican	wholesaler	£ 18,000
George Eddie Sanders	L	Anglican	wholesaler	£ 25,000
John Savage	T	Anglican	manufacturer	£ 9,000
Richard Smith	T	Anglican	surgeon	£ 30,000
William Pyle Taunton	L	Anglican	barrister	£ 2,000
George Thomas	L	Quaker	wholesaler	£ 200,000
William Tothill	L	Quaker	manufacturer	n/k
Harman Visger	L	Anglican	consul	£ 70,000
James Wood	L	Methodist	insurance	£ 6,000

* Value of estate at death

Sources: *Matthews's directory*, 1814, 1822, 1826, 1832, 1841; Bush, *Bristol and its municipal government*, appendix 5; BRO 00568 h)

had been a prominent campaigner against the old Corporation, and had caused a stir during the visit of the Municipal Corporations Commissioners by approaching one of them outside the formal channel of the public hearing with information on the docks' policy that was later included in the report.[83] Visger, along with Richard Ash, was responsible for the bribery petition which had followed the Tory victory in the 1835 election. Active involvement in national elections is also demonstrated by the role of trustees in nominating the Liberal candidates. Between 1831 and 1852 the role was performed by Ash, Sanders, Castle, Cunningham, Thomas and Visger.

Anglicans out-numbered dissenters, rendering unconvincing the Tory argument that charities of the Established Church were in the hands of sec-

---

[83] *House of Lords Journal*, 5 Aug. 1835, 407; *Brougham's speeches*, iii. 418.

tarians whose goal was to open them to nonconformists. However, though not numerous, the Quakers had a high public profile.[84] As will become more apparent in the discussion of subscriber charity, philanthropy in this period had a deeply sectarian tinge, so can a nonconformist agenda be discerned? The problem here lies in disentangling religious motives from political impulses, or simply from the desire to promote fairness and efficiency. For example, the first advertisement for the Peloquin charities under the new regime introduced a procedure of petitioning through an application form carrying the names of 'two respectable persons', whom the trustees could approach for a reference. When the applications were assessed all those supported by the churchwardens of St Thomas's were rejected.[85] Was religion or politics at issue here? The Peloquin gift was one of those which had been under scrutiny in the evidence before the Parliamentary Bribery Committee following the 1835 election, and the Liberals were convinced that the majority of the gifts had found their way to Tory voters.[86] Managerialism, partisan favouritism or sectarian animosity may all have played a part in this.

Membership was drawn equally from the professions and commerce, slightly less from manufacturing, while wealth varied fairly dramatically. However, it is only when the trustees are compared to another elite power grouping – the Tories on the reformed Council – that their distinguishing features become apparent. Table 10a shows that in occupational terms the Tory group had slightly less representation amongst professionals (predominantly the law), a much greater number of merchants engaged in foreign trade, and an absence of those working in internal commerce; there was also a higher proportion of manufacturers (glass, tobacco, metals, paint). The two gentlemen with private incomes also had links to eighteenth-century sources of wealth: Robert Case, a West Indian proprietor, and Gabriel Goldney, member of a family with interests in banking and iron. Although there was only one banker, James Lean, within the Tory ranks, Thomas Daniel and James George, as well as Goldney had either direct or family connections with Bristol's banking network, again in contrast to the Liberals.[87] In addition membership of the gild of Merchant Venturers was here exclusive to the Tories, and representative of the cross-section of foreign trade and manufacturing which typefies the group.[88] The Tory elite was also entirely Anglican.

This is in line with Fraser's analysis of a national political divide between an upper middle class of mostly Tory merchants and manufacturers who owed their position to the town's commercial past, and a Liberal bourgeoisie drawn from the newer service sector. Broadly, a comparison of the wealth of the two

---

[84] *The Bristol municipal annual for 1838*, Bristol 1838, sections on Thomas and Tothill.
[85] BMC, NC i; BMC, MB, 12, 26 Dec. 1836; *Bristol Mercury*, 29 July 1837.
[86] *Select Committee on Bribery at Elections*, questions 6444–6.
[87] C. Cave, *A history of banking in Bristol*, Bristol 1899.
[88] P. McGrath, *The Merchant Venturers of Bristol*, Bristol 1975; Kington, 'A burgess's' letters, 129–35, Municipal Commission Report, 20–1; Alford, 'Economic development', 265–6.

Table 10
Comparison of Liberal charity trustees with
corporation Tories, 1835-6

10a: occupation and religion

	Liberal trustees		Tories	
	no.	%	no.	%
Occupations				
Professions	6	33	4	16
Commerce:				
a) Merchants	2	11	9	36
b) Wholesalers	6	33	-	-
Manufacturers	4	23	10	40
Private income	-	-	2	8
Religion				
Anglican	9	53	25	100
Non-Conformist	8	47	-	-
Merchant Venturers	-	-	11	44

10b: wealth (estate at death)

	Liberal trustees		Tories	
	no.	%	no.	%
Wealth				
<£ 9,999	6	37	6	26
£ 10,000 - £ 39,999	7	44	7	31
£ 40,000 - £ 69,999	-	-	4	17
£ 70,000 - £ 99,999	2	13	1	4
>£ 100,000	1	6	5	22
Average size of estate	£ 35,725		£ 64,143	

Sources: As for table 9; Beaven, *Bristol lists*; McGrath, *Merchant Venturers*

groups confirms this speculation, though table 10b is only an impressionistic view of wealth since the size of estate at death cannot be taken as a sure indicator of riches in life.[89] The most significant factor in determining average wealth is the greater number of Tory 'super-rich', i.e. with estates valued at over £100,000, yet the overall imbalance is quite distinct, with 81 per cent of the Liberal Trustees leaving less than £40,000, against 57 per cent of Tories.

Do these distinctions between the Liberal trustees and the Tory councillors imply an ideological cleavage which might in turn have informed a different approach to charity administration? The record of business relations within or across the groups is too fragmentary. For example, it is unclear whether the partnership formed for a property deal by Liberals Visger, Fripp and Powell represented a firm economic identification or merely a transitory alliance.[90] At what point did political difference supersede similarity of economic position for the leading party protagonists, Daniel (Tory) and Cunningham (Liberal), who were both West Indian planters compensated for loss of slaves on abolition?[91] In some key issues party boundaries became blurred. Dock politics for instance had always been bi-partisan, despite the fact that it was the Liberals, notably Visger, who had made capital from the old Corporation's inertia before the Municipal Corporations Commission. However, Tories had also been active adversaries, with Bush and Gutch attacking port dues in the 1820s and inspiring the foundation of the Chamber of Commerce, in which various leading Tories were 'even more zealous in their attack than were their Whig colleagues'.[92] Later, on the national question of free trade, the Frippite Tories of 1847 supported the lowering of duties. Nor was the municipalisation of the docks in 1846 a party issue – the Free Port Association was bi-partisan. Council protagonists for a buy-out of the Dock Company included the Liberal Harman Visger and the Tory Richard Poole King, while objectors were drawn from both Tory territory (Cliftonites fearing that their rates would subsidise the cost of the purchase of the shares) and Liberal (Herapath's proposal that a new Council dock committee should be chosen by ratepayers).[93]

If city politics did not always divide neatly along party lines, would it be possible instead to characterise the Liberals as representing a new political ethic which emphasised integrity and honesty?[94] Certainly there was a

[89] S. Gunn, 'The 'failure' of the Victorian middle class: a critique', in J. Wolff and J. Seed (eds), *The culture of capital*, Manchester 1988, 17–43 at pp. 20–1.

[90] BRO 4965 34g, conveyance of two tenements; J. B. Kington, the critic of the old Corporation, was also a partner.

[91] Cave, *Banking in Bristol*; *FFBJ*, 24 Mar. 1838.

[92] Latimer, *Annals . . . nineteenth century*, 104.

[93] *Bristol Mirror*, 12 Dec. 1849; Bush, *Bristol and its municipal government*, 22–4, 89–91.

[94] See N. J. Brewer, 'Commercialisation and politics', in N. J. McKendrick, J. Brewer and J. H. Plumb, *The birth of a consumer society: the commercialisation of eighteenth-century England*, London 1982; W. D. Rubinstein, 'Wealth elites and class structure in Britain', *P&P* lxxvi (1977), 99–126; John Torrance, 'Social class and bureaucratic innovation: the commissioners for examining the public accounts, 1780–1781', ibid. lxxviii (1978), 56–81.

conscious aspiration to high standards of administrative probity evident in the records of the trustees, particularly in the early days of the organisation when standards were first laid down. A hefty security of £4,000 was to be demanded of the group's secretary, who had responsibility for handling the monies; no employee of the trustees was to receive gratuities from charity applicants or from trade suppliers on pain of dismissal; all contracts for building repairs and food supplies were put out to tender and the cheapest estimate accepted; annual accounts were published.[95] The Corporation had hitherto enjoyed an annual feast on the Red Maids School's 'founder's day', funded by the Whitson charity, but when consultation of Whitson's will revealed no provision for a dinner, the proposal had been rescinded.[96] A proliferation of committees for the different schools, the loan monies, insurance, accounts, individual gifts, and temporary issues such as 'to Define duties for a Committee of Management' illustrate a pervasive ideal of efficiency through a division of labour.[97] Two of the trustees could claim to be experts on relevant issues: Fripp presented papers to the local Statistical Society on poverty in Bristol, and Taunton had published a booklet on the Westbury-on-Trym charities.[98]

However, it is by no means clear that the new ethic of accountability can be ascribed to party ideology. Division of labour by committee and an automatic acceptance of the cheapest tender was a feature of some select vestries in the early nineteenth century. The new Council's treasurer, Thomas Garrard, had also to provide £4,000 sureties. Perhaps the greatest act of self-sacrifice in rejecting a perquisite of the old system was that of a Tory, John Kerle Haberfield, who in 1837 assumed the mayoralty, refusing the allowance of £400.[99] Looking back on the reform era from the mid-Victorian period, commentators were more inclined to characterise it as a non-partisan reformation of manners, in which civic affairs became more moderate, serious and respectable.[100]

Nor were the trustees themselves willing to sever all links with customary practice, especially where there was a benefit to be derived. Continuity was most clear in their use of charity schoolchildren in urban display. In 1837 they positioned the boys of Queen Elizabeth Hospital over the portico of the Mayor's Chapel during the trades procession celebrating the election victory

95 BMC, MB i, 2, 11 Nov., 9, 14, 31 Dec. 1836; 11 Aug. 1837; accounts, *Bristol Mercury*, 29 May 1841.
96 BMC, MB i, 18, 21 Nov. 1836.
97 Ibid. 8 Sept. 1837.
98 Fripp: BRO, Bristol pamphlets, vol. iv; W. P. Taunton, *Account of Anthony Edmond's Charity*, Bristol 1834.
99 BRO, Common Council proceedings, 20 Dec. 1843; 06527, James Kerle Haberfield, memorial scrapbook, 10.
100 *Bristol Times*, 2 Jan. 1858; *Bristol Times and Mirror*, 2 Apr. 1888; Bush, *Bristol and its municipal government*, 212–13.

of Berkeley, the Liberal candidate.[101] This prominent spot was favoured not out of consideration for the childrens' view of the event, but because they themselves were on view, adorning a symbol of civic power. As the Tory *Journal* observed: 'The object . . . was to shew off the poor children as being under the patronage of the Liberal Trustees . . . who have used the charities as an electioneering engine, and are resolved to keep up the game.'[102] Parades of charity schoolchildren were an enduring practice, encapsulating the relation-ship between charity and civic power that is the theme of this chapter.[103] Both before and after reform the charity schools were expected to support the *status quo* of power in the town, whether through attendance at functions marking corporate loyalty to the crown, or in pageants with a purely civic meaning.[104] Association of these scholars with the ruling elite, of whatever party stripe, provided authentication of the authority structure, reminding spectators that the gift relationship uniting the children with the civic lead-ership was resonant of the historic bonds of dependence and obligation joining all Bristolians, rich or poor. To take just two examples, in 1846 Free School children processed at the celebrations which inaugurated the restora-tion of St Mary Redcliffe church, while in 1864 boys from Queen Elizabeth's Hospital and Colston's School lined the footpaths for the opening of Clifton Suspension Bridge.[105] In this respect the actions of the Liberals trustees were no different from those of the elite they supplanted, and provide further justi-fication for seeing the politics of charity in the light of a struggle for power, as well as a desire to reform.

Finally, is the managerial efficiency of the new trustees quantifiable? After all, substantial increases in annual income were achieved between the time of the Brougham Commission's report and the Commission of 1867–76. This rose from £19,874 to £48,356, of which £18,587 was 'Improved Increase of Reported Endowments'.[106] Out of the total increase of £28,482, income from real estate (rents and rent charges) had increased by £18,757, and that from personalty by £9,730.[107] Most of the added income from new charities or pre-viously unrecorded subscription institutions was in the form of profits from personalty – only £1,410 out of £9,895 was from real estate. Hence 35 per cent of the total increase was produced by the new/unrecorded charities, 4

101 *Bristol Mercury*, 29 July 1837.
102 *FFBJ*, 29 July 1837.
103 Craig Rose, 'London's charity schools, 1690–1730', *History Today* xl (1990), 17–23, and ' "Seminaries of faction and rebellion": Jacobites, Whigs and the London charity schools, 1716–1724', *HJ* xxxiv (1991), 831–55; Phillis Cunnington and Catherine Lucas, *Charity costumes of children, scholars, almsfolk, pensioners*, London 1978, ch. xv.
104 Bowen, *Queen Elizabeth's Hospital*, 30, 61, 73–4, 95–6; Vanes, *Apparrelled in red*, 79, 87, 104.
105 *Bristol Mirror*, 25 Apr. 1846; Bowen, *Queen Elizabeth's Hospital*, 96.
106 *General digest*, PP 1877 lxvi. 34, table III.
107 Ibid. 27, table I; *Summary of the reports made by the Commissioners of Inquiry into Charities*, PP 1845 xvii. 830–1.

per cent by increase in the securities income of the old charities, and 61 per cent by gains in the real estate income of the old charities. Just over half of this was attributable to five of the charities now supervised by the trustees. This demonstrates the tangible benefits of reform, as a large part of the increases were due to the recovery of lands alienated at various times from the charities.[108] It is most unlikely that this would have happened without the handover to the trustees, since, unlike the property that funded Colston's school, the Brougham Commissioners had not detected contested claims to the land.[109] However the achievement of the trustees needs to be qualified in two ways. Firstly, the period in question was one in which rental income from land rose dramatically. Historians have offered several examples of growth. Between about 1790 and 1820 rents on cultivated landed estates rose by an average of 90 per cent; a small sample of great estates in Yorkshire reveals rentals trebling between 1780 and 1830, then doubling between 1830 and 1880; a late nineteenth-century estimate of average rent of cultivated land per acre in 1770 was 13s., rising to 27s. by 1850, and 30s. by 1878.[110] The successful development of urban property in this period could also yield a 'golden harvest'.[111] No suitable index exists with which to adjust the increased Bristol charity revenue, but clearly the context of rising real estate receipts modifies the trustees' gains, and, as will be shown, the pre-reform vestries were not incapable of increasing rental income.

John Vincent has argued that the great national questions were of secondary importance in Victorian parliamentary elections, which should be regarded as 'more a drama enacted about the life of the town, the precedence, "pecking order", and social sanctions which held it together, than a means of expressing individual opinions about the matters of the day'.[112] Here it is suggested that the question of charity corruption, as it arose in the elections of 1812, 1835, 1837 and 1841, was part of just such a process. The aim of this chapter has been to show that the waxing and waning of endowed charity as an issue in the theatre of urban politics owed more to its significance to the 'pecking order' than its immanent importance as one of the 'matters of the day'. The administrative improvements that were undertaken were prompted neither by the external efforts of the Charity Commissioners, nor by an internal movement of social renewal, but by the cut and thrust of local and national electioneering. Where claims were advanced against the Corporation for malversation they related to events which had occurred in the distant past,

---

108 Latimer, *Annals . . . nineteenth century*, 233–5.
109 McGrath, *Merchant Venturers*, 365–70.
110 F. M. L. Thompson, *English landed society in the nineteenth century*, London 1963, 218–20; Barbara English, *The great landowners of East Yorkshire, 1530–1910*, London 1990, 104–6; George C. Brodrick, *English land and English landlords*, London 1881, 85.
111 David Cannadine, *Lords and landlords: the aristocracy and the towns, 1774–1967*, Leicester 1980, 129.
112 John Vincent, *The formation of the Liberal Party*, London 1966, p. xv.

and it was never seriously intended that the full sums should have been paid. Comparison between the Liberal trustees and their Tory rivals revealed a distinction between an 'in' and an 'out' group within the urban elite differentiated by religious and socio-economic background, but these did not add up to a clear ideological divide which might have motivated the reform of the charitable trusts.

If the chronology of the politicisation of charity is set against the timing of the fall in the number of new endowments, then it seems that if 'reform' had any effect at all on the habit of establishing charitable trusts, it was a negative one. Far from reassuring potential donors and attracting them back towards a discredited form of giving, the most plausible inference must be that the publicity surrounding the reform of the municipal charities made philanthropists all the more wary. Confidence did not return until the latter part of the century when the issue had faded in importance, but now it was the more recent voluntary institutions which attracted endowment. So, an important component of the decline of endowed charity was, paradoxically, the public debate over its improvement. To complete the picture of change we must turn from the high-profile, wealthy municipal charities, to the more numerous but much smaller parish charities, where some additional pressures can be detected.

4

Charity and the Parish: An End to 'Old Corruption'?

Analysis of the Charity Commission's findings has shown that the rejection of endowed charity was marked particularly by a fall in the number of new trusts in the gift of the parish. This chapter asks why potential testators increasingly spurned the option of leaving money for vestry distribution through parish channels. First, the role of the parish in local government is examined. Was the undemocratic nature of the vestries their undoing, with the related possibilites of abuse of power for personal or political advantage? Secondly, the administration of the charities is considered. Might the fear that unpaid, volunteer officials were incompetent to manage complex trusts have been the determinant? And how strong is the evidence that parish charity policy favoured party loyalty? Thirdly, the parish is set in the changing context of local government during the reform era. To what extent was it coming to be seen as an administrative anachronism?

The parish in the city

The urban landscape paintings of Bristol in the nineteenth century, particularly those by the doyens of the 'Bristol School', William Muller and Samuel Jackson, show a city of churches. Muller's 'Bristol from Clifton Wood' (plate 1) epitomises the contemporary view: in the foreground pastoral scenes cup the city in a bucolic hand, and somewhere between the habitations and the heavens are the clustered spires, with the cathedral, its perspective distorted to exaggerate its size, at the centre of the work.[1] Distance has softened the noise, the smoke and the industry, and, looming metaphorically and physically above the ships' masts and the chimneys of the glass-houses, are the churches. The image is one of homogeneous community, consisting of the parishes, individual *Gemeinschaften*, revolving around the symbol of cohesion, the Anglican cathedral. Aesthetics reflected a partial reality; parishes were still a locus of the political community, through their secular government, the select vestries.[2] And, as we have seen, the greatest number

---

[1]   F. Greenacre and S. Stoddard, *W. J. Muller*, Bristol 1991, 19, 100.
[2]   Sidney Webb and Beatrice Webb, *The parish and the county*, first publ. London 1906, London 1963, 173–276; Barry, 'The parish in civic life'.

Plate 1. 'Bristol from Clifton Wood', by W. J. Muller (1837). Courtesy of Bristol City Museums and Art Gallery

of charitable trusts was in the administrative purlieu of these bodies, usually through endowment to the churchwardens. Can an understanding of the nature of the select vestry system in the early nineteenth century help explain the decline of parochial charity?

Bristol's select vestries were self-perpetuating cliques of the leading citizens of a parish, united by loyalty to Church and Crown. Rooted in 'immemorial custom', this 'closed' system of local government was by no means typical, though it was also found in Westminster and the City of London, and throughout Northumberland and Durham.[3] The usual procedure was for a nominee to be co-opted initially to the post of churchwarden, which carried the brunt of the administrative and financial responsibility, particularly in the second year, when the new member rose to senior churchwarden.[4] The full group consisted of the churchwardens, the overseers, the way-wardens (Surveyors of the Highway), the vestrymen and the incumbent, though the latter was not expected to meddle in 'temporal affairs'.[5] In the early nineteenth century new city-wide bodies such as Pitching and Paving Commissioners and the Poor Law Union were usurping vestry influence, but there remained various management duties which both conferred and reflected status and power. These could be parochial and customary, such as the perambulation of the parish with staves and rods to check the boundaries, followed by the distribution of cakes and ale 'for the boys' and a ceremonial dinner for the vestry and 'gentlemen of the parish'.[6] There were also national responsibilities devolved to the vestry as the smallest arm of government. For example, from 1801 to 1831 it was the duty of overseers to compile the census returns, a task which usually involved the whole vestry in planning.[7] In addition to supervising the fabric of the church building, the chief functions of the vestry were the levying of the poor rate, and the administration of the church lands and charitable trusts.

To what extent might the unrepresentative nature of the select vestry have deterred potential donors? If this question is approached through a prosopography of vestry members the answer is equivocal. Table 11 breaks down the occupations and residency of members of St James's and St Augustine's vestries from 1800 to 1835. St James's vestry was the largest of the parishes of the old city (population 10,488 in 1831), and one which included smart residential squares and labourers' tenements. By contrast, St Augustine's had the cathedral, much of the dockside and fashionable Park Street within its bounds. With regard to St James's table 11 suggests that the stereotype of a trades-dominated 'jobbing' vestry caricatured by the Webbs is inappropriate, as is that of conscientious administration presided over by a disinterested

3   Webb and Webb, The parish, 174, 182–3, 189.
4   BRO, P/St J/V/6, 3, 17 Feb. 1809; P/St P/V/1a, 3 May 1813.
5   P/Tm/La, 3, 4 Feb. 1817.
6   P/St P/V/1a, 15 May 1811; Rogers, Whigs and cities, 353–4.
7   P/St T/V, 2 May 1831.

Table 11
Occupational and residential structure of St. James's
and St Augustine's vestries, 1800-35

	St James	St Augustine
Merchants	3	19
Gentlemen	9	5
Professions	3	5
Services (retailing, building, others)	14	6
Manufacturing	4	4
Resident in parish	31	36
Resident elsewhere	2	10

Sources: St James and St Augustine vestry minute books;
Bristol poll books, 1812, 1820, 1830; *Matthews's directory*, 1830

elite.[8] There undoubtedly was a degree of jobbery: in 1802 for example, vestryman Joseph Panting was employed for joinery work on the church, vestry-room and porch, while in 1817 Thomas Cole was contracted to erect the booths and buildings for St James's Fair.[9] St Augustine's, with its preponderance of merchants and gentlemen, is even less likely to have experienced trades jobbery, though the high number of non-residents hints that the vested interests of Bristol's merchantocracy saw control of this dockside parish as important. The fine line between dishonest self-interest and customary norms is hard to distinguish. Take for instance the resignation from St James's vestry in 1817 of William Reed, a vestryman motivated by 'the care of the church, the interest of the parish and the comforts of the poor'. Such was the devotion and longevity of his service that the vestry voted to present him with an inscribed plate worth fifty guineas.[10] Should this be read as an unwarranted use of public funds, symptomatic of the venal ethos of pre-reform politics, or does it simply indicate a different ethos? After all, vestrymen were unpaid, yet their responsibility was considerable: St James's annual income and expenditure was well over £1,000; if a rate collector defalcated the blame fell on the parish.[11] There may have been popular acceptance of perquisites for a job which shouldered the burdens of the community.

Could disenchantment with the vestry have arisen instead from a perception of administrative failings? Rubinstein has argued that a pre-modern lack

8   Webb and Webb, *The parish*, 244–5.
9   P/St J/ChW 36; P/StJ/V/6, 13 Aug. 1817.
10 P/St J/V/6, 18 Feb. 1817.
11 P/St J/V/6, 20 Jan. 1814; defalcation: 1816–17 passim, 9 Feb. 1818.

of democratic control impeded bureaucratic efficiency and rationalisation in the early decades of the century, before being swept away by the Whig reforms.[12] In Bristol, however, greater accountability was not the prerequisite of parish bureaucratisation. Paid specialists were used, with the employment of vestry-clerks to ensure effective record-keeping, and bailiffs to manage church property; the use of job descriptions to clarify the role of these new paid officials also occurs.[13] Another example is delegation of responsibility to sub-committees, such as St James's Committee of Renewals, which oversaw property inspections, renewals of lives and fund investments. By the 1820s it was recording tenders for church repairs and accepting the cheapest bid.[14] Indeed, some vestry minutes of the period, those of St Mary Redcliffe for instance, are increasingly the dry, business-like deliberations of a housing committee.

A more serious charge against the early nineteenth-century Bristol vestries was levelled by the Webbs, who called them 'notorious for their active political partisanship . . . in fact, Tory electioneering clubs, in shameless electoral alliance with the Corporation'.[15] The question of vestry politics in this period of often bitter division is central to understanding public perceptions of local government, and can be approached in various ways. Table 12 tests the Webbs' assertion through investigating the political affiliation of St James's and St Augustine's vestrymen, based on votes cast in 1812, 1820 and 1830.[16] It suggests that there was a grain of truth in the charge of partisanship, but that the nature of the borough seat ensured that the vestry vote was not exclusively Tory. The preferred ticket was the Whig/Tory split, the two-party carve-up so reviled by Hunt, which represented stability and the assertion of the *status quo*. Comparison with the overall spread of votes within the town locates the vestry firmly to the right of centre, with Radicalism rejected in 1812 and 1830, and Romilly's more progressive platform in 1812 finding little favour. The one discrepancy between the two vestries is over the Whig candidates in 1830. Baillie was the pro-slavery Whig, and as such may have had an understandably greater appeal to the merchants of St Augustine's.

Despite their split votes between Whig and Tory, vestry interventions in national politics align them to the 'High Church party'. A recurrent cause of petitioning in the second and third decades of the century was Catholic emancipation, to which they were implacably hostile.[17] Loyal addresses to the crown followed deaths or successions of monarchs, and there were pledges of allegiance to George IV during the Queen Caroline affair, when St

12 W. D. Rubinstein, 'The end of "Old Corruption" in Britain, 1780–1860', *P&P* ci (1983), 55–86.
13 P/StJ/V, 13 Mar. 1816; St Mary Redcliffe vestry minutes, 1822–45, 29 Oct. 1824, 5 Sept. 1828.
14 P/StJ/V, 1816–17 passim; tenders, 8 Aug. 1828.
15 Webb and Webb, *The parish*, 242n.
16 Twenty-nine out of the forty vestrymen were traceable in the poll books.
17 P/StJ/V, 4 May 1819; 7 Apr. 1821.

Table 12

Party affiliation of St James and St Augustine vestries, 1800-35

12a: Votes cast 1812, 1820, 1830

	St James	St Augustine
Whig plumpers	6	2
Tory plumpers	14	6
Whig/Tory split	23	24
Total Whig	29	26
Total Tory	37	30

12b: Percentage share of votes cast, vestries compared to Bristol total

1812: Candidate:	Davis (T)	Protheroe (W)	Romilly(W)	Hunt (R)
	%	%	%	%
Bristol total	39	33	22	6
St James	57	38	5	0
St Augustine	52	44	4	0

1820: Candidate:	Davis (T)	Bright (W)	Baillie (W)
Bristol total	47	51	2
St James	63	37	0
St Augustine	60	40	0

1830: Candidate:	Davis (T)	Baillie (W)	Protheroe (W)	Acland (R)
Bristol total	44	30	25	1
St James	50	23	27	0
St Augustine	54	38	8	0

W: Whig; T: Tory; R: Radical

Sources: St James, St Augustine vestry minute-books; *Bristol poll books,* 1812, 1820, 1830; Beaven, *Bristol lists*

James's vestry castigated support for the queen as 'Irreligion and Blasphemy'.[18] Bristol parishes were also staunch defenders of the social order. In the depressed winter of 1816, when 'Orator' Hunt was due to address a protest meeting on Brandon Hill, it was the local vestry, St Augustine's, which organised the swearing in of 'respectable householders' and 'principal

[18] P/StJ/V, 25, 27 Oct. 1820; *Political Register,* 7 Oct. 1820; Harrison, *Crowds and history,* 247–8; Davidoff and Hall, *Family fortunes,* 150–5.

inhabitants' as special constables. This event also entailed a political misuse of the charity monies, for the usual distribution of Christmas gifts was postponed, 'to keep the watchmen to their duty on that day'. Again, in the early 1830s, 'some gentlemen' of St Paul's vestry ensured 'the preservation of the public peace' by policing reform meetings.[19]

Vestry Toryism points to a final, perhaps self-evident, feature which may have shaped their popular image, their Anglicanism. For example, opposition to John Cam Hobhouse's Select Vestries Bill, from St Thomas's and Temple, was made on the grounds that the trusts and property 'held for the support of the Church and other pious and charitable uses' might now be administered by non-Anglicans.[20] These arguments may have been advanced to protect privilege, but the very fact that they were put forward at all indicates that, unlike other towns, conformity was the norm for Bristol vestrymen.[21] The identification of parish government with the Church of England would surely have alienated the high proportion of dissenters. However, Bristol had hosted a large and influential dissenting community since the seventeenth century; nor was there any evidence that Anglicanism in the city was lacking in vigour in this period, so this need not have influenced benevolence.

Turning to the more specific aspects of the vestries' public profile, could it be that concern with property management was a deterrent to potential testators? Hunt's suspicions of vestry abuses in this area have already been noted, and the parishes' role as landlords/feoffees of 'church lands' may have shaped perceptions of their ability to administer endowed property. Supervision of the church lands involved the levying of rent from lessees and the collection of fines for renewal of lives, a transaction normally accompanied by the perk of a 'guinea for a sealing dinner'.[22] There were other compensations too, as the extent of the property brought considerable power and influence. For example, amongst Temple's properties in the 1820s were sixty-eight 'messuages and tenements', including six pubs and six warehouses, and a variety of industrial premises: three lime-kilns and lime-sheds, two stanks, a laboratory, a vinegar works, two malthouses, a brewhouse and two workshops.[23] There were 823 occupied houses in the parish, with perhaps some 440 parishioners living in properties let by the vestry.[24] Evidence of apparent self-interest is not hard to find; six out of twelve Temple vestrymen held church property, both as lessees and occupiers of 'messuages and tenements' or of business premises – a warehouse in the case of Preston Edgar, and for William Gwyer, head of a firm of Russia merchants, property which included

---

19 P/St Aug/V 1b, 22 Dec. 1816; P/StP/V 1a, 1 Dec. 1830, 18 June 1832; *Political Register*, 28 Dec. 1816.
20 P/StT/V 1, 22 Feb. 1831; P/Tm/La 3, 26 Feb. 1831.
21 Fraser, *Urban politics*, 28; Morris, *Class, sect and party*, 123–4.
22 P/Tm/La 3, 17 Oct. 1823, 22 Nov. 1826.
23 Manchee, ii. 480–5.
24 Estimate based on parish population, 1821 census.

accommodation, stables and limeworks. The terms seem to have been favourable; for example Thomas Brooks paid £3 *per annum* rent for his two 'messuages and tenements' which he held on a ninety-nine year lease, subject to a fine for the renewal of lives of £67 10s.[25] In St Mary Redcliffe there was a similar story, with eight vestrymen among the lessees, one with three properties.[26]

Evidence confirming Hunt's fears of party influence in letting policy is less convincing. Table 13 shows party affiliations of lessees in three different parishes, using the 1821 rental records, and the extant poll books of the three nearest preceding elections. Bearing in mind the margin of error (where the lessee and the voter polled are two different people sharing the same name), the analysis points in a similar direction to that of vestrymen's affiliations. Both in terms of total votes cast and in comparison to the city vote, right-of-centre politics was dominant. Again, the most popular ticket was the Whig/Tory split rather than Tory plumping, indicating a preference for the two-party *status quo*. The 1812 result shows that the lessees were politically more mixed than the vestrymen (table 12) with more voting for Romilly and Hunt; indeed one of the Radical voters, William Pimm, a tailor leasing in St John's parish, had actually proposed Hunt's candidature.[27] It would therefore be incorrect to assert that as a general rule party loyalty played a part in letting policy, although some vestrymen did use their position of trust over church land for private gain, and it is likely that in some cases party or church allegiance benefited potential lessees.

To what extent would this constitute venality to the contemporary observer? The notion of conflict of interest has already been shown to run through the literature of the Radical critique. Specifically, Henry Hunt claimed that not only were leases given to favoured individuals, but that the form of letting, on long leases with lives inserted at nominal cost, benefited the lessee rather than the parish.[28] Parliamentary interest in the ethical management of public housing was expressed in Oxford MP Ingram Lockhart's 1813 'Bill to prevent the trustees of estates, given for charitable uses, from granting long and improvident leases'.[29] The ideals of probity and accountability which informed Ingram's bill were also supported in Bristol, and may therefore have weighed against the parish. In 1826, ex-poor law governor James Johnson launched a bitter attack on the leasing policy pursued by the Corporation of the Poor on its property.[30] He pointed out that its general court had laid down a strict code of conduct in 1819 which was not properly

---

[25] Manchee ii. 480–5; vestry members P/Tm/La 3, 1820–4 passim.; lease, 19 Feb. 1824. Local sources do not permit a systematic comparison with private letting.

[26] St Mary Redcliffe lease/land grant book. William Bell held three properties: Manchee, ii. 448–61.

[27] Ibid. ii. 27; Hunt, *Memoirs*, iii. 13, 118–20, 397.

[28] Ibid. ii. 131–2.

[29] PP 1812–13 ii; *House of Commons journal*, 10 July 1813; *Hansard*, 8 Dec. 1812.

[30] J. Johnson, *Transactions of the Corporation of the Poor*, Bristol 1826, 89.

Table 13
Political affiliations of 1821 lessees of church lands, Temple, St John's and St Nicholas's

13a: Votes cast, 1784, 1812, 1820

Whig plumpers	33
Tory plumpers	19
Whig/Tory split	38
Whig/Whig split	2
Tory/Tory split	25
Radical	2
total Whig	76
total Tory	105
total Radical	2

13b: Percentage share of votes cast, lessees compared to Bristol total

1784: Candidate	Cruger (W)	Peach (W)	Brickdale (T)	Daubeny (T)
	%	%	%	%
Bristol total	31	4	35	30
Lessees	21	3	40	36

1812: Candidate	Davis (T)	Protheroe (W)	Romilly (W)	Hunt (R)
Bristol total	39	33	22	6
Lessees	45	39	13	3

1820: Candidate	Davis (T)	Bright (W)	Baillie (W)
Bristol total	47	51	2
Lessees	48	52	0

Sources: Manchee, ii. 26-7, 209-16, 472-85; *Bristol poll books*, 1784, 1812, 1820; Beaven, *Bristol lists*

adhered to. This expressly forbade the practice of holding leases on lives; fourteen years was to be the absolute maximum, and could only be awarded if the lessee undertook to spend on improvements.[31] A life could not be inserted into a lease to prolong it; instead it had to fall into hand at the designated time. No lease could be granted until the property had been advertised

---

[31] The cost of a life was calculated by multiplying the value of the property by seven then dividing by the number whose lives were to be inserted on the lease: BRO, DC/E/40/39/7.

at least twice in the Bristol press. Members of the Corporation of the Poor were entitled to hold a maximum of one lease themselves. Johnson commented: 'I am sorry to observe that the laws of the Corporation are very differently observed from those of the Medes and Persians.'[32] There is good reason to think that this criticism may have been equally apposite to vestry leasing policy, not least because nineteen churchwardens sat in the General Court of the Corporation of the Poor.[33]

However, in defence of vestry practice, it is possible to justify the high renewal/low rent leasing policy as sensible management. Where deterioration of property occurred the parish would often require a large sum to pay for repairs and rebuilding. Fines for renewals could provide this; alternatively a lease which gave responsibility for repairs to the lessee could be offered, but this would only be attractive if the rents were low. Nor can we be sure that early nineteenth-century vestrymen failed to take advantage of rising rentals on their charity properties. A random sample of charities listed in the Gilbert Returns and the Brougham Commission Report illustrates the rise in annual revenue from minor real estate between 1786 and the 1820s: Aldworth (St Augustine's), increase from £12 to £30; Chester (St James's), £13 to £21; Hodges (St Michael's), £4 to £9; Clement (St Peter's), £4 10s. to £30 10s.; John Jane (St Phillip and St Jacob's), £8 to £11.[34] No substantive conclusion can be drawn from this, given the absence of evidence for comparative commercial rentals and lack of firmer detail of the size and condition of the properties. However, this growth of receipts clearly does not suggest financial incompetence. And, even if there were a widespread disapproval of local government leasing policy, this need not have deterred new donors, since from the early eighteenth century it had become unusual for endowments to be made in land.

The select vestries and their charities

Thus far Bristol's select vestries have emerged as bastions of the Tory/ Anglican establishment in which the opportunity existed for self-interested management and political/religious favouritism with respect to housing policy. In this section the cause of the decline of parochial endowment will be sought in records of vestry charity administration. Were there, for example, difficulties in maintaining charity property, and what were the investment implications of the shift to endowment of stock? What actual criticisms were voiced by the Charity Commissioners? Were there concerns over the means of disbursement of charity doles, perhaps because they were dispensed to

---

32 Johnson, *Transactions*, 89.
33 Kington, 'An analysis', in '*A burgess's' letters*, 19; *Minutes of evidence*, PP 1830 iv. 665, evidence of William Fripp.
34 *Abstract of returns*, PP 1816 xvia. 442–3, 446–7, 456–7, 452–5; *Analytical digest*, PP 1843 xvi, xvii. 238–9, 240–1, 246–7, 250–3.

Table 14
St James charities, 1680-1870

Decade	Church	Poor	Elderly	Loans	Value*		
					£	s	d
1680-9		6	1		9	10	0
1690-9		4	1		8	4	0
1700-9		1			4	0	0
1710-9	1	5			7	11	0
1720-9	2	2	2		20	0	6
1730-9	2	3	1		7	19	0
1740-9		2	1		6	7	0
1750-9	1	7			20	0	0
1760-9		3	1		4	6	0
1770-9			3		37	0	0
1780-9							
1790-9			2		7	0	0
1800-9	1	2	1	1	195	4	0
1810-9							
1820-9							
1830-9	1		1		16	10	0
1840-9			1		2	14	7
1850-9			1		17	0	0
1860-9			1		6	14	0

* = new income p.a.

Sources: Manchee, i. 397-481; *Analytical digest*, PP 1843 xvi, xvii; *Copies of the general digest*, PP 1873 li; St James vestry list of charities, 1915, BRO P/St J/Ch/92

party loyalists? The search for the answers to these questions will centre on the period before and after the visit of the Brougham Commissioners, and is based largely on St James's parish. Due to its position on the northern fringe of the old city, population growth in St James's continued well into the nineteenth century, unlike the smaller city centre parishes which were crammed into an increasingly commercial urban core. It therefore experienced an escalation of need. Also, its vestry had more charities in its trust than any other group in the city, including the Corporation, though their value was less.[35]

Table 14 sets out St James's charity portfolio, showing both value and charitable heads. Its experience broadly conformed to that of the city as a

[35] The numbers in 1822 were St James's 66, Temple 61, St Nicholas's 60, St Thomas's 59, and St Augustine's 56 while the Corporation only administered 43: Manchee, i, ii.

whole, with the numerical peaks of the late seventeenth and mid eighteenth centuries and the brief rally at the start of the nineteenth preceding the long-term decline. The value of the endowments is erratic, though the 1800–10 figure again reflects the temporary revival which characterised the period; in this case almost the whole amount is accounted for by one major donor, Mary Lewis, who left an estate worth over £4,000. Of the seventy-seven endowments surveyed, twenty-one took the form of property yielding rents, though this form of gift was not made after 1734. Since this predates the decline of endowed charity by several decades it is unlikely that changing peceptions of housing management acted as a deterrent factor, though, as will be shown, property proved to be most difficult to administer.

After 1720 charitable trustee accounts started to figure prominently in long-term government loans, particularly the fixed-interest annuities of the South Sea Company which were seen as the safest return.[36] According to the Charity Commissioners St James's bought Old South Sea annuities in 1777, but this is unlikely to have been the earliest move in this direction. The first will to speak of the endowed sum being 'put out at interest' was that of Alice James in 1727, while 1789 saw the first St James's gift bestowed in the form of stock, in this case 3 per cent consols.[37] By the 1820s the vestry's portfolio was spread over Navy 5 per cents, Old South Sea annuities and 3 per cent consols. The extent to which charity investment had shifted towards stock had already been made clear by the Gilbert returns of 1787–8. The findings for the city as a whole (table 15a) do not differentiate very precisely the public funds chosen, but emphatically demonstrate their role in the generation of income. Although the Brougham Commissioners did not produce a similar tabulation, St Michael's submitted its investment details in 1821–2 (table 15b) and these indicate a shift towards 4 per cent stock in the interim period. Whether this trend towards higher denomination securities constitutes sounder management on the part of St Michael's was unclear at the time and cannot be answered now; against the higher return in the short term of 4 per cent and 5 per cent stock has to be set the far greater market in 3 per cents, and the relative improbability of their conversion downwards.[38] In the absence of data on local property values in the period we cannot compare the relative profitability of stock and land, but the extent to which resources had shifted to securities indicates that the chief concern was not the margin of return, but the desirability of avoiding property management.

Was the legacy of the 'financial revolution' to stimulate or to dim the charitable impulse? The mid eighteenth-century peaks in volume of Bristol endowments correspond to the period in which trusts in general and charities in particular were beginning to appear as major public creditors to the

36 Dickson, *Financial revolution*, 283–4, 299–300; J. Brewer, *The sinews of power*, London 1989, 114–26.
37 Manchee, i. 444, 463.
38 E. Hargreaves, *The national debt*, London 1930, 113–14.

Table 15
Capital resources of Bristol charitable trusts

15a: Capital resources of Bristol trusts, 1787-8

	£	s	d
£ 3% stock.	85,429	7	3
£ 4% stock	15,403	6	4
£ 5% stock	2,146	5	5
Mortgage, personal, turnpikes etc	65,011	9	4

15 b: Capital resources of St Michael's parish trusts, 1821-2

	£	s	d
4% consols	1,685	12	2
3% consols	319	10	0
3% reduced	475	15	4

Sources: PP 1816 iii. 826-7; Manchee, ii. 148-52

National Debt. It is therefore tempting to speculate that the existence of a growing market in public securities encouraged potential testators. Unfortunately this conception of the charitable as rational actors making a cost-benefit evaluation of the prospects for their endowments begins to break down in the late eighteenth and early nineteenth centuries. The decades 1770–1800 have been identified as the period in which the long-term decline of endowed charity sets in, yet this was also the period in which the yield of consols crept up from the region of 3.5 per cent in the 1750s and 1760s to new heights: 5.4 per cent in 1784 and 5.9 per cent in 1797–8.[39] Admittedly the unusually high returns available during the Napoleonic Wars do coincide with the brief revival of endowment, but this may equally have been motivated by evangelicalism or the heightened demand for welfare. What is certain is that the yield of consols settled back to a reliable, predictable return somewhere above 3 per cent in the mid nineteenth century, while endowed charity lost popularity.

Turning from investment of charity funds to the distribution of the income generated, is it likely that a growing disenchantment with the process of giving was a deterrent to the beneficent? It seems that informal approaches were preferred prior to the Brougham Commission, with considerable power in the hands of individual vestrymen. In St James's proportions of the annual gifts in money and clothing were allocated to each of the members shortly

[39] Mitchell, *British historical statistics*, 678.

98

before St Thomas's Day 'for his personal distribution'.[40] The amount given to each was £2 11s. in 1809, with an indivisible surplus of 18s. 6d. handed over to the vestry clerk.[41] Family income of the Bristol labouring poor was somewhere in the region of 10s. per week, so this was a generous sum.[42] The weekly bread doles (twenty-four loaves in 1822) were given to appointees of the churchwardens or the clerk, 'mostly women', and chosen from those 'in greatest want', with a preference for those who actually worshipped regularly at the parish church.[43]

This emphasis on the personal distributive capacity of the select vestry is suggestive of a face-to-face basis for the charitable relationship, in which recipients of the gift were already known to the vestrymen. If so, then a range of questions arise. Were the gifts used primarily as a means of cultivating deference and social cohesion rather than relieving poverty? Were they deployed to maximise personal or party gain? And did this style of giving engender resentment? Certainly the public display of vestry charity was an important means of cultivating the prestige which had customarily attended the job. When the parish perambulation of St Augustine's took place the vestrymen were followed by the boys of three endowed schools, Colston's, St Michael's and St Augustine's. After the procession 'the school-boys and boys of the parish were regaled with plumb [sic] cakes and a most excellent subscription dinner'.[44] Here was a ritual which sought to enforce the customary deferential bonds within the city between church, poor, and the merchant elite who dominated that particular parish.[45]

There is also evidence that it was not always those most in need who were the recipients. The Brougham Commissioners were concerned by the discretionary bestowing of gifts, and highlighted two defects of the system of distribution: its tendency to overlook the precise directions of the testator and its unregulated nature.[46] Twelve of St James's sixty-six charities were described as failing to fulfill the wishes of the donor as set out in the original will, two because they were given in cash not bread, the rest because they did not reach the specified target group. For example, Alice James's will of 1727 had established a Christmas cash gift to two poor widows; the principal had gone into the parish account and its interest, calculated at 4 per cent, became part of an indiscriminate grouping of all the money gifts dispensed annually by the vestrymen without reference to the target group.[47] An alternative was proposed, apparently designed to eradicate opportunities for favouritism: 'a list of

---

[40] Manchee, i. 414.
[41] P/St J/V/6, 20 Dec. 1810.
[42] Frederick Morton Eden, *The state of the poor*, n.p 1797, repr. London 1928, 189.
[43] Manchee, i. 414.
[44] P/St Aug/V/1b, 21 Apr., 4 May 1815.
[45] Bob Bushaway, *By rite: custom, ceremony and community in England, 1700–1880*, London 1982.
[46] Manchee, i. 444–5, 447–8.
[47] Ibid. i. 444–5.

persons, whom the members of the vestry were desirous of proposing to receive the benefit of the charity, should be produced at the vestry, and there agreed upon, previous to the distribution'.[48] Suitably chastised, the vestry acknowledged that in future 'their application of the limited gifts . . . particularly in the money charities are intended for a class of person answering the description of the almspeople'.[49]

However, it is important not to romanticise nor condemn face-to-face distribution, as inherently personalised and paternal.[50] The system operated by the applicant approaching the vestryman for aid, rather than waiting hopefully for a dole from a patron: a vestry minute of 1803 ordered that a list of names of all recipients should be handed to the churchwarden 'to prevent imposition by the application of the same person to some other vestryman'.[51] Needy parishioners might support a claim by a signed recommendation from a third party, such as ex-employers, landlords or known figures in the parish. Thus surgeon J. Tucker's reference for the Wilkins family:

> The Bearer and her husband are industrious people who have endeavoured as much as in their power to support themselves and two children by honest means, but as her husband cannot work on account of the frost they are much distressed. They are real and deserving objects of charity.[52]

From this it may be possible to extrapolate the role of the vestryman as intermediary between the parish and its poor. Rather than acting as 'Lord Bountiful' to a known client group, his job was to assess applicants, sometimes directly, sometimes via a third party recommendation, in terms of family conditions, character and cause of need to determine whether they were deserving poor. Nor should it necessarily be assumed that attendance at Anglican service was a prerequisite: the Brougham Commissioners admonished the vestry for failing to observe this instruction with regard to James Jeanes's clothing charity.[53]

Before concluding that contemporaries probably viewed charity distribution as essentially equitable, if occasionally incompetent, the Radical charge that the gifts rewarded electoral loyalty must be considered.[54] Probably only a few parochial charities were actually prone to this type of abuse. These were trusts which specified freemen or their families as target recipients, an instruction which would oblige the vestry to have some record or means of checking who held freedoms. Though perhaps innocent in intent such a

---

[48] Ibid. i. 447.
[49] P/St J/V/7, 1 Feb. 1836.
[50] Fissell, *Patients, power and the poor*, ch. vi.
[51] P/St J/V/6, 12 Dec. 1803
[52] P/St J/Ch/8.
[53] Manchee, i. 449–50.
[54] Hunt, *Memoirs*, iii. 131–2; *Select Committee on Bribery at Elections*, 383–4, questions 6438–42, 6447–51.

record would amount to a list of voters which might then be misused. This was a particular concern, as general elections in the city had historically witnessed spectacular increases in the number of freedoms held as a means of increasing the support for one or other party.[55] Table 16 examines the voting records of recipients of Alderman Kitchen's charity in St Mary Redcliffe, to assess whether the suspicions of bribery voiced by contemporaries were well-founded.[56]

As in the political affiliation studies of the vestrymen and the church lands lessees, it presents both an overview of total votes, and a comparison of recipients, from a sample of twelve years' charity payments in the period 1804–36. There were usually four annual beneficiaries of the gift, who received 10s. at Christmas, in some cases for several years running. The assumption is therefore made that if the fund was used to bribe it was as a reward for long-term loyalty, rather than as an immediate pay-off given at the time of the poll; hence the overall survey rather than a study of election years only. As with the two previous affiliation tables it is striking that the most popular ticket was the Whig/Tory split vote. In the elections where the Tories fielded two candidates, 1784 and 1835, recipients were loyal to the 'blues', but such a platform was unusual for the borough. A preference for a result representing the *status quo* was the norm; where there was a choice between Old and Reform Whigs, in 1832 for instance, it was Baillie, a candidate cool towards reform, rather than Protheroe, who picked up the votes. This trend to the *status quo* is also evident if recipients in the actual election years are studied. In 1812, 1830 and 1835 the same pattern was repeated: of the two out of four freemen who cast a vote, both selected a Whig/Tory split.

None of this solves the problem of whether the trusts were used to buy votes. There is a marked right-of-centre slant, though again it may be that the key determinant in choice of recipient was not his responsiveness to a bribe, nor his politics, but his Anglicanism, which in turn inclined him towards the High Church party. The circumstantial evidence, coupled with the answers given to the two Select Committees, prompts a cautious acceptance that some bribery took place, but the notion that vestry charity policy was seriously subverted by Tory electoral needs is not borne out.[57]

When the Charity Commissioners visited St James's they were more concerned with inefficiency than corruption. Nor did their presence inspire swift remedial action, suggesting a vestry perception that considered procedural reform, rather than a drastic purge, was required. The first summons to the St James's vestry clerk was in January 1821, and the main interviews and consul-

[55] Ibid. questions 6357–72; Rogers, *Whigs and cities*, 286–8; Gash, *Politics in the age of Peel*, 117. Jonathan Barry (personal communication) has found an election-time boom in freedoms as early as 1660.

[56] Manchee, i. 415, 135; ii. 86; *Minutes of evidence*, PP 1830 iv. 662–3, 11 Mar. 1830.

[57] Ibid. 665; *Select Committee on Bribery at Elections*, 382–4.

Table 16
Party affiliation of recipients of Alderman Kitchen's charity, 1804-36

16a: Votes cast, 1784, 1812, 1820, 1830, 1832, 1835

Whig plumpers	1
Tory plumpers	4
Whig/Tory split	47
Whig/Whig split	1
Tory/Tory split	11
total Whig	51
total Tory	73

16b: Percentage share of votes cast, recipients compared to Bristol total

1784: Candidate	**Cruger (W)**	**Peach (W)**	**Brickdale (T)**	**Daubeny (T)**
Bristol total	31	4	35	30
Recipients	0	0	50	50

1812: Candidate	**Davis (T)**	**Protheroe (W)**	**Romilly (W)**	**Hunt (R)**
Bristol total	39	33	22	6
Recipients	50	50	0	0

1820: Candidate	**Davis (T)**	**Bright (W)**	**Baillie (W)**	
Bristol total	47	51	2	
Recipients	52	48	0	

1830: Candidate	**Davis (T)**	**Baillie (W)**	**Protheroe (W)**	**Acland (R)**
Bristol total	44	30	25	1
Recipients	50	19	31	0

1832: Candidate	**Vyvyan (T)**	**Baillie (W)**	**Protheroe (RW)**	**Williams (RW)**
Bristol total	29	25	24	22
Recipients	50	46	4	0

1835: Candidate	Miles (C)	Vyvyan (C)	Baillie (L)	Hobhouse (L)
Bristol total	33	29	22	16
Recipients	46	31	15	8

W: Whig; T: Tory; R: Radical; RW: Reform Whig; L: Liberal

Sources: St Mary Redcliffe gift books, 1797-1822, 1822-47; *Bristol poll books*, 1784, 1812, 1820, 1830, 1832, 1835; Beaven, *Bristol Lists*

tation of the documents took place in March 1822.[58] Almost two more years elapsed before the vestry formed a sub-committee to consider the report; it was in February 1826 that their recommendations were presented, and a further three months until their enactment.[59] When changes finally did come their rather limited nature suggests that they were not viewed as matters of pressing public concern. Four problem areas had emerged in the report: the method of distributing the money gifts, the failure to comply with precision with the testators' wishes, the slipshod method of accounting which had led the books into 'ambiguity and error', and the poor management of property which had brought about a deficit in the payments. The vestry went some way towards changing its method of distribution: in 1827 the church-wardens presented a list of recipients to the vestrymen prior to distribution, indicating that a wider vetting process was now in operation.[60] However, the personalised dispensation was retained, as the more formal itemisation in the mid nineteenth-century charity books confirms. In 1845 the allocation of money gifts ranged from £6 14s. for the churchwardens to £3 14s. for the ves-trymen; each also gave out one coat, one cloak, two gowns, a pair of men's shoes, a pair of women's shoes, a man's and a woman's hose, three-quarters of a ton of coal and fifty-four half quartern loaves.[61] There may have been a more satisfactory check on recipients, but clearly the prestige, patronage and personal fulfilment which the old system offered vestrymen had forestalled greater rationalisation.

Comments on defects of accounting and record-keeping were made with regard to twenty-one trusts, most typically the observation that sums gener-ated by separate endowments 'do not distinctly appear in the accounts till the year 1809'.[62] This was the year in which the new parish of St Paul was created out of St James's, necessitating a thorough review of charity funds prior to dividing them on a 35:65 ratio. Unfortunately this attempt to improve the

---

[58] P/StJ/V/6, passim.
[59] P/StJ/V/7.
[60] Ibid. 5 Jan. 1827.
[61] P/StJ/Ch/11/6.
[62] Manchee, i. 441.

book-keeping did not rectify the accumulation of errors; the commissioners showed that the parish was obliged to distribute £241 1s. *per annum*, but its income was only £191 18s. 10d.[63] It was the difficulties of long-term property management, combined with poor accounting which had created the deficit.

None the less, it is unlikely that this created widespread public concern, since the vestry could claim to have acted responsibly, within the letter of the law as it was understood. The problem with investing charitable trust funds in housing was that ultimately money had to be spent on repairs and rebuilding which would either diminish the capital or soak up the interest. St James's had faced this difficulty in 1777 by offering low-rent leases obliging the lessees to pay for upkeep.[64] Income from high renewal fines was invested in government stock, but here the confusion began, for the fines were merged in with the rest of the parish funds, with no attempt to distinguish the charity income and protect it from being drawn on for general purposes such as church repair. Did this assumption that only rentals from charity property should count as its proceeds, while fines for renewals should augment the general income, constitute sharp practice, a genuine mistake or legally valid behaviour?[65] St Mary Redcliffe was caught in the same trap by the commissioners with one of its housing trusts and decided to fight the matter through the Court of Chancery, arguing that it was simply following a precedent dating back to the mid seventeenth century. Although this was rejected the fact that the case was brought at all indicates the uncertainty over the legal niceties of the issue. St James's was more co-operative, reimbursing the charities through sales of stock, and reversing its housing policy, with lowered fines and higher rents.[66]

This study of vestry charity administration offers few clues as to why trusts endowed to the parish were entering a decline. The system offered scope for abuse for personal or party advantage, but there is no evidence that this occurred on a large scale. Inefficiency or ignorance were to blame for problems: the trustees were volunteers never in place long enough to learn the complexities of the task. Yet it was their role as members of the church community which had always made them the most fitting choice as trustees. Housing investment, the area most prone to error, was giving way to investment in stock which offered a painless and predictable source of income. Despite this, and with the Commission now pointing the way to restore the trusts, their decline actually accelerated. Even the more benevolent vestrymen rejected the opportunity to make endowments. John Bangley, who first served as a churchwarden in 1804, had been with St James's vestry throughout the reform era. On his death in 1837 he entrusted his bequest not to his

---

[63] P/St J/V/7, 1 Feb. 1826.
[64] Manchee, i. 467.
[65] Jones, *Law of charity*, 91–3, 153–6.
[66] St Mary Redcliffe vestry minutes, 1822–45, 9 Dec. 1828, 26 Feb. 1830; P/St J/V/7, 1 Feb., 30 June 1826.

parish but to the Bristol Royal Infirmary.[67] Rather than reflecting a conflict of loyalties, this was a simple acknowledgement that the balance between the urban structures which delivered welfare had altered irreversibly and it is this changing balance which underpinned decline.

The parish and the management of poverty

This section will argue that the decline of parochial endowment is best understood in the light of what the Webbs called the 'strangling' and 'death of the parish' in the early nineteenth century – in other words that the increasing irrelevance of the parish as a unit of local government discouraged testators.[68] There is broad acceptance of the Webbs' chronology, which stressed the impact of legislative efforts to democratise the vestry, and the removal of poor rate responsibilities in the Poor Law Amendment, though they may have been guilty of 'Fabian teleology' in underplaying the efficacy of the unreformed system. Fraser sees a longer process, culminating in the 'mortal wound with the abolition of church rates in 1868'.[69] Discussion here will centre on two themes which determined the timing of vestry marginali-sation in Bristol: the resolution of an ongoing tension between churchwar-dens and the Corporation of the Poor over rating, and the broader acceptance, from the 1810s, that the parish was now ill-suited to address the complexities of urban government.

It was as mediator between the policies of the city and the capacity of the parish to pay for them that the vestry exercised its most significant role, at least until the 1820s. Before then the churchwardens played a vital part in the assessment of the various local taxes, such as the poor rates, dock dues, pitching and paving and watch taxes. This was an increasingly awkward role. On one hand they pursued their traditional defence of the ratepayers' inter-est, but on the other they had to acknowledge the increasing demand for poor relief, sanitary reform and so on. The kudos which responsibility had once brought to unpaid officers was withering in the face of an administrative burden that the tradition of amateur service was ill-equipped to deal with. Historically parish officers attempted to obstruct over-eager Corporation spenders; it had been their objections to the rating policy of the Corporation of the Poor in 1712 and 1713 that had led to the act which first constituted the churchwardens as Guardians.[70] The exigencies of urban growth in the nineteenth century brought new strains. Early minutes of the newly-

---

67 Ibid. 4 Mar. 1837.
68 Webb and Webb, *The parish*, 146, 171.
69 Ibid. ch. iv; David Eastwood, *Governing rural England: tradition and transformation in local government, 1780–1840*, Oxford 1994, 3; Fraser, *Urban politics*, ch. i, p. 29.
70 Butcher, *Bristol Corporation of the Poor*, 88–91; Kington, 'An Analysis', in 'A burgess's' *letters*, 19; Barry, 'The parish in civic life', 168–9.

established Pitching and Paving Commissioners in 1806–7 display friction between the valuation of the Commissioners, and the churchwardens, who were personally liable for whatever they failed to collect.[71] Vestry minutes also abound with complaints. For instance, in 1818 Temple found the collection of dock dues 'not well executed in principle and is peculiarly heavy on those parishes which abound in poor population', and set about co-ordinating the other parishes to lobby the Dock Director to change the law.[72]

Unsurprisingly, it was over the matter of the poor rates that tensions between the churchwardens and other authorites came to a head. Prior to 1823 the procedure for collecting the rate was that a total amount for the city was arrived at by the Guardians, the aldermen assessed the contribution of the different parishes, while the churchwardens and overseers then rated the individual properties and employed collectors to extract the payments.[73] Problems arose over the inevitable shortfalls, for though the general rule was that no one renting a tenement worth over £10 *per annum* should be exempt, the churchwardens and overseers also exercised a pastoral function and could allow exemption if 'in their discretion that any such persons are by poverty or otherwise unable to pay'.[74] Deficiencies owing to exemptions or other causes were then added on to the next year's rating: St Paul's, a parish with 1,076 households in 1821, exempted 158 persons in 1819, and had a cumulative deficiency of £502 13s. added to its bill.[75] This led to a tougher line with non-payers. 1822 was the first time that St Paul's vestry asked the churchwardens to bring lists of defaulters, while for Temple matters had come to a head in 1818 when the vestry decided to 'go round the parish in order to ascertain who among the list of defaulters may be enabled to pay', following stern letters from the authorities. The sources therefore point to the curtailing of the vestries' pastoral interventions and a tightening of their role as tax-collecting functionaries.[76]

The turning-point came with the Corporation's presentation of the Bristol Poor Bill to parliament in 1821. It gained support from vestries for its proposal to relieve churchwardens of rate collection, yet in retrospect this piece of legislation marked an important surrender of power.[77] When it finally became law two years later the parish still retained the right to carry out the local assessment, but all else was gone: the court of the Corporation of the Poor now set the total rate and appointed collectors, while the apportionment between the parishes was made by the mayor and two justices. Appeals

[71] BRO, Acts, orders and proceedings of the Commissioners of Pitching and Paving, no. 1, minute book, 1806–7, 30 Sept., 23 Dec. 1806, 10 Feb. 1807.
[72] P/Tm/La 3, 27 Mar. 1818.
[73] Kington, 'An analysis', in 'A *burgess's*' letters, 19; *Bristol Poor Act*, Bristol 1823.
[74] P/St P/V 1a, 1 Aug. 1817.
[75] Ibid. July 1819.
[76] Ibid. 10 Dec. 1822, 16 June 1824; P/Tm/La 3, 16 Dec. 1818.
[77] P/St J/V, 7 Feb. 1821; P/StP/V, 17 Mar. 1821.

against the assessment were heard by the vestry in the first instance, but now the Justices were given the ultimate right to reduce or discharge liability 'on account of poverty, or any other account whatsoever'.[78] This marked the end of a long process by which the most crucial function of the parish in English local government, the control over rates, was devolved to a city-wide authority. For Bristol, the 'death of the parish' ante-dated 1834.[79]

In this transfer of power lies the key to understanding the decline of the select vestry. It was not a simple matter of efficiency which necessitated the reform: a vestry such as St James's was doing much to adopt classic bureaucratic features, such as division of labour, incentives and formal accounting. The critical factor was the enormous rise in the poor rate (table 4), which caught the churchwardens uncomfortably between the demands of the Guardians and the resentment of the ratepayers. Where once the job had carried status, responsibility and a certain amount of patronage, it now brought excessive stress for an unpaid public servant. Yet its derogation was a signal of the increasing marginalisation of the parish in local government.

The long withdrawal from poor rate management is one aspect of the waning of the select vestry, but not the whole story. An attempt was made to create a new working partnership between the Corporation and the vestries to meet additional poor relief demands in the exceptionally depressed winter of 1816–17.[80] This exposed the limited capacities of the parish, and in so doing accelerated their removal from poor relief activities. The project began with a letter from the mayor to all the vestries requesting them to 'ascertain the extent of the distress of the poor therein, arising from want of employment' and then to report back with plans of work creation to overcome the problem.[81] A house-to-house survey was undertaken, with vestries engaging the help of their 'respectable inhabitants', graphically revealing the scale of poverty.[82] When the returns began to reach the Council House the Corporation responded by establishing the 'Bristol subscription for the benefit of the labouring poor', modelled on a voluntary society, with a committee made up of parish representatives, and lists of names and amounts subscribed placed in the local press.[83] Individual parishes planned their own relief schemes within this framework. St Augustine's began with the distribution of money gifts to the amount of £5 for immediate relief, with distributions of soup tickets and biscuits from the vestry room each morning. By January coal and potatoes were also being given out to claimants with a written recommendation from subscribers.[84] St James's had decided that 'no pecuniary advantage should be

---

78 *Bristol Poor Act*, 71.
79 Webb and Webb, *The parish*, 171–2.
80 Gorsky, 'Experiments in poor relief'.
81 P/St J/Ch/3, minute book, 8 Dec. 1816.
82 Ibid; P/St J/Ch/3, abstract of returns; *Bristol Mercury*, 13 Jan. 1817.
83 Ibid. 20 Jan. 1817.
84 P/St Aug/V/1b, 7 Jan. 1817.

granted except as wages or in very peculiar cases'. Their approach was to buy bulk amounts of bread, potatoes and coal, which were then either given to the poor or offered for purchase by them at a reduced rate. Instead of the needy applying to the church the vestry was divided into four sub-committees which methodically visited each street in the parish, recording all those receiving aid in a register.[85]

The post-war slump seemed to point to a new direction in relief policy spearheaded by the parish, combining its administrative skills and its local commitment with the dynamic fundraising approach of voluntarism. Why was this not maintained? Subsequent years saw equally staggering leaps in the poor rate, for instance 1817–18 and 1826–7 (table 4), yet responsibility was increasingly passed to the Corporation of the Poor. The explanation lies with the scale of the problem of welfare relief, which was better confronted by the bureaucratic efficiency of city-wide institutions than the unpaid efforts of the vestrymen. This can be shown with reference to employment schemes, and the subsequent relations between the vestries and other organisations.

The 1816–17 slump again provides a relevant illustration. Impetus for the poverty survey had come from the mayor's proposal that the vestries put forward employment schemes to deal with the crisis. The St James's report had pointed out that 'from the peculiar nature of their usual occupations it will be an arduous undertaking to find adequate employment', though it had suggested two road-building schemes. In the end the vestry could do no more than employ one individual as an extra, and probably superfluous, constable 'to keep the churchyard clear of idle boys and other disorderly persons'.[86] St Augustine's took a more imaginative step, petitioning the Merchant Venturers for permission to work a quarry they owned at Hotwells.[87] They quickly found their idea appropriated by the governor of St Peter's who claimed that all employment schemes should be under the aegis of the Corporation of the Poor. Not only this, but by February the Corporation of the Poor was claiming a proportion of all subscriptions raised, a concrete representation of the need for a city-wide institution to tackle a problem of this scale.

Vestrymen aware of the strains imposed on relief organisation in the post-1815 period were also acutely conscious of the free-rider problem which dogged their voluntary efforts, and this in turn led them to resist further such initiatives. Thus the response of St Paul's vestry in the winter of 1820 to a call from the governor of St Peter's Hospital for parish subscription to help the poor over another inclement winter:

> Resolved unanimously that however much the present state of the poor is to be deplored yet it is the opinion of the meeting from experience on former occasions that parish subscriptions being in their amount so inconsiderable

85 P/St J/Ch/3, 24 Dec. 1816.
86 Ibid. St J/Ch/3, 16 Dec. 1816, 3 Feb. 1817.
87 P/St Aug/V/1b, 13 Jan., 14 Feb. 1817.

and in their application so ineffectual and tending only to draw from the purses of the humane and charitable whilst it screens the rich and affluent are not desirable. And that in order to make the burthen equal and the relief to the poor more permanant the legitimate authorities from their information and experience are best calculated to distribute the same.[88]

While the surrender of power was acknowledged then, a more obstructive attitude to other civic bodies was the result. Further sources from 1832 point to reluctance to adapt to the new role. The Board of Health wrote to St Paul's to enlist the vestry's help in whitewashing and ventilating premises and supporting a cleanliness and dietary campaign amongst the poor. Not even the threat of cholera could prompt the vestry to co-operate: 'they see no reason at present for their personal exertions or for interfering with the duties of the Guardians of the Poor of St Peter's Hospital'.[89] Nor could the hapless board persuade St James's to cancel the annual fair on the grounds that it would promote the spread of cholera. Both sides lobbied Lord Melbourne, who finally forced the vestry to climb down.[90] St Thomas's was slightly more amenable, but grudgingly so, offering £41: 'under the peculiar exigencies of this time be distributed in aid of prevention of the pestilential cholera, but with this express consideration that this be not brought in as a precedent'.[91]

The first part of this chapter pointed to some of the weaknesses of Bristol's select vestries. Work was rewarded with status, not pay, procedures were not efficient, and there were opportunities for self-interest and partisanship in jobbing and leasing policy. Though these attributes attracted criticism and placed stress on the vestry, other evidence pointed to its capacity for bureaucratic modernisation. More significant was the growing irrelevance of the vestry in what had previously been its chief function, the management of the poor through the rating system. This accelerated the decline of the select vestry as an arm of urban administration in the early nineteenth century, and by extension, its viability as a channel of philanthropy. Potential donors perceived the marginalisation of the parish, but did not shift the site of endowment elsewhere. Trusts required a perpetual body to administer them, but the reputation of the chief alternative to vestries – the Corporation, then the Charity Trustees – had been damaged by the entangling of charity with party politics. Thus donors increasingly preferred the newer subscription charities.

---

88 P/St P/V/1a, 12 Jan. 1820.
89 Ibid. 20 July 1832.
90 P/St J/V, 10, 27 Aug. 1832.
91 P/St T/V 1, 9 Jan. 1832.

PART II

BRISTOL'S VOLUNTARY SOCIETIES
AND INSTITUTIONS

5

The Emergence of Subscriber Associations and Institutions

The remaining chapters of this book deal with the vast range of philanthropic associations and institutions founded in the city between about 1790 and 1870. These voluntary charities, which superseded the endowed trusts, were organised around the principle of open membership based on subscription and had various characteristic features, including formal annual meetings and annual reports in which their accounts were published. Although it will be argued below that from the end of the eighteenth century their numbers proliferated significantly, the roots of these organisations lay deep in the soil of the early modern town. Recent work by historians of the eighteenth century has begun both to elucidate the development of prominent subscriber institutions like the hospital and to recover the existence of hundreds of local clubs and charities. This chapter will draw upon these findings to provide a brief introduction to the theme, discussing the nature of the voluntary charities that were prominent in Bristol and pointing to some of the reasons for their appearance. Its main argument will be that although the influence of national culture and metropolitan example were important factors, the city's institutional history also points to the influence of earlier associational forms. Local and civic traditions were a central factor.

An intellectual and cultural basis for the appearance of new charitable forms has been detected in mercantilist theory and writings of political economists: 'a new system of thought' which reorganised charity according to 'a reshaped view of what constituted the nation's greatest need'.[1] More generally historical interest in the extent, novelty and significance of voluntarism during the eighteenth century has been closely linked to changing ideas about the social position of the middle class. Once relatively invisible in the bi-polar model of patrician and plebian society, work on the languages of class, on 'politeness', and on popular politics has now restored middle-class citizens to a more central position.[2] Thus alongside influential national currents of religious and political thought, the distinctive values which the urban bourgeoisie embraced are held to have been reflected by the voluntary

---

[1] Donna T. Andrew, *Philanthropy and police: London charity in the eighteenth century*, Princeton 1989, 4, 22–30.
[2] For example, P. J. Corfield, 'Class by name and number in eighteenth-century Britain', in P. J. Corfield (ed.), *Language, history and class*, Oxford 1991, 101–30; Langford, *Polite and commercial people*, ch. iii; Brewer, *Sinews of power*; Rogers, *Whigs and cities*.

societies. Some of these related to public behaviour and mores, such as moderation, a sense of the responsibilities of the free and independent citizen and a respect for precedence legitimating membership of the civic community.[3]

In addition to the explicit purpose of charities, emphasis has also been placed on the sources of personal satisfaction which voluntary association gave to philanthropists. The importance of *caritas* as a religious duty which benefited the soul of the giver was one aspect of this. The language of unity and religious heterogeneity is also suggestive of an economic purpose, with membership a badge of credit-worthiness, and attachment to 'tradesman-like, bourgeois values' as distinct from the client economy.[4] At the same time their inclusiveness and scope for subscriber democracy provided a natural platform for the assertion of political and religious identities. Freemasonry, for example, was a force in Hanoverian politics, with its celebration of tradition and public ritual providing an important precondition for the popular loyalism that flourished in the 1790s.[5] Associations also acted as agents of social integration during a phase of intense urban population growth, when 'a concatenation of pressures seemed to threaten to pull the city apart'.[6] To some extent this 'English urban renaissance' spawned an essentially emulative public life, which while satisfying the middle-class consumer was modelled on fashionable society.[7] But alongside the influence of metropolitan urbanity the transformation of existing civic traditions was accomplished by the autonomous and specific wishes of groups of citizens.[8]

Subscriber institutions in the eighteenth century

Bristol's institutional history provides several examples of the reshaping of earlier associational forms. The most distant ancestors of subscriber charity were the pre-Reformation parish gilds or fraternities. These coupled mutualist practices such as visiting the sick, obligatory attendance at deceased members' funerals and regular convivial events, with eleemosynary activity: alms to the sick and poor were paid from a common chest to which all contrib-

3   Barry, 'Bourgeois collectivism?', 95–107.
4   N. McKendrick, J. Brewer and J. H. Plumb, *The birth of a consumer society: the commercialisation of eighteenth-century England*, London 1982, 217–30, 228; Davidoff and Hall, *Family fortunes*, 208, 425–7.
5   John Money, 'Freemasonry and the fabric of loyalism in Hanoverian England', in Hellmuth, *Transformation of political culture*, 235–71 at pp. 255, 259–60.
6   Peter Clark, *Sociability and urbanity: clubs and societies in the eighteenth century city*, Leicester 1986, 6.
7   P. Borsay, *The English urban renaissance: culture and society in the provincial town, 1660–1770*, Oxford 1989; Porter, 'The gift relation', 158–61.
8   Barry, 'Bourgeois collectivism', 87, and 'Provincial town culture, 1640–1780: urbane or civic?', in A. Wear and J. H. Pittock (eds), *Interpretation and cultural history*, Basingstoke 1991, 198–234.

uted.[9] Closer precedents may be found in the early modern craft gilds. These had an elaborate organisational structure in which democracy was tempered with respect for hierarchy: masters and wardens were chosen at an annual meeting by open vote and a system of fining enforced decorum, attendance and the duties of office. Members' subscriptions took the form of 'quarter-edge' paid over at the quarterly hall-days, and out-going masters were obliged to provide a yearly inventory of the gild's funds and belongings, in much the same way that later society treasurers would present annual accounts.[10] Gild mutualism was to be the template for the practices of the later benefit clubs, such as the levying of fines to ensure attendance at a member's funeral and the use of a box with multiple locks whose keys were held by separate officials for the society's funds and documents.[11] Conviviality was interwoven with civic ceremonial, for instance when gild officials took their oaths before the mayor in the Tolzey and the whole company celebrated public holidays and patron saints' days. This might involve a dinner at the gild hall or in a local tavern, or something more elaborate: at midsummer the Merchant Taylors would distribute bread to the poor, repair to an inn to 'wash the new master's plate', then take a 'walk into ye country' with wives and children.[12] Welfare procedures were typically mutualist and ranged from running almshouses, providing small pensions for widows and operating schemes to maintain the families of bankrupt members, though by the eighteenth century these functions were comparatively trivial, save in the case of the few wealthy companies.[13]

[9] McIntosh, 'Local responses to the poor', 214–16; *LRB*, pp. xxvi–vii; Barret, *History of Bristol*, 453; Nicholas Orme, 'The Guild of Kalendars, Bristol', *Transactions of the Bristol and Gloucestershire Archaeological Society* xcvi (1978), 32–52 at p. 36; Mary Grace, *Records of the Gild of St George in Norwich*, Norwich 1937, 24–5. On parish fraternities see H. F. Westlake, *The parish gilds of mediaeval England*, London 1919, ch. iv and pp. 42–4; Burgess, ' "A fond thing vainly invented"', 67; Tanner, *Church in late medieval Norwich*, 67–82, 91–110; Scarisbrick, *Reformation and the English people*, ch. ii.

[10] F. H. Rogers, 'The Bristol craft gilds during the sixteenth and seventeenth centuries', unpubl. MA diss. Bristol 1949, 111; BRO 9748, Company of Bakers, ordinances, 1623, rules 3, 4, 5, 7, 8, 9, 10, 12, 23; 01244, Drapers Company, ordinances, 1654, rules 6, 7, 8, 9, 13, 14; 08156 2, Feltmakers and Haberdashers, minute book, passim, accounts, 1728; 35684 15, Company of Merchant Taylors, memorandum and account book, 1707–1818, esp. 1716, 1721; *GRB* i. 74–5, 118; iii. 150–1, 160–1.

[11] F. F. Fox, *Some account of the Merchant Taylors of Bristol*, Bristol 1880, 54; Rogers, 'Bristol craft gilds', 90, 110–111; BRO 08019, Company of Whitawers, Pointmakers, Glovers, Pursers and Pointers, account book, entries for 1734–5, 1767; *GRB* iii. 74; BRO 08155 Company of Bakers, minute book, fo. 299, 1720; 043691, Company of Joiners etc, 1606, nos 9, 86; FS, 18a, 30a.

[12] Ibid. 08155, fos 299, 301, 1728; 9748, rule 3; 35684 15, 1721, 1745, 1746, 1747; 08156 2 passim for payment to inns; *GRB* iii. 75, 116; i. 26–7, 153, 160.

[13] F. F. Fox and J. Taylor *Some account of the weavers in Bristol*, Bristol 1889, 56–8, 90–1; *LRB* i. pp. xxvii–iii; ii. 186–92; doles/pensions: BRO 08156 2; 08019 passim; 35684, Merchant Taylors' poor house, passim; Rogers, 'The Bristol craft gilds', 110.

The payment of quarteredge in non-gild contexts begins to be documented from the mid seventeenth century, as in a professional association of Bristol lawyers (1661–70), in the Artillery Society, a royalist militia (from 1679), in the convivial club, St Stephen's Ringers (from 1693) and in the Society for the Reformation of Manners (1700–5).[14] The raising of a subscription to tackle an emergency or a favoured cause – a 'charitable breife' – was already a well-established practice for members of the Corporation or particular congregations.[15] Annual reports with a published subscription list showing the names of donors date in the city from 1742 with the first surviving 'State of the Bristol Infirmary'.[16] These yearly reckonings of income and expenditure were a more sophisticated and public manifestation of the annual presentations of accounts made by gild masters to the company, and by Anglican churchwardens to the vestry; also, as Morris has argued, they bear similarities to the practice of the joint-stock company, and the nonconformist chapel.[17]

As well as pioneering the use of subscription, sectarian religion influenced the practices and aspirations of voluntary associations in a more profound manner. The activities of the Society of Friends (the Quakers) will demonstrate this. A history of persecution extending up to the late eighteenth century had enforced a sense of separateness in Bristol Quakers and promoted independent welfare arrangements.[18] The ties between members of the community were strengthened by the practice of home-visiting which helped sustain a common morality amongst Friends, and gave support during life crises. Home-visiting occurred in a variety of situations: assessment of the 'clearness and conversation' of a prospective bride, relief for a member with bad debts, mediation in marriage breakdown, investigation of non-attendance at meeting and the succour of 'invalid Friends'.[19] Visiting was later to become a common strategy for charities intent on combining poor relief with moral reform through the domestic missions; the Methodist Strangers' Friend Society (1786) was the first to expand these efforts beyond denominational boundaries.

Quakers also made innovations in the care of their poor, a task which fell

---

[14] Barry, 'Cultural life', 173, and 'The politics of religion in Restoration Bristol', in Tim Harris, Paul Seaward and Mark Goldie (eds), *The politics of religion in Restoration England*, Oxford 1990, 163–89 at p. 170; BRO 8029/11, Friendly Society of the Exercisers of Arms, articles and orders; H. E. Roslyn, *History of the Ancient Society of St Stephen's Ringers*, Bristol 1928; BRL 10162, fos 2–3, Society for the Reformation of Manners, repr. in *Reformation and revival in eighteenth-century Bristol*, ed. Jonathan Barry and Kenneth Morgan (Bristol Record Society xlv, 1994), 17.

[15] Latimer, *Annals . . . eighteenth century*, 87–8, 153; BRO, SF/F1/1.

[16] BI *State*.

[17] Morris, 'Voluntary societies', 104–5.

[18] BRO, SF/A1/15, Mens Monthly Meeting, 6 Mar. 1780.

[19] SF/2/A2/3, Monthly Meeting of women friends, 1790–9, passim; SF/A1/15, 10 Jan., 24 July 1780; SF/2/A2/6.

within the purlieu of the Bristol Meeting, whose practical strategies included payment of apprenticeship fees and maintenance, admission of deserving pupils to nearby Sidcot School and payment of their fees, and placing the young in work.[20] Paupers were relieved in the Friends' Workhouse, built in 1698, and used as an almshouse until its conversion to the New St Mission in 1866.[21] By the 1810s a committee met at the workhouse each 'sixth day' afternoon to oversee out-relief disbursements at a similar rate to that paid by friendly societies.[22] Attendance, medication and funeral costs were paid to the sick and terminally ill, assistance was provided for the elderly, and furniture was lent out.[23]

These local arrangements worked in the context of the Society of Friends' larger commitment to poor relief and charity. Regular responses to the sect's central body contained an assurance that 'Our Poor are well provided for and care is taken for the Education of their Offspring.'[24] A national network of institutions sustained this effort. Sidcot and Ackworth schools were supported by local collections as well as fees, and Bristol Friends contributed to the building of Tuke's 'Retreat' in York, then paid for the stay of members of the local meeting at the asylum.[25] A settlement system operated whereby Bristol Quakers met the cost of their members needing relief elsewhere.[26] There was an annual collection taken 'for the relief of our Poor and other Publick Services', and it was common for the Bristol Meeting to collect for the relief of Quakers elsewhere, or more generally of the 'distressed Poor'.[27] The dissenting community therefore developed characteristic organisational features of voluntarism such as home-visiting and mutualist relief structures, and it also provided a channel for the dissemination of wider philanthropic ideals such as anti-slavery and support for the Infirmary movement.

Amongst the most prominent civic charities were the county and Colston collecting societies, which combined mutuality, charity and gild traditions.[28] The Gloucestershire, Somerset, Wiltshire (all established in 1657–8) and

---

[20] SF/A1/15, 10 Jan. 1780; SF/F2/4, 26 Apr. 1816, 20 Sept. 1822, 24 Jan. 1823; SF/F2/4, General committee minute book, 1816–32.
[21] Mary E. Fissell, 'Charity universal?: institutions and moral reform in eighteenth-century Bristol', in Lee Davison, Tim Hitchcock, Tim Keirn and Robert B. Shoemaker, *Stilling the grumbling hive: the response to social and economic problems in England, 1689–1750*, Stroud 1992, 121–64 at p. 125; Arrowsmith, *Dictionary*, 55; SF/2/A2/3, 24 Apr. 1791.
[22] SF/F3/5, Minute book of the weekly committee, 1814–1827.
[23] SF/F2/4, 26 Dec. 1823; SF/F8/5, Women's collection book, 1829–1860.
[24] SF/2/A2/3, 30 Nov. 1790.
[25] SF/A1/18, passim; SF/F1/1, 29 Oct. 1793, 30 Aug. 1796.
[26] SF/A1/15, 10 Jan. 1780.
[27] Ibid. 1751, 1724; SF/A1/18, June 1795.
[28] Barry, 'Cultural life', 170–2, and 'Bristol charities in the eighteenth century' (Bristol Record Society lecture, 27 Feb. 1993). I am indebted to Jonathan Barry for several references to societies mentioned in this chapter. I have not reproduced the original citations which may be found in Barry, 'Cultural life', 163–81.

Herefordshire (1726) societies were joined by the Welsh 'Antient Britons' (1733) and Scottish clubs, the aim being to provide a social nexus for those whose origin was in the respective regions.[29] Conviviality was integral to their activities, with the recognisable ceremonial forms of the annual sermon, procession and feast with drinking songs. Probably this adoption of traditional ritual patterns attracted participants and signified a claim to membership of the civic community that appealed to those born outside the city. The novel features were the practices of fundraising through the sale of tickets for the dinner and by collection at the service. Annual profits were used to relieve those who might hitherto have been ineligible for aid from the parish or from endowments.[30] A similar approach was adopted by the Colston commemorative associations, starting in 1726 with the Colston Society, which celebrated the local philanthropist's birthday with bell-ringing, a procession to the cathedral with the Colston scholars for a sermon, then a dinner and some minor charitable distributions. This 'parent society' spawned three others, the Dolphin in 1749, the Grateful in 1759 and the Anchor in 1768, all of which held dinners at which collections for doles or apprenticeship fees were made.[31]

In addition to these societies, patronised by the elite, activity also flourished in the taverns and coffee-houses, which hosted a range of clubs for discussion, conviviality, shared interests or mutual benefit arrangements.[32] Box and benefit clubs were particularly numerous, and Walker stresses that these early friendly societies had 'the weight of guild heritage behind them'.[33] Nationally friendly society activity was certainly underway by the 1690s, and the earliest recorded Bristol club, the Friendly Union Society, started in 1717.[34] Jonathan Barry has found several examples of trades' benefit clubs, such as the Society of Masters of Ships (1748), the Mates Club (1749) and the Plush-Weavers Friendly Society (1752). There were also multi-occupational groups such as the Helpful Society (1751), Useful Society (1754) and Society for the Benefit of Widows (1765), and although no membership lists for these survive it is clear from similar groups elsewhere that such benefit clubs were attractive to the middle class.[35] Some types of club

---

29 Ibid. 179 nn. 5, 7, 8.

30 Ibid. 179–81.

31 Ibid. 178–9; Latimer, Annals . . . eighteenth century, 153–4, 280.

32 Earle, Making of the English middle class, 240–50; Clark, Sociability and urbanity; Munro Smith, Bristol Royal Infirmary, 231–4.

33 M. J. Walker, 'The extent of guild control of trades in England, c. 1660–1820', unpubl. PhD diss. Cambridge 1986, 345, 389; R. A. Leeson, Travelling brothers: the six centuries' road from craft fellowship to trade unionism, London 1979, 77–8.

34 Daniel Defoe, Essays on projects, London 1697, in The works of Daniel Defoe, London 1843, 21–5; BRO, FS 30a.

35 Bristol Oracle, 30 Apr. 1748; Oracle and Country Advertiser, 11 Mar. 1749; FFBJ, 11 Nov. 1752; BRL 20095, William Dyer's diary, 6 Nov. 1751, and passim.; William Davies, Sermons on religious and moral subjects, Bristol 1754, 159; Bristol Journal, 4 May 1765; Hampshire Record Office 44M69/H2/29–34, New Alresford Provident Society 1767–96.

were stimulated by national developments, notably the various lodges of Freemasons which flourished in the city during the eighteenth century. Here again though earlier craft gild practice influenced features such as meeting decorum, initiation fees and quarteredge, regular accounting and the election of master and wardens.[36] Charitable activity took the form of relief for 'distressed' brothers or their widows, and one Masonic lodge in Bristol – the Temple Lodge Benefit Society, doubled as a friendly society.[37]

Reference to Freemasonry, and to the influence of the Quaker's national network, serves as a reminder that not all the new associations were 'indigenous' urban institutions. For example, national developments were important to the charity school movement in the early eighteenth century.[38] The inspiration of the SPCK lay behind the Revd Arthur Bedford's initiative in Temple, where parishioners' subscriptions established boys' and girls' schools in 1711 and 1713, and a year later a school opened serving St Michael's and St Augustine's, apparently as a joint venture. Subscription alone was uncertain, so the financing of the Temple schools was also underpinned by a large annuity from Edward Colston; likewise the Protestant Dissenters (later Unitarians) at Lewin's Mead had built their school with voluntary subscriptions in 1722, then provided an endowment for future income.[39] Later in the century the influence on a local churchman of initiatives pioneered in London led to a quite different foundation, that of James Rouquet's Society for the Relief and Discharge of Persons Confined for Small Debts. Modelled on the Thatched House Society, its aim was to obtain the release of those imprisoned for small debts and thus to relieve their families from 'most deplorable situations'.[40]

Perhaps the most significant meeting of metropolitan example and local aspiration was the establishment of the Bristol Infirmary. A considerable literature now exists on the birth of the voluntary hospital in the eighteenth century, contextualising it within the new urban civility which followed the political and religious discord of the Stuart era.[41] Aristocracy and gentry were instrumental in the founding of early institutions, but it was middle-class subscribers who dominated the provincial hospitals.[42] Some of the attractions have already been noted, such as the administrative ethos of open accounting and free membership which contrasted favourably with the self-perpetuating

[36] Arthur Powell and Joseph Littleton, A history of freemasonry in Bristol, Bristol 1910, 32–3, 43.
[37] Ibid. 43, 101–3, 181–3; BRL 7952, Jeffries collection, fo. 7.
[38] Jones, Charity school movement.
[39] Manchee, i. 202–5; Latimer, Annals . . . eighteenth century, 80; Fissell, 'Charity universal', 138.
[40] FFBJ, 1 Jan., 16 Feb., 7 Apr. 1774.
[41] Borsay, English urban renaissance.
[42] Porter, 'The gift relation'; Amanda Berry, 'Patronage, funding and the hospital patient, c. 1750–1815: three English regional case studies', unpubl. DPhil. diss. Oxford 1995, 59–61.

corporate bodies and the closed, partisan trustees of endowed charities.[43] In addition, the system of admitting non-emergency patients by ticket obtainable from a subscriber provided a new form of paternalism.[44] Medical practitioners were also instrumental in this process. The late eighteenth and early nineteenth centuries witnessed the emergence of medicine as a profession, with the distancing of scientific medicine from quackery, the development of training and certification and the reappraisal of the role of the professional bodies.[45] In the absence of substantial advances in therapeutic outcomes this heightened status is to be explained in part by the benefits gained from honorary hospital appointments, which enabled doctors to 'climb over the backs of the poor into the pockets of the rich'.[46] They brought practitioners into contact with a wide range of diseases, with the opportunity for sustained clinical observation. They also offered the ideal teaching environment for paying apprentices, and private clients were attracted by the reputation for expertise which they conferred. It is possible too that charitable support of the hospital was a deliberate strategy of business elites designed to elevate the rewards and respectablity of the medical profession so that it became a suitable career for family members.[47]

Opened in 1737, the Bristol Infirmary was founded in the first wave of provincial hospital-building alongside the Hampshire County Hospital in Winchester and Cambridge's Addenbrookes. It was popular with philanthropic citizens: subscriber numbers rose from 209 in 1742 to 918 by 1797, and few years went by without the receipt of legacies, sometimes of a substantial size – £1,690 in 1771 for example (appendix 2). The Infirmary's annual sermons suggest a mix of impulses for subscriber benevolence: the concern of employers for their human capital, the reduction of the poor rates, fears over the level of population, religious duty with its promise of eternal reward, and the opportunity for the moral reform of unbelievers.[48] It was also appreciated by the citizens: at the end of its first ten years annual in-patient numbers were 593, and out-patients 1,117, rising by 1792 to 1,445 in-patients and 3,145 out (appendix 2). Not all of these came from within the city itself, although Bernice Boss's study of 1761–2 shows that the majority did; indeed, if her

---

[43] Borsay, ' "Persons of honour and reputation" ', 281–94; Wilson, 'Urban culture and political activism', 172–3, 180–1

[44] Fissell, *Patients, power, and the poor*; Berry, 'Patronage'.

[45] P. J. Corfield, *Power and the professions in Britain, 1700–1850*, London 1995; Loudon, *Medical care*.

[46] John Fothergill, cited in Albert Deutsch, 'Historical inter-relationships between medicine and social welfare', *Bulletin of the History of Medicine* xi (1942), 491.

[47] Peter Dobkin Hall, *The organisation of American culture, 1700–1900: private institutions, elites and the origins of American nationality*, New York 1982, 70–3.

[48] Josiah Tucker, *A sermon preach'd in the parish church of St James in Bristol*, London 1746; Carew Reynell, *A sermon preached before the contributors to the Bristol Infirmary*, Bristol 1738; Bernice Boss, 'The Bristol Infirmary, 1761–2, and the "laborious-industrious poor" ', unpubl. PhD diss. Bristol 1995, 116–28.

estimate of the city's population is correct, then some 7.4 per cent of Bristoli-ans were treated in that year.[49]

The administration of the Infirmary was similar to that which obtained in hospitals elsewhere.[50] It combined features of associations, such as meetings, annual sermons and feasts, with the administrative characteristics of trusts – investment of funds, management of property and supervision of staff. Sub-scribers paid a sum, typically two guineas a year, which entitled them to rec-ommend for admission one in-patient and up to three out-patients at a time.[51] Donors were predominantly private individuals, though an initially small number of organisations, principally parishes and firms, also sub-scribed.[52] Recommendation took the form of a signed note which the patient presented on admission, though accident and emergency cases were accepted without this formality. Generalisation on the nature of the patient/subscriber relationship is hazardous, but surviving evidence suggests that personal bonds of residential proximity, employment and religious affiliation underpinned recommendations.[53] Despite the motto 'Charity Universal' inscribed above its entrance the Infirmary intended to limit its intake to those 'Not able to pay for their medicines, or subsist themselves during the time of cure'; in addition the linkage of admission to recommendation was a means of differ-entiating patients from the less worthy paupers who resorted to the work-house. In practice this distinction also related to age and affliction: Infirmary patients were limited to those suffering from acute, non-infectious illness, while age breakdown of patients reveals that young adults aged between fifteen and thirty-four were disproportionately represented, and children hardly figured.[54]

Scholars of the eighteenth-century Bristol Infirmary have differed in their interpretation of the institution's role in the city. Mary Fissell contextualises its foundation by reference to other initiatives such as the interventions of the Society for the Reformation of Manners, the charity school movement and the establishment of the Corporation of the Poor. It was therefore another aspect of the 'moral reformers' programme of incarceration', with one of its prime goals the 'disciplining of the poor'. This leads her to empha-sise the commonalities between the workhouse and the hospital, in that both were the resort of those who lacked the necessary family networks for the pro-

[49] Ibid. 40.
[50] Porter, 'The gift relation', 149–57; Brian Abel-Smith, *The hospitals 1800–1948: a study of social administration in England and Wales*, London 1964, ch. i; John Woodward, *To do the sick no harm: a study of the British voluntary hospital system to 1875*, London 1974, chs iii, iv, v.
[51] Berry, 'Patronage', 72, 197.
[52] Ibid. 24, 66, 94–110.
[53] Fissell, *Patients, power and the poor*, 113–16; Berry, 'Patronage', 215; Boss, 'Bristol Infir-mary', 81–4.
[54] Anon., *An account of the Bristol Infirmary from the first institution to this time*, Bristol 1738, 8; Fissell, *Patients, power and the poor*, 103; Berry, 'Patronage', 222.

vision of care within the home.[55] Boss regards the element of moral reform as a minor aspect of hortatory rhetoric which did not impinge on the patient's experience, and distinguishes the Infirmary from the workhouse in respect of both the social origins of patients and higher quality of medical care.[56] Resolution of these differences must await further evidence. Fissell's argument for the lack of family ties of Infirmary patients is a weak inference based on a search of the parish registers of St Philip and Jacob's for patients recorded in the admission registers as parishioners; some 40 per cent were untraceable and she thus concludes that they must have been largely 'single, transient individuals' who 'did not have local family'.[57] Also, in the absence of records of workhouse admissions or medical treatment comparison between the two types of institution with respect to clientele and therapeutic efficacy remains problematic. Boss effectively demonstrates that risk of contracting a communicable disease within the hospital was negligible and points to the success rates of procedures such as lithotomy; however the lack of casebook evidence compels her to infer likely treatments from a later pharmacopeia, and again this does not provide a firm gauge for the relative benefits of hospital and domiciliary care.[58] What can be said with more certainty is that the Infirmary was extensively supported and utilised, the scale and imposing facade of the building itself marking it out as a major civic institution. By the 1790s its patient numbers and its capital resources had established it as an attractive option for legators who might previously have endowed a trust.

The motivation for voluntary association

Discussion thus far has emphasised that while broad religious and intellectual currents were important factors, local and urban traditions and needs influenced institutional forms. Indeed, if the charities are considered not for their manifest purpose but as venues for sociability and civic interaction, then it is notable that their growth occurred as older institutions fell into decline. From the 1720s the membership of Bristol's craft gilds was waning as their regulatory functions became outmoded, and the number of companies fell from twenty-four in 1700 to eight by 1800. While the journeyman's gild influenced the development of subsequent labour organisations, only a minority of gilds – the Merchant Venturers for instance – retained their position as the focus of elite sociability.[59] The parish vestry continued to fulfil

---

55 Fissell, *Patients, power and the poor*, 74, 85 and ch. v.
56 Boss, 'Bristol Infirmary', 5–8, 49–50, 67.
57 Fissell, *Patients, power and the poor*, 104–5, 224.
58 Boss, 'Bristol Infirmary', 60, 179, 204–9, 211–12.
59 Walker, 'The extent of guild control', 89, 123, 126, 332–5, 376, 383. See also Geoffrey Crossick and Heinz-Gerhard Haupt, *The petite bourgeoisie in Europe, 1780–1914: enterprise, family and independence*, London 1995, ch. ii.

an administrative role in the city but, as noted above, membership was closed to the vast majority. Underpinning the need for new forms was the pace of urbanisation and the rise in the city's population, the scale of which has been gauged from an analysis of baptismal registers and contemporary estimates. These suggest that the town of 27,373 in 1700 grew to around 50,000 by 1750, and reached 63,645 by the time of the 1801 census.[60] In the changing city the subscriber charity fulfilled leisure and welfare functions and provided an alternative means of registering social standing.

Underpinning the need for new associational forms was the pace of in-migration, which was the key to the emergence of the county societies and benefit clubs. The former offered incomers a yearly event which celebrated their identity as both citizens and migrants, and also provided charitable aid for 'poor lying-in women' and 'apprenticing friendless orphans'. Applicants, who had to be fellow natives, could petition for aid following the annual dinner.[61] It is also likely that migration was central to the growth of alehouse benefit clubs, although the absence of detailed membership records for the period prevents an empirical test of this theory. It was E. P. Thompson who first stressed the creative and integrative role of the clubs as communities underwent industrial transition, and at the national level there is a broad correspondence between the areas of greatest population growth and the density of friendly society membership as recorded in the surveys of 1803 and 1813–15.[62] A link between mutual association and the needs of in-migrants is also evidenced by a number of specifically ethnic friendly societies, such as French Huguenot clubs in London and Orange lodges in Liverpool.[63] The international literature provides other examples of voluntary organisations as institutions of adaption, either to a new country – the *Landmanschaften* of New York Jews for instance – or in the urbanisation process, as in the clan associations of West and East Africa.[64]

With respect to artisan benefit clubs both migration and the long-run influence of trade gilds were significant, given the arrangements increasingly made at least up to the 1730s to support travelling journeymen by the payment of relief or the issue of certificates which temporarily bound the

---

[60] B. Little, *The city and county of Bristol*, London 1954, 326–7; Law, 'Some notes', 13–26.

[61] Ibid. 179–81. See, for example, *FFBJ*, 5, 19 Mar., 9 July, 6, 8, 15, 27 Aug., 10, 17 Sept., 16 Nov. 1774.

[62] E. P. Thompson, *The making of the English working class*, London 1963, 456–7; Martin Gorsky, 'The growth and distribution of English friendly societies in the early nineteenth century', *EcHR* li (1998), 489–511.

[63] P. H. J. H. Gosden, *Self-help: voluntary associations in the nineteenth century*, London 1973, 6–7; Frank Neal, *Sectarian violence: the Liverpool experience, 1819–1914*, Manchester 1988, 23, 31.

[64] Michael R. Weisser, *A brotherhood of memory: Jewish Landmanschaften in the New World*, New York 1985; Kenneth Little, *Urbanisation as a social process: an essay on movement and change in contemporary Africa*, London 1974, 88–94.

tramp to a gild master.[65] By the early nineteenth century the need to prevent tramping workers imposing on branch friendly societies led to federation, starting with the 'Manchester Unity' of the Independent Order of Odd Fellows, for the purpose of standardising renewable travelling cards and changeable pass-words.[66] In Bristol labour mobility was to be an important factor in the later spread of the affiliated friendly societies; for instance the first Foresters' court was set up by an engineer and fitter from South London, while Oddfellowship was established in the city in 1838 by migrant Lancashire cotton workers.[67] Benefit club membership assured migrants against risk by providing weekly payments in the event of sickness and a death benefit on the demise of the member or his wife; some also offered lying-in payments and annuities. That participation was also a means of claiming membership of the local community is implicit in the convivial arrangements and in surviving artefacts, such as the brass pole-heads symbolising the name of the pub where the club met.[68] Thus it offered sociability and a safety-net to new arrivals drawn by the promise of the city's labour market, but who had in the process relinquished the security of poor law settlement, family support and rural paternalism.

While national debate about the role of charity was premised on the assumption of a hierarchical relationship between rich and poor, a rhetoric of mutualism pervaded much of the language of Bristol's associations, suggesting that philanthropic ties were viewed as both horizontal and vertical. This was not only the case in artisan benefit clubs, where group cohesion was essential to guard against fraudulent claims on the box, but across the range of voluntary societies. For example, in a sermon to local Freemasons in 1747 John Price urged that:

> Whatever . . . is the concern of one, is the care of all; for every one is indispensably obliged not only to be compassionate and benevolent, but to administer that relief and comfort, which the condition of any member requires, and he can bestow without manifest inconvenience to himself. . . . For everyone here is another self; and he, that hates another, must necessarily abhor himself also.[69]

---

65 Walker, 'The extent of guild control', 326–8, 332–5; Leeson, Travelling brothers, chs iv, vi; Eric Hobsbawm, *Labouring men: studies in the history of labour*, London, 1964, ch. iv.
66 R. W. Moffrey, *A century of Oddfellowship*, Manchester 1910, 25–7; *Odd Fellows' Magazine* lxxxxii (1951), 91–2; P. H. J. H. Gosden, *The friendly societies in England, 1815–1875*, Manchester 1961, 76–78, 222–3, appendix A; Eric Hopkins, *Working-class self-help in nineteenth-century England*, London 1995, 28–9.
67 AOF, minute book of Court City of Bristol, 1840; *Foresters directory* (1893), liii–lix; IOOFMU, *Annual Movable Committttee reports*, Bristol 1896.
68 Margaret Fuller, *West country friendly societies*, Reading 1964.
69 BRL 5800, John Price, *The advantages of unity considered, sermon preached before the antient and honourable society of free and accepted Masons*, Bristol 1747, 9.

The county societies also viewed benevolence in mutualist terms, as another John Price sermon, this time to the Antient Britons, reveals:

> And Lastly, That no Dissentions may disgrace this Feast of Charity, give me leave to recommend to you, Order and Harmony, as the most likely Means of uniting and supporting our Society, to that noble purpose of enabling it in a few Years, to relieve the Distressed and Indigent amongst us.[70]

This blurring of function between horizontal and vertical charity can be perceived in more specialised associations, such as the Sons of Clergy (established 1691), the Mariners and Shipmasters (1748), the Captains Society (1777) and the Society of Mariners (1749), where the function of the benefit club combined with the hierarchical structure of the later subscription societies. The Sons of Clergy promoted a sense of occupational solidarity and also raised funds through its annual dinner, sermons and collections for the purpose of apprenticing clergymen's sons in respectable trades.[71] The Captains Society exhorted donations from both above and below:

> Many are the Advantages which would accrue to themselves, and to the Public, if the Sailors . . . would establish a Fund equal to the Demands of their future Necessities. . . . And did the Merchants in general duly consider to whose Bounty they are indebted for the plentiful Returns of Commerce . . . we should see a large Addition to those respectable Names which now grace your List.[72]

Traditions of mutual aid were therefore evident in the newer forms of charitable association. The new charities also mingled notions of mutual and hierarchical giving in their appeal. Why should this have been so? First, in order to attract membership they adhered to recognisable patterns of civic ritual and group behaviour, in which, owing to the gild tradition, mutuality had been firmly embedded for centuries. Secondly, the chosen functions of the new charities, apprenticing and support for child-bearing women, suggest a conception of need centred on the integrity of the family or household as the 'core' unit of city life. The charitable relationship was not a straightforward hierarchy of rich and poor, but sprang instead from this mutualist vision of the city as community of households.[73] Third, economic insecurity and risk of downward social mobility lent weight to the rhetoric. Even the Infirmary, which epitomised the hierarchical philanthropic relationship, played on this

---

[70] BRL 9628, John Price, *The antiquity of the festival of St David asserted: a sermon preached before the Society of Antient Britons*, Bristol 1754, 21.
[71] Barry, 'Cultural life', 172–3; *FFBJ*, 15 Aug. 1774, 2 Sept. 1797; *Bristol Gazette*, 21 Aug. 1806.
[72] BRL 931, John Camplin, *The duty of providing for a family recommended and enforced in a sermon preached before the Society of Captains belonging to the port of Bristol*, Bristol 1789, 11, 15.
[73] Barry, 'Bristol charities'.

theme in its annual sermons, stressing not only the reciprocal bonds between employer and employee but also the ever-present threat that poverty might strike even the comfortably off.[74]

The integrating power of voluntary association was therefore a force for cohesion in city life in the century that followed the bitter divisions of Civil War and Restoration. Freemasonry, for instance, explicitly claimed to unite its members, regardless of status, creed or politics, and injunctions against fractious topics of religion and party also appear in benefit clubs' rules of meeting decorum.[75] Fissell has argued that the establishment of the Infirmary cemented a new relationship between members of the city's elite in which affiliations of party and sect were set aside. Thus the popularity of the institution amongst subscribers and the heavy representation of Quakers amongst the early governors and officials reflected the shared aspiration to bury difference in polite society.[76]

None the less voluntarism remained a vehicle for the expression of political and religious affiliation. The milieu of the alehouse society was also the seedbed of popular political culture, with the proliferation of tavern clubs such as the Jacobite 'Nagg's Head' and the high Tory 'Half-Pint' and the party associations which drove electoral politics: the Loyal, the White Lion (or Stedfast) Societies and the Union Club.[77] Because charitable activity was identified with civic solidarity it also provided an ideal means whereby groups could lay claim to being legitimate representatives of urban identity and popular feeling. Hence the overt party attachments of the Colston societies (Dolphin: Tory; Anchor: Whig) and the recurrent Tory/Anglican bias of the Gloucestershire Society.[78] Hence also the factional infighting which dogged Colston's charity schools.[79] Even the success of Quaker Infirmary governors in securing an outlet for social action that was untainted by the sectarian animosities which fractured the Corporation of the Poor and the charity schools was shortlived. By the 1770s acrimony between dissenters and Anglicans had arisen here too, over the question of the appointment of a new chaplain.[80]

The tension between integration and sectionalism in the voluntary world was reflected in the increasing tendency of charities to follow the Infirmary's lead in publishing annual reports that listed name and donation of subscribers. Although the printed subscription list was in part a fundraising device which encouraged others to match the largesse of current donors, the capacity of the gift relationship to confer status on the giver suggests that it was also used by donors to signal social rank. Ordinary subscribers were of the

[74] Boss, 'Bristol Infirmary', 116–26.
[75] BRO, FS 5, 12; Brewer, 'Commercialisation and politics', 219.
[76] Fissell, Patients, power and the poor, 87–90.
[77] Munro Smith, Bristol Royal Infirmary, 237; Rogers, Whigs and cities, 267–303.
[78] Barry, 'Cultural life', 173–81; Arrowsmith, Dictionary, 110–11.
[79] Latimer, Annals . . . eighteenth century, 86.
[80] Ibid. 139; Munro Smith, Bristol Royal Infirmary, 34–8.

middling stratum of society, where the threat of downward social mobility was ever-present, and the concern to mark out status pervasive.[81] Later, social stratification within the middle classes was reflected in differentiation within the charities, where the make-up of the board and the presence of very wealthy 'life benefactors' marked out a hierarchy of bankers, professionals and large industrialists as the managerial elite.[82] However, the concept and usage of 'subscription' implies that donors also sought to identify themselves as equal participants in a shared venture with an intrinsic purpose. The semantic origin of subscription was the signature at the bottom of a document, but from at least the early sixteenth century this was understood as signifying consent or adhesion to the document's content.[83] Around this time its usage also took in a more generalised sense of agreement, as in Shakespeare's 'Advise thee Aaron, what is to be done, and we will all subscribe to thy advise.'[84] By the nineteenth century subscription was understood firstly as signatory assent, secondly as a practical arrangement for activities such as the publication of books, promotion of concerts or even business organisation, and thirdly as the expression of approval or consent.[85] This last sense suggests that the printed charity subscription may have been perceived, or at least intended, primarily as a form of public endorsement of a standpoint or practice. From the outset then, voluntary charities in urban society were vehicles for both social integration and the expression of ideological difference.

The public house was the venue for all these associational activities, from the feasts of the disappearing craft gilds, to the 'sealing dinners' of parish vestries, the annual junkets of the Colston and county societies and the monthly club-nights of more lowly benefit clubs. There is therefore a commercial dimension to the early flourishing of voluntarism, in that popular demand for societies was met by suppliers eager to provide the necessary space and catering. Elizabeth Baigent's analysis has shown that the victualling and hospitality sectors were large and vigorous areas of the city's eighteenth-century economy.[86] Given the long-established function of the public house as a venue for business activity it was well-suited to pursue profit by accomodating and provisioning clubs. There was also a link with early eighteenth-century trade clubs whose tramping journeymen relied on the 'house of call' to secure

---

81 John Seed, 'From "middling sort" to middle class in late eighteenth- and early nineteenth-century England', in M. L. Bush (ed.), Social orders and social classes in Europe since 1500, London 1992, 107–56 at pp. 124–5; Davidoff and Hall, Family fortunes, 24–5, 49, 103–4, 212, 264–5.

82 Morris, 'Voluntary societies', 101–2; Seed, 'From "middling sort" ', 132–3.

83 OED ix/2, s.v. 'subscribe', 'subscriber', 'subscription'.

84 Ibid. 43: Titus Andronicus iv. ii. 130.

85 Manchee, i, pp. v–vii; Bristol Mercury, 15 Feb. 1819; Bristol Gazette, 20 Mar. 1806; Bristol Mercury, 25 Nov. 1816, 22 Feb. 1819; Hazlitt, Spirit of the age, 1825, 173; OED, 43; FFBJ, 4 June 1803.

86 Baigent, 'Bristol society', 236–7, 245, and 'Economy and society', 115–16.

work.[87] Landlords were particularly active in establishing benefit clubs and acting as treasurers; the reward was the fixed sum spent on refreshments for club night and the annual feast.[88] There is some evidence that this type of marketing activity increased with the 'industrialisation of urban brewing' in the eighteenth century and the concomitant growth of the tied trade.[89] The wholesale brewers were able to guarantee the security of the funds of societies meeting in their tied houses, with 'Clubs' deposits kept in their own capital accounts.[90] In Bristol surviving bonds from victuallers and spirit merchants guaranteeing club funds show smaller suppliers promoting benefit clubs, perhaps to consolidate their position against competitors.[91]

The separation of charity and mutuality

Many of the associations established in the eighteenth century continued to flourish in the next, and continuities can also be observed in the procedures and the strategies of later voluntary societies. The following chapter will detail the new visiting, poor relief and medical charities that began to appear from around 1790. In one respect though the Bristol case suggests that the 'change of trend' at the turn of the century was not simply a matter of the increasing number of charities.[92] By the early nineteenth century benevolent associations were shedding the specifically mutualist aspects of their identity and rhetoric. A small minority of societies still appealed to a sense of mutual obligation, such as the National Benevolent Institution For the Relief of Distressed Persons in the Middle Ranks of Life, which reminded subscribers that they too might 'one day be under the hard necessity of having recourse for aid'.[93] But henceforth the majority inclined more towards a vertical model of charity along the lines of the hospital subscription system with its promise of a more direct channel of patronage between have and have-not.

A central aspect of this was the gradual distancing of middle-class citizens from the world of the benefit club.[94] While later nineteenth-century friendly societies often contained a few middle-class members – for instance, some five per cent of Bristol's Ancient Shepherds had white-collar jobs – club-

---

87 Peter Clark, *The English alehouse: a social history, 1200–1830*, London 1983, 137–8, 229–30, 232–6; Leeson, *Travelling brothers*.
88 Young, 493; Fuller, *West country friendly societies*, 53, 58–60, 103–5.
89 Peter Matthias, *The brewing industry in England, 1700–1830*, Cambridge 1959, p. xxiii, ch. iv.
90 Ibid. 277–8.
91 BRO, FS 7b, 7c, 15, 30c, 32a, 33a, b.
92 Morris, 'Voluntary societies', 96.
93 BRL, B1534, National Benevolent Institution, 17; Prochaska, 'Philanthropy', 374, relates such associations to changes to crown pension arrangements.
94 F. M. L. Thompson, 'Town and city', in Thompson, *Cambridge social history*, i. 64.

based mutual insurance for the better off disappeared.[95] At first it had seemed that it would be otherwise, with the formation of several large societies such as the Bristol Philanthropic and the Bristol Annuitant offering death benefits and pensions. The scale of subscriptions and the insistence that trustees were householders indicate that these were targeted at the more comfortable, even though they were registered as friendly societies and marketed as such to imply financial soundness (see plate 2).[96] Alignment with charities was achieved through the timing, place and procedure of meetings, which were modelled on those of the Colston and county societies. Thus the Philanthropic Society members in 1803 convened at the Mulberry Tree Tavern for the taking of initial subscriptions, then accompanied their president, the mayor, to St James's Church for a sermon by the evangelical Anglican vicar Thomas Biddulph.[97]

These efforts to extend the principle of mutual insurance for middling citizens into the nineteenth century did not last long, and such societies soon disappeared from newspaper reports and the friendly societies register. The well-to-do preferred to address the exigencies of old age through the inheritance strategies of the property-cycle, while the relative abundance of trained doctors meant that private medical attendance was affordable without recourse to insurance.[98] Meanwhile commercial life assurance offered a tempting range of products as the industry expanded, driven by the growing wealth of the propertied classes and advances in actuarial knowledge.[99] Bristol trade directories listed thirteen life offices in 1820, rising to forty-four in 1840, and sixty-five by 1870. A further consideration is the rejection by the middle class of the public house as locus of benefit club and of charitable activity. Drunkenness had become less popular with fashionable society and was attacked by intellectuals, medical men, Evangelicals and temperance crusaders, at the same time as tea and coffee drinking was gaining popularity.[100] Meanwhile the long-run trend towards a greater emphasis on private life intersected with the emerging middle-class domestic ideology: Christian manliness now stressed sensitivity and familial obligation, while the female ideal of mother and home-maker was even more at odds with the rough sociability of the inn.[101]

---

95 Loyal Order of Ancient Shepherds AU Register of Deaths, 1894–1899.
96 BRO, FS 2, 6, 20, 31.
97 *Bristol Journal*, 29 Jan., 2, 23 Apr., 18 June, 15 Oct. 1803; *FFBJ*, 24 June, 1 July 1797.
98 Morris, 'The middle class and the property cycle', 91–113; Anne Digby, *Making a medical living: doctors and patients in the English market for medicine, 1720–1911*, Cambridge 1994, 20–3.
99 Barry Supple, *The Royal Exchange Assurance: a history of British insurance, 1720–1970*, Cambridge 1970; Clive Trebilcock, *Phoenix Assurance and the development of British insurance*, I: *1782–1870*, Cambridge 1985.
100 Brian Harrison, *Drink and the Victorians*, London 1971, 45–6, 91–4; W. R. Lambert, *Drink and society in Victorian Wales c. 1820–c. 1895*, Cardiff 1983, 15–19.
101 Phillippe Aries and George Duby (eds), *The history of private life*, iv, Cambridge, Mass.

LOSE NO TIME!

Entrance Free for Three Months!!

BRISTOL FRIENDLY

Union Society,

(ENROLLED AGREEABLE TO ACT OF PARLIAMENT)

An Excellent Provision in Case of Death;

INSTITUTED IN AUGUST, 1816,

For the Benefit of Subscribers, their Widows, Widowers, & Nominees,

HELD AT

MR. JOHN STOCKWELL's,

No. 20, NARROW WINE STREET, BRISTOL.

EXTRACTS FROM ARTICLES:

The above Society, at present, consists of 560 members, and by the Articles to *consist* of 2500 members of both sexes, comprising *Three Classes*, under the following regulations, viz. the First Class to contain *one thousand* members, between the ages of ten and forty years;—the Second Class *nine hundred* members between the ages of ten and fifty years;—and the Third Class *six hundred* members between the ages of ten and sixty years.

When the Society arrives to its full number of members,

On the Death of any Member or Nominee, belonging to the First Class, the Sum of

One Hundred Pounds will be paid to the Survivor;

For the Second Class, Fifty Pounds;

For the Third Class, Thirty Pounds.

In the event of the death of any member or nominee, previous to the Society being full, every member shall contribute towards the payment of his or her funeral money according to the respective class to which such deceased member or nominee belonged, viz. If the deceased member or nominee belonged to the *First Class*, then the members of the First Class shall pay thirteen pence, the members of the Second Class seven pence, and the members of the Third Class five pence. If the deceased member or nominee belonged to the *Second Class*, then the members of the First Class to pay seven pence, the members of the Second Class seven pence, and the members of the Third Class five pence. And if the deceased member or nominee belonged to the *Third Class*, then the members of each Class to pay five pence towards such funeral money.

PERSONS WISHING TO BECOME MEMBERS

Of either Class, may be enrolled by applying at the Society-House, on the first Wednesday in every Month; or the first Tuesday, Wednesday, and Thursday, after each Quarter Day.

The above Society has a Stock in Hand, and pays the Claims for Deceased Members or Nominees immediately upon Demand.

A SIGHT OF THE ARTICLES MAY BE HAD ON APPLICATION AT THE SOCIETY-HOUSE, AS ABOVE.

☞ *Members of any Benefit Society may be enrolled in the above.*

PRINTED BY T. LANE, REDCLIFF STREET, BRISTOL.

Plate 2. Handbill for the Bristol Friendly Union Society, n.d., BRO, B15136
Courtesy of Bristol Reference Library

At the same time as the charities were shedding their mutualist aspects and the middle class were withdrawing from benefit clubs, philanthropic attention turned to the friendly society as a suitable vehicle for charitable intervention. Indeed, the earliest government legislation on friendly societies, Rose's Act of 1793, had intended to encourage societies 'of good fellowship for raising by the subscriptions of the members thereof or by voluntary contributions a fund'.[102] Hierarchical involvement was initially a feature of rural benefit clubs, notably the female benefit societies run by Hannah and Martha More in Shipham and Cheddar. In suburban Bristol the club at The Goat Inn, Westbury-on-Trym, hoped that 'such gentlemen who feel the expediency and utility of this institution' would want to become honorary members, in return for a one-guinea subscription each year.[103] This approach soon provoked more elaborate ventures.

The Prudent Man's Friend Society (PMFS) was founded in 1813 to attack poverty from a variety of directions, one of which was the formation of benefit clubs. It was one of a new breed of inclusive voluntary societies of the early nineteenth century, in which all branches of the elite could participate regardless of sect or politics.[104] Three aspects of the PMFS's programme were aimed at promoting self-help. One was 'the establishment of a benefit club, particularly for females, upon such a plan as shall remove the objections to some of the existing societies of this kind'. These failings were the 'perpetual instances of bankruptcy in the common clubs' and 'the enormous expenses attendant on the funerals of the deceased members etc'. The second was a savings bank for the poor with deposits invested in government securities. Finally, a fund providing interest-free loans was established 'to enable the deserving poor to better their condition', which, it was hoped, would promote 'that goodwill and kindness which should ever subsist between the higher and lower classes of the community'.[105] Poorer savers welcomed the latter two initiatives, deposits to the savings bank rose from £537 in 1813 to £2,275 in 1815 while the loan fund lent out £3,133 10s. in its first three years in sums averaging £4. However the patronised benefit clubs were not popular, probably because they did not fulfil any social or convivial functions, and the PMFS dropped the scheme, complaining that 'the minds of the lower classes are not yet sufficiently prepared by education to receive a plan which

1990; Clark, *English alehouse*; Davidoff and Hall, *Family fortunes*, 300, 427–8 and passim. See also 'Mass Observation', *The pub and the people: a Worktown study*, London 1943, 138–43, 154–5.

102 33 Geo. III, c.54.

103 BRO 07898; S. R. Woods, 'Westbury-on-Trym, V: Friendly societies', unpubl. MS 1975, copy in BRO; Martha More, *Mendip annals*, ed. with additional material by Arthur Roberts, London 1859, passim.

104 BRL 9180–1, *State of the Prudent Man's Friend Society for the year 1814*, Bristol 1814; *3rd. annual report of the Prudent Man's Friend Society*, Bristol 1815; Gorsky, 'Experiments in poor relief', 17–30.

105 *Bristol Journal*, 1 Jan., 24 Dec. 1814.

principally promises distant advantages'.[106] The world of the charity and the friendly society were not the same.

Another unsuccessful hierarchical benefit club was the South Gloucestershire Friendly Society, founded in 1825 during the spate of county friendly society formations.[107] Its figureheads included local nobility, with the duke of Beaufort as patron and the Lord De Clifford as president, while ex-PMFS subscribers sat on the committee. The society claimed that workmens' clubs were poorly run and unreliable, compared to its own rational and better managed system. Membership was open to both men and women aged from ten to fifty, who could choose from ten classes of payment and benefit, as well as annuities, and endowments on children's lives. Sick pay was graded into 'bedlying pay' and 'walking pay' (payable when illness did not confine members to bed). Monthly payments were assessed according to age, and personal attendance was not required. Sureties were provided by the treasurer and secretaries with stock invested in government securities.[108] However, despite its flexibility and inclusiveness the club lasted only twenty-seven years. Dissembling members exploited their philanthropic patrons, and the excessive volume of claims for the loosely formulated entitlement to 'walking pay' made the club unviable – a characteristic problem: 'Patronized societies are, however, obliged to be strict, since their constitution does not enlist so strong a feeling in their members against imposition. Many have failed from this cause.'[109]

By the 1820s then, the charitable and mutualist aspects of the voluntary sector had bifurcated, and a gulf lay between them. The philanthropic elite saw friendly societies as valuable institutions of thrift which might reduce the parish rates, but which were marred by 'vicious principles, intemperate practices and the sad and disastrous failures of many ale-house and other clubs'.[110] However, charitable intervention was resisted by working people who rejected the patronised societies in favour of clubs which may have been less secure, but which remained culturally and socially independent. In national politics these divisions were thrown into sharp relief by Courtenay's Friendly Societies Bill of 1828, which aimed to bring clubs seeking the benefits of registration under the supervision of local elites. Trustees, who were required to be householders, were to have greater supervisory powers and magistrates were to be empowered to adjudicate in disputed cases.[111] A campaign against the bill was led by a committee of London friendly society delegates with the

[107] Gosden, *Friendly societies*, 52–5.
[108] BRL, B7437 SGFS, *5th Report of the Stapleton, Winterbourne etc Association*; B7435, *SGFS Tract explanatory of the nature and benefits of this society*, Bristol 1825.
[109] *Young*, 7.
[110] *SGFS Tract*; BRL, B7439 *SGFS 7th Report*; *Bristol Temperance Herald*, Jul. 1837; Johnson, *Transactions*, 45–7.
[111] I. Prothero, *Artisans and politics in early nineteenth-century London*, Chatham 1979, ch. xii, p. 234.
[112] *House of Commons journal*, 2 June 1828.

support of the Bristol clubs. A petition was presented to the House of Commons in June 1828 from the 'officers and members of benefit societies, in the city of Bristol' calling for the bill to be rejected.[112] In the event it was replaced in 1829 by an act which removed registration from local quarter sessions to central government, a move which later historians have viewed as a landmark in the progress of the state's encouragement of self-help.[113] Its significance also lies in its acknowledgement of the urban artisan's rejection of mutual insurance managed by philanthropic elites, and as such it marked a division within the voluntary world that was based on ideologies of class.

Many of the features that are associated with the voluntary charities of the nineteenth century have their origin in the patterns of social organisation of the post-Restoration town. The decline of the craft gilds and the insufficiency of the parish and Corporation as a basis of sociability called forth a range of new forms which suited the needs of the citizens during a period of rapid expansion and in-migration. Administrative procedures were adapted from the gilds, the parishes and the chapels, and convivial activities built upon earlier ceremonial practices. Several key attributes distinguish the new style of voluntary association from its forebears. First, its membership was open in a way that of the gilds or vestries was not. Of course constraints of nativity determined which county society one might join, and political preference which Colston society, while Freemasonry and benefit clubs developed through networks of acquaintance. Ultimately though, willingness to subscribe was the key to participation. Secondly, many of the new associations were a part of the public sphere, appearing in the newspapers, through the publication of sermons on their behalf, and through the published subscription list and accounts. The Infirmary epitomised these characteristics, and if a turning point in the development of voluntary charity in Bristol is sought, then the 1740s, its first full decade, is a promising candidate.

However it was also suggested that by the early nineteenth century change was discernible in one respect at least. The rhetoric of eighteenth-century charity had frequently been framed in terms of interdependence and mutual obligation: 'For the industry of the poor, is the wealth of the rich.'[114] This was to be replaced with the harsher tones of the wartime societies, concerned with the 'pernicious examples of idleness and vice, exhibited by street beggars and other impostors'.[115] Whether or not this presentational shift genuinely heralded a more discriminatory attitude towards almsgiving will be discussed

---

112 *House of Commons journal*, 2 June 1828.
113 10 Geo. IV, c.56; Gosden, *Friendly societies*, 177–8; B. Supple, 'Legislation and virtue: an essay on working-class self-help and the state in the early nineteenth century', in N. McKendrick (ed.), *Historical perspectives, studies in English thought and society, in honour of J. H. Plumb*, London 1974, 211–54 at p. 229.
114 Reynell, *Sermon*, 17.
115 *FFBJ*, 1 Jan. 1814.

below. In the world of the benefit society, however, the differentiation of mutuality and charity was quite marked. Following the disappearance of the annuity societies and the failure of paternalist intervention the world of voluntary associations developed along two paths: the friendly societies, circumscribed by law and largely invisible to public media, and the organisations of the middle class.

6

Voluntary Charities

There is no clear consensus on the chronology of the growth of voluntary societies, perhaps because the process is conceived as an aspect of the making of the middle class. Historians of class formation have characterised the flourishing of associational life in the era of the French wars and their aftermath as a time of significant change, when paternalistic, face-to-face charity gave way to a benevolence determined by class relations.[1] Yet, as noted in chapter 5, recent work on the post-Restoration middling sorts is revealing much older forms of charitable 'bourgeois collectivism', pointing instead to long-run continuities in the habit of association, as the source of civic values, class identity and support for the embattled urban household.[2] Different approaches have also been taken to the later nineteenth century. John Pickstone's study of medical charity in the Manchester region discerns a hiatus in the 1830s and 1840s attributable to the impact of Malthusian thought and its emphasis on more discriminatory giving.[3] Helen Meller has argued for the emergence of a new and distinct philanthropy after the mid-century, engendered by fresh notions of social citizenship arising from mass urbanisation.[4] Others tie voluntarism to the cyclical upsurges of religious enthusiasm, stressing the evangelical fervour of the early nineteenth century, and the revival of the late 1850s and early 1860s.[5]

The most influential attempt to impose a coherent pattern on the development of voluntary charity is that set out by R. J. Morris.[6] The period from around 1780 is viewed as a change in trend, as benevolent societies responded to an escalating rate of social and economic transformation, which provided 'the basis for the formation of a middle-class identity', and a means of 'gaining and asserting authority'. Voluntarism in the early nineteenth century therefore helped to overcome political and sectarian division, to weld a unitary middle-class consciousness, and to promote the 'organisation of consent' at a time of bitter class relations. The 1850s were another turning

---

1 Morris, *Class, sect and party*; Koditschek, *Class formation*, chs ii, ix, x, xi, xv; Fissell, *Patients, power and the poor*, ch. vi; Roberts, 'Reshaping the gift relationship'.
2 Jonathan Barry, 'Review article: the making of the middle class?', *P&P* cxlv (1995), 194–208, and 'Bourgeois collectivism'.
3 John V. Pickstone, *Medicine and industrial society*, Manchester 1985, ch. v.
4 H. E. Meller, *Leisure and the changing city, 1870–1914*, London 1976, p. 13 n. 123.
5 D. J. Carter, 'Social and political influence of Bristol churches 1830–1914', unpubl. MLitt diss. Bristol 1971; John L. Duthie, 'Philanthropy and evangelism among Aberdeen seamen, 1814–1924', *Scottish Historical Review* lxiii (1984) 155–73.
6 Morris, *Class, sect and party*; 'Clubs, societies and associations'; 'Voluntary societies'.

point; by this stage the acculturation of the lower middle class had been achieved and the artisan threat neutralised. Henceforth voluntary societies proceeded along different paths, some seeking to reach their goals by means of aid from the state and others mutating into commercial organisations.[7] This chapter tests these ideas against the experience of Bristol's voluntary charities by providing a chronological survey of new formations and the development of existing institutions.

The main sources for this are newspapers, trade directories and annual reports, whose survival allow the reconstruction of a reasonably comprehensive database which accurately ascribes the foundation of new societies at least to a particular decade, if not always the precise year. The database includes 346 voluntary societies or institutions founded between 1780 and 1899, and records name, date of foundation, prime function, place, day and time of meeting, names of key individuals (patron, president, treasurer, secretaries), place of subscription/collection and name of collector, and, if relevant, details of the ladies' committee and time and place of sermon. Various limitations of the database need to be noted. First, reliance on sample years for newspaper searches fails to catch the short-term, individual collections which were such an important form of aid. These might emanate from congregations concerned with a transient issue, from clergy making Christmas appeals to aid poor parishioners, from popular responses to events such as civilian casualties in war or shipping tragedies, or simply from individuals in straitened circumstances.[8] Secondly, trade directories have long been recognised as dangerous for the selectivity of their entries, although the problem becomes less acute from the mid-century.[9] Omissions can be offset through cross-referencing with newspapers but these too were deliberately selective and pitched at a readership of better-off citizens – Bristol's most pervasive associational form, the friendly society, was virtually invisible in the local press. It is the prominent voluntary societies of the middle class that are caught in this methodological net, with the risk that spontaneous charity and more small-scale effort, parish-level female philanthropy for instance, is underplayed. Lastly, despite the broad definition of philanthropy adopted in this study the database ignores institutions for cultural improvement or leisure provision, such as libraries and literary and philosophical societies. Although these helped create the climate of social understanding in which philanthropy flourished their exclusion is pragmatic rather than conceptual –

---

7 Ibid. passim and diagram 107.
8 BRO, SF/A1/24, 5 July 1831; SF/A1/28, 4 Nov. 1862; FFBJ, 26 Jan. 1811; Bristol Mercury, 18 Dec. 1858; FFBJ, 10 Sept. 1803; 19, 26 Feb. 1814; 10 Feb. 1838.
9 Jane E. Norton, Guide to the national and provincial directories of England and Wales, excluding London, published before 1856 (Royal Historical Society Guides and Handbooks v, 1950); P. J. Corfield and Serena Kelly, ' "Giving directions to the town": the early town directories', Urban History Yearbook (1984), 22–35; Gareth Shaw, 'The content and reliability of nineteenth-century trade directories', The Local Historian xiii (1978), 205–9.

good studies of these already exist and it would be pointless to duplicate effort.[10]

Any attempt to categorise voluntary effort immediately confronts the difficulty of developing a viable taxonomy. Motive and outcome might be different – for example, the evangelising impulse lay behind adult school formations – and many charities were multi-functional, like domestic missions, mixing proselytising with home-visiting and material aid.[11] Table 17 offers a general overview of development during the century, with classification based on what appears to be the principal objective. The largest single category is education, reflecting its central position in the philanthropic project. As the PMFS put it: 'when the rising sun of knowledge shall have attained its meridian splendour, . . . ignorance, credulity and vice shall vanish like the morning mist before its beams'.[12] The Sunday, evening and adult school movements at the start of the period opened the way for a sectarian-driven growth of charity day and infant schools that dominated the mid-century, while reformatories and ragged schools featured strongly between the 1840s to 1870s.[13] The flurry of activity in the wake of Forster's Education Act in fact signalled an end to new charity establishments as the school boards took over.[14] Public health charities also loom large, dominated by the dispensaries and hospitals, which continued to appear throughout the period, along with lying-in and Dorcas societies in the early and mid-century and nursing institutions from the 1860s. Charities with a primarily religious function included domestic and foreign missions, and a few geared to church building and the support of clergy. While new formations were a persistent feature of the period, an intense burst of domestic and foreign evangelising characterised the 1810s and 1820s. The subsequent establishments of the mid and late century, though numerous, were on the whole smaller and more specialised.

Was the apparent 'take-off' of society formations from around the 1790s a real phenomenon, or, as Barry suggests, a reflection of their heightened visibility in the printed record?[15] It is difficult to argue that the period c. 1790–1820 was a major disjuncture, given the eighteenth-century activity discussed above, but both quantitative evidence and contemporary testimony point to a cyclical upsurge of voluntary effort with quite distinctive features.

10 M. Neve, 'Natural philosophy, medicine and the culture of science in provincial England: the cases of Bristol and Bath, 1790–1850, and Bath, 1750–1820', unpubl. PhD diss. London 1984, and 'Science in a commercial city'; Meller, Leisure and the changing city.
11 Thomas Pole, A history of the origin and progress of adult schools, Bristol 1816, 19.
12 FFBJ, 24 Dec. 1814.
13 Michael Sanderson, Education, economic change and society in England, 1780–1870, London 1983; Mary Sturt, The education of the people, London 1967; Brian Simon, Studies in the history of education, 1780–1870, London 1960; Neil J. Smelser, Social paralysis and social change: British working-class education in the nineteenth century, Oxford 1991.
14 Ibid. 256.
15 Barry, 'Review article', 92–3.

Table 17
Numbers and types of voluntary societies and institutions formed by decade, Bristol, 1780-1899

	Poverty	Education	Health	Church	Temperance	Reform	Housing	Campaign	Total
1780s	1	1							2
1790s		1	3	2					6
1800s	1	3	3	1			2		10
1810s	5	12	5	8			1		31
1820s	5	17	3	13				2	40
1830s	3	19	8	3	3	2			38
1840s	8	16	3	6		1	1	7	42
1850s	2	24	5	2	1	4	3		44
1860s	3	16	5	5	1	4	3	2	39
1870s	7	20	4	8	1	1	7	2	50
1880s	4	3	2	2	2	1	2	3	19
1890s	3	1	4	4	2	7	3	1	25
Total	**42**	**134**	**47**	**55**	**10**	**25**	**18**	**17**	**346**

Poverty: visiting charities, mendicity, emigration, providence societies; Education: adult, infant, day, Sunday schools; Health: hospitals, dispensaries, Dorcas societies, institutions for deafness, blindness; Church: evangelising organisations, home and foreign missions; Temperance: abstention from drink; Reform: rescue of prostitutes, prisoners, 'civilising' the poor; Housing: institutional residence for moral reform; Campaign: philanthropic/political groups, ie. anti-slavery, peace, animal welfare.

Sources: *Matthews's & Wright's directory*; local press; miscellaneous annual reports etc. of societies and institutions: see bibliography

The evidence of the trade directories suggests a marked accumulation of charitable provision, with around thirty-four voluntary charities listed in 1794, 104 in 1851, and 204 in 1900. Formations are therefore not a proxy indicator of the actual scale of provision. Some groups merged with others (for example the Bristol Temperance Society and the Gospel Temperance Union in 1883), some transformed their function (the mutation of the anti-mendicity PMFS into the Bristol Savings Bank) and some dissolved when their work was done (such as the Bristol and Clifton Ladies Anti-Slavery Society).[16] Also, a number of separate charities could represent the work of a small group of activists, such as the city's Anglican vicars, who in the 1850s led the Bristol Diocesan District Visiting Society, the Bristol Chuch Missionary Association, the Society for the Propagation of the Gospel in Foreign Parts, the Bristol Auxiliary Irish Church Mission, and the Church Pastoral Aid Society.[17]

These developments will be discussed in three sections loosely organised around the first three quarters of the nineteenth century, each phase distinguished, it is argued, by particular factors. Certain questions recur in each section and form the basis of the analysis. Did societies appeal to all sections of the town's elite or were they sectarian? Why were particular goals and target groups more prominent at some times than at others? Is it possible to identify a specifically female philanthropy? What was the contribution of doctors to the vigorous growth of medical charity? What was the interplay between the voluntary world and social policy formulated by the state?

The swelling river of charity: c. 1790–c. 1820

When we consider the unexampled exertions that are now making in every part of the kingdom, in behalf of the lower classes of the community, the present may be denominated the age of philanthropic benevolence. In times past, we have been accustomed to form an idea of benevolence as a rivulet flowing through the several societies of Christians; dividing and sub-dividing into small, and thence more diminutive streams; but, of later years, we have seen this rivulet spread wider and wider, until, like the waters of the Nile, it has swollen and broken down the ordinary boundaries, diffusing its fertilising deluge over the whole country; yea, it has rendered the nation fruitful in liberal charity.[18]

These observations were made in 1814 by Bristol's adult school proponent, Thomas Pole, and surviving records confirm that the period was indeed distinguished by a spate of new formations. On the one hand it was marked by a new trend to high-profile societies in which the town's leading citizens

---

16 Arrowsmith, *Dictionary*, 395.
17 *Bristol Mercury*, 13 Feb., 20 Mar., 13 May, 2, 23 Oct. 1858.
18 Pole, *Adult schools*, 99.

participated regardless of sectional or party allegiance, while on the other the traditional identification of charities with a particular church or dissenting group continued.[19] There is therefore scope for attributing the efflorescence of voluntarism both to a unitary class project – notably in the innovatory approaches to poverty – and to more discrete religious aims, manifested in education and the evangelical societies. These were not the only factors however. Women became active in the voluntary arena, albeit usually in a subsidiary role. The career aspirations of doctors were furthered by the establishment of specialist charities. The state's impact was oblique, with censure of the endowed charities starting to gather pace locally and nationally, and institutional interventions for criminals and lunatics paralleling developments in the voluntary sector, with its asylums for marginal groups like orphans, prostitutes and the blind.

What was the nature of the prominent, non-sectarian societies in which different sections of Bristol's elite could combine to pursue social goals? The first notable example was the Society for the Prevention and Suppression of Vice (1803), and although movements for the reformation of manners had appeared before in Bristol as elsewhere, this was directly inspired by evangelical activity in London.[20] Another such group drawing support from across the political and religious spectrum was the Bristol Auxiliary Bible Society (BABS) formed in 1810, which saw tract distribution as a route to 'civic' and 'moral' reform.[21] It had distributed a total of 81,660 Bibles and Testaments by 1823, at a time when, according to the 1821 census, there were 21,466 families in the city and suburbs.[22] Foreign missions could also follow the pattern of cross-faith establishment. The Bristol Missionary Society (1812) initially rejoiced in 'the undisguised harmony of churchmen and dissenters', collecting nearly £600 from churches and chapels in 1814.[23]

The other prime concern of the non-partisan societies was to establish fresh approaches to the problem of poverty. The Samaritan Society (1807) was an early attempt to rationalise provision through a committee made up of the treasurers of other charities, prefiguring the later strategy of the Charity Organisation Society.[24] Careful scrutiny of those soliciting aid, coupled with the project of engendering self-sufficiency, guided the Samaritans, as it did

---

[19] Fuller details of the religious allegiances of prominent philanthropists may be found in Martin Gorsky, 'Charity, mutuality and philanthropy: voluntary provision in Bristol 1800–70', unpubl. PhD diss. Bristol 1995, notes to ch. viii.

[20] *FFBJ*, 1, 8, 15 Jan. 1803; *Bristol Gazette*, 21 Aug. 1806; *FFBJ*, 26 Jan. 1811; BRO 4579 2; Gorsky, 'Charity', 203 n. 30; Ford K. Brown, *Fathers of the Victorians: the age of Wilberforce*, Cambridge 1961, 84, 238, 434–6.

[21] *FFBJ*, 5 Feb. 1803; James Moulton Roe, *The British and Foreign Bible Society, 1905–1954*, London 1965, ch. i; BRL, B3951 BABS, *8th report*, 1817.

[22] BABS, *8th, 9th, 11th, 14th reports*.

[23] *FFBJ*, 17 Sept. 1814.

[24] BRL, B4620, *Bristol Samaritan Society, its rules and an address to the public*, Bristol 1807.

the PMFS (1812), whose thrift schemes have already been discussed.[25] As in other mendicity societies PMFS subscribers addressed begging by distributing redeemable tickets in lieu of money when solicited for alms; refusal to take the ticket was held to be 'a strong presumptive proof that his case will not bear investigation'.[26] Rewards were offered for the conviction and removal of vagrants to their parish of settlement.[27] Fundraising on behalf of others was the activity of the Reynolds Commemoration Society (1816), set up after the death of the eminent Quaker philanthropist. It exhorted Bristolians to act 'in their collective capacity' to sustain Reynolds's example of benevolence.[28] The National Benevolent Institution for the Relief of Distressed Persons in the Middle Ranks of Life provided doles and medical aid for the more respectable aged and infirm who had fallen on hard times – teachers, governesses, clerks, tradesmen or professionals.[29]

Alongside the non-sectarian ventures were others specifically associated with urban sub-groups. The eighteenth-century county societies (Gloucestershire, Somersetshire etc.) still flourished. The Clergy Society (1692) was a high-profile charity under the patronage of the Anglican elite.[30] Party affiliation continued to influence the Colston societies although the Grateful (1758) remained explicitly neutral. Funds were expended on the payment of annuities to the elderly, and the apprenticing of poor boys, while the Grateful Society retained a particular commitment to mothers in childbirth.[31] Various local doctors were prominent members of these, especially the Tory Dolphin society, though status and politics probably overshadowed medical philanthropy as the prime concern here.[32] Sectarian identity was also overt in the Stranger's Friend Society (1786) whose members were Wesleyan Methodists, though the pledge of the society to treat all 'without distinction of sect or party' ensured that its subscription list contained both Anglicans and members of other dissenting sects.[33]

While these societies reflected the nature of eighteenth-century associationalism, it was the new wave of educational subscription charities which ensured the continuity of sectarianism into the nineteenth. In addition to schools funded by subscription, it was typical for them to be financed by endowments managed by the Corporation, independent bodies of trustees or parishes.[34] By the 1790s old traditions and new developments were combined

---

25 Gorsky, 'Experiments', 17–30.
26 Owen, *English philanthropy*, 109–13.
27 *FFBJ*, 1 Jan. 1814.
28 *Bristol Mercury*, 9 Dec. 1816; *FFBJ*, 9 Mar. 1811.
29 BRL, B1534, National Benevolent Institution, 12, 15.
30 *Bristol Mercury*, 13 Sept. 1819.
31 *FFBJ*, 5 Nov. 1814; *Bristol Mercury*, 6 Nov. 1858; Arrowsmith, *Dictionary*, 111.
32 Munro Smith, *Bristol Royal Infirmary*, 83, 123, 126, 128, 17–1, 183, 192, 310.
33 BRL, B4048, *Report of the Strangers Friend Society*, Bristol 1826, 6.
34 BRO, P/Tm/Kb 1, Temple Blue Girls' School, minutes and accounts; Barry, 'Cultural life', ch. ii; Manchee, passim; Jones, *Charity school movement*, 360.

by the Benevolent Society of St James and St Paul (1789) which provided education to parish children from voluntary contributions.[35] The next stage of development was driven by the Sunday school movement, starting with the Congregationalist school of the Tabernacle chapel (1801–2).[36] Surviving records suggest that dissenters played the leading role, and in particular William Smith, sexton of the Methodist King Street Chapel, who was spurred into action in 1804 by his volunteer Sunday visiting on behalf of the Stranger's Friend Society.[37] The Quakers' experience was similar, with two enthusiasts inspired to raise funds from the more well-to-do, such as Richard Reynolds, and start a school, initially in the Friends' almshouse.[38] The general pattern of lay activists from the philanthropic world acting through dissenting congregations was replicated in the growth of the adult school movement. Again the prime mover was William Smith, who this time used the recently established proselytising charity, the BABS, to provide support and a subscription base for his plans.[39] Though Anglican effort has left fewer traces it is not likely that it was absent. Two of the Sunday school movement's chief propagandists, Hannah and Martha More, lived only a short way from the city and had extensive links with members of the Bristol elite, such as the philanthropic banker John Scandrett Harford of Blaise Castle, thought to have been the model for Coelebs in the eponymous novel.[40]

By the closing years of the Napoleonic Wars trends in educational charity set the tone for a future in which sectarian concerns were much more prevalent. The development of adult and Sunday schools had led to the formalisation of educational charities in societies, which could provide a steady source of subscription and a coherent framework of aims and rules upon which expansion could be based. The Bristol Diocesan Society, formed in 1813 'for the education of the poor in the principles of the Established Church', may well have been activated partly in response to the contemporaneous efforts by nonconformists in adult education.[41] At the same time the Bristol Royal Lancastrian Free Schools established a boys' and a girls' school, run on a

---

35 *FFBJ*, 28 May 1803; *Bristol Gazette*, 19 May 1806.

36 W. Matthews, *The new history, survey and description of the city and suburbs of Bristol*, Bristol 1794; John S. Broad, *A history of the origins and progress of the Sunday schools in the city of Bristol and its vicinity under the patronage of the Methodist Sunday School Society*, Bristol 1816, 59–61; Thomas W. Laqueur, *Religion and respectability: Sunday schools and working-class culture*, London 1976, 24.

37 Broad, *Sunday schools*, 10–24.

38 A. Naish, J. S. Fry and W. Sturge, *Some particulars concerning the establishment and early history of the first-day schools conducted by the Society of Friends in Bristol*, Bristol 1860.

39 Pole, *Adult schools*, 7, 11–20.

40 B. Little, *The history of Barley Wood*, 1978, 13; More, *Mendip Annals*; Annette M. B. Meakin, *Hannah More: a biographical study*, London 1911, chs xxi, xxv; Mary Alden Hopkins, *Hannah More and her circle*, New York 1947, chs iii, iv, xvi–xx; *FFBJ*, 1 July 1797; Laqueur, *Religion and respectability*, 75–6; Bristol University Library, 'Hannah More, Blagdon Controversy'.

41 *FFBJ*, 5, 12 Feb. 1814.

similar principle to the poor relief and medical charities. An annual half-guinea subscription provided one recommendation for a place in the school, while the yearly open day provided the opportunity for patrons to relish the 'gratifying spectacle' of the children going through their lessons.[42] It seems then that if sectarian feeling could be sunk in the cause of tract distribution and poor relief, it was exacerbated by the prospect of young minds exposed to Anglican, or non-sectarian, teaching, particularly since the personal intervention of donors was built into the structure. An anonymous painting of St James's Benevolent School, c. 1810 (plate 3) shows a well-dressed lady visitor looking on as the girls sew and one of the pupils reads to the schoolmistress; all is order and decorum before the benevolent gaze.

If some evangelical initiatives encouraged non-partisan involvement, it was more usual for the multiplying religious charities to proselytise on behalf of a particular church. Nationally there were clear antecedents to the Anglican evangelising societies in the Society for the Promotion of Christian Knowledge (1698), and the Society for the Propagation of the Gospel in Foreign Parts (1701).[43] Methodism had arisen from the world of pietist voluntary societies in the 1730s and went on to dominate local tract distribution in the mid eighteenth century.[44] The leading force in tract distribution may have been the BABS, but similar, competing organisations arose from the various centres of religious life in the city: the diocese, evangelical Anglicans and dissenting chapels.[45]

Medical charities flourished in this period for a variety of reasons. The Bristol Infirmary had already built up a solid base of invested capital and was able to finance a phase of rebuilding begun in 1784, which led to the opening of two new wings by 1814.[46] The 1790s saw an unprecedented (and unsustained) increase in subscriber numbers and income in response to the building appeal and perhaps assisted by civic unity engendered by war. Bristol Dispensary (1775) also extended its capacity, providing home-visits by an apothecary for out-patients and a midwifery service for lying-in women, based on subscriber recommendation.[47] Participation by female philanthropists was first notable in several new charities for women in childbirth: the Female

---

[42] Ibid. 28 May, 4, 11 June 1814.

[43] W. K. Lowther Clarke, A history of the SPCK, London 1959; V. E. Neuburg, Popular literature, London 1977, 249–64; Owen, English philanthropy, 20–31; Jones, Charity school movement, passim.

[44] John Walsh, 'Origins of the Evangelical revival', in G. V. Bennett and J. D. Walsh (eds), Essays in modern church history, London 1966, 132–62 at pp. 144–8; Jonathan Barry, 'The press and the politics of culture in Bristol 1660–1775', in J. Black and J. Gregory (eds), Culture, politics and society in Britain, 1660–1800, Manchester 1991, 49–81 at pp. 54–5.

[45] Gorsky, 'Charity', 211n. 67.

[46] See appendix 2.

[47] BRL, B7891, State of Bristol Dispensary for the year ending . . ., annual reports, 1791–1855; 35893 36n, Richard Smith papers, vol. xiv. 232; Fissell, Patients, power and the poor, 118; C. Bruce-Perry, The voluntary medical institutions of Bristol, Bristol 1984, 7–8.

Plate 3. Anonymous, 'The Benevolent School', c. 1810
Courtesy of Bristol City Museum and Art Gallery

Misericordia (1800), the Bristol (Bridge Street Chapel) Dorcas Society (1809), the St Phillips Dorcas Society (1810s) and the Bristol Lying-In Institution (1820).[48] Another important factor was the need for doctors to establish a career niche in an overcrowded profession. This consideration applies not only to the dispensaries and those lying-in charities supported by male-midwives/accoucheurs, but more particularly to the emergent specialist hospitals.[49] Entrepeneurial doctors combined an expertise in a particular field with the existing framework of charity, for example Thomas Beddoes's Pneumatic Institute (1793), the Institute for the Cure of Diseases to the Eye among the Poor, founded in 1810 by William Goldwyer, and its rival Dispensary for the Cure of Complaints in the Eye, begun by John B. Estlin in 1812.[50] Estlin, a Unitarian, had been decisively beaten in elections to the Infirmary surgeoncy in 1810, and self-funded his Dispensary during its first year; he may have sought to provide for patients who lacked access to the patronage network of Goldwyer's Institute.[51]

The development of institutional care in this phase demonstrates that voluntarism was unnecessary where sufficient consensus existed on the need for public policy towards marginal groups such as criminals and lunatics. Bristol's elite followed the 'ideology of the penitentiary' promoted by humanitarian and utilitarian reformers, and successfully over-rode ratepayer objections to building the New Gaol, opened in 1820.[52] Henceforth prisoners received little attention from philanthropists, though the Society for the Relief and Discharge of Persons confined for Small Debts (1774) remained active.[53] Unlike nearby Gloucester, Bristol did not take advantage of the 1808 County Asylum Act to finance a public asylum from the rates. St Peter's Hospital had already pioneered the separate accomodation of lunatic patients under the poor law, and the city was well-served by private asylums, notably Edward

---

48 BRO 38463, Female Misericordia, minute book; 39399/CD/S/3d, Bristol Dorcas Society, *Annual reports*, 1841–70; 35893 36n, vol. xiv, Bristol Lying-In Institution, *Annual report*, 1821.
49 Fissell, *Patients, power and the poor*, ch. x; Pickstone, *Medicine and industrial society*, ch. iii; Sir Zachary Cope, 'The history of the dispensary movement', in F. N. L. Poynter (ed.), *The evolution of hospitals in Britain*, London 1964, 73–6; Jean Donnison, *Midwives and medical men: a history of the struggle for the control of childbirth*, London 1977, 2nd edn, London 1988, chs ii, iii; Ornella Moscucci, *The science of woman: gynaecology and gender in England, 1800–1929*, Cambridge 1990, ch. ii.
50 Lindsay Granshaw, ' "Fame and fortune by means of bricks and mortar": the medical profession and specialist hospitals in Britain, 1800–1948', in Granshaw and Porter, *Hospital in history*, 199–220; Munro Smith, *Bristol Infirmary*, 159, 318–19, 258–9, 439; Charles J. G. Saunders, *The Bristol Eye Hospital*, Bristol 1960; Neve, 'Science in a commercial city'.
51 Ibid. 33; *DNB*, 645.
52 Michael Ignatieff, *A just measure of pain; the penitentiary in the industrial revolution, 1750–1850*, London 1978, ch. iii; Latimer, *Annals . . . eighteenth century*, 488, and *Annals . . . nineteenth century*, 65–8.
53 *Bristol Journal*, 1 Jan., 9, 16 Feb., 7 May 1774; *Bristol Gazette*, 12 June 1806.

Long Fox's Brislington House. This offered 'moral therapy' in the manner of the York Retreat, and took pauper as well as private patients.[54]

These establishments were predicated upon the discipline of work as the means by which marginal groups could be reintegrated into society.[55] While public finance took care of the 'mad' and the 'bad', the voluntary sector applied the institutional approach to the physically disabled. In 1792, for example, local Quakers established the first Blind Asylum, where blind boys were instructed in plaiting whips, spinning flax, basket-making and stay-lace manufacture. This superseded the eighteenth-century preference for pensions for the blind, and it rapidly became a favoured cause of the civic establishment, relocating in 1838 to a prominent spot on Park Street.[56] Bristol Penitentiary (1800), the Refuge House (1814) and The Guardian House (1830s) were institutions for prostitutes. Here 'fallen women' (or the vulnerable) could receive food and shelter while they learnt to read the Bible and express repentance. Rehabilitation was to be achieved through the acquisition of literacy skills, the teaching of domestic service, needlework and shoe-making, and ultimately the procuring of a 'situation' with a respectable family.[57] Another such charity enjoying the patronage of the civic elite was the Asylum for Poor Orphan Girls (1795) opened 'to rescue destitute children . . . from . . . idleness and vice; to instil . . . religion and morality; and to inure them to habits of industry and cheerful obedience, . . . which may qualify them for acceptable servants in respectable families'.[58] The building itself was set in a rural location on the edge of the city, its house and gardens echoing the idyllic aspect much favoured in the contemporary design of lunatic asylums.[59]

Cultural factors and practical stresses both contributed to this reassertion of the Puritan work-ethic in an institutional form.[60] Theories of lunacy, after Locke, had evolved to assert the curability of the mad, while penal thought under materialist influence now proposed the function of imprisonment to be

[54] *Appendix to the first report from the Commissioners on the Poor Laws*, PP 1834 xxviii. 512; Kathleen Jones, *Lunacy, law, and conscience, 1744–1845: the social history of the care of the insane*, London 1955, 21–2, ch. v; Roy Porter, *Mind forg'd manacles: a history of madness in England from the Restoration to the Regency*, London 1987, 146–7, 165–6, 271–2; Andrew T. Scull, *Museums of madness: the social organisation of insanity in nineteenth-century England*, London 1979, 51, 67, 77, 79, 94, 205, and plate 5; William Parry-Jones, *The trade in lunacy: a study of private madhouses in England in the eighteenth and nineteenth centuries*, London 1972, tables ix, x, pp. 50–64, 327.
[55] Samuel Tuke, *Description of the Retreat*, York 1813, 156; Scull, *Museums of madness*, 105–7; Ignatieff, *Just measure of pain*, 70, 102, 110–11.
[56] Manchee, i. 104–6; H. J. Wagg and M. Thomas, *A chronological survey of work for the blind*, London 1932, 7, 9; Latimer, *Annals . . . eighteenth century*, 498.
[57] *FFBJ*, 9 Feb. 1811, 19 Nov. 1814; Pole, *Adult schools*, 52–3; *Matthews's directory 1841*.
[58] BRL, B9780–1, *State of the Orphan Asylum for the year, . . . 1821, 1826*.
[59] Ibid.; Tuke, *Description of the Retreat*, ch. iii; Elaine Showalter, *The female malady: women, madness and English culture, 1830–1980*, London 1987, 35–6.
[60] Scull, *Museums of madness*, 30–48.

not punishment of the body, but reform of the mind.[61] Science provided theoretical vindication for the asylum; it was the challenge of urban poverty which brought it forth. Wartime Bristol hosted an expanding, unsettled population ill-equipped to provide for the indigent within familial structures; large numbers of impoverished vagrants fuelled perceptions of a crime wave which at its most extreme was addressed with an unprecedented resort to transportation.[62] The war years galvanised a section of the city's elite, Evangelicals and Quakers especially, to forms of social action which expressed a compound of self-regard, compassion and fear.

Fragmentation and specialisation: c. 1820–c. 1860

Between the aftermath of war and the mid-century the trend towards high-profile, non-partisan association was reversed. New formations were either more closely identified with a particular congregation or had a more tightly defined purpose, while older ones like the PMFS fell into abeyance or, like the BABS, lost their broad appeal. A highly politicised sectarian atmosphere pervaded education, anti-slavery and temperance. It also encouraged a distinctly female philanthropy and inspired both small-scale missions and one prominent hospital, although professional ambition continued to be a factor influencing medical charity. In this phase the direct role of the state was limited to the meagre education grant, but indirectly the reform of the endowed charities was significant.

Civic debate on poverty, as earlier chapters showed, had now turned from voluntarist solutions to discussion of the poor law and the old endowments. The initiative thus passed to small societies formed by nonconformist churches, which combined visiting, evangelising, educational, providential and medical aid. Baptists and Congregationalists were active in the Bristol City Mission (1826) and the Unitarians began a Working and Visiting Society (1835) and later a Domestic Mission (1840).[63] The Society of Friends formed a Rice Committee (1849), a Mission to Navvies (1861), and finally the New Street Mission, where the Quakers converted their original almshouse into a mission building hosting a ragged school, adult school, Sunday school, a 'Bible woman', a cocoa room and soup kitchen.[64] Other charities were organised around one distinct activity, such as the St Mary Redcliffe Soup Society (1847) or the Clifton Loan Blanket Society (1855), where the

---

61 Porter, *Mind forg'd manacles*, ch. iv and pp. 279–80; Ignatieff, *Just measure of pain*, 66–79.
62 See John K. Walton, 'Lunacy in the industrial revolution: a study of asylum admissions in Lancashire, 1848–1850', *Journal of Social History* xiii (1979), 1–22; John F. Mackeson, *Bristol transported*, Bristol 1987, 37.
63 BRL, B7054–9, LMCWVS, *Annual reports*, Bristol 1835–50; B7060–7, LMDMS, *Annual reports*, Bristol 1841–58.
64 Ronald Cleeves, *Mission of mercy*, Bristol 1979; Carter, *Bristol churches*, ch. iii; Arrowsmith, *Dictionary*, 256; BRO, SF/A9/3, 4a, 4b, 5.

Plate 4. 'General Hospital, Bristol', by W. B. Gingell
Courtesy of Bristol City Museum and Art Gallery

parish or suburb rallied cross-sectarian support.[65] Malthusian ideas were prominent, but rather than restraining charitable impulses they existed in an uneasy tension with the imperative of poor relief. Thus while Unitarian domestic missionaries worried over 'the inexpediency of indiscriminate relief' their home-visiting revealed that 'fluctuation or uncertainty in the means of subsistence' lay at the root of poverty.[66]

Disability could still stimulate cross-faith effort. The Deaf and Dumb Institute (1841) was very much a civic institution, chaired by the mayor and supported by Anglican and dissenting clergy. Like the asylums it emphasised training for work and its subscribers made an annual 'examination' visit, in the manner of charity school trustees.[67] Elsewhere sectarianism reasserted itself. It was Evangelical Anglicans who provided the impetus for the Society for the Instruction of the Blind (1830s) and the Society for Embossing and Circulating the Authorised Version of the Bible For the Use of the Blind (1836).[68]

The great importance attached to particular styles of religious instruction in schools meant that educational foundations were closely linked to particular congregations. Table 18 draws on the 1851 census to demonstrate the voluntary (i.e. non-endowed) day schools' denominational links. National and British schools educated no more than 56 per cent of charity school children, and a mere 25 per cent of the total number of Bristol scholars, of whom 2,457 attended the eight National schools, as against 2,077 in the nine British schools. The Church of England was the dominant religious influence, with 59 per cent of the charity children, in 60 per cent of the schools. One possible reason for the discrepancy is the devotion of Methodist resources to Sunday rather than day schools, at least before the foundation of three Wesleyan schools in the 1850s and 1860s. It is also the case that the great expansion of parochial schools coincided with the transformation in the role of the Anglican parish outlined above. Finally, the ratio of boys to girls in voluntary schools was 57:43, against 50:50 in the private schools recorded in the census. Parents of boys may have preferred charity school education to working-class elementary schools because they felt it had greater utility in the labour market, or perhaps a stronger disciplinary ethos.[69]

The claim that charity education promoted 'among the lower orders a salutory disposition of subordination' was present from the first, and appeals for voluntary schools were often couched in a language of class management.[70] Similarly adult education in this period was transformed from a

---

[65] St Mary Redcliffe Vestry Archive, Soup Society minutes, 1854–61; BRO, P/StAug/Soc/1a, b, Clifton Loan Blanket Society, minute books.
[66] LMDMS, 3rd report, 1842; LMCWVS, 2nd report, 1836.
[67] Bristol Mercury, 19 June 1858; FFBJ, 9, 23 May 1846.
[68] Wagg and Thomas, Work for the blind, 11, 19, 28–9; Bristol Gazette, 18 Feb., 12 May 1836.
[69] See Gardner, Lost elementary schools.
[70] FFBJ, 12 Feb., 3 Dec. 1814; Pole, Adult schools, 91.

Table 18
Sources of financial support for Bristol voluntary schools, 1851

Denomination	Schools	Scholars		
		Male	Female	Total
Church of England:				
National	8	1,464	993	2,457
Others	19	1,073	1,267	2,340
Independents:				
British	1	52	96	148
Others	1	116	135	251
Quakers	2	306	32	338
Unitarians:-				
British	3	456	233	689
Moravians	1	22	73	95
Roman Catholics	5	259	305	564
Non-denominational:				
British	5	904	336	1,240
Total	45	4,652	3,470	8,122

Source: 1851 *Census of Great Britain. Education report (England and Wales)*, summary tables, p.clviii

religious to a secular attempt to influence working-class culture, via the establishment of the Mechanics Institute in 1825.[71] Within a few years it offered a programme of classes and lectures, and had its own museum and library, at a cost of 10s. *per annum* subscription.[72] Unfortunately the intent of the promoters was not matched by response of the target public and in 1845 it was wound up, its library and apparatus taken over by the Athenaeum.[73] An editorial in the *Bristol Mercury* looking back in 1858 accounted for this failure thus:

these valuable institutions were never Mechanics Institutions at all. The promoters, with the best intentions, generally exercised a sort of condescending patronage and authority, by which the government of the institution was entirely removed from the ordinary subscribers, whilst another class of persons, of which the young clerk or shopman is a fair representative, commonly

71 J. F. C. Harrison, *Learning and living, 1790–1960 : a study of the English adult education movement*, London 1961, 57–89, 172–84.
72 *FFBJ*, 25 June 1825; *Matthews's directory 1831*, 276; *Bristol Gazette*, 3 Mar., 22 Sept., 27 Oct. 1836.
73 Latimer, *Annals . . . nineteenth century*, 288.

usurped the advantages which were originally intended for the working population.[74]

Expansion of the prominent medical charities was the result not of any marked initiative on the part of subscribers, but of the steady accumulation of fixed capital via single gifts and legacies, which were then invested. Further building work in 1830–2 extended the Bristol Infirmary out-patients admission facilities and enlarged its dispensary, freeing up space for conversion into two new wards in 1841, so that by 1850 the number of beds had risen from around 150 in 1794 to 245, in 'spacious and well-ventilated surroundings'. Further developments in the 1860s were the opening of a chapel, museum, three new wards, a new storey to accommodate forty nurses, and the installation of speaking tubes and a telegraphic apparatus.[75] Bristol Dispensary patient numbers rose impressively during the first half of the nineteenth century, though within this trend a decrease in the proportion of midwifery cases was the salient feature: 1795: 595 sick, 216 midwifery; 1820: 2,313 sick, 492 midwifery; 1855: 3,587 sick, 247 midwifery.[76] In part this reflected the vigour of the smaller 'natalist' charities driven by female philanthropy, and in part the impact of commercial medicine. The rise of the man-midwife in the eighteenth century had established obstetrics as an integral part of general practice, ill-paid yet essential to building up a clientele. In the period between 1820 and 1850 burgeoning numbers of general practitioners competed to establish themselves as relatively cheap family doctors: the marketplace therefore drew midwifery away from charity.[77] The increasing tendency of benefit societies to employ qualified doctors from the mid-century may also have been a factor.

Competition for a career niche meant that medical specialisation continued to be a major factor in formations towards the mid-century. A concern for the diseases of children, who were relatively neglected by the Infirmary, led to the creation of the Institute for the Cure of Diseases in Children in 1821, a development which foreshadowed the spread of children's hospitals elsewhere post-1850.[78] A Vaccine Institute was started in 1838 by Estlin, the eye doctor; in the 1840s a Dispensary for the Cure of Diseases of the Skin opened in St James, while two institutions for treating deafness and diseases of the ear were begun in the 1850s, followed in 1860 by a Hospital for Diseases of the Teeth.

This undermining of traditional types of patronage by new attitudes to medical philanthropy and the pressures of commerce was not an even process however, as the founding of the most important new institution of the

---

[74] Bristol Mercury, 20 Jan. 1838; Koditschek, Class formation, 308–19.
[75] Munro-Smith, Bristol Infirmary, 138–45, 148–57, 161–3, 280–2, 333, 335–9; Bruce-Perry, Voluntary medical institutions; Matthews's directory, 1794, 1851.
[76] State of Bristol Dispensary.
[77] Loudon, Medical care, ch. iv, p. 99; ch. x, pp. 275–9.
[78] Pickstone, Medicine and industrial society, 113–22.

mid-century, the Bristol General Hospital, demonstrates. Old-style benevolence, particularly from two wealthy Quakers, Joseph Eaton and George Thomas, played an essential part in its establishment in 1832 in two houses in Guinea Street, followed in 1858 by its expansion on a much larger site by the Bathurst Basin. The professional jealousies of non-Infirmary doctors were a factor in the debate which preceded the foundation of the new hospital, as did an awareness of patient demand: 233 patients had been turned away from the Infirmary in the first three months of 1830, and the Bristol Hospital and Surgery was started in May of that year to meet this need, seeing patients without notes of recommendation. The setting up of the General, which subsumed the Hospital of Surgery, reasserted the links between paternal largesse and subscriber power: a two-guinea subscription permitted the benefactor to admit two in- and two out-patients. This can be understood within the context of the years 1831–2, when Bristol's elite was faced with discontent from the lower orders as economic depression, cholera and the Reform agitation coincided, and at the same time experienced an intensification of internal divisions of party and religion. The General therefore provided a new channel of patronage to soften class antagonism and also offered Liberal nonconformists an alternative nucleus of civic power.[79]

Religious charities increasingly reflected the cellular religious sub-culture of the city as the pattern of cross-faith establishment gave way to the efforts of individual sects. For example the Independents dominated fundraising for the Bristol Missionary Society from the 1830s, and its annual meeting was no longer held at the neutral Guildhall, but at their Castle Green chapel.[80] New foreign missions were henceforth clearly identified with particular Anglican or dissenting groups, while proselytising societies in the mid-century concentrated on support services, such as church-building, scripture-reading, and target groups such as seamen.[81] Quaker pacifism was promoted in the Bristol Auxiliary to the London Peace Society (1820) which also featured Wesleyans and Independents. The Anti-War Association (1843) attacked recruiting sergeants for 'decoying young men into public houses, and intoxicating them', and opposed flogging in the army, and colonial expansion: 'trade which could be obtained without conquest was all that was wanted'.[82]

Temperance activity also assumed a sectarian stamp, although its inspirations were various: middle-class withdrawal from the alehouse as leisure venue, the pub's association with undesirable social and political attitudes,

79 Munro Smith, *Bristol Infirmary*, 278–80; Bruce-Perry, *Voluntary medical institutions*, 4–5; J. O. Symes, *A short history of the Bristol General Hospital*, Bristol 1932.
80 *Bristol Gazette*, 15 Sept. 1836; *FFBJ*, 17 Sept. 1814.
81 Gorsky, 'Charity', 221 nn. 119, 120; *FFBJ*, 10 Jan., 24 Oct., 14 Nov. 1846; Meller, *Leisure and the changing city*, 138.
82 *Matthews's directory 1831*; *FFBJ*, 5 Sept., 3 Oct. 1846; Carter, 'Bristol churches', ch. iv; *Bristol Mercury*, 25 Feb. 1854.

and the argument that alcohol caused crime and ignorance.[83] Bristol Temperance Society (1830) started fairly moderately, with a declaration by doctors and surgeons against 'ardent spirits' that included the *bon viveur* Richard Smith among its signatories. However, the growing dominance of Quakers of conviction, like George Thomas, Samuel Capper, Joseph Eaton and Robert Charlton pushed the movement towards total abstinence.[84] The West of England Temperance Association (1837) sought to propagandise more widely with the *Bristol Temperance Herald*, funded by Eaton. Events like tea-parties and abstinence Christmas festivals were held in public spaces as counter-attractions to the pub; these were central to the campaign from the start and prefigured later interventions in working-class leisure.[85] The established form of school outings was co-opted to the cause: the 'rural fete' of the Bristol Juvenile Total Abstinence Union of Day and Sunday Schools at the Zoo on Whit Tuesday 1846, attracted 15,000 people to drink tea, coffee, soda and ginger beer, and listen to bands.[86]

The politicisation of philanthropy was most complete in the anti-slavery movement. This began with Clarkson's visits to the city from 1787, which led in turn to the establishment of an abolitionist committee in 1789.[87] Following abolition a Bristol Auxiliary Anti-Slavery Society (1823) was formed to lobby for emancipation and was active up to the campaign against apprenticeship in the 1830s, and the issue remained central to divisions in local politics between traditional and reform Whigs.[88] Interest was maintained from 1840 by the Bristol and Clifton Auxiliary Ladies Anti-Slavery Society, first as a forum for discussion and fundraising for schools in Jamaica, and later lending annual support for the Boston Bazaar and American abolitionism.[89] Garrisonian agitation from 1846 encouraged the Ladies Society to move to a more fundamentalist condemnation of slave ownership and an endorsement of the female campaigners' right to the public platform, and it eventually disaffiliated itself from its more hidebound parent society.[90] This nucleus of

[83] Harrison, *Drink and the Victorians*, 166, 186, 233, 244, 256.

[84] BRL 24078, Bristol Temperance Society declaration by doctors against 'ardent spirits'; *Bristol Gazette*, 16 June 1836.

[85] Ibid. 11 Mar., 8 Sept. 1836; *FFBJ*, 3 Jan. 1846; Meller, *Leisure and the changing city*, 123–5, 163–9.

[86] *FFBJ*, 23 May, 6 June 1846.

[87] Latimer, *Annals . . . . eighteenth century*, 473–6; Peter Marshall, *The anti-slave trade movement in Bristol*, Bristol 1968; *FFBJ*, 9 July 1814.

[88] BRL 3217, *Proceedings of the anti-slavery meeting held at the Guildhall Bristol on February 2nd. 1826*; BRL 3218, Bristol Auxiliary Anti-Slavery Society, *Report of proceedings from the formation of the institution to the 31st December, 1830*, Bristol 1831; Marshall, *Bristol and the abolition of slavery*; *FFBJ*, 9 Dec. 1837.

[89] BRL microfilm, Estlin papers, reel 5, BCLASS, minute book, 1840–61.

[90] *FFBJ*, 29 Aug. 1846; *The Liberator*, 16 Nov. 1855, in BRL, RLSA B32045, papers of J. B. and Mary Estlin, box 3, scrapbook 'The late J. B. Estlin'; *FFBJ*, 5, 19 Sept., 10 Oct. 1846; Howard Temperley, *British anti-slavery, 1833–70*, London 1972; Clare Midgley, *Women against slavery: the British campaigns, 1780–1860*, London 1992.

women later formed the local branch of the Women's Suffrage Society, chaired by Congregationalist minister Urijah Thomas, another active philanthropist.[91]

Proliferation and change: c. 1850–c. 1880

The latter half of the century saw the continuing proliferation of charities associated with a particular congregation or a specialised approach. New target groups such as young people, animals and juvenile delinquents came to the fore both in societies and in a fresh burst of institutional establishments. The subscriber system began to give way on the one hand to anonymous benevolence, and on the other to approaches which merged providence and private payment. Again the active role of the state was visible. The supervisory function of the Charity Commission and the Registrar of Friendly Societies now firmly underpinned aspects of voluntarism. The extension of publicly funded asylums and reformatories continued the withdrawal of the deviant from private charity, and the 1870 Education Act began the demise of voluntary schooling.

There was no revival of the high-profile, cross-faith poor-relief initiatives. New projects arose from individual churches or offered a distinct service. The 1870s witnessed the arrival of the Broadmead Baptist Church Mission, and the St Luke's Mission Hall, which combined a soup kitchen with ragged school; there was also renewed concern for genteel types fallen on hard times, with the Bristol Benevolent Institution, and a 'depot for the sale of work by ladies of limited means'. In the 1880s two groups emerged with a novel solution to poverty, the Bristol Emigration Society, which offered loans and clothing for would-be migrants, and the Canadian Home, 'for the purpose of collecting and training neglected girls under 13 years of age', for migration to Canada.[92] In the later Victorian period there was a spate of new mission foundations, stimulated, according to Meller, by a 'cultural renaissance' in Bristol between 1865 and 1875. This 'civilizing mission to the poor' marked by a 'growing desire to foster communities and community spirit' was in many respects a development of the earlier missionary initiatives of Quakers, Baptists and Unitarians.[93] In the world of fundraising for foreign missions the

---

91 Ellen Malos, 'Bristol women in action, 1839–1919: the right to vote and the need to earn a living', in Ian Bild (ed.), Bristol's other history, Bristol 1983, 97–128; S. J. Tanner, Suffrage movement in Bristol: how the women's suffrage movement began in Bristol fifty years ago, Bristol 1918; papers of J. B. and Mary Estlin, Mary Estlin's correspondence. See also Clare Taylor, British and American abolitionists: an episode in transatlantic understanding, Edinburgh 1974, 382–3; Meller, Leisure and the changing city, 83, 138, 152–4, 170.
92 Wright's directory 1890, 552.
93 Gorsky, 'Charity', 224 nn. 135, 136; Meller, Leisure and the changing city, chs vi, vii, pp. 123, 137.

progress of British imperialism saw the original initiatives augmented by a host of others, representing ever more specific concerns.

The passing of Forster's Education Act and the shift in favour of funding of schools from taxation signified growing popular assent for the collective educational goods pioneered by charity and private schools. However, sectarian division in education persisted up to the elections to the first local school boards which were dominated by the controversy that had attended debate over the legislation at national level. A Conservative/Roman Catholic alliance in favour of denominationalism emerged, though the non-sectarian bloc won the day.[94] A last significant phase of voluntary school establishment in Bristol occurred in the 1870s, suggesting that the denominational impulse behind charity foundations was initially stimulated, rather than quelled, by the introduction of the state system. Philanthropy left another legacy in this phase, for like the medical charities the voluntary schools had provided the stability of employment and the networks for training and interraction that encouraged the professionalisation of teaching. Early associations included a society of Quaker teachers and the Western Union of Teachers (1858), while the Gloucester School Prize Association represented an early effort to standardise local examinations.[95]

The other area in which public policy was shaped by voluntary initiatives was juvenile delinquency, hitherto tackled by the ragged schools, reformatories and industrial schools.[96] The roots lay with those educational and missionary charities which had long emphasised visiting and personal knowledge of the family, the work with children being seen as a means of social intervention with parents.[97] Meanwhile the notion that institutionalisation could achieve reform of 'vicious' habits was brought to bear on the newly articulated problem of juvenile crime.[98] These strands came together in the well-known career of Mary Carpenter, which began with her involvement in the Girls Branch of the Lewin's Mead Sunday School, and as a visitor with the Unitarian's Working and Visiting Society.[99] The idea of her first ragged school (1846) was to reach those children whose deprivation had thus far

94 Latimer, Annals . . . nineteenth century, 455–6; BRO, proceedings of the Common Council, 13 Dec. 1870; Beaven, Bristol lists, 107–8; Meller, Leisure and the changing city, 176 and passim; S. Humphries, 'Schooling and the working class in Bristol, 1870–1914', Southern History i (1979), 176–80.

95 BRO, SF/FD/AR/1a, First Friends' Day School; Bristol Mercury, 27 Mar., 22 May 1858; Harold Perkin, The rise of professional society: England since 1880, London 1989, 349–50; A. M. Carr-Saunders and P. A. Wilson, The professions, Oxford 1933, 252–3.

96 BRO, SF/A10/3b; Naish, Fry and Sturge, Some particulars; BRO, 38603/Z/S/1.

97 Broad, Sunday schools, 43–5; FFBJ, 12 Feb. 1814, 2nd annual report of the Diocesan Society.

98 Susan Magarey, 'The invention of juvenile delinquency in early nineteenth-century England', Labour History xxxiv (1978), 11–27.

99 Ruby J. Saywell, Mary Carpenter of Bristol, Bristol 1964; Jo Manton, Mary Carpenter and the children of the streets, London 1976; J. Estlin Carpenter, The life and work of Mary Carpenter, London 1879.

excluded them from both dame and charity schools, and provide them with 'religious and moral training, intellectual and industrial training, self-respect and cleanliness'.[100] She later participated in the public debate over reformatories, in which her advocacy of moral reform was an important influence on the content of the Youthful Offenders Act of 1854.[101] Following the Industrial Schools Acts of 1857 and 1866 children convicted of begging or minor offences were sent to a tier of schools between the reformatories and day schools. Part-funded by government, these Certified Industrial Schools were located in Pennywell Road, Clifton, Cotham and Park Row, while the Bristol Training Ship 'Formidable' received homeless and destitute boys between eleven and fourteen to be trained for the Royal Navy or merchant fleet.[102]

Voluntarism augmented the efforts of the state in several other respects. Although the City and County of Bristol Lunatic Asylum was publicly funded, a Committee of Visitors played a quasi-charitable role, for example holding a 'Lunatics New Year's Ball' in 1858.[103] The penal system was also supported by a variety of initiatives. Like the penitentiaries, the Asylum for Hopeful Discharged Female Prisoners (1854) offered training in household work leading to a placement in service, and two other prisoners' missions started in the 1890s.[104] At the end of the century the Royal Victoria Home was built for the moral reform and social integration of female convicts, 'poor inebriate women' and 'hopeful' small offenders, while a sister home for alcoholics was funded by the state under the 1898 Inebriates Act. Religious education was high on the agenda, as was training for domestic service, and teaching married women 'how to be better housewives'.[105] Public policy also recognised physical disability as a category of need, with the Home for Crippled Children (1876) largely financed by the Poor Law Board. As with the hospitals, it was accepted that groups suffering from chronic ailments and needing long-term care were the responsibility of the state. Charitable initiative came in the 1890s, with Ada Vachell's Guild of the Brave Poor Things, which may well have offered disabled children a greater degree of self-determination and shared identity.[106]

A variety of other crusading groups sought to sway public opinion in the

---

[100] Saywell, *Mary Carpenter*, 5; *FFBJ*, 26 Dec. 1846; Gorsky, 'Charity', 225 n. 143.

[101] R. J. W. Selleck, 'Mary Carpenter: a confident and contradictory reformer', *History of Education* xiv (1985), 101–13.

[102] *Wright's Directory, 1876, 1882*; *Bristol Mercury*, 22 May 1858.

[103] *Bristol Mercury*, 9 Jan. 1858; Latimer, *Annals . . . nineteenth century*, 346–7; Arrowsmith, *Dictionary*, 241.

[104] *Bristol Mercury*, 23 Jan. 1858; Arrowsmith, *Dictionary*, 258.

[105] *Wright's directory 1900*.

[106] Bruce-Perry, *Voluntary medical institutions*, 17–18; *Wright's directory 1900*; F. M. Unwin, *Ada Vachell of Bristol*, Bristol 1928; Seth Koven, 'Remembering and dismemberment: crippled children, wounded soldiers, and the Great War in Great Britain', *American Historical Review* xcix (1994), 1167–202.

period. Temperance agitation continued – for example, the Bristol auxiliary to the United Kingdom Alliance (1850s) campaigned for reform of the laws permitting traffic in liquor, though again new formations indicate religious fragmentation.[107] Animal rights were defended by the Bristol and Clifton Auxiliary of the Society for the Prevention of Cruelty to Animals (1842) whose list of concerns ranged from local to international.[108] The early closing campaign arose from another philanthropic interest, the leisure hours of clerks and shop workers.[109] An Anti-State-Church Association (1846) brought together dissenting clergymen aiming to argue that 'any legislation by secular governments in matters of religion is contrary to the principle of the New Testament'.[110] At the end of the century lobby groups such as the Bristol Peace and Arbitration Association promoted the adoption of international law for arbitration in disputes, while conversely a branch of the Navy League urged that an arms build-up was 'the best guarantee of peace'.[111]

This period witnessed the undermining of the power of subscribers to dominate access to a charity's bounty, a trend first discernible in medical philanthropy. Admission to the Bristol Free Institution for the Treatment of Diseases Peculiar to Women and Children (1857) could either be by subscriber note, or a note from 'a housekeeper who can certify the merits of the case', or simply by paying a reduced market rate.[112] A new committee member, Mark Whitwill, inspired its transition in 1866 from dispensary to the Bristol Childrens' Hospital, in which subscribers had no rights of admission: 'Enough that a child be sick and poor, it will be admitted, provided there be a vacant bed, and that medical officers consider the case a suitable one for the hospital.'[113] Redland Dispensary opened in 1860, also using the standard subscriber note system, then became part provident institution, whereby the subscriber note – one's own or one's patron's – bought a month's treatment. Bristol Medical Missionary Society (1870s) was a charitable dispensary whose services were free to the poor without recommendation. Nurse attendance in the home could be procured from the Bristol District Nurses Society (1890s) on either a private or a charitable basis. Likewise the Read Dispensary for Women and Children (1874) was funded both by the patients themselves and by voluntary contributions, as was the Bristol Private Hospital for Women and Children (1895).

The diminishing power of the subscriber in medical charities suggests a growing preparedness on the part of the beneficent to accept the doctor as sole arbiter of admissions, perhaps because the profession increasingly

[107] Gorsky, 'Charity', 226 n. 150.
[108] Ibid. n. 151; FFBJ, 14 Nov. 1846.
[109] Meller, Leisure and the changing city, 126–7.
[110] FFBJ, 7 Mar. 1846.
[111] Wright's directory 1900.
[112] Matthews's directory 1862; Bristol Mercury, 20 Feb. 1858; Charles J. G. Saunders, The Bristol Royal Hospital for Sick Children, Bristol 1960, 10.
[113] Ibid. 9–10.

regarded specialist hospitals as *bona fide* institutions rather than career vehicles for outsiders.[114] It also points up the increasing pressure on medical services to cater to the stratum of the population who were neither wealthy nor paupers or charity cases. This was the period in which friendly society medical attendance became widespread, in which the Workmen's Saturday Fund commenced, and in which pay-beds were introduced at Guy's and St Thomas's.[115] Lastly, as the cost of medical treatment advanced, so hospitals sought fresh sources of funding.[116]

Bristol's most celebrated new charity of the period advanced a theological justification for subscriber anonymity. George Muller's Orphan Homes had begun as the Scriptural Knowledge Institution, dedicated to Bible distribution and education as well as the care of orphans. Between 1836 and 1870 this expanded from three houses in St Paul's with seventy-five children, to the purpose-built homes on Ashley Hill with capacity for 2,050.[117] Muller eschewed the usual methods of attracting subscribers in favour of individual contacts, appeals from the pulpit and use of the evangelical press in which he mythologised his fundraising success as the direct result of the power of prayer.[118] A key financial role was played by Muller's fellow emigré and co-religionist Conrad Finzel, the Bristol sugar magnate, who had been convinced that a serious fire at his refinery was God's judgement on him for failing in his charity and had henceforth vowed to donate a third of his income to good works.[119] The orphanages appealed to both rich and poor donors, partly due to the fact that the charity published no subscription lists, and deliberately stood apart from the sectarian identities of the Bristol voluntarist world. As at the Children's Hospital, admission was based directly on need, rather than personal recommendation: Muller donors therefore experienced genuine *caritas* divorced from the usual concerns of power and status in the gift relationship.

Muller's charity was also representative of another important trend which marked this period, the proliferation of residential institutions for specific groups. Some offered shelter and rehabilitation for 'fallen women' and again aimed to channel poor or at risk girls towards domestic service.[120] Another was provided for that other favoured target group of mid-century missionaries, seamen, who received their Sailors' Home in 1853. In the 1870s homes

114 Granshaw, ' "Fame and Fortune" ', 212–13.
115 Abel-Smith, *The hospitals*, 9.
116 Keir Waddington, ' "Grasping gratitude": charity and hospital finance in late-Victorian London', in Daunton, *Charity, self-interest and welfare*, 181–202.
117 Latimer, *Annals . . . nineteenth century*, 223–6; Owen, *English philanthropy*, 160–2.
118 Nancy Garton, *George Muller and his orphans*, London 1963, 56, 65–72 and ch. viii; Arthur T. Pierson, *George Muller of Bristol*, London 1912, chs xi–xv, xxii, esp. pp. 161, 221, 327, 440.
119 Jean Burrows, 'The Finzels of Counterslip and Clevedon', *The Bristol Templar 1992: Bristol faces and places*, Bristol 1992, 7–17.
120 Gorsky, 'Charity', 229 nn. 165, 166.

were also established for Working Boys, Working Women and Working Girls in Business, Apprentice Boys, and Invalid Ladies of Limited Means, as well as a Childrens' Home and the Bristol Boys' Home.

How is this new phase of institutionalism to be explained? Surveys of Bristol's population growth between 1841 and 1931 have shown that the 1860s and to a lesser extent the 1870s were the two decades in which increase by net immigration was most intense, and it seems certain that part of this increase represents the presence in the city of a large transitory population of migrant workers.[121] The large proportion of young people in the population has also been mentioned (table 2). In meeting this new demand for cheap, 'respectable' accomodation philanthropists drew on their familiar goals of investment in human capital and socialisation through employment. Efforts to prepare poor women or prostitutes for domestic service were a continuation of earlier initiatives, and the Sailors' Home also intended an intervention in a casual labour market: 'According to his conduct is he (i.e. the resident) recommended, and often through that recommendation advanced, and captains and owners wanting crews knew where to get them at the shortest notice.'[122] A third explanatory factor was the growing national debate from the mid-century on prostitution and sexual mores, which inspired local initiatives such as the Bristol Female Mission and the Temporary Home for Fallen Women.[123]

Meller's work on Bristol's 'socio-religious' life after 1870 has provided a thorough account of the burgeoning number of associations directed at the 'religious and intellectual improvement' of young men and women. She charts the way in which alarm at rapid urban growth was coupled with concern for the cultural impoverishment of the working class, epitomised in Arnold's *Culture and anarchy*. These anxieties gave rise to societies oriented to the young, offering meetings, lectures and the establishment of libraries.[124] Temperance activists drew children into the Bands of Hope which grew out of the Total Abstinence Society's work with schools.[125] The last quarter of the century witnessed the growth of suburban church youth clubs, an area in which the Congregationalists were particularly prominent. For instance in 1883 Redland Park Chapel formed a Boys' Brigade aimed at 'the promotion of

---

121 Shannon and Grebenick, *Population of Bristol*, 10–11; Alford, 'Economic development', 267–70; *Condition of the poor*, 28–9.
122 *FFBJ*, 28 Nov. 1846.
123 Eric Trudgill, *Madonnas and magdalens: the origin and development of Victorian sexual attitudes*, London 1976, chs viii, ix; Judith R. Walkowitz, *Prostitution and Victorian society: women, class and the state*, Cambridge 1980, chs i–iv.
124 Meller, *Leisure and the changing city*, 48–51, 126–30, 145–9; Gorsky, 'Charity', 230 n. 173; BRL, B1533, *Address delivered at the Broadmead Room Tuesday, June 14th, 1853 at the inaugural gathering of the Young Men's Christian Association*, Bristol 1853.
125 *Bristol Mercury*, 27 Mar., 24 July 1858.

habits of reverence, discipline, self-respect, and all that tends towards a true Christian manliness'.[126]

Meller's analysis can be augmented by recent work which elucidates the motive for philanthropic youth work. The reference to 'muscular Christianity' in the preceding quotation may now be better understood in the light of cultural studies which have shown how insecurity and religious doubt gave rise to a more assertive masculinity. In the public schools, in literature and in social action male self-perceptions now stressed moral fibre through the healthy body.[127] Imperial discourse gave further encouragement to youth workers seeking to cultivate manly virtues in their charges.[128] Lastly, the advance of education, the trend to smaller, more affective families and the marketing of commodities for children created a perception of childhood, for the middle classes at least, as a distinct and extended phase of the life-cycle.[129] In addition to stimulating charities for orphans and young people these concerns gave rise directly to the National Society for the Prevention of Cruelty to Children (the Bristol branch began in 1889) which was instrumental in developing the notion of children's rights embodied in the Children Act of 1908.[130]

The impetus for the growth of voluntary organisations came from two areas: members of the town's business and professional elite and its religious institutions. A rapid expansion of voluntarist activity occurred around the turn of the century, a period encompassing the French wars and their aftermath, and a phase of renewed evangelical fervour. In Bristol this was distinguished by several societies patronised by all sections of the elite regardless of their party or sectional affiliation. From the 1820s the identification of associations and institutions with specific churches or chapels was more obvious. The elite continued to provide leadership for major institutions such as hospitals and asylums, but henceforth philanthropy was closely interrelated with the city's religious sub-culture. This second phase also saw a change in the nature of women's voluntarism from an apparently subordinate position in male-led societies to a proactive participation in identifiably female charities. The third stage was marked by the move away from active subscriber involve-

---

126 Meller, *Leisure and the changing city*, 169–75; *Wright's directory 1900*.

127 Norman Vance, *The sinews of the spirit*, Cambridge 1985; Donald E. Hall (ed.), *Muscular Christianity: embodying the Victorian age*, Cambridge 1994; Lynne Segal, *Slow motion: changing masculinities, changing men*, London 1990, 104–11; J. A. Mangan and James Walvin (eds), *Manliness and morality*, Manchester 1987. See also John Tosh and Michael Roper (eds), *Manful assertions: masculinities in Britain since 1800*, London 1991.

128 Geoffrey Pearson, *Hooligan: a history of respectable fears*, London 1983, 106–16; Anne Summers, 'Edwardian militarism', in Raphael Samuel (ed.), *Patriotism: the making and unmaking of British identity*, I: History and politics, London 1989, 236–56.

129 Harris, *Private lives*, 84–91; Hugh Cunningham, *The children of the poor: representations of childhood since the seventeenth century*, Oxford 1991, p. 3, chs vi, viii.

130 Harris, *Private lives*, 75.

ment, initially discerned in the hospitals and dispensaries, where for the first time the principle of reciprocity was absent from the gift relationship and power shifted to the administrator and the recipient. New residential institutions and missionary societies built on earlier initiatives as they responded to changing demographic pressures and cultural forces. Throughout the period the career ambitions of doctors were a driving force in medical charity.

The context for all this activity was a plural society in which voluntarism provided an outlet for different groups to address problems that fell outside statutory provision. The early phase was one of debate at national level about the extent to which the state should intervene to aid the poor through such mechanisms as out-relief payments and contributory insurance, and this was the period in which Bristol's elite experimented with different approaches, including the PMFS and parochial voluntarism.[131] By the 1830s a new consensus on the proper limits of public provision had been reached, and the costs of addressing crime and lunacy was met by the rates. Expenditure on the poor law was more restrained and now embodied the approach piloted by earlier voluntary societies like the PMFS.[132] Subsequent philanthropic initiatives emanating from the city's religious groups continued to stimulate public debate on the issues of poverty, drink, schooling, slavery and empire. This led to further state intervention with the adoption of institutions developed in the voluntary sector: the reformatories in the 1850s, elementary schools in the 1870s and homes for alcoholics in the 1890s. Whatever their narrow interests or affiliation, voluntary charities provided a site in which public opinion was formed and in which social policy might evolve.[133]

---

131 See J. R. Poynter, *Society and pauperism: English ideas on poor relief, 1795–1834*, London 1969, 64, 116, 140, 164, 269–71, 289–94.

132 Ian Archer, Spencer Jordan and Keith Ramsay, *Abstract of Bristol historical statistics*, I: *Poor law statistics, 1835–1948*, Bristol 1997, 15.

133 Robert Wuthnow, 'The voluntary sector: legacy of the past, hope for the future?', in Robert Wuthnow (ed.), *The voluntary sector in comparative perspective*, Princeton 1991, 3–29 at pp. 22–5.

7

Women and Voluntarism in Bristol

The importance of social organisations to the construction of gender and the negotiation of the perceived differences between the sexes has directed historiographical attention to female philanthropy in both Britain and America.[1] Interest focused initially on rescuing women's charity from its caricature as the condescending interference of 'Lady Bountifuls' and according it the status of meaningful work.[2] It also delineated the economic and cultural factors underpinning the different scale of female philanthropy since the early nineteenth century. Middle-class families were increasingly wealthy enough for wives to disengage from business and for widows and spinster daughters to draw an independent income; at the same time higher education and the professions were closed avenues. Men may have created most voluntary societies, but it was women with the means, the time and the hunger for a social role who took on the running of them.[3] The Evangelical revival encouraged social action through its emphasis on a woman's 'calling' and duty, while the traits of character deemed to be peculiarly female, such as care, sympathy and domesticity, were seen as necessary for philanthropy.[4] The extension of woman's mothering role into the public arena directed female voluntarism to the support of the embattled urban family. Home-visiting may also have reflected women's desire to recreate the harmoniously regulated nature of the mistress/servant relationships of middle-class households in the wider environment.[5] Aid for widows and children, moral reform and the temperance campaign all provided opportunities for 'maternal socialisation' in the mobile and socially fragmented city.[6]

The relationship between female philanthropy and feminism is a more

---

[1] Joan Wallach Scott, *Gender and the politics of history*, New York 1988, 43–4.

[2] Ann Summers, 'A home from home: women's philanthropic work in the nineteenth century', in Sandra Burman (ed.), *Fit work for women*, London 1979, 33–63 at p. 33; F. K. Prochaska, *Women and philanthropy in nineteenth-century England*, Oxford 1980, 223–4.

[3] Summers, 'Home from home', 37–8; Davidoff and Hall, *Family fortunes*, 422–3, 431–2.

[4] Prochaska, *Women and philanthropy*, 1–17; Davidoff and Hall, *Family fortunes*, 429–31; Morris, 'Clubs, societies and associations', 430; D. W. Bebbington, *Evangelicalism in modern Britain: a history from the 1730s to the 1980s*, London 1989, 128–9; Patricia Hollis, *Women in public: the women's movement, 1850–1900*, London 1979, 223.

[5] Summers, 'Home from home', 36–41.

[6] Mary P. Ryan, *Cradle of the middle class: the family in Oneida County, New York*, Cambridge 1981, ch. iii, p. 140; Anne M. Boylan, 'Women in groups: an analysis of women's benevolent organizations in New York and Boston, 1797–1840, *Journal of American History* lxxi (1984), 497–519 at pp. 503–4.

controversial subject. Most would accept that philanthropy was one strand of female activity from which organised feminism was to emerge, and some give particular weight to the cultural, social and administrative impact of charity work.[7] However socialist–feminist critics point to the conservatism, anti-feminism and 'collusion with masculine power structures' of female philanthropy, and warn against a 'class-blind feminist analysis'.[8] For Leonore Davidoff and Catherine Hall female philanthropy may have slightly shifted the boundaries of gendered behaviour, but it was ultimately 'unpaid social work'; instead they locate the emergence of modern feminism in the demographic factors which produced 'surplus' women, and thus forced the issues of female employment and property onto the political agenda.[9] This debate overlaps with current unease about the applicability of the notion of 'separate spheres' (of public and private) as the dominant category for theorising gender identity. Do the works of propagandists such as Hannah More indicate a lived reality of women 'severely circumscribed' in their domestic sphere?[10] Or, as Linda Colley has argued, was the impact of the French Revolution and Napoleonic Wars both to accentuate gender difference and to provide new opportunities for women's public presence?[11] If the emphasis on suppressed aspiration is actually the product of modern assumptions and the rhetoric of an earlier generation of suffragists, then it may be that philanthropy was more important than hitherto supposed in providing extensive access to public life.[12] There is therefore a tension between the conservative and emancipatory aspects of female voluntarism, which may be partly resolved by attention to the different forms which it took.[13] For instance, empirical work on American cities has found no linear progression from benevolent to reformist organisations, but has shown that particular groups, typically socially-mixed but inclined to religious liberalism, were the forerunners of the feminist tradition.[14]

Opinions vary on the chronology of female philanthropy. In Britain Morris discerns an initial burst of women's 'entryism' in the early nineteenth century, though by the 1830s the 'gender frontier' of voluntarism had rolled

[7] Olive Banks, *Becoming a feminist: the social origins of first wave feminism*, Brighton 1986; Prochaska, *Women and philanthropy*.

[8] Johanna M. Smith, review of Lewis, *Victorian Studies* xxxvi (1993), 227–9; Nancy F. Cott, *Bonds of womanhood: 'woman's sphere' in New England, 1780–1835*, London 1977, 149–57. This was also debated by contemporaries: June Hannam, *Isabella Ford*, Oxford 1989, 51.

[9] Davidoff and Hall, *Family fortunes*, 436, 453.

[10] Ibid. 167–72.

[11] Linda Colley, *Britons: forging the nation, 1707–1837*, London 1992, 237–81; Joan B. Landes, *Women and the public sphere in the age of the French Revolution*, Ithaca 1988, 117–21.

[12] Vickery, 'Golden age to separate spheres?', 383–414; Mary Clare Martin, 'Women and philanthropy in Walthamstow and Leyton, 1740–1870', *London Journal* xix (1994), 119–50.

[13] Summers, 'Home from home', 57–61.

[14] Boylan, 'Women in groups'.

back again, confining them to 'a number of distinctive and limited roles'.[15] Prochaska detects an increasing 'feminisation' of charity throughout the century, both in respect of female organisations and of women's financial contribution.[16] America provides an interesting contrast. Ryan highlights the 1830s and 1840s as the 'era of associations' in small towns, in which female voluntary action was the major agent of social intervention during the hiatus in which 'family history was suspended between the patriarchal household and the middle-class home'.[17] Meanwhile in New York upper-class women controlled benevolent institutions up to the Civil War, after which they surrendered their position to professional, male charity workers who ran the industrial schools and work programmes.[18] This claim that the 'Masculine officialism' of state intervention curtailed women's social role at the end of the nineteenth century has also been applied to Britain, providing a pessimistic conclusion to the narrative of female action.[19]

This chapter will explore female philanthropy in Bristol in the light of these debates. It will argue that within the totality of charitable voluntarism the power and influence of women remained circumscribed, despite their numerical significance in some areas. However the city does provide a very clear example of the progression in the 1840s from benevolent missionary work to reform issues such as anti-slavery, and finally to women's rights. This development was associated with a network of nonconformist women, particularly the Unitarians.

The extent and significance of female philanthropy

Bristol charity administration in the eighteenth century was largely a male preserve. The endowments were in the hands of male vestrymen and Corporation members, and the Infirmary, the Colston and the county societies were led by men. Absent from management, women none the less remained significant as fundraisers and donors. In 1774, for example, at the Sons of Clergy feast a 'ladies collection' was held at the door of the cathedral for wives and daughters of clergymen.[20] Of the parochial endowments made to St James's during the eighteenth century, twenty-seven came from men and seventeen from women. Very few of the Corporation charities were bequeathed by women, though Mary Peloquin's gift of £19,000 in 1778 was one of the city's largest funds, its enormity perhaps due to her being the last surviving member

---

15 Morris, 'Clubs, societies and associations', 430–1.
16 Prochaska, The voluntary impulse, 64–6.
17 Ryan, Cradle of the middle class, 143.
18 Amy Gilman, 'From widowhood to wickedness: the politics of class and gender in New York City private charity', History of Education Quarterly (1984), 59–74.
19 Prochaska, The voluntary impulse, 72–4, 89.
20 FFBJ, 15 Aug. 1774.

of her family.[21] The endowment was conventional in honouring Peloquin's parish by supporting the rector and paying doles to poor parishioners – twenty 'poor widows and single women' and ten poor men. It also dignified prominent women with a civic function of some weight, since it made available fifty lying-in gifts of 30s. to wives of freemen, to be chosen by the wife of the mayor or leading alderman.[22] Female involvement in subscriber charity can be traced to the early years of the Infirmary, where women contributed with subscription, donation and legacy. In the late eighteenth century they made up about 12 per cent of total subscribers, and about a third of testators; around a quarter of woman subscribers in the 1760s did not exercise their admission rights, a slightly higher proportion than that of males who did not use their tickets.[23]

The new century saw the emergence of specifically female voluntarism, with the foundation of several new charities specialising in lying-in women. These were the Female Misericordia, which loaned clothing, gave small money doles and ran a kitchen to feed nursing mothers, the Bristol and St Phillips Dorcas Societies, which provided surgeons/accoucheurs in 'extreme cases', and loans of sheets and linen, and the Bristol Lying-In Institution, which organised midwifery provision.[24] This more active role of women in the charitable arena was associated with wartime voluntarism and with the encouragement to female participation given by the Evangelicals – indeed the patroness of the Lying-In Institution was the duchess of Beaufort, the evangelical activist and supporter of Hannah More.[25] Public debate over infanticide motivated the Lying-In Institution, and it may also be that these societies were manifestations of the wartime pro-natalism then current on the continent.[26] The Lying-in Institution appears to have had a broader target group than the Dispensary and the Dorcas Societies which specified that only married women might apply.[27] Its formation indicates a growing concern for the 'casual poor' and recent migrants 'who as strangers know not

---

[21] Manchee, i. 397–481; Latimer, Annals . . . eighteenth century, 435.

[22] Manchee, i. 106–8.

[23] Berry, 'Patronage', 37; Boss, 'Bristol Infirmary', 73–4.

[24] BRO 38463, Female Misericordia, minute book; 39399/CD/S/3d, Bristol Dorcas Society, Annual reports, 1841–70; 35893 36n, Bristol Lying-In Institution, Annual report, 1821.

[25] Colley, Britons, ch. vi; Brown, Fathers of the Victorians, 10, 83, 102, 153, 195, 241, 324, 358, 360.

[26] Donnison, Midwives and medical men, 51–2; Stuart Woolf, 'The Societé de Charité Maternelle, 1788–1815', in Barry and Jones, Medicine and charity, 98–112; Bristol Lying-In Institution, Annual report, 1821.

[27] Ibid; BRO, P/St BM/X/1 July, 1820; Fissell, Patients, power, and the poor, 123, suggests that its 'real agenda was the training of midwives', though it is not clear whether the minute book's reference to 'midwives about to be instructed' refers to training or simply denotes 'engaged'.

where to procure Dispensary notes'.[28] Thus lying-in charity addressed the stresses placed on the family by rapid urbanisation.

Women's initial claim to public participation was therefore based upon their special sympathy with mothers in childbirth, but to what extent did they control the associations? The Lying-In Institution had a patroness, and a ladies committee 'to regulate the affairs of the Institution', while the 1821 subscription list was made up of sixty-six women and three men. There was no gentlemen's committee, though the physician, surgeon/accoucheur, secretary and treasurer were all male.[29] Bristol Dorcas Society had been started by the minister of a Congregational Chapel but was run by a female committee which organised the loans and gifts of clothing and bed-linen, made at their monthly meetings.[30] A man was called in each year to audit the accounts: in 1841 this was done by the Revd Henry Roper, husband of the secretary and minister of the chapel, and in 1845 male trustees were appointed to perform the annual audit and invest legacies.[31] Five male surgeons and accoucheurs were associated with the group, presumably giving their services free; the 1841 report records that 324 lying-in women were helped, with only a small sum paid for midwife attendance, so the chief activity appears to have been home-visiting by the women themselves.

The novelty of female association in the new century was also discernible in the formation of benefit societies by working-class women. A return made in 1803 recorded fourteen women's clubs containing 939 members in Bristol; this would suggest that about one in every five friendly society members in the city was female, an unusually high proportion.[32] Women's benefit clubs were typically found in areas of high female employment, such as northern textile towns and the Potteries, and it is likely that the Bristol clubs attracted employees in dress, boot and hat manufacture, and service industries such as laundry-keeping and food and drink.[33] Like men's clubs most met in ale-houses, though some used parish school rooms. Gender exclusivity was enforced through the feminisation of rulebook language ('Sisterhood', 'Presidess', 'Stewardess') and articles explicitly barring husbands and children from attending.[34] There was also an awareness of the 'equal, if not greater sufferings' to which women were exposed, suggesting that the lower levels of subscription and benefit were offset by the importance of sisterly solidarity during childbirth and lying-in. As in the charities then, motherhood legitimised association; indeed the Society of Women of St Augustine's parish

28 Bristol Lying-In Institution, *Annual report*, 1821.
29 Ibid.
30 Bristol Dorcas Society, *Annual reports*.
31 Ibid. The earliest report dates from 1841.
32 *Abstract of answers and returns pursuant to: 'An act for procuring returns relative to the expence and maintenance of the poor in England'*, PP 1803–4 xiii.
33 Gorsky, 'English friendly societies'; Baigent 'Economy and society', 117–18; 1841 *Census: occupations*.
34 BRO, FS 8, 17; FS 1 Gloucestershire 548, 587.

(formed 1800) kept a 'baby linen basket' and 'sick basket' for members to borrow.[35] Unlike the benevolent associations though, these friendly societies appear to have been entirely independent of men.

The first decades of the nineteenth century were also marked by a profusion of ladies' committees attached to new charities, although here women's involvement was not instrumental and creative but instead a necessary part of structures conceived and managed by men.[36] This division of labour reflected existing arrangements in nonconformist chapels. Even where, as in the case of the Quakers, a women's committee wielded considerable responsibility, it was the male supervisory body which had 'care and direction of the poor' and responsibility to supervise the 'property of the Society, and to transact the whole of their money matters', while women took care of 'the business of visiting and relieving poor Friends'.[37] Amongst the associations and institutions which employed women's committees or visitors were the Penitentiary, the Diocesan School Society, the National Benevolent Institution, the Friendly Female Clothing Society, the Bristol Auxiliary Bible Society, the Clifton Parochial Provident Society, and the Diocesan District Visiting Society. For instance, while evangelical vicars were happy to fundraise for the Penitentiary (the rescue home for prostitutes), the superintending and visiting of the institution itself was woman's work. The imagery of its appeals regularly evoked womanly virtue despoiled: 'an innocent and amiable female, the delight of her parents . . . seduced and betrayed by an artful villain and abandoned to the scoff of the world'.[38] It was therefore appropriate that women, as moral guardians of the bonds of family, should engage in the rescue of their 'fallen' sisters. However, key decisions still rested with the Gentlemen's Committee, which had the final approval on admissions and frequently overruled suggestions made by the Ladies, as in 1836, when the latter proposed a change of policy to admit 'infected females' to the Penitentiary. This balance of power only began to alter in 1854, when the right of admission was delegated principally to the matron and the 'Visiting Lady'.[39] Similarly, a gender division of labour could apply in educational charities, as in the Methodist girls' Sunday schools, whose visiting was undertaken by women; this was not always the case though, as the records of the all-male committee of guardians of Temple Blue Girls' School demonstrate.[40] Women were comparatively well-represented amongst Sunday school teachers, but again the boundaries were clear. In Bristol's seventeen Methodist Sunday schools in the 1810s there were 174 male teachers and 158 female; however all the school

---

35 BRO, FS 14.
36 Davidoff and Hall, *Family Fortunes*, 421–3.
37 BRO, FS/A2/3, 29 Apr. 1800.
38 *FFBJ*, 19 Nov. 1814.
39 BRO 35722/4/b, c, Bristol Female Penitentiary, minute books, 29 Feb. 1836, 20 Feb. 1854.
40 Broad, *Sunday schools*, 29; BRO, P/Tm/Kb/1, minute book, 1816–49.

superintendents were men, and of the women teachers all but twenty-five were unmarried, suggesting that this work was regarded as most suitable for those who were single.[41] Finally, fundraising offered more casual roles for women in public. Ladies reluctant to participate in rowdy civic celebrations, such as the illuminations marking victory over Napoleon, could involve themselves actively in collecting at such events as the Infirmary music festivals.[42]

If male committees or male congregational initiatives provided the context for this expansion of women's philanthropy this does not mean that female involvement was insignificant, as the history of the Bristol Auxiliary Bible Society (BABS) demonstrates. Founded in 1810 to distribute Bibles to the poor of the city, the leadership of the Society was entirely male. Women figured quite strongly in the membership list, providing 124 out of the 407 subscribers in the 1823 annual statement, with a contribution amounting to £155 out of a total subscription income of £540, with a further £206 contributed by the collectors of the Bristol ladies' branch, whose sales of Bibles yielded £203. Women's direct financial input was around 20 per cent of BABS's total income from all sources.[43] Initially the reports adopted a defensive tone in reference to female involvement, reflecting evangelical uncertainty over the propriety of women's engagement in this type of work.[44] At the same time it was frankly admitted that if 'the ladies of Bristol were to withdraw themselves from the work, the supply of scriptures to the poor would be tardy and partial'.[45] So, while initially precluded from foundation, management and financial control, women activists quickly seized on the BABS as an outlet for public work and made themselves indispensable. This in turn brought a gradual increase in power. A Ladies Branch had been founded in 1817, and though nominally superintended by the BABS committee its treasurer, secretary and own committee were all women. The target group was 'females exclusively', with efforts directed at first to servants. The procedure was to seek permission of the 'master or mistress', then carry out the visit, with 'the benefit of the individual applied to' always kept in mind.[46]

Encouraged by success the branch was later reconstituted into six associations, and the range of activity expanded to more general home-visiting now that the committee was sure that 'the reception the Ladies have met with in their visits among the poor has been generally respectful'.[47] By 1828 they were reported to have made 11,000 home visits in the course of the year, an

---

41 Ibid. 151–4.
42 *FFBJ*, 7 May, 4, 11, 18 June 1814.
43 BRL 9354, BABS, *Fourteenth annual report*, 1824.
44 Prochaska, *Women and philanthropy*, 25–6; Davidoff and Hall, *Family fortunes*, 429–30.
45 BRL 9351, BABS, *Eighth report*, 1817.
46 Ibid.
47 BRL 9354, BABS, *Fourteenth annual report*, 1824.

extraordinary figure, considering that the total number of houses in the city and suburbs was somewhere between 15 and 20,000.[48]

Developments in the mid-century provide further evidence of expanding female effort within associations managed by men. Newspaper accounts of voluntary sector meetings repeatedly evoked the image of an audience of ladies facing a platform of clergymen.[49] The regularity with which the 'softer sex' were thanked for their presence, their parochial visiting or their fundraising makes it clear that female support was vital.[50] Charity bazaars dated from the mid-century in Bristol, when they became an established, if minor, aspect of the fundraising year, devoted to 'one-off' appeals, and often attracting the patronage of the town's leading women.[51] These events happily combined voluntary action with the chance for unchaperoned interaction with males which could occur at bazaars: 'For weeks past fair fingers have been deftly plying these arts of mystic elegance in which the sex are adepts. . . . And here, if any incitement be needed to add to the appeal of beauty and bright eyes, it ought to be abundantly supplied by the nature of the cause appealed to.'[52]

In contrast to such high-profile events in support of institutions like the General Hospital, much female philanthropy occurred at the parochial level. Bristol City Mission was a Congregationalist association which in the 1840s supported four full-time missionaries engaged in visiting the sick and elderly. Management was in the hands of an all-male committee, though a woman had charge of the tract depot; however, the ladies' associations at each of the sect's chapels consisted of treasurers and collectors who controlled the fundraising, and who proved adept at bolstering the funds by collecting quite small sums for the cause.[53] Similarly, the Clifton Loan Blanket Society based at Clifton parish church and managed by local Anglican clergy and churchwardens was funded almost entirely by women. Subscribers were entitled to two tickets of recommendation to be exchanged for blankets to be loaned to the poor of the parish, thus lending additional weight to female parochial visiting.[54]

A few mid-century societies enjoyed complete female control. The Lewin's Mead Working and Visiting Society was an initiative of the Unitarian congregation, run by an all-woman committee and female treasurer and with a subscription list in 1836 of one man and forty-two women.[55] An explicit purpose was the 'increased union' amongst the participating women, who

48 BRL 9356, BABS, *Eighteenth annual report*, 1828; *1821 Census*.
49 *FFBJ*, 23 May, 24 Oct. 1846; *Bristol Mercury*, 19 June 1858.
50 *Bristol Mercury*, 4 Jan., 20 Mar., 22 May, 24 July 1858.
51 Prochaska, *Women and philanthropy*, ch. ii; BRL, microfilm, Estlin papers, reel 5, BCLASS, minute book, 1 July 1841, 3 Mar. 1842, 5 May 1842; *Bristol Mercury*, 13 Mar., 24 Apr. 1858, 29 Feb., 11 Apr., 16 May 1868.
52 *Bristol Mercury*, 27 Mar. 1858; Davidoff and Hall, *Family fortunes*, 430–1.
53 BRL, B16885, *15th annual report of the Bristol City Mission*, Bristol 1842, 20–31.
54 P/StAug/Soc/1a/b, Clifton Loan Blanket Society, minute books, 1855–70.
55 BRL, B7055, B7057, LMCWVS, *2nd, 4th reports*.

drew 'pleasure and improvement' from their monthly meetings where they met to make articles of clothing for distribution and to discuss their visits.[56] The visits led to a variety of outcomes, such as encouraging children to Sunday school, and parents to services, along with the distribution of clothes and the development of provident society membership. However, with an annual budget that peaked at £39 in 1838, and remained at around £25 *per annum* over the next fifty years, female autonomy did not translate into meaningful control of resources.[57] The limitations of the group were also shown by its decision to advocate the establishment of a Domestic Mission with a paid minister, given the necessity of reaching those in the 'lowest grade of society', into whose 'wretched habitations . . . it would be neither safe nor right for ladies to go alone'.[58] The Bristol Dorcas Society wielded more financial power, enjoying an income boosted by legacies which only dipped below £100 *per annum* once after 1845. It was run by a ladies committee with a woman treasurer and secretary, and once again the 115 female subscribers far outnumbered the twenty men.[59] The relief of 'poor destitute females' increasingly took precedence over childbirth cases as the century progressed, a trend shared by the Dispensary and reflecting the increased activity of commercial practitioners in this field. None the less, the foundation in the mid-century of five new Dorcas Societies associated with parishes and chapels, for visiting and aiding 'poor lying-in women', demonstrates the continuing appeal of such interventions. However the scale of these should not be overstated. The Zion Chapel Dorcas Society meetings frequently drew less than ten members and were often sporadic, while its annual income hovered at a little over £10.[60]

Lower down the social scale independent female associations continued to figure amongst the benefit clubs. Although female mutuality declined elsewhere it remained strong in Bristol, with fourteen new women's friendly societies registered between 1830 and 1880.[61] The popular affiliated orders were predominantly male, but Bristol women emulated the exclusive Odd Fellows by starting a non-affiliated order of 'Odd-Sisters', and there were six sanctuaries of 'Shepherdesses' operating in 1870, only one of which was registered. The Friendly Society Commissioners of 1874 wrote disparagingly of 'The United Sisters' and 'Female Dolphins' who 'go in largely for regalia and finery, even more so than men'.[62] The orders eventually opened to women, with the Foresters, for example, admitting female courts in 1892 and mixed

---

[56] BRL, B7054, LMCWVS, *1st report.*
[57] BRO 39461/5/a, b, c; LMCWVS, *Annual reports*, 1835–84.
[58] LMCWVS, *2nd report.*
[59] Bristol Dorcas Society, *Annual reports*, 1841–70.
[60] BRO 38603/Z/S/1, Zion Chapel Dorcas Society, minute book 1832–56.
[61] Dot Jones, 'Did friendly societies matter?: a study of friendly societies in Glamorgan, 1794–1910', *Welsh History Review* cccxxiv (1985), 324–49 at p. 333; Gorsky, 'Mutual aid', table 1b.
[62] Young, 502.

Table 19
The extent of female subscription to Bristol Infirmary, 1801-71

Women as % of total:

	Subscribers	Subscriptions (£)	Life trustees
1811	10	10	13
1821	12	11	21
1831	11	11	22
1841	13	12	17
1851	14	13	28
1861	18	15	15
1871	18	15	15
1881	18	15	19
1891	22	18	21

Source: BI *State*

courts from 1899.[63] Despite all this activity the women's clubs were far out-numbered by men's organisations, owing to women's lack of independent financial rights. For most of the period the legal doctrine of coverture gave a husband possession of his wife's property at and during marriage, hence responsibility for assuring the family economy against risk fell to the husband.[64] It was a charity, the Savings Bank, rather than the friendly socie-ties, which responded most quickly to changing ideas on married women's property; from the 1850s it allowed married women to deposit and withdraw in their own names, their accounts later 'deemed to be the separate property of such women'.[65]

The constraints which financial dependence placed on eleemosynary con-tributions also restricted claims to direction and control, as consideration of female participation in Bristol's pre-eminent charity, the Infirmary, demon-strates. Table 19 shows the extent of women's subscriber power, as well as their role as life trustees (donors with lifetime admission rights following a thirty-guinea gift). The picture is of a contribution rising from about 10 to 18 per cent of subscription income through the century. Of course this under-played women's true importance since many male gifts could be viewed as

[63] *Foresters' directory*, 1893, pp. lxi–ii; Walter G. Cooper, *The Ancient Order of Foresters Friendly Society, 150 years, 1834–1984*, Southampton 1984, 19, 22.
[64] Susan Staves, *Married women's separate property in England, 1660–1833*, London 1990, 221–30; Mary Lyndon Shanley, *Feminism, marriage and the law in Victorian England, 1850–1895*, London 1989.
[65] BRO 4492 17 h, Bristol Savings Bank, savings book, 1885–8; 24759 53, *Rules for the management of the Bristol Savings Bank*, Bristol 1857.

171

representing households in which the female economic role was present if unacknowledged.[66] And indeed women did figure more strongly amongst Infirmary legators: in the 1830s they left £5,995 compared to £6,811 from men, suggesting that control of property in widowhood allowed charitable impulses greater rein. Despite this the lesser extent of their *inter vivos* charity deprived women of their due share of power as trustees, both with respect to admission rights and the status these conferred, and to voting rights in the elections to faculty. Suffrage did not come easily even to existing female trustees, though when the issue arose in 1806 'the right could not be disputed but it was contended that it had never been the custom. A precedent however was adduced and the ladies vote was taken'.[67] Other charities were equally grudging, as in the Asylum for Poor Orphan Girls where women members were entitled to a vote but could only issue it by proxy.[68] In the Infirmary then, the 'limited role' was clear, but 'feminisation' also proceeded. Although no women acted as patrons or as house committee members, a group of 'lady visitors' was established in 1842, while at the end of the century women played a significant part as canvassers; this tradition endured into the 1920s, when employees in Wills and Fry factories formed ladies' sewing guilds.[69]

Philanthropy and women's rights

The picture that emerges is therefore one of women pushing at the boundaries of what was socially acceptable. However, only a limited number of comparatively small societies were actually run by women and most female activity was as footsoldiers of organisations managed by men. While there was no bar on entering the public sphere, cultural proscription still militated against women who wished to initiate and organise philanthropic activity beyond the parameters of lying-in charity or parochial visiting. Female philanthropy offered the opportunity for women to meet and act in solidarity, and voluntary activity must surely have enhanced the sense of self-worth which barriers to education and the labour market denied them. It is also possible that the satisfaction which partial empowerment offered may have prevented the shared recognition of subordinate status.[70] To trace the transition from female benevolence to reformist initiatives which raised feminist issues it is necessary to concentrate on the activities of nonconformist women.

The interconnections of charitable work, feminism and sectarianism first emerged with female anti-slavery, where links of personnel connect aboli-

---

66 Davidoff and Hall, *Family fortunes*, 432.
67 *Bristol Gazette*, 1 May 1806.
68 BRL, B9780, *State of the Orphan Asylum for the year . . ., 1821*.
69 BI *State*, 1842, 1893, 1922.
70 Cott, *Bonds of womanhood*, 156.

tionism to the suffrage campaign.[71] The Bristol and Clifton Ladies Anti-Slavery Society (BCLASS) was founded in affiliation with the British and Foreign Anti-Slavery Society in 1840 to conduct a 'religious, moral and pacific' campaign.[72] The group was based at the Independent Bridge Street vestry (home of the Bristol Dorcas Society) and Broadmead Baptist Church, and as table 20 shows, was initially dominated by Quakers and Congregationalists. Seven of the women were wives of Congregationalist or Baptist ministers and some were active in other groups: two Dorcas Society members, three collectors for Bristol City Mission Ladies' Associations, one member of the Working and Visiting Society and one who sat on the General Hospital's ladies' committee. In its early years the Society worked quietly and undemonstratively raising small sums in support of schools for freed slaves, despatching 'useful, fancy and ornamental articles' to the Massachusetts Female Emancipation Society for the annual Boston Bazaar and petitioning against the return of fugitive slaves. Meetings centred around discussion of issues, correspondence with fellow campaigners and consideration of anti-slavery journals; in 1843 the invitation to send a delegate to the Anti-Slavery Convention was rejected.[73]

Radicalisation of the group followed a shift towards the Garrisonian position and eventual disaffiliation from its parent society. This more assertive stance can be traced to the arrival of two Unitarians, Mary Estlin and Frances Armstrong, won over to Garrisonianism by the visits of prominent American abolitionists.[74] Frederick Douglass had been a house-guest of the Estlins, an event which had crystallised for Mary's father John B. Estlin the tensions of race, gender and class: 'You can hardly imagine how he is noticed, – petted I may say by ladies. . . . My fear is that often associating so much with white women of education & refined taste & manners, he will feel a "craving void" when he returns to his own family.'[75] The divisive impact of William Lloyd Garrison arose from two issues: the campaign against American churches which refused to condemn the Fugitive Slave Act and support for women abolitionists' right to a public platform.[76] The group's disaffiliation from the British and Foreign Anti-Slavery Society occurred in 1851. Henceforth the independent society was the base for Mary Estlin's emergence as a national proponent of Garrisonian abolitionism in Britain, extending her

---

71 Clare Midgley, *Women against slavery: the British campaigns, 1780–1860*, London 1992, and 'Anti-slavery and feminism'; Barbara Taylor, *Eve and the New Jerusalem*, London 1983, 277; Malos, 'Bristol women in action', 97–128 at pp. 98, 104–6.

72 BCLASS, 17 Sept. 1840.

73 BCLASS, 27 Feb., 2 Mar., 6 Apr. 1843.

74 BCLASS, 10 Sept. 1846.

75 Taylor, *British and American abolitonists*, 305.

76 Midgley, *Women against slavery*, 133–4, 158–72: Louis Filler, *The crusade against slavery, 1830–1860*, London 1960, 130–6.

Table 20
Religious affiliation of Bristol and Clifton Ladies Anti-Slavery
Society members, 1840s

Congregationalist	11
Quaker	13
Unitarian	4
Baptist	2
not known	5

Sources: BRL microfilm, Estlin papers, reel 5; Congregationalist: BRO, B16885 *15th. Annual Report of the Bristol City Mission, Matthews's directory;* Quakers: BRO, SF/R3/3 list of members of Bristol Society of Friends Monthly Meeting; Unitarians: BRO 39461/F/4b) Unitarian subscription book

links with American colleagues such as Maria Weston Chapman and supporting the extension of the female platform.[77]

Mary Estlin's subsequent activities demonstrate the way in which experience in the anti-slavery movement led on to female emancipation. In the late 1860s she joined Josephine Butler's campaign to repeal the Contagious Diseases Acts, the legislation empowering police and doctors in garrison towns to apprehend and examine prostitutes, and forcibly hospitalise those suffering from sexually transmitted disease. Butler's establishment of the Ladies National Association followed women's outrage at the sexual double standard this represented; it was also triggered by a familiar grievance, the prohibition of women from public discussion of the acts, which flared when the Social Science Association met in Bristol in 1869.[78] Other local anti-slavery veterans joined Estlin, including the Priestman sisters, Margaret Tanner and Mrs Charles Thomas; Butler spoke of the Bristol women as her 'body guard, . . . *corps d'élite*'. They were also active in the foundation (in 1870) and management of Old Park Lock Hospital for the treatment of women with venereal disease, an institution that remained open until 1921 when state funding to voluntary hospital VD clinics had begun.[79] Estlin was a founder member of the Bristol Suffrage Society in 1868 and acted as the group's treasurer in the 1870s; Tanner and the Priestmans were also members.[80]

The career of another Unitarian woman, Mary Carpenter, provides a

[77] Midgley, *Women against slavery*, 134–5, 169, 171–2.
[78] Shanley, *Feminism, marriage and the law*, 82–3.
[79] BRO 40145/P/24, *Bristol Old Park Lock Hospital annual report*, 1878; Midgley, *Women against slavery*, 172–3; Walkowitz, *Prostitution*, 121, 130–1.
[80] June Hannam, ' "An enlarged sphere of usefulness": the Bristol women's movement, *c.* 1860–1914', in Dresser and Ollerenshaw, *Making of modern Bristol*, 184–209 at pp. 189–94.

further illustration of the route from parochial charity to reformism.[81] Her
voluntarism began with the Girls' Branch of the Lewin's Mead Sunday
School, and by 1831 she was home-visiting as superintendent of the school.
She became a founder member of the Lewin's Mead Chapel Working and Visiting Society, visiting in an area notorious for the poverty of its inhabitants.[82]
The first ragged school, started in 1846 in St James's Back and funded initially
by the Unitarian congregation, was an extension of her earlier work.[83] She
went on to establish the Kingswood Day Industrial School (1852) which was
later reorganised as a reformatory for convicted juvenile boys, and the Red
Lodge (1854), the first reformatory for girls. Carpenter's leadership in the
field drew her into the public discussions of the proposals for government-
sanctioned reformatories as the solution to youth crime, and her stance in
favour of reform rather than retribution contributed to the eventual shape of
the Youthful Offenders Act of 1854 and the 1857 Industrial Schools Act.[84]
Her accounts of overcoming her reservations about public oratory due to the
'need to speak' for the reformatory cause provide an intimate portrait of a
woman confronting the barriers to civil society.[85] She later gave support to
the local suffragettes and also chaired the first Ladies Committee of the
Social Science Association, where Elizabeth Blackwell spoke on female
medical training.[86]

The passages to reformism illustrated here cannot be fully explained by the
inherent nature of charitable work. Despite its language of equal rights
female anti-slavery was socially conservative, characterised by imperialist
sentiment and middle-class mores.[87] Carpenter's work has also been criticised
for her refusal to acknowledge the social role of poverty in causing juvenile
crime and for developing reformatories whose goal was a 'constructed nor-
mality . . . of sexless deferential womanhood'.[88] None the less, the voluntary
arena offered opportunities for independent organisation and for the development of networks: Estlin's correspondence suggests that the ongoing influence of more advanced American feminists was an important legacy of
transatlantic abolitionism.[89] It also prompted women whose knowledge of
issues was equal to that of their male counterparts to participate more vocally

---

81 Saywell, *Mary Carpenter*; Manton, *Mary Carpenter*; Carpenter, *Life and work of Mary Carpenter*.
82 LMCWVS, 2nd report.
83 Saywell, *Mary Carpenter*, 5.
84 Selleck, 'Mary Carpenter', 107–8.
85 Seth Koven, 'Borderlands: women, voluntary action, and child welfare in Britain, 1840 to 1914', in Seth Koven and Sonya Michel (eds), *Mothers of a new world: maternalist politics and the origin of welfare states*, London 1993, 94–135 at pp. 100–1; Julia Parker, *Women and welfare*, London 1989.
86 Malos, 'Bristol women', 101; *Times*, 1 Oct. 1869.
87 Midgley, *Women against slavery*, 176–7, 203.
88 Selleck, 'Mary Carpenter', 114; Michelle Cale, 'Girls and the perception of sexual danger in the Victorian reformatory system', *History* lxxviii (1993), 201–17 at p. 217.
89 Malos, 'Bristol women', 98–100, 106 n. 21; Estlin papers.

in public debate. In addition, the Bristol case highlights the importance of dissenting circles to the growth of feminism. Willingness to embrace minority causes was fostered by the unusual strength of the city's nonconformist tradition and the residual identification of anti-slavery with the political struggle against the pre-Reform Tory/Anglican establishment. Dissent also offered institutional experience: for instance female Quakers had long been used to the financial, administrative and welfare responsibilities delegated to the Women's Monthly Meeting.[90] Lastly there was the cultural milieu of Bristol Unitarianism with its provision of a more equal education for girls in the dissenting school run by Lant Carpenter, father of Mary and minister of Lewin's Mead Chapel. Gleadle has traced the flowering of 'new Unitarian' culture from the 1830s, characterised by faith in science, education, rationality and industrial progress, along with an openness to radical and socialist ideas shunned by others. The intellectual contradiction between the movement's commitment to freedom and reason and the conventional evangelical view of women espoused by mainstream Unitarians was the stimulus to feminist thought amongst its radicals. This went beyond the encouragement of girls' education to calls for the suffrage and reform of the marriage contract.[91] Although Bristol patriarchs Carpenter and Estlin gave hostile responses to these radical Unitarian arguments in the 1830s, their daughters clearly grew up in an environment where progressive views on the 'woman question' were aired.[92]

A final aspect of the long-run relationship between voluntarism and the advance of women's rights is its impact on female paid employment. To a limited extent, charity was a door to opportunity. Voluntary schools employed schoolmistresses, and in 1851 the women teachers listed in the trade directory outnumbered men in a ratio of 4:3. The remuneration was lowly, however; no women's salaries have been traced, but a master in the 1860s earned around £70, placing him in the ranks of the poorly paid *petit-bourgeoisie*.[93] Analysis of the background of trainee schoolmistresses at Fishponds Diocesan College in the 1850s confirms that girls entering teaching came from the families of artisans and small tradesmen.[94] In the same period the Lady Superintendent at the Infirmary, with responsibility for forty nurses, received £70, while the trainee nurses' remuneration seems to have been largely bed and board.[95] Bristol had at least 120 nurses working in voluntary

---

[90] BRO, SF/A2/2–7, Women's Monthly Meeting, minutes, 1781–1873.
[91] Kathryn Gleadle, *The early feminists: radical Unitarians and the emergence of the women's rights movement*, London 1995, 15–21, 45–54, 62–70.
[92] Ibid. 34–6.
[93] M. J. Campbell, 'The development of literacy in Bristol and Gloucester, 1755–1870', unpubl. PhD diss. Bath 1980, 70.
[94] Ibid. 84–6.
[95] Munro Smith, *Bristol Infirmary*, 337–8.

hospitals when the collation of national records began in 1889.[96] The flexibility of medical charity proved vital to the career of the city's first woman doctor, Eliza Walker Dunbar, who had earlier been ousted from her appointment to the Children's Hospital in 1873 by male colleagues who would not work alongside her.[97] She built up her practice as a physician at a low-cost dispensary for women and children, and at the Bristol Private Hospital for Women and Children, funded by fees and contributions. Dunbar was an active suffragette, closely involved with local efforts to organise working-class women, and a national committee member of the Women's Protective and Provident League.[98]

Female philanthropy took off in Bristol at the start of the nineteenth century with the lying-in charities that offered succour to the urban family, disrupted as it was by war, migration and poverty. A few societies were principally controlled by women, but these were mostly small and poorly funded, and the expansion of female voluntarism took place mainly under the aegis of associations founded and run by men. If women's financial contribution was comparatively less, their visiting and fundraising efforts afforded them considerable access to public life, while voluntary medical and educational institutions provided some paid employment for the lower middle class, albeit not of a high status. Reformism and feminism was not an inevitable outcome of voluntarism, but was instead associated with Unitarian, Quaker and Congregationalist women who moved from visiting and lying-in charity to broader issues such as anti-slavery and the reformatory movement. Practical experience of organisation was important in conjunction with the intellectual stimulus of nonconformist thought.

---

96 Henry C. Burdett, *Burdett's hospitals and charities: the yearbook of philanthropy*, London 1889
97 Saunders, *Hospital for Sick Children*, 12, 62.
98 Hannam, ' "Enlarged sphere of usefulness" ', 194–5.

8

Charity and Society

In his famous study of the motives of blood donors Richard Titmuss argued that the explanation of the gift relationship in terms of status and reciprocity alone was insufficient as it left no room for altruism.[1] This aspect of philanthropic motivation is one of the hardest to recover, since surviving sources for the benevolent impulse such as appeals and annual reports push interpretation towards the external identities of donors, rather than interior reasons. Occasional insights may be gained when the exhortation to give was couched in terms of personal feelings instead of broader social goals. Thus a Samaritan Society appeal revealingly articulated the importance of philanthropy to the evangelical conscience: 'There are delicious emotions excited in our hearts by the consciousness of doing good, so that habitually to withhold our hands from misery, lest our benevolence be misplaced, would tend at once to contract the heart to selfishness, and would prove a greater loss to ourselves than to those whom we deny our compassion.'[2] None the less the surviving evidence directs us to social meaning rather than the individual selflessness or benevolence inspired by personal faith. This is because 'voluntarism is caused', in other words it was always more than like-minded individuals spontaneously following a common interest.[3] As the discussion of female philanthropy has shown, membership was socially rooted in other groupings within the community.

While acknowledging the importance of *caritas* to the inner motivation of participants, the aim of this chapter is to consider further the social meaning of voluntary action. It begins by exploring the occupational background of philanthropists, then brings the local case study to bear on two questions relating to charity and class. First, was there a change in the nature of the charitable relationship in the early nineteenth century that reflected the changing aspirations of the middle class, and second, to what extent does the behaviour of working-class recipients confirm that charity was a site of shared values? The final section revisits the theme of the relationship between associations and political and religious affiliations, suggesting why urban charities became vehicles for the expression of identities.

---

[1] R. M. Titmuss, *The gift relationship*, London, 1970.
[2] BRL, B4643, *Report of the Samaritan Society*, Bristol 1835.
[3] Jack C. Ross, 'Toward a reconstruction of voluntary association theory', *British Journal of Sociology* xxiii (1972), 20–30 at p. 28.

Table 21
Occupations of officers of Bristol voluntary charities, 1841, 1883

	1841	1883
	%	%
Professions	18.2	20.4
Church	27.3	16.7
Gentleman/Lady	18.8	25
Trade	13	10.2
Servicemen	4.5	4.6
Charity workers	3.2	5.6
Not found	14.9	17.6

Sources: *Matthews's directory* 1841, *Condition of the poor*

The social origin of Bristol philanthropists

Before discussing the possible meanings participants attached to voluntarism it is important to form a clearer picture of who they were. Table 21 shows the occupations of secretaries and treasurers for 1841 and 1883, the latter year chosen to test the possibility that a working-class presence increased later in the century, and because the source, the 1884 *Condition of the Bristol poor* report, provides an alternative to reliance on trade directory entries. Names of officers were extracted then linked with occupations listed in the 1841 and 1883 directories. 'Gentleman' was assumed where an address in one of the wealthy suburbs was given, but no occupation, though this probably over-lapped in reality with 'trade'.[4] This latter category could embrace a range of social gradations: in 1841 it contained one of Bristol's wealthiest business-man, George Thomas, the wholesale grocer, and others for whom size of busi-ness, wealth and status cannot be easily discerned from the entry. There is a fairly large 'not found' group in both years, arising from non-appearance in the directory, or the impossibility of isolating a person with a common name, or the difficulty of identifying women from the predominantly male listings. However, the existence of this category should not be taken as indicating a potential working-class presence; in 1883, of the nineteen not found, the addresses of nine were given in the 1884 report, eight of which were in the wealthy suburbs.

One striking result is the role of professionals working in banking, medicine and the law, who furnished about one-fifth of the activists in both surveys. This suggests that the comparative security of income and social status enjoyed by successful professionals brought the leisure and the dis-position for voluntarism, as it did with local government, while the skills

4 See Morris, *Class, sect and party*, 23.

associated with their work made them likely choices for leadership roles.[5] The Church also provided a substantial number of officers, with Anglicans the more active: twenty-three in 1841 (including wives and parish clerks) against thirteen nonconformists, and in 1883, nine Anglicans against two nonconformists. High-ranking servicemen, probably retired, appear in both surveys as do gentlemen and ladies. Possibilities for a working-class role are limited to a few of the 'not found', some of the tradesmen, and the charity workers themselves. Three charity officers in 1841 may have been artisans, a watch- and clock-maker, a boot- and shoe-maker, and a bookbinder, while in 1883, a further three may have been lower status tradesmen: a builder, a cabinet-maker and a painter.[6] In the category of charity workers, it is possible to identify in 1841 two people who gave their occupation as 'collector', and three in the book trade who serviced the demand for Bibles and tracts, while in 1883 three missionaries and two home superintendents were found. There are no further indications of their social standing.

Table 22 offers a second example, the occupations of the Infirmary's House Committee 1812–70; this body was elected by subscribers to oversee management, and therefore represents active medical philanthropists. The new professions that began to appear in subscription lists in the late eighteenth century are well to the fore here, with the law again furnishing consistently large numbers.[7] Equally important were those with no occupation listed, represented here as 'gentleman'. Contrary to the claim of Fissell, who detected a nineteenth-century 'abdication of the governors' from Infirmary administration, in favour of medical professionals and new men, Bristol's old elite remained well represented.[8] The numbers of merchants did not diminish until the mid-century, nor did they all represent new trades: in 1841 four out of the seven were wine merchants, one of the port's oldest commodities. A sense of commitment to the charity is also evidenced by the reappearance of individuals and families on the House Committee over time, for example F. C. Husenbeth (1812, 1820, 1830), the Revd Thomas Hope (1847, 1870), town clerk Daniel Burges (1820) and his son, Daniel, Jr (1841, 1847). Long-term devotion by elite families was also evident amongst permanent office-holders: members of the Cave banking dynasty held the post of treasurer from 1829 to 1844 and from 1880 into the new century, while two members of the Harford family, which had been involved with the Corporation of the Poor and the Infirmary in its early days, were in the office from 1844 to 1859 and from 1859 to 1869.[9]

---

5 E. P. Hennock, *Fit and proper persons: ideal and reality in nineteenth-century urban government*, London 1973, 28, 202–4, 324–6.

6 *Condition of the poor*, 210, 213, 230.

7 Mary E. Fissell, 'The physic of charity: health and welfare in the West Country, 1690–1834', unpubl. PhD diss. Pennsylvania 1988, 96.

8 Fissell, *Patients, power and the poor*, ch. vi.

9 Ibid. 89, 111; Beaven, *Bristol lists*, 330; Cave, *Banking in Bristol*.

Table 22
Occupations of Bristol Infirmary House Committee, selected years, 1812-70

	1812	1820	1830	1841	1847	1870
Gentleman	7	5	2	5	7	4
Services	1			1	1	
Professions:	10	7	13	10	4	5
Agent			*3*			
Architect				*1*		
Finance			*1*	*1*		
Insurance	*1*	*1*	*1*	*1*		
Law	*7*	*4*	*4*	*3*	*3*	*3*
Medicine	*2*	*2*	*4*	*4*	*1*	*2*
Trade:	9	12	12	6	3	
Artisan			*1*	*1*	*1*	
Books/print	*1*		*2*			
Manufacture	*2*	*2*	*1*	*1*		
Merchant	*4*	*9*	*7*	*3*	*1*	
Retail					*1*	
Wholesale	*2*	*1*	*1*	*1*		
Church:	2		1	3	2	3
Anglican			*1*	*2*	*1*	*1*
Dissent	*2*					
Other*				*1*	*1*	*2*
Not found	4	5	0	4	4	7

* = affiliation not known

Sources: BI *State*; *Matthews's directory*, 1812, 1820, 1830, 1841, 1847, 1870

Arrangements for the charities' public meetings also reflected the social status of the participants. Table 23 draws on notices of meetings or fundraising activities in the local press to examine the changing use of civic space by charities with the highest profile. In the late eighteenth century the annual meeting was a public event visible to all citizens, typically commencing with a service in one of the parish churches or the cathedral, followed by a procession to one of the old gild halls, an inn or the Assembly Rooms for a feast. Popular churches for sermons were all central: Bristol Cathedral, St James's, St Augustine's, St Stephen's, and All Saints', where the Colston memorial was situated, and the short journey from these to the White Lion Inn or the Bush Tavern, both overlooking the River Frome, meant the participants traversed the central dock area *en route* to their feast. In their visibility these celebrations harked back to an era when the old parishes were *loci* of both

Table 23
Meeting places of voluntary associations, Bristol, 1774-1858

	1774	1797	1806	1819	1836	1846	1858
Inn	2	2	2	1	2	1	2
Church-inn	1	3	4	3	3	2	1
Church-hall	6	2	2	1			
Cathedral	1					2	
Cathedral-hall	2						
Cathedral-inn		2	2	2	2	2	1
Public hall	1	1	1	3	11	21	41
Own institution		3	4	3	10	10	11
Church-school		1	1	1	1	1	1
School				5	4	6	8
Own rooms				1	2	4	3
Chapel/church				2	5	7	12
Outdoor						1	3

Sources: *FFBJ*, 1774, 1797 1846; *Bristol Gazette*, 1806, 1836; *Bristol Mercury*, 1819, 1858

religious life and civic power.[10] After the 1800s only a few high-status societies (Gloucestershire, Colston, Clergy) continued with this traditional format, though its retention demonstrates the longevity of civic memory in a city where ritualised procession of urban hierarchy from chapel to gildhall drinking had a long antiquity.[11] The first decade of the nineteenth century saw the trend towards holding meetings on the premises of the institutions themselves, and a growing preference for public buildings such as the Broadmead Rooms, the Assembly Rooms and the newly opened schools. These practices extended in the early to mid-Victorian period, with the continuing rise of the public hall being the most striking feature, along with a new approach: charity sermons without a subsequent feast. Schools were used more frequently and a small number of charities had their own committee room or met at the Savings Bank.

What factors lay behind these changes? The rejection of the inn as the venue for middle-class public life has already been mentioned in discussion of the withdrawal for mutualism. New buildings offered alternative meeting spaces which symbolically resonated the wealth and power of subscribers, and, on a practical level, were less expensive in hire charges or catering.

[10] Barry, 'The parish in civic life'; Harrison, *Crowds and history*, passim.
[11] David Harris Sacks, 'The demise of the martyrs: the feasts of St Clement and St Katherine in Bristol, 1400–1600', *Social History* xi (1986), 151.

Decorum was increasingly important and the affairs of the charities were discussed much as the concerns of a business.[12] Buildings with a cultural
purpose, such as the Bristol Institution (1823) and most notably the Victoria
Rooms in Clifton (1843) also undermined the popularity of the public house
which had hitherto hosted discussion and debating clubs popular with merchants and professionals.[13] Their gender neutrality offered respectable ladies
the chance to participate in public activity and attracted their help to charities which could not fulfil their functions without them.[14]

The timing of meetings reinforced exclusiveness. Most occurred during
the weekday, either in the late morning or early afternoon, limiting attendance to those whose working lives permitted them sufficient freedom. Again
this marks out voluntary charity as the preserve of the middle class, though
some qualifications can be made.[15] A number of associations, including the
Infirmary, the Blind Asylum, Sunday School societies, the Mechanics Institute and the Church of England Young Men's Society, met in the evenings,
while anti-war, anti-slavery, or temperance reformers hoping to appeal to the
public at large had to lay on their functions during leisure hours. Others
coupled the annual meeting with a series of Sunday and evening sermons and
collections, while a particular congregation, or group of chapels within a
denomination, could devote the regular Sunday service to the annual
report.[16]

If ideas and organisation emanated from the city's elite families and from
the churches, was working-class involvement more obvious in the staffing?
Charities offered a number of job opportunities. In 1841 for instance there
were forty-six masters, mistresses and governesses teaching in the charity
schools, and five matrons/superintendents running asylums and hospitals.
These numbers had risen to sixty and fourteen respectively by 1862, though
this is likely to under-represent the real figure given the unsystematic
approach to trade directory listing. The 1851 census of occupations did not
differentiate charity school teachers from the rest, though it did distinguish
seventeen men and sixteen women as 'officer of a charitable institution'.
There were also 197 nurses listed and fourteen midwives, but again the proportion identified with charity is uncertain. The social status of all these
workers is by no means clear, and the Bristol sources offer little new evidence.

In the entirely voluntary field were large numbers of Sunday school teachers and lay visitors. By the 1810s there were twenty-nine superintendents and
332 teachers working in the seventeen Methodist Sunday schools alone,
while in 1835 the Friends First Day School had eighteen volunteer teach-

---

[12] Munro Smith, *Bristol Royal Infirmary*, 24–5, 111.

[13] Ibid. 231–4; Meller, *Leisure and the changing city*, 57, 219.

[14] Davidoff and Hall, *Family fortunes*, 433; *Bristol Mercury*, 2 Oct. 1858.

[15] Morris, *Class sect and party*, 186; Harrison, *Crowds and history*, ch. v.

[16] *FFBJ*, 24 Jan., 7 Mar. 1846; *Bristol Mercury*, 13 Mar. 1858.

ers.[17] Historians of the Sunday school are divided on the social origins of the teachers: were they mostly working-class ex-pupils, or was the majority from a superior stratum, at least before the 1830s?[18] The 1884 report asserted that the teachers varied 'in station, from poor and simple to rich and cultured', and also alluded to Bible classes 'conducted by working men', one of which attracted 400 people.[19] It also asserted that working-class home-visiting was not extensive. Poorer districts had the fewest volunteers from within the locality, and it was in them that middle-class agencies such as 'congregations' from 'Clifton, Redland and Cotham', 'Clifton College' and ' "ladies from Clifton" ' were most active.[20] Where the help of the 'artizan class' was acknowledged the committee members were lukewarm as to its efficacy. The problem was that 'the gulf between this class is deeper than that between the rich and poor', owing to the 'rougher kindness of the manners of the artizan class'. In contrast the 'tact' and 'adaption' of the 'richer classes' proved to be 'more efficient and influential'.[21]

If 'charitable co-operation'[22] across the classes was not the norm in visiting work, how significant were working-class subscriptions to voluntary charities? Bristol Infirmary accounts offer some support for the contention that 'humble subscribers' played a significant part in hospital funding, but this must be carefully qualified.[23] Working-class subscription began on a small scale from the 1840s, when it was deemed so remarkable that the 1846 annual report drew special attention to it. From the 1850s the 'Workmen's contribution' was listed separately, perhaps with the intention of embarrassing 'those who have been blessed with the abundance of this world's goods' into greater generosity.[24] It rose from 3 per cent of all subscriptions, and a mere 0.1 per cent of total income in 1847 to 28 per cent of total subscriptions and 7 per cent of total income by 1884.[25] Contributions were made by workplace or occupational groups, and while sometimes presented as offerings made in gratitude for treatment, their organisation around individual firms or trade unions suggests they should be understood not as individual gifts, but as a form of mutually funded employee health insurance.

From the timing and nature of these subscriptions it seems that the working-class financial contribution to philanthropy only gathered pace after the mid-century when real wages began to rise. Before that time, the gap

[17] Broad, *Sunday Schools*, 151–4; BRO, SF/FD/AR/1a, Friends' First Day School, *Annual reports*.
[18] Laqueur, *Religion and respectability*, 91–3; Malcolm Dick, 'The myth of the working-class Sunday school', *History of Education* ix (1980), 31–4.
[19] *Condition of the poor*, 118, 121.
[20] Ibid. 116–17.
[21] Ibid. 118–19.
[22] Prochaska, 'Philanthropy', 366, 370–1.
[23] Ibid. 364, citing Abel-Smith, *The hospitals*, 250.
[24] BI *State*, 1846, 1847, 1852.
[25] *Condition of the poor*, appendix 1.

between surplus from the weekly wage and the usual amount given to charity must surely have been too great to permit individual subscription. In 1854 wage levels had reached 11s.–15s. per week for the unskilled or semi-skilled labourer, and 15s.–30s. for the skilled operative.[26] Examples of minimum subscriptions in the mid-century were two guineas for the Infirmary and one guinea for the General Hospital, Bristol Auxiliary Bible Society (1823), Stranger's Friend Society (1826), Asylum for Poor Orphan Girls (1821) and Samaritan Society.[27] Not all charities were so exclusive, and there were occasions on which the poor 'cheerfully contributed their mite'.[28] Where societies did solicit small donations however, their impact was not great. For example, out of 120 annual subscribers to the Congregationalist Bristol City Mission in 1841, twenty-eight gave less than 10s. In sum this accounted for £8 7s., out of a total of £104 10s.[29] The Mission was also supported by collections by the ladies' associations of each chapel with a lower threshold of contribution, of 5s. or less. Even here though small gifts did not automatically signify working-class status: of the 469 donors in 1841 who gave 5s. or less, 61 per cent gave between 3s. and 5s., and indeed the largest number (153) gave 5s. The smallest donors, who gave under 3s., were mostly concentrated in Zion, Hope and Broadmead chapels, suggesting that the energy of individual collectors was the key factor, as much as grassroots popular approval.

The Bristol evidence therefore suggests that the management and funding of voluntary charity was controlled by middle-class males. Visiting, fundraising and participation at meetings increasingly fell to those women who fastened onto philanthropy as a field of social action, but only a small minority of charities had female committees, and most of these also had male officers, or were supported by a congregation. The working-class contribution is hard to document, though it is most probable that charity workers such as teachers and visitors came from a mixed social background; however there is no good evidence that the financial impact of the less well-off was particularly significant.

Class ideals and charity

The dominance of the middle class over the voluntary sector, and the efflorescence of activity in the early nineteenth century have led some to characterise charitable effort as a manifestation of class formation, producing a new, coherent class identity.[30] Indeed Morris argues that a 'British bourgeois ideol-

26 *Bristol Mercury*, 25 Feb. 1854.
27 BABS, *Fourteenth annual report*, 1824; BRL, B4048, *Report of the Stranger's Friend Society*, Bristol 1826; B9780, *State of the Orphan Asylum for the year . . .*, 1821; 4644, *Report of the Samaritan Society for the year 1840*.
28 *FFBJ*, 30 July 1814.
29 BRL, B16885, *15th annual report of the Bristol City Mission*, Bristol 1842.
30 Morris, *Class, sect and party*, chs i, vii, x, xi, xiii, and 'Voluntary societies'.

ogy', achieved through voluntary action, set the agenda for public life over the next century. Its components were:

> the moral value of social discipline; the moral value of work; the rightness of inequality; the relationship of inequality to merit; the need for paternalistic regulation of that inequality; a total assurance of the correctness of British economic progress and world political authority; an uneasiness over the stability of their own authority but never of its correctness and a confident central place for religion in social life.[31]

A similar thesis has been applied to Bristol by Fissell, who describes the replacement in the early nineteenth century of the old-fashioned 'face-to-face' charity of patronage networks by a depersonalised, interrogative philanthropy, a change brought about by the 'birth of class'.[32] Likewise Whittle identifies a 'demise of old obligations' and traditional responsibilities of *noblesse oblige* within a society conceived of as an organic whole giving way before a new individualism which treated poverty as the result of personal failings.[33]

In some respects this study also supports the emphasis on the early nineteenth century as a period of distinct change. The sheer number of new initiatives emanating from voluntary organisations confirm that this was a time when middle-class intervention in the lives of the poor was particularly intense. The growing gulf between mutual aid societies and charitable associations also highlights the impact on the voluntary world of the increasing social distance between different income groups. However it is by no means clear that these changes were representative of a 'new' middle class with a unitary worldview, nor that styles of charity changed from a traditional to an impersonal paternalism. It is true that the burst of voluntary activity at the time of the French Wars and their aftermath was characterised by an unusual degree of co-operation amongst leaders of the town's different political and religious groupings. However, unlike classic industrial revolution towns such as Preston there was no striking transfer of power from old elite to new cotton masters, synonomous with the middle class.[34] Bristol's ruling oligarchy stayed in place and adapted. The new associations were led by the established elite and supported by prominent dissenters. The PMFS for instance had as its vice-presidents Thomas Daniel, the leading Tory-Anglican, Charles Harford, master of the Merchant Venturers, the Revd Dr Randolph, prebendary of Bristol Cathedral, and the Quaker Richard Reynolds; pre-eminent Unitarians included Lambert Schimmelpenning, trustee, and John and Alfred Estlin, committee members. Among the 'members for life' of the Samaritan Society were Quakers Thomas Bonville, Edward Ash and Joseph and Richard

[31] Ibid. 7.
[32] Fissell, *Patients, power and the poor*, ch. vi, p. 228.
[33] Whittle, 'Philanthropy in Preston', pp. i, 13–14, 33–4, 89, 95, 105, 113, 118, 384–6.
[34] Ibid.

Reynolds, alongside Anglicans Thomas Daniel, John Scandrett Harford, Edward Protheroe and Richard Vaughan. Anglicans and Old Dissenters were most visible in the leadership, but other nonconformists were eager subscribers; in the PMFS for instance the Revds Cowan, Grinfield, and Rowe.[35]

Therefore, rather than seeing this as the first manifestation of the ideology of liberal individualism, borne by new men, it may be more helpful to stress the particular conjunction of economic and cultural forces which gave rise to it. Specifically it was stimulated by the impact of evangelicalism against the background of war. The surge of metropolitan voluntarism inspired by 'vital religion' is well known, as is the leading role of Quakers alongside Anglicans. Moreover such groups as the BABS, the Vice Society, the Society for the Relief of Poor Pious County Clergymen (1820s) and the Church Missionary Society were auxiliaries to, or inspired by, those established by metropolitan evangelical leadership.[36] The appeal of these initiatives reached beyond Bristol's Anglican elect partly because church/chapel hostilities in the late eighteenth century were already muted by a common pietism, and partly because of the prevailing political truce.[37] The Corporation of the period contained several Unitarians, both Whig and Tory, some of whom served as mayor, while national electoral politics were conducted unusually amicably between 1790 and 1812.[38] War also strengthened social solidarity, at least within the middle class, not only generating related voluntary activities, but also creating a sense of insecurity and impending doom to which philanthropic effort offered an antidote.[39] Thus calls for moral reform were made under a perceived threat of 'ruin and destruction' and warnings that 'corrupt morals are a sure presage of the downfall of a state'.[40] Lastly, the war had exacerbated external pressures that required a response; these were reflected in the stress on statutory poor relief mechanisms, with an overcrowded workhouse, escalating numbers of out-paupers and visible vagrancy.[41]

There were also limits to the extent to which these non-partisan associa-

35 BRL 9180–1, *State of the Prudent Man's Friend Society for the year 1814*, Bristol 1814; 3rd. *annual report of the Prudent Man's Friend Society*, Bristol 1815; BRL, B4620, *Bristol Samaritan Society, its rules and an address to the public*, Bristol 1807; Bush, *Bristol and its municipal government*, appendix 4; *Matthews's trade directory*; BRO 39461/F/4b, Unitarian subscription book; SF/R3/3, Bristol Society of Friends Monthly Meeting, membership list.
36 Brown, *Fathers of the Victorians*, 244, ch. ix.
37 Barry, 'The parish in civic life', 161–2, and 'Piety and the patient: medicine and religion in eighteenth-century Bristol', in Roy Porter (ed.), *Patients and practitioners: lay perceptions of medicine in pre-industrial society*, Cambridge 1985, 145–75.
38 Bush, *Bristol and its municipal government*; Beaven, *Bristol lists*, 170–1. The exception was 1807: Latimer, *Annals . . . nineteenth century*, 29–30.
39 Colley, *Britons*, 260–2.
40 FFBJ, 14 Jan., 15 Apr. 1797; V. Kiernan, 'Evangelicalism and the French Revolution', *P&P* i (1952), 44–56.
41 Butcher, *Bristol Corporation of the Poor*, 12, and *Bristol Corporation of the Poor, selected records*, 29–30, 134, 153; *Reports from the committees of the House of Commons, X: Provisions; poor; 1774–1802: 1787; Further appendix to the report from the committee on certain returns*

tions altered the nature of the charitable relationship between rich and poor. For example, the emphasis on the 'moral value' of social discipline and of work is better understood as a cyclical recurrence than a new departure. Such had been the mercantilist philosophy propounded by John Cary when he established Bristol's Corporation of the Poor in 1696, the aim being to provide inmates with spinning and carding, to wean them from idleness and begging by inculcating a work ethic, and guide them to 'civility and a love to their labour'.[42] Similarly, while Malthusian thought had some purchase amongst articulate Liberals in the 1830s and 1840s, it never became a dominant influence, but co-existed throughout the period with an entirely non-discriminatory, open-handed approach to street-begging. This is amply demonstrated through the scare stories about imposture that can be traced back to the eighteenth century as well as on to the late nineteenth.[43] Nor would the efforts to introduce a ticketing system, made by the PMFS in the 1810s or the Clifton Mendicity Society in the 1840s, have got underway if casual giving was not seen to be extensive. As late as 1884 the Bishop's Committee was castigating such promiscuous benevolence as 'the *certain source* of the evil conditions it assumes to remedy', having estimated (without explanation) the sums informally distributed at £50,000 a year.[44] This is suggestive of the persistence of spontaneous Christian almsgiving, devoid of judgements as to the character of the needy or responsibility for destitution.

The recognition that external factors such as seasonal trade cycles and unemployment were to blame for poverty was also a recurrent theme, acting 'to check the sweeping condemnation of the poor in which some are apt to indulge, who suppose that poverty is entirely the fault of the sufferer'.[45] Coal committees and appeals from vicars on behalf of parishioners regularly appeared in the newspapers in cold winters.[46] Unitarian missionary reports repeatedly stressed the way in which: 'periodical loss of employment, and illness in the family of the industrious artizan, frequently operate to produce degradation and misery'.[47] They also identified the intractability of the poverty cycle: 'The next generation bring up their children, as they themselves were brought up, and afterwards pass away to a pauper's grave ... each generation is a link of vagabondism and pauperism, ... and CHAINS are

---

relative to the state of the poor, and to charitable donations, & c., 599; Kington, 'A burgess's' letters, 311.

[42] J. Cary, *An essay on the state of England in relation to its trade 1695*, and *An account of the proceedings of the Corporation of Bristol*, 1700, cited in Slack, *Poverty and policy*, 196; Michel Foucault, *Madness and civilization*, Paris 1961, repr. London 1993, 51–2; Sacks, *The widening gate*, 340.

[43] Fissell, *Patients, power and the poor*, 76.

[44] *Condition of the poor*, 179–80.

[45] LMDMS, *2nd annual report*, 1841, 3. See also *Condition of the poor*, 23.

[46] *FFBJ*, 26 Jan. 1811, 5 Dec. 1846.

[47] LMDMS, *2nd annual report*, 1841, 3.

made that entrammel and retard the commonwealth.'[48] Attitudes and strategy towards poverty amongst the Bristol middle class were therefore not all founded upon the concepts of individual merit and the importance of investigation. Charitable responses were diverse, shaped by differing religious outlooks and by pragmatic and immediate concerns.

Similarly, the disappearance of paternalist obligation cannot be documented convincingly. The case of the Bristol Infirmary is particularly relevant here as Fissell has used it to argue more generally that subscriber paternalism was in retreat before the 'transformation' of the hospital from charity to 'medical workplace'.[49] She stresses both the withdrawal of the old elite, due to suburbanisation and the counter-attraction of new charities, and the decline of the traditional paternalism of parish, neighbourhood and workplace in which ties between subscribers and patients were 'personal' and 'long-standing'.[50] This was replaced by a class-based and impersonal evaluation of the recipient's worthiness, evidenced by the rise in the number of patients admitted directly by doctors from 15 per cent in 1751 to 32 per cent by 1826, and by the decline in the mean number of patients recommended by each subscriber, from 3.8 in 1750 to 0.33 in 1806. All this was underpinned by the need for surgeons to enhance their reputations and attract paying pupils by selecting the more scientifically interesting cases. [51] Thus medical charity became 'a class-specific demonstration of respectability . . . rather than the gentler expression of social hierarchy it had been'.

As shown above with respect to the House Committee, Fissell's view that the old elite withdrew from patronage of the Infirmary is hard to sustain. Consideration of the hospital's financial records, and of the longer-term context suggest her other conclusions might be modified. A supposed decline in the charitable nature of the Infirmary actually coincided with a jump in the number of subscribers in the 1790s (appendix 2); an additional 200 subscribed between 1796 and 1797 in response to the building appeal and the debt crisis which attended expansion, at a time when the city's economy was in slump. Nor is it correct, as Berry has shown, to suppose that earlier subscribers were all active paternalists, 'intimately involved in hospital management'. Subscriber drop-out rates ran at about 6 per cent annually and even in 1768 as many as a third of subscribers made no use of their sponsorship rights.[52] The purported fall in subscriber influence on admissions is much less striking over the long run, as samples from three randomly chosen years will demonstrate. Taking in-patients first, the ratios of charity patients to medical/staff admissions in 1814 were 65:35, in 1836, 58:42 and in 1854,

---

48 LMDMS, *12th annual report*, 1855.
49 Fissell, *Patients, power and the poor*, 12, 110, 126, 147.
50 Ibid. 113–15, 125.
51 Ibid. 117, 126 and ch. vii.
52 Ibid. 117; Berry 'Patrons', 53, 191.

74:26.[53] Far from declining, patronage remained central to in-patient admission. The fluctuating numbers admitted by doctors were not contingent upon the growing ascendancy of medical men over the charity, but on funding considerations. As the capital assets of the Infirmary grew through building, the accumulation of legacies and investment income, so it could accommodate a much greater number of patients than subscribers could recommend (appendix 2). Out-patient admissions can be viewed from the numbers recorded in annual reports, and if the mid-century is studied, percentages of patients admitted by note were: 1850, 45 per cent; 1860, 45 per cent; 1870, 38 per cent.[54] Here too patronage was still of considerable importance, even though admissions by note did not keep pace with the growth of out-patient numbers in the 1860s. Again, this was a function of the expansion of facilities, including the employment of more dispensary staff, the reform and expansion of nurse training and the opening of new wards in the 1860s.[55] There were also limits to the extent of medical administrative control: for instance in 1811 medical staff were actually removed from the Infirmary Committee due to their poor attendance at meetings.[56]

Ongoing paternalism can also be seen in the growing number of business subscribers making charity admissions: these rose from 6 per cent in 1814 to 15 per cent in 1836, to 22 per cent by 1854, by which time firms like the Great Western Railway Co., the sugar manufacturer Finzel and Sons, and the Coalpit Heath Company regularly sponsored patients. As Fissell points out with reference to the eighteenth century, this can hardly be explained as accident insurance, since employees suffering from a workplace injury could be admitted as casualties; contrary to her assertion, workplace paternalism as the basis of the charitable relationship grew rather than diminished.[57] So, while doctors did play a substantial part in admissions, due both to the rising status of medicine and the increasing wealth of the institution, this did not yet signify the hospital's transition from charity to 'medical workplace'. A more significant transition was the displacement of private subscribers by workmen and employers that was discernible by the mid-century.

Indeed, this persistence of old fashioned benevolence was a major theme in the earlier discussion of endowment, which highlighted the ongoing friction between those who accepted that parish or corporate charity remained a channel of patronage, and those who attacked this practice to explicate the Radical theme of 'Old Corruption'. Later in the century disgruntled Liberals, musing on their 1868 by-election loss to J. W. Miles, had suspected that it was the implicit capacity for patronage that he wielded as a prominent banker

---

[53] 1814: BRO, FCH/BRI/3k 6, 7, 8; 1836: FCH/BRI/3o 10, 11, 12; 1854: FCH/BRI/3t 4, 5, 6.
[54] BI *State*.
[55] Munro Smith, *Bristol Royal Infirmary*, 333–9.
[56] *FFBJ*, 1 Mar. 1811.
[57] Fissell, *Patients, power and the poor*, 115.

that had ensured his success: charity may have been absent, but the importance of the personal relationship in party politics lived on.[58] As late as 1884 Joseph Russell's bequest to St Paul's parish had specified that income from the endowment (in the form of a food dole) was only to go to those who voted 'constitutionally'.[59] In the same year the bishop's report asserted that 'rivalry of political spirit' still motivated distribution of Colston society gifts.[60]

Face-to-face distribution of alms co-existed with impersonal enquiry. At parish level, despite the efforts of the Charity Commission, vestrymen were still allowed a good deal of individual discretion in the allocation of Christmas doles.[61] Nor was the indiscriminate money dole given up: the Gloucestershire Society was taken to task by the Bristol Mercury in 1837 for promoting dependency and false expectations with its pecuniary gifts.[62] The whole purpose of district visiting was to reforge personal bonds of a community or congregational nature, and missionaries' reports make it quite clear that visits were repeated, sometimes over a period of years, to establish a genuine rapport.[63] Unitarian lady visitors targeted their Sunday school families and 'the poor connected with the congregation', not just to distribute gifts but 'as friends desirous of manifesting sympathy'.[64] It was the suspicion that not all voluntary charities operated an impersonal assessment of the client's worth that brought the Charity Organisation Society into existence to introduce a more discriminatory approach, though interest was short-lived in Bristol.[65] If a rupture in the development of subscription charity has to be identified, then a better candidate is the period around 1870 when subscriber intervention became less important in several areas, such as Muller's orphanages, which thrived on anonymous donations, Whitwill's Children's Hospital which abandoned recommendation, and elementary education which also drew on both taxes and fees. This timing is to be explained by the growing confidence of professionals and charity activists that provision could be delivered more effectively, quickly and universally by abandoning subscriber mediation.

The argument then is that while voluntary societies provide useful insights into the aspirations and beliefs of the middle class, it would be inappropriate to characterise the charities as reflecting a unitary set of attitudes which underwent a clearly discernible change in the early nineteenth century.

---

58 Bristol Mercury, 2 May 1868.
59 BRO, P/St P/Ch/1.
60 Condition of the poor, 178.
61 See P/St J/Ch/11/6.
62 Bristol Mercury, 16 Sept. 1837.
63 BRL, B16885, 15th annual report of the Bristol City Mission, Bristol 1842, 36–9.
64 LMDMS, 1st, 2nd annual reports, 1835, 1836.
65 Condition of the poor, 187, 213–14; Alan J. Kidd, ' "Outcast Manchester": voluntary charity, poor relief and the casual poor, 1860–1905', in A. J. Kidd and K. W. Roberts (eds), City, class and culture: studies of cultural production and social policy in Victorian Manchester, Manchester 1985, 48–73.

Would it be more convincing to depict philanthropy as an arena of shared values between the classes? There is no doubt that large numbers of the poor were reached by voluntary effort. For example, in the first few months of 1868, 350 'aged poor' had enjoyed a free roast dinner and 'address' from the vicar of St Phillip's, there were 803 depositors to the Bristol Penny Bank, and the Bristol and Clifton Mendicity Society gave out 3,403 meals.[66] Temperance campaigns regularly drew impressive attendances for fetes, teas and processions.[67] Thousands were schooled or medically treated by charity. However, there are various difficulties in assuming that working-class recipients of charities embraced the values of respectability, religion, self-help and gratitude for the kindly gift. Numerical attendance at campaigning rallies does not prove their efficacy. For example, despite the scale and vigour of temperance activities Bristol's fabled reputation for hard drinking was not appreciably altered; a Bristol Temperance Society census discovered that on one Saturday night in the city 98,226 persons entered a pub, out of a population of 206,374.[68] Nor does an individual's participation in a charitable activity give a certain indication of his or her private beliefs. The sources on which historians rely for their discovery of the 'respectable' working class tend to be those produced by middle-class observers, whose understanding and motivation may be questionable.[69] Bailey has urged that the application of a role analysis of working-class behaviour can provide a greater sensitivity to the reality behind the appearance of compliance and respectability, and he points to the charitable relationship as one class interface in which a perceptional gulf between rich and poor is most likely.[70]

Evidence of duplicity offers a useful way of exploring this gulf. The suspicion that beggars were generally idle, dissolute individuals exploiting the generosity of the charitable runs through the literature of the period, and is still found in the late twentieth century.[71] Partly this reflected real examples of dissembling mendicants feigning distress. A personal house-call bearing a begging letter with the forged signature of a local vicar was one successful technique, while in 1835 a beggar was found with a list he had bought for 6d. of 'about a score of respectable families who might be called on by a person', detailing a convenient route to their houses and instructions on who to ask

---

[66] *Bristol Mercury*, 4 Jan., 21 Mar. 1868.

[67] *FFBJ*, 23 May 1846; *Bristol Mercury*, 24 July 1858.

[68] *Condition of the poor*, 80–2.

[69] Alistair Reid, 'Intelligent artisans and aristocrats of labour: the essays of Thomas Wright', in J. Winter (ed.), *The working class in modern British history: essays in honour of Henry Pelling*, Cambridge 1983, 171–86.

[70] Peter Bailey, ' "Will the real Bill Banks please stand up?": towards a role analysis of mid-Victorian working-class respectability', *Journal of Social History* xiii (1979), 343.

[71] *FFBJ*, 1 Jan. 1814; *Bristol Mercury*, 13 Jan. 1817, 14 June, 29 Nov. 1819; *FFBJ*, 11 Nov. 1826, 21 Feb. 1846; *Bristol Mercury*, 13 Mar. 1858; 'An imposter', *Bristol Gazette*, 10 Nov. 1836; *Condition of the poor*, 179–80; 'Operation Grail Nets "Rich Beggars" ', *Venue*, 7 Jan. 1994.

for.[72] Others felt a more general unease that the desired reciprocity was not being achieved, and examples of deception and failure relayed in annual reports attest that this was a well-founded fear. The Unitarian domestic missionaries noted several cases of pragmatism rather than submission:

> A poor woman, . . . having become very straitened in her circumstances, one day observed that she must go to 'some place' (meaning some church or chapel) and see *what she could get*. 'Go', said the party addressed, 'to the —— chapel.' 'But', she replied, 'I must go round and see where I can get most!' She did go round, and obtained her object. It is thus that the poor learn to patronize their patrons, and make religion a stalking horse, for the most selfish purposes.[73]

1868 brought another blow to the certainties of the philanthropic, with the discovery that a black market existed in hospital notes and mendicity tickets obtained from gullible subscribers. An Infirmary in-patient note changed hands at between 9d. and 1s., while a Mendicity Society bread/coal ticket fetched 3d.[74]

Nor did recipients always evince appreciation. For example John Board, a casualty patient of the Infirmary in 1815, was lent a cotton shirt during his stay which he was allowed to wear home, then when asked to return it, sent it back to Matron 'torn into strips'.[75] Similarly, Mary Rider had spent two years in the Girl's Reformatory and was then taken on as a servant in Mary Carpenter's own house, only to abscond shortly after, stealing a silk mantle and various items of clothing.[76] Others bluntly informed philanthropists that their poverty could be solved neither with small alms nor religious ministration, and again the candid reports of the Unitarian domestic missionary record several such responses. 'Don't tell me to pray, I have enough to do to bear my pains without praying' was the message from one woman. Another reacted to the visitor's reading of a tract with: 'Sir, it is all very well for men to write and talk, but starvation takes the spirit out of a man, and leaves him no heart for anything!' Yet another informed him that 'he considered it insulting for gentlemen to talk of religion to the distressed poor'. And how often did the missionary's blandishments of self-improvement meet with the response made by one 'poor man' who

> declaimed violently against the institutions of society, which, he said, took from the poor man the reward for his labours. He proposed various alterations, such as making a division of the land &c., among the people, in order that each might enjoy the fruit of his labours.[77]

---

[72] *FFBJ*, 10 Feb. 1838, 10 Jan. 1846; *Bristol Mercury*, 22 May 1858; *Bristol Gazette*, 18 Feb. 1835.

[73] LMDMS, *5th annual report*, 1844, 14; *12th annual report*, 1855, 5.

[74] *Bristol Mercury*, 21 Mar. 1868.

[75] BRO 35893/2/e, Bristol Infirmary, weekly committee minute book, 8 Mar. 1815.

[76] *Bristol Mercury*, 14 Aug. 1858; *FFBJ*, 5 Sept. 1846, for pawning of Dorcas Society linen.

[77] LMDMS, *4th., 3rd., 5th., 11th. annual reports.*

Plate 5. *Bristol as it was 1845–1900*, plate 158
Courtesy of Reece Winstone Archive

On one occasion at least the philanthropic relationship was more publicly inverted, by a Mr R. Scully, who was about to be evicted from his house in Wellington Street to make way for the rebuilding of Fry's Factory No. 7. Before his roof was removed to dislodge him from his home he made his protest with a banner (plate 5) that mocked the cocoa magnate's benevolent public image.

These are anecdotes, and are not necessarily indicative of widespread deception or bitterness towards the charitable. However they affirm the validity of a role-model analysis of the philanthropic relationship and warn against reading too much social consensus into working-class participation in the voluntary world. Probably the dominant response of the poor to charity was ambivalence guided by maximisation of individual utility, and the imbibing of values should not be assumed, even where participation was extensive.[78] The examples also suggest why some felt the receipt of charity to be so demeaning. The accompaniment of aid with unwanted moralising was disliked, while the association of philanthropy with the more privileged and powerful in society provoked resentment. This perception of charity as part of an unequal social structure in which the poor remained dependent – what Salamon terms 'philanthropic paternalism' – was to become an important rationale for state intervention in the twentieth century.[79]

Charity and identity

A central paradox of voluntary associations from the eighteenth century was their capacity to act both as agents of integration and as expressions of different political and religious affiliations. Historians of nineteenth century voluntarism have tended to minimise the impact of party and sectarian fissures in such areas as education and missionary work. This is portrayed as competition which aided class formation, while the unity of class purpose was ensured in other associations by an explicit language of inclusion – 'no religion, no politics'.[80] This section will reassert the importance of voluntarism as a badge of religious and political identity. The argument flows from the theoretical assumption that voluntarism arises in a plural society where small

[78] Ellen Ross, 'Hungry children: housewives and London charity, 1870–1918', in Peter Mandler (ed.), *The uses of charity: the poor on relief in the nineteenth-century metropolis*, Philadelphia, 1990, 161–96; Bernard Harris, 'Responding to adversity: government–charity relations and the relief of unemployment in interwar Britain', *Contemporary Record* ix (1995), 529–61.

[79] Prochaska, *Philanthropy and the hospitals of London*, 109; Salamon, *Partners in public service*, 46–7.

[80] Morris, *Class, sect and party*, ch. xi; Philip Hills, 'Division and cohesion in the nineteenth-century middle class: the case of Ipswich, 1830–70', *Urban History Yearbook* (1987), 47–8.

groups pioneer welfare strategies that do not command sufficient unanimity for statutory provision. It also accords with three earlier observations: that party and sectarian identities continued to divide Bristol's middle classes until the mid-century, with endowed charity one of their battlegrounds; that the formation of charities with an inclusive leadership was an exception associated with war and its aftermath; and that the persistence of paternalism and differing attitudes to poverty are suggestive of long-run continuities in the charitable world.

It is certainly true that the literature of voluntarism proclaimed the non-sectarian nature of appeals with monotonous regularity, but the very ubiquity of this claim is indicative of a consciousness of sectarianism. Thus we find the Benevolent Evening School Society in 1811 stressing that pupils could come from any denomination; the Dorcas Society and Strangers Friend in 1814 declaring that they would not proselytise on behalf of sect or party or likewise discriminate in almsgiving; the Methodist Sunday School movement in 1816 hoping that their efforts would not be seen as 'a party thing'; the Bristol Missionary Society in 1836 promising that 'no episcopalian need be afraid to lose caste by mingling his praises with those of other distinguished men'; the newly formed YMCA in 1853 bemoaning the fact that the rival Church of England Young Men's Society was refusing to disband and unite with them; the volunteer enumerators of the Sunday School census in 1858 complaining that 'the clergy of the Established Church declined to unite with them' despite their non-denominational aims; the Bristol United City Mission justifying its establishment in the same year on the grounds of the need for a non-denominational mission.[81] It is true that emergencies could, and did, make strange bedfellows, like the St Mary Redcliffe Soup Society, started in 1847–8, which found such prominent dissenters as George Thomas, Joseph Eaton and Conrad Finzel on a committee of the once 'blue' vestry, to build a 'soup-house' for poor parishioners.[82] None the less the overriding tone of the sources points to an abiding awareness of division. The Unitarian surgeon John B. Estlin explained matters thus to an American correspondent in 1846: 'in educational and religious projects, the members of the Establishment do not like any other to unite with them in charitable & even literary instit. parties, especially political ones act together, & the management generally falls to the strongest'.[83]

Educational voluntarism repeatedly focused division. For example, in 1825 the bishop of Bristol attacked the formation of the Mechanics Institution as a dangerous threat to the education based on 'moral improvement'

81 *FFBJ*, 9 Feb. 1811, 16 July, 20 Aug. 1814; Broad, *Sunday schools*, 59–61; *Bristol Gazette*, 29 Sept. 1836; BRL, B1533, *Address delivered at the Broadmead Room Tuesday, June 14th. 1853, at the inaugural gathering of the Young Men's Christian Association*, 12–13; *Bristol Mercury*, 24 Apr., 12 June 1858.
82 St Mary Redcliffe Vestry, Soup Society minutes, 1854–61.
83 Taylor, *British and American abolitonists*, 257.

obtainable in a National School; this was also the line of the Tory *Journal* which condemned it as a threat to social stability.[84] Seventeen years later the educational clauses in the 1843 Factory Act found the nonconformists alarmed by government proposals that factory school committees should be chaired by local Anglican clergy. At a mass meeting in defence of religious liberty in schools the leading figures of Bristol Liberal dissent, George Thomas, Richard Ash and H. O. Wills shared a platform to attack the legislature.[85] As shown above, religious division was still prominent in the elections to the first Bristol School Board in 1871.

Even societies founded in a flush of enthusiasm for unity were not immune from dissension. For example the evangelical BABS had explicitly opened its committee and visiting activities to 'parochial clergy and dissenting ministers'.[86] However, at a time of intense party feuding in 1838, the Liberal press pointed out that dissenting collections had contributed far more to the society's coffers than had those of the Established Church.[87] Tabulated accounts for 1810-35 were carefully reproduced, naming particular churches and evangelical vicars, and the predictable row ensued. Party alignments could also determine popular perceptions of the temperance movement: a pub landlady prosecuted in 1836 for opening on Sunday during divine service 'considered it necessary to enter into a long and eloquent defence, which she concluded by exclaiming "if this is what comes by Reform, I say God bless the blues" '.[88] This is an important reminder that religious reformism was a minority aspect of middle-class culture, and that to the ordinary citizen the hegemonic tussle over the status of the pub in society was perceived to be an intra-class, not an inter-class, issue.[89] Nor were cultural institutions, which were perhaps the most integrated of all, exempt from dissension, though here the lines of fracture were less clearcut. In 1846 the committee of the Zoological Society had a heated debate on the propriety of opening the gardens on Sundays, with divison not on the usual party or sectarian lines, but in accordance with the seriousness with which members took their sabbatarianism.[90]

Why did voluntary charities act as a platform for competing political and religious identities? The tendency arose from the access they offered to fields of civic power. These ranged from the microcosmic concerns of governing asylums and schools, to voting and management rights in more prestigious institutions, to the necessary accoutrements of those who sought to represent

---

[84] *The Trades' Newspaper and Mechanics Weekly Journal*, 28 Feb. 1825; *FFBJ*, 18 June 1825.

[85] Campbell 'Development of literacy', 98–102.

[86] BRL, B3951, BABS, *Eighth report*, 1817.

[87] *Bristol Mercury*, 13 Jan. 1838.

[88] *Bristol Gazette*, 29 Sept. 1836.

[89] Hugh Cunningham, 'Leisure and culture', in Thompson, *Cambridge social history*, ii. 279–339 at pp. 299–300.

[90] *FFBJ*, 13 June 1846; *Bristol Mercury*, 2, 16, 30 Jan. 1858 for the Athenaeum's Essay and Discussion Society.

the city at corporate or parliamentary level. Examples of these will be considered in turn.

The Asylum of Poor Orphan Girls was a small-scale voluntary charity, with annual subscriptions accounting for about half of its income in the early nineteenth century.[91] A two-guinea subscription purchased a guardianship for the year which entitled one to recommend orphaned children for admission to the asylum. Nominations could be applied to children resident in the guardian's parish or within a one-mile radius, thus conferring the status of local almoner, similar to that attached to membership of a select vestry. Applications were then put before the committee, whose quarterly boards were open to guardians, and whose membership was chosen by election from the subscriber body.[92] The critieria used made direct reference to the poor law: the preferred inmate was a child whose parents had resided in Bristol, but who did not have a settlement. Beyond this, a personal interview with the child accompanied by the guardian was the means of selection.[93] So, by purchasing a subscription the donors acquired a small slice of municipal power outside the official network of vestries and corporate bodies which conferred status at parochial level, a capacity to exercise patronage and some institutional control.

A greater political significance attached to the hospitals. Bristolians in the mid nineteenth century liked to quip that 'patients going to the Infirmary could expect a sovereign remedy, while those going to the Hospital would receive a radical cure'.[94] To test whether this would have been obvious to a politically conscious citizen table 24 shows voting choices of surgeons, physicians and officers in 1812, 1832 and 1847, all years in which elections were hotly contested, and the platforms offered clear choices. This confirms the Infirmary's Tory stamp. In 1812 the favoured vote was the Tory/'Old Whig' split with one Tory plumper: Edward Protheroe, the 'Old Whig' candidate, was quite acceptable to Tories as he opposed Catholic emancipation and was lukewarm on reform.[95] By the 1830s a contrast emerged between the Infirmary, again favouring the Tory/Conservative/Whig split, and the General, divided between those who plumped for Baillie, the 'Old Whig', and those who split between Edward Protheroe, Jr, the abolitionist reform Whig, and John Williams the Reformer. In 1847 the General's faculty plumped for Francis Fitzhardinge Berkeley, while Infirmary staff were divided between those able to accept the manifest contradictions of a split Tory ticket, and those who plumped loyally for the 'Old Tory', Philip Miles.

Hospitals flagged their party colours to supporters through their patrons. The General's first president was Lord Grenville, whose family association

---

91 BRL, B9780, *State of the Orphan Asylum for the year 1821*.
92 Ibid.
93 *Bristol Gazette*, 13 Mar. 1806; *FFBJ*, 12 Mar. 1814.
94 C. Bruce-Perry, *The Bristol Medical School*, Bristol 1984, 9.
95 Brett, 'Liberal middle classes', 93–4; Beaven, *Bristol lists*, 171.

Table 24
Voting choices in general elections of officers and faculties, Bristol Infirmary, General Hospital, 1812, 1832, 1847

	Plumpers				Splitters			Not found
	T	W	RW	R	T/W	T/T	RW/R	
1812								
Infirmary	1				3			6
1832								
Infirmary	1				7			2
General		2					3	3
1847								
Infirmary	4				1	3		4
General		3						4

T = Tory; W = Whig/Liberal; RW = Reform Whig; R = Radical/Reformer.

Sources: *Bristol poll book*, 1812, 1832, 1847; *Matthews's directory*, 1812, 1831, 1832, 1847

with Bristol Whiggery was well-established.[96] Between 1849 and 1869 the Quaker George Thomas was president/treasurer. His role as a Liberal councillor and charity trustee, and his prominent position in the Anti-Corn-Law League and support of Liberalism in national elections has already been mentioned.[97] In 1844 the vice-presidents were two 'old Whigs', James Evan Baillie MP, and councillor Christopher George, and they were shortly joined by Joseph Eaton, the Temperance Quaker who campaigned against slavery and the Corn Laws.[98] Of course, complete partisanship was never favoured as this might alienate potential subscribers: Tory MP Richard Vyvyan was a vice-president in the 1840s, and Conservative mayor Richard Poole King in the 1850s, though King was perceived as reformer due to his support for dock municipalisation.[99] Party politics and medical charity also came together in the election of doctors, where a candidate's party stripe was also a career attribute: for example, in the 1812 Infirmary sugeon's election a dismal third place in the poll went to John Bishop Estlin, a Unitarian who voted for Romilly.[100] Prospective faculty members would embark on a canvass of sub-

---

96 Bush, *Bristol and its municipal government*, 20; Brett, 'Liberal middle classes', 89.
97 Nicholls, *Life of George Thomas*.
98 *Report of the Bristol General Hospital for the year ending 1843*; *Bristol Mercury*, 22 May 1858.
99 Bush, *Bristol and its municipal government*, 170–2.
100 Beaven, *Bristol lists*, 259; *Bristol poll book*, 1812.

scribers once an impending vacancy was made known.[101] This might involve announcing one's candidacy and placing letters of recommendation in the local press, or, more discreetly, drawing on loyalty networks of family and association.[102]

For nineteenth-century public figures personal benevolence and a willingness to support philanthropic causes were desirable, perhaps essential attributes. An example from local politics is the Tory John Kerle Haberfield. In a municipal career between 1835 and 1857 he was six times mayor, alderman, magistrate, town councillor, charity trustee, seven times governor of the Corporation of the Poor, and chair of the Bristol Waterworks Company. His obituaries concurred that 'he will be remembered and revered as the princely philanthropist', and that his good nature 'loosened his purse-strings to all our benevolent institutions'.[103] Philanthropists and publicists sought political capital by identifying their causes with civic reputation 'to the honor of the merchants, gentry, clergy, and opulent citizens of Bristol, who know the way to their pockets, and have hearts and hands ready to compassionate the distressed'.[104] Reference to the efforts of rival cities and local tradition became a standard device in charitable appeals.[105] Thus identification of charity with civic pride sustained the value of philanthropic prominence to politicians.

The association of charity and character was also common currency in national political discourse. Here a perceived lack of charity could work against ambition, as in the vituperative campaign directed against William Fripp in the 1841 general election. A poster urged voters to 'Try Mr Fripp again by his charitable contributions and you may look in vain for his name, except among the subscribers to the Bristol Infirmary, in which Institution, it is notorious he carries his party principles to a shameful excess.'[106] As late as 1868 a Liberal puff for Samuel Morley reminded readers that he 'has already made himself a national reputation for his almost unbounded philanthropy and munificence . . . his generous yet discriminating sympathies towards the working classes have made his name dear to tens of thousands who have never seen his face'.[107]

Voluntary societies could therefore represent fragmentation and dissonance. To what extent was this offset by an articulation of a shared national

101 *Bristol Gazette*, 13 Mar., 10 Apr. 1806.
102 Bristol Lying-In Institution, Annual report.
103 BRO, 06527, John Kerle Haberfield, memorial scrapbook; *Bristol Times and Mirror*, 24 Feb. 1877.
104 W. Matthews, *The new history, survey and description of the city and suburbs of Bristol*, Bristol 1794, 88.
105 'Distress in Germany', *FFBJ*, 5 Mar. 1814; Reynolds Commemoration Society, *Bristol Mercury*, 18 Nov. 1816; 'Distressed manufacturers', *Bristol Mirror*, 20 May 1826; Infirmary building extensions, *Bristol Mercury*, 20 Feb. 1858.
106 Poster in BRL 10103, Collection . . . election of 1841; see also 10109, Collection . . . election of 1847.
107 *Bristol Mercury*, 25 May 1868.

identity? Certainly voluntarism acted as a countervailing force of paternal aid and of order in the atmosphere of social dislocation that attended the French wars.[108] The language of charity reflected the heightened and inclusive sense of British national identity which the war effort encouraged.[109] Thus a supporter of the Colston societies daubed them in patriotic colours:

> In what other country . . . are individuals to be found . . . thus bountifully to give assistance to their fellow creatures? Let the indigent amongst us reflect . . . that were the Corsican tyrant and his slaves to acquire the ascendancy here, all such sources . . . would instantly be dried up.[110]

Philanthropy became a forum in which the now acceptable plebian patriots could be idealised. The PMFS asserted that begging was alien to the 'dignified spirit' of the English, owing to 'our national industry, the free spirit of our constitution, and the comparatively large portion of information which is diffused among all ranks'.[111] An emergency subscription levied during the unemployment crisis of early 1817 aimed 'to prevent an increase of the degradation of that honest sentiment which is the birthright of every Briton, however low he may rank in society'.[112]

Belief in the superiority of Britishness flowered on the international stage in the wake of imperial expansion, which some voluntarists understood as part of the divine plan: 'the providence of God has made the scourge of war the means of affording enlarged opportunities for missionary efforts'.[113] For example, the Indian Mutiny was regarded as a sign of Britain's special global destiny. An address to the YMCA asserted that 'we claim to have part in every transaction which takes place in the world, because we have been appointed by God to make a noble stand for the cross of Christ'.[114] Britain's task was paternal stewardship: 'If they abandoned India there would be no irrigation, no improvement of their culture; there would be no roads or railroads, and that country . . . would be the degraded half-dead thing it had been.'[115] As Britishness came to be defined increasingly in terms of racial stratification, the language of good intentions deployed by philanthropists helped shape a perception of otherness.[116] Blackness was a pervasive motif in speeches: 'Light is beginning to dawn upon the Caffres and the darkness dispelled'; 'ere long they should see the black man . . . as white in soul and

---

[108] Prochaska, *Voluntary impulse*, 21; Owen, *English philanthropy*, 97–8; *FFBJ*, 1 Oct. 1803, 19 Feb., 5 Mar. 1814.
[109] Colley, *Britons*, chs vii, viii.
[110] *FFBJ*, 19 Nov. 1803.
[111] Ibid. 24 Dec. 1814.
[112] *Bristol Mercury*, 3 Feb. 1817.
[113] Ibid. 27 Mar. 1858. See also *FFBJ*, 28 Nov. 1846.
[114] *Bristol Mercury*, 23, 30 Jan. 1858.
[115] Ibid. 23 Oct. 1858.
[116] Catherine Hall, 'From Greenland's icy mountains . . . to Afric's golden sand': ethnicity, race and nation in mid-nineteenth century England', *Gender and History* v (1993), 212–30.

beautiful in character as the fairest European'.[117] Indeed, this language of otherness was equally applied to the uncharted regions of Bristol's slums. The first pupils of the Methodist Sunday schools were: 'Wild as the untaught Indian's brood', with hair 'like eagles' feathers', while poor children were commonly labelled 'street Arabs'.[118]

The voluntary sector therefore provided a forum in which notions of Britishness were expressed, particularly in the language and assumptions of missionary charity. However, the degree to which this shaping of identity was uncontested should not be overstated. For example, the recognition that Protestantism was the original defining force in British national identity does not mean that all shared in the evangelical zeal for the 'unprivileging of minorities who would not conform'.[119] The several charities directed at weaning the Irish from Catholicism had a strong political context, since they emerged at the time of the furore surrounding Catholic emancipation in the 1820s, and in Bristol they also drew on the long Establishment tradition of anti-Jacobinism.[120] While the role of anti-slavery in the redefinition of British self-image is increasingly recognised, here again the issue was hotly disputed in Bristol elections.[121] Quaker pacifism during the Crimean War was at odds with the general perception of the national interest.[122] Bristol Unitarians forged links with Indian reformers such as Rammohan Roy (who died while visiting the city in 1833) who have been described as early forerunners of Indian nationalism.[123] Nor did everyone approve of the tendency of the charitable to be 'far more interested in the condition of "Borriaboola Gha" than in the White Slaves of London'.[124]

Voluntary charitable associations were the means by which the middle class sought to mould social relations in the provincial city, and their structure of open membership based on subscription offered a public site in which status might be claimed and shared values developed. Some aspects of middle-class culture which they represented dated back to the mid eighteenth century, such as the procedure of the public meeting and the publication of annual accounts. The early nineteenth century was marked by an intensification of activity and by a clearer demarcation between charity and mutual aid. However, the gamut of philanthropic attitudes and interventions cannot be easily captured within a single set of ideological assumptions which crystal-

---

117 *Bristol Gazette*, 29 Sept. 1836; *Bristol Mercury*, 27 Mar. 1858.
118 Broad, *Sunday schools*, 11, 16; *Bristol Mercury*, 7 Mar. 1868.
119 Colley, *Britons*, ch. i, pp. 18–30, 53.
120 Ibid. 324–34; BRO P/StJ/V/7, 1 Dec. 1828.
121 Hall, 'Greenland's icy mountains', 216–19, and *White, male and middle-class: explorations in feminism and history*, Cambridge 1992, ch. ix; Colley, *Britons*, 350–60; Marshall, *Bristol and the abolition of slavery*.
122 Carter, 'Bristol churches', ch. iv; *FFBJ*, 25 Feb. 1854.
123 Rohit Barot, *Bristol and the Indian independence movement*, Bristol 1988, 1–7.
124 *Bristol Mercury*, 6 Feb., 13 Mar., 8 May 1858.

lised at that time. Face-to-face benevolence co-existed with discriminating philanthropy, structural causes of poverty were recognised along with individual failings, there was no sudden retreat of paternalism in the hospital, and, because they were embedded in religious and political life, charitable societies also reflected the diversity of opinion within the middle class.

Consequently, where charity took the form of the voluntary association it inevitably became laden with other concerns. A trenchant sermon given to the Canynges Society in 1858 captured the tension well:

> Compared with these high ennobling motives of the love of Christ, the value of souls, the stewardship, and account we must all soon give at God's judgement seat, how base is the metal of which many incentives to charity are composed? Men do not ask what is the love of Christ to me, but what does my neighbour intend to give? Show me, they cry, the subscription list. Will it be published to the world? Will my name be there, and will I claim credit and popularity by the subscription? Will my political friends (suppose you) think well of it? Such is the world, and when they have exhausted all the flattering arts of beggary and nothing more can be wrung out by fear or favour, then let us have a bazaar, and dress up our charity with the amusement and the tricks of trade. Let us buy in the cheapest and sell in the dearest market, let us make money by fantastic devices, amidst laughter and merriment and cavilling, and let us call it charity. Call it what you please, this is not true love to God in the soul of man.[125]

These caustic comments on the motives of the philanthropists, albeit made in the interest of exhortation, invite further consideration of the problems of charitable fundraising, and it is to this theme that the next chapter turns.

---

[125] *Bristol Mirror*, 7 Aug. 1858.

9

The Limits of Charity

The preceding discussion has already shown that a plethora of initiatives flourished in the city, acting as a significant channel for the redistribution of resources from rich to poor. It also demonstrated that voluntary actors identified and sought to aid vulnerable groups, often by means of innovative strategies. But is it possible to evaluate their achievements in a more systematic fashion? And how did they address the challenges which contemporary theory suggests are inherent to voluntarism, such as insufficiency of income, the free rider problem, inability to provide a comprehensive service, amateurism and paternalism?[1] The latter two aspects have already been observed, in the efforts of the Charity Commissioners to impose stricter bureaucracy and accountability on the endowed trusts, and in the resentment of some recipients towards demeaning benevolence. The first section of this chapter deals with income and asks whether voluntary sources of funding were sufficiently robust and flexible to meet the demands placed on them. The second section assesses the outcomes of philanthropic effort, concentrating on the contribution of the charity schools towards raising literacy and the impact of the hospitals on mortality and morbidity.

The uncertainty of income

Voluntary charities announced themselves to prospective donors by means of annual general meetings, annual reports and newspaper accounts of their activities. The annual report would typically contain a standard introduction, followed by a copy of the rules and perhaps the abstract of a legacy; others included a chairman's address, or, in the case of auxiliaries, the reproduction of the thoughts of its parent body; a few appended quite lengthy case studies of their work.[2] Common features were the itemising of expenditure and income by the treasurer, and a list of donors and the sums given, which usually distinguished annual subscribers from life trustees and givers of legacies or donations. Open accounting assured donors that their gifts were being handled responsibly while the subscription list satisfied status concerns and

---

1 Salamon, *Partners in public service*, 45–7.
2 BRL, B9780, *State of the Orphan Asylum for the year . . .*, 1821; BI *State*, 1742–1873; BABS, *Annual reports*; BRL, B16885, *Bristol City Mission Society*.

helped elicit further funds. Beyond this the texts of reports ranged from cursory statements to extensive discussion of social ills and their possible solutions.

Newspaper advertisements and notices were also an essential part of the fundraising process. From the late eighteenth century they were used by charities to advertise their meetings and functions, to articulate their objectives and to publish subscription lists. Editorial accounts of meetings were initially limited to a few lines in the local news section, where the main focus of interest was upon who attended and the amount raised. As the size of newspapers expanded in the nineteenth century, so the amount of space devoted to charity increased, with advertisements of the annual meeting, notices placed by the charity summarising its accounts and its annual report, followed by the newspaper's own description of the annual meeting. By the mid-century, charity reports could occupy several columns, with verbatim extracts from speeches offering participants access to a much wider public than that addressed at the original meeting. This allowed the Church in particular a heightened command of the media and capacity to comment on events: missionary analysis of the Indian Mutiny is a case in point.[3] In the later nineteenth century charity events remained a common part of the local reporter's round.[4] As a more public product than the annual report, newspapers were not innocent of social or political significance. A charitable association's use of the print media signalled its wealth and status in ways which others, friendly societies for example, usually could not.

Gifts were also elicited at festive occasions aimed at respectable society. Musical events in aid of the Infirmary were important dates in the city's cultural calendar, and as the century progressed benefit concerts and balls remained an occasional feature of the fundraising round.[5] For instance, in 1836 the Diocesan School Society held concerts to support National Schools, while the Blind Asylum in 1858 raised money from a lecture on Milton followed by 'madrigals and glees'.[6] The attraction of processions was undimmed and they maintained their place in the charitable year into the twentieth century. Schools and temperance groups continued to process, along with prominent societies that retained the annual walk from church to feast.[7] Whitsun was a favourite time for religious festivals, paternal treating, school outings and temperance fetes.[8] As in the processions of endowed school- children and the fairs and galas of the benefit clubs, the importance of civic tradition and holiday custom was not lost on philanthropic voluntarists seeking public approval.[9]

3   *Bristol Mercury*, 15 May 1858.
4   BRO 40301, journalist's diary (1878).
5   *FFBJ*, 19 Mar., 28 June 1774; 26 Feb., 9, 16 Apr. 1803; 3 Oct. 1846.
6   *Bristol Gazette*, 11 Mar. 1836; *Bristol Mercury*, 4 Sept. 1858.
7   Reece Winstone, *Bristol suburbs long ago*, Bristol 1985, plates 157, 158, 301.
8   *FFBJ*, 6 June 1846.
9   Alun Howkins, 'The taming of Whitsun in nineteenth-century Oxfordshire', in Eileen

Table 25
Subscriptions to selected charities, Bristol, 1800–70, 5-year means, showing percentage variation

	Infirmary	%	Dispensary	%	Total medical	%	Dolphin	%	Anchor	%	Grateful	%	Gloucester-shire	%	Total county/Colston	%
1801-5	2,054		562		2,616		196		287		190		187		861	
1806-10	2,714	32	598	6	3,312	27	264	35	322	12	195	3	211	13	993	15
1811-15	3,050	12	560	-6	3,610	9	326	23	327	2	266	36	226	7	1,115	12
1816-20	2,910	-5	545	-3	3,455	-4	315	-3	331	1	232	-13	198	-12	1,076	-4
1821-25	2,480	-15	598	10	3,078	-11	420	33	506	53	245	6	228	15	1,398	30
1826-30	2,441	-2	612	2	3,053	-1	440	5	535	6	373	52	284	25	1,632	17
1831-35	2,201	-10	535	-13	2,736	-10	471	7	369	-31	342	-9	304	7	1,486	-9
1836-40	2,027	-8	450	-16	2,477	-10	579	23	524	42	766	124	435	43	2,304	55
1841-45	2,302	14	438	-3	2,740	11	483	-17	501	-4	417	-46	412	-5	1,812	21
1846-50	2,579	12	513	17	3,092	13	406	-16	430	-14	474	14	334	-19	1,644	-9
1851-55	2,681	4	590	15	3,271	6	349	-14	442	3	664	40	283	-15	1,739	6
1856-60	2,711	1					432	24	451	2	617	-7	274	-3	1,774	2
1861-65	2,916	8					503	16	605	34	723	17	280	2	2,110	19
1866-70	2,856	-2					824	64	776	28	698	-4	271	-3	2,569	22

Sources: BI *State*; *State of the Bristol Dispensary*; Beaven, *Bristol lists*, 138-65

Despite their public visibility and their strategies for raising money the voluntary associations depended ultimately on persuasion alone. This raises a series of questions about their financing. Was the annual subscription reliable or were diverse income sources always required? What factors determined popular enthusiasm for donation to a particular cause? Fashion? Concerns of specific age cohorts? Notions of social control? Was fundraising always hampered in years of poor economic performance, or did temporary surges of distress call forth greater generosity from philanthropists?

To assess the relationship between Bristol's fluctuating economic fortunes and charitable subscription/collection table 25 presents income trends in the Infirmary, the Dispensary, the three Colston societies and the Gloucestershire Society. These may be set against the economic indicators collected in table 4 above. Up until 1810 the increasing income levels were in line with a generally prosperous phase. Between 1811 and 1815 they continued to rise (apart from the Dispensary) while the economic indicators began to turn down, suggesting that heightened need did call forth more benevolence. This was partly related to the Infirmary's building works, and also perhaps to the use by the elite of the Colston and county charities to promote civic unity and patriotism during wartime.[10] However, in the 1816–20 phase subscription moved in line with the general shape of the city economy, falling almost across the board. It seems, then, that as recession deepened the charitable purses closed: the link between generosity and need was not sustained.

This failure of charity in the post-war slump casts light on the relationship between charity and social control – the claim that philanthropy was used at times to dampen down the flames of insurrection.[11] There is no doubt that the city leadership nursed real fears of 'the fury of the Bristol mob', and it may be that the slump led to a shift in spending away from established charities towards those with a greater 'social control' potential; this was when the PMFS emerged as the prominent relief organisation.[12] However, the logic of the social control thesis suggests subscriptions should also have risen in the charities considered here, given the channels of personal patronage offered by the medical charities' admission system, and the identification of the Colston and Gloucestershire societies with the civic elite. This is not to imply that a rhetoric of control was absent from charity appeals, nor that the charities played no part in socialisation.[13] It does suggest though that easy linkages between philanthropy and social control cannot be made.[14] In the

Yeo and Stephen Yeo (eds), *Popular culture and class conflict, 1590–1914: explorations in the history of labour and leisure*, London 1981, 187–208.

[10] Munro Smith, *Bristol Royal Infirmary*, 161–3.

[11] McCann, 'Popular education'; Whittle, 'Philanthropy in Preston', 14, 30–1, 46, 55, 76, 106–7, 198–9, 383.

[12] Letter to R. H. Crew, PRO, HO 41/223/12/1816; letter from Alderman Daniel, HO 42 155, 14–16; Whittle, 'Philanthropy in Preston', 106–7.

[13] *FFBJ*, 1 Jan., 12 Feb., 1814.

[14] F. M. L. Thompson, 'Social control in Victorian Britain', *EcHR* xxxiv (1981), 189–208.

era of 'demagogues and martyrs' Bristol voluntarism appears to have been restrained by the straitened circumstances of the time, and indeed this was a period in which very few new charities were actually founded. Of those voluntary groups which can be dated accurately, twenty were formed between 1811 and 1815, against three between 1816 and 1820. Charity income, then, could be vulnerable to economic downturns.

Henceforth the relationship between business cycle and charity income becomes increasingly erratic. Through the 1820s and 1830s the collections for the Colston/county societies broadly conformed to the pattern of the city economy, though they began to fall off before the the 1846 downturn. External factors were at work – for example, Tory in-fighting in the 1840s may explain the fall-off in collections for the Dolphin Society at this point. In the buoyant 1820s Infirmary subscription levels slipped back, probably a reflection of subscriber lethargy after the long phase of building work and the sustained income from legacies and investments.[15] The Dispensary's failure to increase subscriptions in the late 1830s can also be explained in these terms, as the decade was a particularly fortunate one for the receipt of legacies. Possibly the opening of the General Hospital diverted some funds away from the other two medical charities, both in the late 1830s, and 1850s, when economic indicators were generally favourable, although the Colston/county societies were equally flat. Conversely, Infirmary income fell off in the slump of the late 1860s, but the Dolphin and Anchor societies both enjoyed increases. It is occasionally possible to find coincidental leaps in peak years, such as the Infirmary subscription level rising by £700 in 1806, or conversely to detect moderate dips in tune with the business troughs, as in 1816. Where sizeable annual shifts occurred there was always an external reason. For example the massive decreases of the Colston/county societies in 1830–1 reflected the shock administered by the Reform Riots, which took place shortly before the annual feasts.[16] The big rise in Infirmary subscriptions in 1848–9 was the result of efforts to chase up accumulations of arrears.[17] Again, a huge leap in the Liberal Anchor Society collections in 1867–8 arose from political events: a Conservative by-election victory necessitated the wooing of the newly expanded electorate.[18]

All this indicates that individual charities had their own economic histories, sometimes quite divorced from the trade cycle. The range of different experiences societies might undergo may be illustrated by reference to smaller-scale initiatives directed at proselytising and relieving poverty, for which only partial series remain (table 26). The Samaritan Society illustrates the tendency of diminishing returns. After its launch in 1807, the society attracted a large sum in its first accounting year, no doubt reflecting its cross-

15 BRO 35893/21c.
16 Latimer, *Annals . . . nineteenth century*, 146–83.
17 BI *State*.
18 Latimer, *Annals . . . nineteenth century*, 439–40, 442.

sectional appeal to the city's elite and the presence of the eminent Richard Reynolds as treasurer.[19] From then on subscription income waned and annual reports regularly lamented the 'insufficiency of their resources' due to 'the decrease of annual subscribers from death and other causes'.[20] The society's failure to attract new subscribers owed much to faddishness, shaped initially by the social cachet of joining and by perceived efficacy, then later undermined by the counter-appeal of new ventures.

Charities that could rely on the efforts of particular congregations for their support base had a much firmer opportunity to plan their work, predict their level of activity, and if necessary mobilise for expansion. The core income of the Lewin's Mead Domestic Mission and the Working and Visiting Society was from annual subscriptions, which remained constant at a little over £100, and between £10 and £20 respectively, while the Unitarian congregation could also be tapped for extraordinary expenditure.[21] The Friends First Day School planned in the knowledge that local Quakers would maintain support for the venture. After small beginnings expansion followed in the 1840s when old legacy funds were used to buy and restore the Cutlers' Hall, at which point subscription levels rose to around £70 *per annum*. The security of this capital investment meant that surplus subscription monies could finance expenditures such as treats and prizes.[22] In contrast a society like the SPCK, which lacked a congregational mainstay, had extremely erratic income levels, dependent on such factors as the power of visiting speakers to evoke sympathy. The Anglican parish base of the Clifton Loan Blanket Society also permitted rising levels of support after a modest beginning. Subscribers were predominantly female, so perhaps as well as impressing prospective donors with competent management, it also exerted a social pull over Clifton ladies.[23] A more extreme illustration of charitable growth irrespective of external events is provided by George Muller's Scriptural Knowledge Institution. Expenditure on orphans rose from £1,664 in 1837–8, to £3,035 in 1851–2, to £8,022 in 1860–1, reaching £20,198 by 1869–70.[24] In 1846–7 'they went through the winter as easily as through any other from the beginning of the work', while another very successful phase was the late 1860s, also a time of difficulty for the city.[25] For Muller supporters 'deeds of charity were done in secret and without any show', while the emphasis on faith and the power of prayer offered donors the hope of a more direct channel to divine grace.[26]

[19] *Bristol Samaritan Society*, 1807.

[20] BRL, B4628, *Samaritan Society*, 1816; B4644, *Samaritan Society*, 1840.

[21] BRO 39461/S/2a, 1860.

[22] Naish, Fry and Sturge, *Some particulars*; BRO, SF/FD/AR/1a, 1839, 1844; SF/MM/6, 7 Mar. 1848.

[23] BRO, P/StAug/Soc/1a, b, Clifton Loan Blanket Society, minute books.

[24] *Autobiography of George Muller, or a million and a half in answer to prayer*, ed. G. Frederick Bergin, Bristol 1906, passim.

[25] Pierson, *George Muller*, 221.

[26] Ibid. 327, 440–5.

Table 26
Subscriptions to selected small charities, Bristol, 1808-70

Year	LMDMS	LMCWVS	Samaritan	Friends First Day	Loan Blanket	SPCK
1808			1,918			
1809			391			
1810			364			
1811			346			
1812			308			
1813			294			
1814			310			
1815						
1816			254			
1817			252			
1818						
1819			130			
1820			189			
1821			168			
1822			199			
1823			191			
1824			183			
1825			166			
1826			161			
1827						
1828			153			
1829			148			
1830			150			
1831			141	21		
1832				21		
1833			132	21		
1834				20		
1835		11	131	20		
1836		16		21		
1837		16		21		88
1838		16		21		433
1839		17		25		877
1840		21	93	25		564
1841		20		23		752
1842		20		23		913
1843		16		62		731
1844		16		58		1,090
1845		19		73		880
1846		18		69		
1847				86		
1848				70		
1849		19		60		
1850	80	16		54		
1851		16		49		
1852		17		49		
1853		14		56		
1854		14		57		
1855		13		65		
1856	93	14		62	88	
1857	100	14		63	38	
1858	103	17		78	52	
1859	109			79	69	
1860	106	16		64	81	
1861	529	15		72	71	

Year	LMDMS	LMCWVS	Samaritan	Friends First Day	Loan Blanket	SPCK
1862	104	16		74	90	
1863	101	16		86	65	
1864	148	17		74	62	
1865	159	20			76	
1866	115	16		78	91	
1867	114	17		67	135	
1868	114	28		70	137	
1869	111	17		106	156	
1870	120	18		72	161	

Sources: B7060-7 LMDMS *Annual Reports*; BRL B7054-9 LMCWVS *Annual Reports*; BRL B4621-44 *Reports of the Samaritan Society*; BRO SF/FD/AR/1a) Friends First Day School annual reports; BRO P/St Aug/Soc/1a),b) Minute booksof Clifton Loan Blanket Society; *FFBJ*, 25 Apr. 1846

Subscription income was therefore not dictated by the ebb and flow of the local business cycle; instead voluntary institutions had internal economic histories determined by a range of factors. This meant that if an enterprise was to survive and fulfil its purpose it had to secure more varied sources of funding, and this was the case in several of the charities discussed here. For example, the runs of accounts used in tables 25 and 26 show that Infirmary subscriptions supplied only 29 per cent of total income, those for the Dispensary 46 per cent, and for the Samaritan Society 42 per cent; only in the Domestic Mission did they provide more than half the income, with 57 per cent. Thus, despite the failure of its subscription base, the Samaritan Society survived, thanks to income from an old style endowment of property.[27] More typically a core sum was raised in collection and subscription, then supplemented by either donations alone or donations, legacies and income from stock.[28]

Bristol Infirmary provides the best example of mixed funding, and its income composition is shown for the period 1742–1870 in appendix 2. While subscription was almost always the largest single component of income, other sums came from sundry donations, from legacies, church collections and from investment of capital. Sundry donations included one-off benefactions, earnings from festivities, sums deposited in the poor-box, and even fines ordered by the courts: for instance in 1811 compensation was paid for an assault, and 'a fine on A.B. inflicted by the Mayor for imprudent conduct to a female'.[29] Securities initially took the same form as trustee investment of endowed charities (i.e. consols, Old South Sea annuities) though later the portfolio was expanded to include Corporation and railway company stock. In general

[27] Manchee i. 227–31; *Bristol Mercury*, 9 Dec. 1816.
[28] BRO 39461/S/2a, LMDMS; *State of Bristol Dispensary*.
[29] BI *State*, 1811.

Table 27
Private and institutional subscribers to the Bristol Infirmary, 1811-91

	1811		1821		1831		1841	
	no.	*£*	*no.*	*£*	*no.*	*£*	*no.*	*£*
	%	*%*	*%*	*%*	*%*	*%*	*%*	*%*
Private	85	82	81	78	79	76	81	79
Institutions:	16	18	19	23	21	25	19	21
Firms	*8*	*9*	*9*	*10*	*10*	*11*	*13*	*13*
Parish/	*3*	*3*	*5*	*8*	*6*	*9*	*0.3*	*3*
Corporation								
Other	*1*	*3*	*0*	*0*	*0*	*0*	*0*	*0*
Church	*4*	*3*	*5*	*5*	*5*	*5*	*5*	*5*
Private subscribers per 1,000 pop:	13		10		8		7	

Source: BI *State*

hospital trustees were not tied to specific terms of deeds or wills, though there were a few endowments made for a bed or ward, or in support of 'incurables'.[30] Projected running costs were therefore met by income from subscription, because patient and subscriber numbers were linked through the admissions system.[31] Additional income from donations and legacies could either be used to meet additional running costs, or invested to provide more current income or to accumulate for future building work: thus the total invested capital fluctuated from £22,855 in 1780, to £11,484 in 1795, £59,854 in 1837, £61,451 in 1851, to £28,422 in 1870.[32]

Three alterations to the structure of funding occurred during the period. Church collections had initially made a minor contribution, but fell into abeyance after the French wars, perhaps owing to the withdrawal of nonconformists in a period of sectional antagonism. They picked up again in the mid-century as Bristol politics became calmer, and grew more significant following the introduction in 1860 of 'Hospital Sunday', when all churches and chapels collected on the second Sunday of January, with the proceeds divided between the General and the Infirmary.[33] From the 1850s the category of 'workmen's collections' began to be separately recorded, although 'accumulative contributions in small sums' from factories and workplaces were first noted in 1846. By the end of the period these ranged from minor amounts,

---

[30] Munro Smith, *Bristol Royal Infirmary*, 202, 390-1, 414.
[31] BI *State*, 1842.
[32] Ibid.
[33] Munro Smith, *Bristol Royal Infirmary*, 332.

1851		1861		1871		1881		1891	
no.	£	no.	£	no.	£	no.	£	no.	£
%	%	%	%	%	%	%	%	%	%
79	75	77	72	73	66	68	65	70	66
21	26	23	28	28	34	32	36	30	36
15	17	18	21	21	25	25	26	22	23
0.3	3	1	3	1	4	1	4	1	5
1	1	0	1	1	1	1	2	3	4
5	5	4	3	5	4	5	4	4	4
7		5		4		3		3	

like the £1 1s. 5d. from Mangotsfield Pennant Stone Co., to the £20 from C Division City Police, to large subscriptions such as the £87 13s. 6d. from Bristol Wagon Works Co. Some firms kept their Infirmary box in their counting house, indicating that contributory schemes were encouraged by employers; the presence of trade unions and friendly societies suggests that they also sprang from the world of club-based mutual insurance.[34] The third change relates to the composition of the ordinary (i.e. not workmen) subscribers, shown in table 27. In the early nineteenth century the majority of these had been private persons, though around 20 per cent of subscription income came from institutions, mainly firms, parishes and the Church (assuming that a clergyman's subscription was pastoral commitment rather than individual benevolence). After the Poor Law Amendment parish subscriptions almost disappeared, presumably rendered redundant by the poor law medical service, but the contribution of firms continued to grow in terms of numbers and sums given. This was a long-run trend, and by the 1920s almost half the subscriptions were from institutions. Whether this is understood as a legacy of paternalism or as incipient welfare capitalism, in which employers effectively provided hospital insurance for their workforce, the key point is that the basis of organised support for the hospital was shifting from the private world of the home to the public world of work.[35]

Infirmary subscription data also permits consideration of the free rider

34 BI State, 1884; Bristol Mercury, 11, 18 Jan., 1868.
35 J. Melling, 'Welfare capitalism and the origins of the welfare states', Social History xvii (1992), 453–78.

problem. This is the tendency for people who could well afford to contribute to the financing of a collective good to leave the burden to be shouldered by their more generous neighbours. Table 27 shows the declining number of private, non-institutional subscribers per 1,000 population of the city, demonstrating clearly that the free rider effect occurred. The Infirmary was a large and heavily used charity, yet as the city grew, and with it the middle class who formed the pool of potential contributors, subscriber numbers remained fairly static. To a certain extent this was offset by the emergence of other medical charities, but given the service the Infirmary offered to both the city and the surrounding countryside, there can be no doubt that many who could afford to support it did not. Smaller fluctuations in subscriber numbers related to the intensity of appeals, with rises coinciding with phases of building work in the 1790s and early 1840s.[36] The success of the voluntary hospitals may have initially reflected strong support amongst local middle classes, but the breadth of individual commitment from the well-off was not sustained. To continue to expand their services the hospitals relied on a core of private subscribers and a small number of generous legators, and increasingly on funding from the Churches and the workplace, either in the form of workmen's contribution or employer's subscription. Nationally these trends became more marked in the late Victorian and Edwardian periods, with the spread of Hospital Sunday, Hospital Saturday and other workmen's contributory schemes.[37]

If the Infirmary solved its financial shortfalls through income diversification, the schools supplemented subscriber funding initially by the contribution of scholars themselves, then increasingly by that of the state. The rates of parental charge recorded in the local Statistical Society report of 1841 suggests the mean fee for a charity scholar was 1s. 3d., against 3s. 8d. for the dame schools and 7s. 5d. for the common day schools.[38] 'School pence' therefore covered about a third of the costs and philanthropic funding met the rest, so clearly the parental contribution counted for much more than a token gesture of commitment. Voluntary gifts by congregations or the National and British and Foreign Societies were also supplemented by the government education grant. This was of course quite negligible at first: Bristolians' individual spending on schooling in 1841, even exclusive of charity, was far in excess of the total United Kingdom education grant.[39] None the less the state had become a significant contributor well in advance of the 1870 Education Act. In 1845–7 Bristol schools received £469 for buildings and £646 for

---

36 Munro Smith, *Bristol Royal Infirmary*, 282.

37 Waddington, ' "Grasping gratitude" '; Steven Cherry, 'Beyond National Health Insurance: the voluntary hospitals and the hospital contributory schemes: a regional study', *Social History of Medicine* v (1992), 455–82.

38 A committe of the Statistical Society, Bristol, 'Statistics of education in Bristol', *Journal of the Statistical Society of London* iv (1841), 250–63.

39 Ibid. 255.

teachers and materials, rising by 1860 to £2,348 for teachers and £465 capitation.[40] Initially the policy was to supplement building funds raised by the National and British and Foreign Schools Societies, but Bristol schools equally took advantage of the offer to fund teaching and supply materials, although the latter was a small component, covering desks, books and maps.[41] More significant was the growth of the teaching grants, which provided either for augmentation of teachers' salaries, or payment for 'Apprentices and Teachers for their Instruction'. For example, by 1860 the Redcross Street British School received £66 capitation, and a teaching grant comprising £12 to certified teachers, £55 to assistant or probationary teachers, £223 15s. to pupil teachers, and £52 10s. 'gratuities' to masters and mistresses.[42]

There was therefore a marked growth of state spending from the late 1840s which supported the great expansion of voluntary schools in the mid-century by underwriting teaching costs and funding training. Only at the end of the century do Education Returns record the relative sums contributed from public and private sources, and by this time there is no doubt that the intervention of national and local government had reduced the need for charity.[43] Schools in poorer areas, particularly those with a track record of obtaining state funding, now subsisted almost entirely on government grants, with school pence still levied by a few.[44] For example, the Hannah More Schools gained grants of £1,201, with only £131 from school pence, and £9 contributions. Schools with endowed trusts had their grants reduced commensurately, which was unfortunate for the trustees of St Nicholas's and St Leonard's parish charities, who in 1858 secured a private act of parliament to abolish all their parish doles and devote the money instead to the school and the parish almshouses.[45] This well-intentioned manoeuvre effectively deprived the parishioners of more than half the income of their old endowments.

To summarise, it is not possible to discover a sustained relationship between funding levels and economic fluctuations.[46] The broader economic environment affected different charities in different ways and the Bristol evidence highlighted the importance of internal or 'institution-specific' factors in determining income and expenditure. These included the degree of capitalisation, reaction to other sources of funding, charismatic leadership, the

---

[40] *Schools aided by parliamentary grants* (p. clxxxvi), *school building grants* (pp. xl, xli), *grants for fittings apparatus books and maps* (p. lxxxiv), *annual grants payable from the parliamentary fund* (p. cxiv), PP 1850 xliii; *Return of the amount of education grants paid to each parish or place in the year 1860*, PP 1862 xliii.

[41] Ibid.

[42] Ibid. 18.

[43] *Return for each public school examined etc. for the year ended 31st. August 1893*, PP 1894 lxv. 186–9, 202–3.

[44] Ibid; Gorsky, 'Charity', 252 n. 69.

[45] *Bristol Mercury*, 17 July 1858.

[46] See also Sandra Cavallo, 'The motivations of benefactors: an overview of approaches to the study of charity', in Barry and Jones, *Medicine and charity*, 46–62 at p. 49.

215

social appeal of joining and public image. Institutions with a high level of capital in staff and buildings such as the hospitals and voluntary schools could not remain dependent on private subscribers in the long run. The initial investment of money and enthusiasm came from philanthropists but by the second half of the century these popular institutions became more distanced from the direct aspirations of the provincial middle-class voluntarists which had spawned them.

The weaknesses of voluntarism as a means of providing sustained, reliable funding were also apparent to contemporaries. Trends in fundraising fashions and the fluctuating popularity of particular causes were of great importance, as witnessed by the enthusiasm for establishing women's committees if one were to vie successfully with the competition. Some regarded the 'marketing' aspect of philanthropy with disdain: 'Excitement, probably, had something to do with it, and it might be fashion, for whenever Dame Fashion could be brought to patronise an institution it was sure to do', lamented the Revd Luke, in a year of failing support for the Deaf and Dumb Institute.[47] Competition for the philanthropic gift was eloquently attacked by John Addington Symonds when he compared the £7,000 given to foreign missions with the £772 donated to the General Hospital's rebuilding campaign in 1858: 'We are so liberal and beneficent that we can fling our largess [sic] broadcast towards those far-off sable and tawny races, . . . and we comparatively overlook our own brethren.' The General, by contrast, had 'few novelties connected with it. No striking recital of romantic enterprise and daring adventures; no interesting pictures of strange races and curious customs; no terrific descriptions of savage cruelties and hideous abominations of devil-worship . . . no ladies auxiliaries; no juvenile collectors'.[48]

Not only did Symonds puncture the rhetoric with which missionary charities played on British imaginations of the foreign, rather as Dickens had ridiculed 'telescopic philanthropy' five years before. He also laid bare the way in which, by its very nature, voluntary subscription acted against long-term provision and informed debate over priorities of public spending.

Evaluating outcomes

How successful were voluntary charities in dealing with the problems which they set out to tackle? They themselves regularly trumpeted their achievement, but crude figures of growing numbers of recipients leave much unsaid. For example, in 1840 John B. Estlin treated 2,151 patients at his Eye Dispensary, the majority of whom suffered ophthalmia, inflammation of the cornea,

---

47 *Bristol Mercury*, 19 June 1858; *Bristol Gazette*, 15 Sept. 1836; *FFBJ* 12 Sept. 1846; Simey, *Charity rediscovered*, 56, 82–3.
48 *Bristol Mercury*, 8 May 1858; Charles Dickens, *Bleak House*, London 1853.

inflammation of the lids, or defective vision.[49] A scrapbook of letters to Estlin from grateful patients leaves no doubt of his capacity to transform people's lives for the better.[50] However, his rate of success is not recorded, and even if it were almost complete several questions would still remain. How well did the Eye Dispensary cater to the needs of the poor in its catchment? Did it treat patients who might otherwise have been able to obtain the same service from the market? How did the reputation as an ophthalmic surgeon which Estlin's voluntary work conferred, benefit his private practice? In this section several outcomes of philanthropic endeavour will be analysed, starting with the relationship between provision and need.

At the outset the localism and independence of voluntary organisations allowed them to develop their services without the financial and bureaucratic burden that a commitment to comprehensiveness entailed. However, their idiosyncratic features, such as the capacity of a given locale to finance charity and the contingent role of individuals in generating support, make the geographical unevenness of provision a likely development. This can be demonstrated in the case of the voluntary hospitals. Table 28 examines ratios of beds and in-patients to population in towns with county borough status for 1891, the first point at which robust comparative hospital statistics for towns can be gathered.[51] This indicates a considerable range of bed provision, with twenty-two towns above the mean and thirty-six below. The situation in some of the under-hospitalled places may not be as drastic as the figures suggest, given the proximity of towns like South Shields, St Helens and Oldham to large cities. However the capacity of sick people to travel even comparatively small distances to use services elsewhere should not be overestimated, and this is especially true of accidents and emergencies.[52] Bristol was above the national average in both cases, ranking tenth with respect to bed provision and eighth for in-patient utilisation. Of course, the latter indicator is not an accurate gauge of need, as admissions might also vary according to length of stay regulations and the ability of medical staff to admit patients without recommendation. None the less from this crude survey it seems that while voluntary hospital provision remained highly uneven in 1891, Bristol was one of the better served English cities. This was most probably due to the strong medical culture that the teaching hospitals had fostered in the town, coupled with the wealth that had enabled philanthropists to build up institutions over the past 150 years.

If it was comparatively well-served, was it healthier? Scepticism about the

---

49 Papers of J. B. and Mary Estlin, box 3, *Dispensary for the Cure of Complaints in the Eyes: twenty-eighth annual report, for the year 1840*, p. 1.
50 Ibid. box 1.
51 I thank John Mohan and Martin Powell of the Leverhulme-funded project 'The historical geography of the voluntary hospital system in Britain, 1890–1947', based at the University of Portsmouth, for providing the data.
52 Urban hinterlands: W. T. R. Pryce, 'Towns and their regional settings', in W. T. R. Pryce (ed.), *From family history to community history*, Cambridge 1994, 131–8.

Table 28
Hospital provision and utilisation in English county boroughs, 1891

Borough	Beds	In-patients per 1,000 persons	Borough	Beds	In-patients per 1,000 persons
Exeter	7.2	48.8	Birmingham	1.3	19.4
Bath	6.1	55.0	Coventry	1.2	10.4
Gloucester	4.6	34.1	Birkenhead	1.2	4.9
Canterbury	4.6	33.5	Sheffield	1.2	10.2
Chester	4.0	25.1	Halifax	1.1	9.7
Oxford	3.7	37.7	Nottingham	1.1	12.0
Wolverhampton	3.1	29.9	Grimsby	1.1	6.2
Worcester	2.8	29.3	Leeds	1.1	15.5
Norwich	2.6	18.4	Huddersfield	1.0	9.2
Bristol	**2.6**	**30.1**	Preston	1.0	11.2
Northampton	2.6	30.4	Kingston-upon-Hull	1.0	10.2
Lincoln	2.5	20.6	Great Yarmouth	0.9	8.6
Reading	2.5	21.4	Cardiff	0.9	10.4
Wigan	2.4	21.4	Bolton	0.9	8.3
Liverpool	2.2	71.4	Newport	0.9	7.5
Brighton	2.1	26.8	Burnley	0.9	7.4
Newcastle	2.1	22.6	West Bromwich	0.9	12.1
Bootle	2.1	16.8	Stockport	0.9	9.6
York	2.1	18.7	Portsmouth	0.8	6.4
Ipswich	1.9	11.7	Blackburn	0.7	12.6
Dudley	1.8	13.6	Bury	0.7	5.1
Plymouth	1.8	15.5	Barrow-in-Furness	0.7	4.2
Sunderland	1.8	16.8	Salford	0.6	7.0
Middlesborough	1.7	6.2	Oldham	0.6	5.4
Southampton	1.7	18.3	Walsall	0.6	6.9
Manchester	1.6	17.4	St. Helens	0.5	3.6
Derby	1.6	13.9	Croydon	0.5	4.9
Bradford	1.5	11.3	Rochdale	0.4	3.0
Hastings	1.4	8.1	South Shields	0.3	2.4
Leicester	1.4	17.4	Gateshead	0.0	0.0
Swansea	1.3	12.4	West Ham	0.0	0.0
			Mean	**1.7**	**16.1**

Sources: Henry C. Burdett, *Burdett's hospitals and charities: the yearbook of philanthropy and hospital annual*, London 1893; Census, 1891

contribution of voluntary institutions to public health has been well ingrained in the historiography since Thomas McKeown's famous attack on works which attributed declining mortality to the advance of medical science; instead he pointed to the importance of improved sanitation and, crucially, rising nutritional standards.[53] Subsequent interventions refined this view with closer attention to variations of regional experience and of particular diseases, stressing in some cases the role of sewerage and fresh water, in others improvement in housing, or differing migration patterns, or the impact of controls on food and milk.[54] Accusations that cross-infection made the hospitals 'gateways to death' date back at least to Florence Nightingale's claims in the 1870s; subsequent work on recorded hospital death rates has shown they were not excessive, but some historians remain highly critical of hospital practice.[55]

Did Bristol's hospitals have an impact on mortality levels? In the mid nineteenth century Bristol city centre was one of the nation's more dangerous areas. Registration records of the city's mortality began in the 1840s, when out of 623 registration districts in England and Wales, only five had a mortality rate as high as Bristol's, and only seven exceeded it.[56] A significant reduction of mortality occurred from the 1870s when the city reduced the mean decadal death rate of 29 in the 1860s to 25.5, but this was still well in excess of the mean for England and Wales of 21.3.[57] As appendix 2 shows, while this stubbornly high mortality rate persisted the Infirmary gradually increased its in-patient capacity and quadrupled its out-patient attendances. So, despite the 'number, magnitude, and diversity of [Bristol's] benevolent institutions' which 'provide relief for almost every description of distress, sickness &c.', and its particularly favourable ratio of doctors to head of population, its citizens' health remained comparatively poor.[58] Another measure is infant death rates, and here again it appears that the dispensaries and the various Dorcas and lying-in societies were unable to ameliorate exceptional mortality: in 1845 the death rate per 1,000 live births of Bristol children under one year

---

53 Thomas McKeown, *The modern rise of population*, London 1976, 13–14 and ch. v.
54 Robert Woods and John Woodward (eds), *Urban disease and mortality in nineteenth century England*, London 1984; Simon Szreter, 'The importance of social intervention in Britain's mortality decline, *c.* 1850–1914: a re-interpretation of the role of public health', *Social History of Medicine* i (1988), 1–37; Anne Hardy, *The epidemic streets: infectious diseases and the rise of preventive medicine, 1856–1900*, Oxford 1993; Anthony S. Wohl, *Endangered lives*, London 1983; David Large and Frances Round, *Public health in mid-Victorian Bristol*, Bristol 1974.
55 Florence Nightingale, *Notes on lying-in institutions*, London 1871; Woodward, *To do the sick no harm*, chs x, xi; F. B. Smith, *The people's health, 1830–1910*, London 1979, 249–84.
56 *Supplement to the twenty-fifth annual report of the Registrar-General of Births, Deaths and Marriages in England*, London 1864, pp. xxxviii–lvi. Rates in Clifton and Bedminster districts were closer to county means.
57 *Supplement to the forty-fifth annual report of the Registrar-General of Births, Deaths and Marriages in England*, London 1885, pp. lxviii–lxxxiii, at p. lxxvii.
58 *Matthews's directory 1831, 1841*; Loudon, *Medical care*, appendices iv, v.

Table 29
Deaths from different causes in Bristol, Clifton and Bedminster, 1851-80, showing mortality rates and total deaths

Cause of Death:	1851-60						1861-70						1871-80					
	Bristol		Clifton		Bedminster		Bristol		Clifton		Bedminster		Bristol		Clifton		Bedminster	
	rate	total	rate	total	rate	total	rate	total	rate	total	rate	total	rate	total	rate	total	rate	total
Attributable to micro-organisms																		
Airborne																		
Diphtheria	0.07	48	0.07	61	0.06	22	0.18	119	0.10	113	0.13	60	0.11	65	0.07	96	0.09	56
Measles	0.55	361	0.53	457	0.42	168	0.73	467	0.52	583	0.48	229	0.4	239	0.43	631	0.37	226
Phthisis	3.22	2,123	2.55	2,204	1.97	782	2.84	1,830	2.30	2,560	1.77	841	2.49	1,493	2.13	3,130	1.57	950
Scarlet fever	0.99	649	0.89	765	0.92	366	1.27	819	1.22	1,361	0.85	406	0.63	377	0.59	872	0.85	517
Small-pox	0.40	266	0.20	175	0.27	109	0.24	152	0.21	238	0.16	78	0.21	124	0.19	282	0.13	77
Whooping cough	0.57	376	0.44	377	0.42	166	0.70	448	0.53	590	0.43	204	0.53	317	0.53	780	0.59	355
	5.80		**4.68**		**4.06**		**5.96**		**4.89**		**3.82**		**4.37**		**3.94**		**3.60**	
Water/food borne																		
Cholera, diarrhoea, dysentry	1.30	859	1.28	1,101	0.72	286	1.16	746	0.97	1,077	0.67	317	0.93	558	0.78	1,130	0.76	456
Enteric fever							0.33	213	0.34	380	0.32	152	0.36	219	0.32	465	0.32	195
Hydrocephalus	0.36	236	0.32	276	0.29	114	0.48	310	0.34	380	0.36	170	0.34	202	0.43	634	0.34	204
Scrofula, Tabes Mesenterica	0.63	417	0.47	406	0.30	118							0.36	216	0.37	545	0.35	209
	2.30		**2.07**		**1.30**		**1.97**		**1.65**		**1.34**		**1.99**		**1.90**		**1.77**	
Other infectious																		
Other infections	0.89	589	0.60	517	0.68	270	0.60	383	0.40	444	0.46	217	0.07	42	0.06	87	0.06	39
Puerperal fever													0.04	24	0.03	86	0.21	125
Simple continued fever	0.97	642	0.84	729	0.79	313	0.93	599	0.83	921	0.71	336	0.03	20	0.04	58	0.03	21
Typhus																		
	1.87		**1.44**		**1.47**		**1.53**		**1.23**		**1.16**		**0.14**		**0.13**		**0.30**	

Non-attributable to micro-organisms

Diseases																		
Urinary	0.42	277	0.22	192	0.24	97	0.55	353	0.31	348	0.34	163	0.72	432	0.39	575	0.44	265
Circulatory	1.49	979	1.10	946	1.22	485	1.38	891	1.15	1,278	1.27	602	1.64	986	1.21	1,856	1.4	843
Digestive	1.08	714	0.93	800	1.10	436	1.07	689	0.80	888	0.90	427	1.04	627	0.81	1,194	0.81	489
Generative	0.08	54	0.08	71	0.06	22	0.08	51	0.07	73	0.08	36	0.11	68	0.05	67	0.05	32
Nervous system	3.05	2,008	2.57	2,219	2.59	1,030	2.88	1,850	2.79	3,113	2.57	1,223	3.03	1,822	2.78	4,092	2.02	1,591
Respiratory	4.79	3,158	3.80	3,283	3.36	1,333	4.79	3,079	3.69	4,105	3.61	1,717	5.23	3,142	3.63	5,333	3.87	2,347
	10.92		**8.70**		**8.57**		**10.74**		**8.80**		**8.76**		**11.77**		**8.87**		**8.59**	

Miscellaneous

Cancer	0.52	340	0.31	270	0.34	133	0.54	345	0.45	498	0.36	173	0.56	334	0.47	688	0.46	281
Childbirth	0.15	100	0.10	88	0.13	50	0.13	85	0.13	142	0.17	83	0.1	58	0.09	133	0.08	47
Other causes	5.24	3,450	3.29	2,844	3.34	1,327	4.51	2,902	3.93	4,381	3.61	1,719	4.96	2,984	4.17	6,156	4.27	2,601
Suicide	0.00	0	0.00	0	0.00	0	0.08	49	0.05	53	0.07	31	0.11	68	0.05	78	0.06	35
Violence	1.44	948	0.40	344	0.62	248	1.45	934	0.33	366	0.63	299	1.51	909	0.35	514	0.62	374
	7.34		**4.11**		**4.43**		**6.71**		**4.88**		**4.85**		**7.24**		**5.13**		**5.49**	
Mortality rate from all causes	**28.23**		**21.00**		**19.84**		**26.91**		**21.45**		**19.94**		**25.51**		**20.04**		**20.35**	

Note: The mean populations recorded by the Registrar-General are the means of populations enumerated in the census at the beginning and end of the decade surveyed

Sources: *Supplement to the twenty-fifth annual report*; *Supplement to the thirty-fifth annual report of the Registrar-General of Births, Deaths and Marriages in England*, London 1875; *Supplement to the forty-fifth annual report*

was 160, compared to 142 nationally, rising by 1875 to 173 compared to 158.[59] Possibly the charities' tendency to encourage childbirth attendance by doctors rather than midwives added to the danger when the delivery did not go smoothly.[60]

A closer examination of changing death rates by cause strongly suggests that the improving health of Bristolians was linked to action by local government, which followed the establishment in 1851 of the Corporation's Sanitary Committee after the 1849 cholera epidemic. Table 29 compares cause of death over three decades, 1851–80, in Bristol, Clifton and Bedminster, showing both the total number of deaths and the rate per thousand living. Subtotals are given for infectious diseases according to mode of transmission, while non-communicable diseases are also subdivided by organ and miscellaneous causes.[61] The problems of disease classification and the poor reliability of the Registrar-General's data are well known, but with these reservations in mind two patterns stand out.[62] Deaths from non-communicable disease rose slightly over the sequence, though only the increase in kidney disease and respiratory affliction is notable. However, Bristol, Clifton and Bedminster experienced a steady fall in mortality from diseases spread by micro-organisms, and it is to this that we must look to explain the downward trend in mortality over the time series. In 1861–70 the most noticeable drop was in the categories of water/food-borne disease and other infections; the latter is likely to have included enteric fever, which was only listed separately for 1871–80, so the fall in this category is probably understated. This coincided with the Corporation's extensive programme of arterial sewer building, begun in 1855 and continuing into the next decade with the ongoing connections of house drains to the main sewer.[63] The 1870s witnessed significant reductions in mortality from airborne infection and from typhus in the three districts, while in Bristol itself the decline in deaths from measles and scarlet fever was marked, though whooping cough and phthisis (tuberculosis) diminished more gradually, despite the population outflow. Again improvements coincided with local government activity following the appointment of Dr David Davies as the city's first Medical Officer of Health in 1865. Davies was strongly influenced by another Bristol doctor, William Budd (surgeon at the Infirmary from 1847 to 1862), who is credited along with John Snow with the discovery of the mode of transmission of cholera, and was a leading proponent of preventive disinfection. A proactive approach was adopted, with sanitary inspectors isolating typhus cases and disinfecting their dwellings with chloride of lime, and also pressurising the Sanitary Committee into a

59 *Annual report of the Registrar-General*, 1845, 254–7; 1875, 134–5.
60 Smith, *People's health*, 55, ch. i passim.
61 McKeown, *Modern rise*, ch. iii.
62 Ibid. 53; Anne Hardy, ' "Death is the cure of all diseases": using the General Register Office cause of death statistics for 1837–1920', *Social History of Medicine* vii (1994), 477–80.
63 Large and Round, *Public health*, 5–7; Latimer, *Annals . . . nineteenth century*, 315–16.

more authoritarian stance against landlords who failed to provide adequate privies with main sewer outflows.[64] Even the fight against smallpox, acknowledged as one area in which medical intervention was potentially effective, cannot be regarded as a great success – there were 550 smallpox deaths in the city and suburbs in 1851–60, and 483 in 1871–80.[65]

Evaluation of the voluntary hospitals' impact on the health of their locale is therefore problematic. Certainly, the pre-Listerian hospital in Bristol provides a good deal of anecdotal evidence for a critical verdict: for example, the vulnerability of staff and inmates to 'hospital fever' (typhus) and erysipelas, the surgeon, clad in germ-ridden gown, smoking a cigar above the operating table, the out-patients made to endure long waits and abrupt manners, and the enthusiasm of some practitioners for bleeding and cupping, which persisted well into the nineteenth century.[66] On the other hand it could be argued that both the expansion of the voluntary hospitals and the in-patient utilisation rates indicated a real demand for their services. Nor are aggregate mortality rates of direct use in assessing hospital efficacy; most of the voluntaries did not admit infectious cases, while the chronic sickness of the aged was seen as the province of the poor-law infirmaries and workhouse sick wards.[67] The hospitals' own statistics for treatment outcomes are no more helpful since discharged patients were usually classified vaguely as 'cured' or 'relieved', revealing nothing of subsequent readmissions or the completeness of the cure.[68] Historians who have closely studied cases and outcomes argue that the voluntary hospital benefited the communities they served in various ways. First, they isolated them from contagion. Second, they offered a recuperative space where in-patients received care, bed-rest, warmth, regular food and a protected environment – vital for common complaints such as leg-ulcers and rheumatism. Third, hospital surgeons had valuable skills, in the early days performing difficult operations such as lithotomy and trephination, and by the last quarter of the nineteenth century successfully carrying out a whole range of procedures; some of the more frequent ones were herniotomy, removal of cataracts, treatment of necrosis and caries and the excision of malignant tumours.[69] Finally, they also offered training which was to bear fruit in scientific advances in the twentieth century, their medical men

---

[64] Large and Round, *Public health*, 16–20; Munro Smith, *Bristol Royal Infirmary*, 354.

[65] McKeown, *Modern rise*, 11–13, 99.

[66] Munro Smith, *Bristol Royal Infirmary*, 54–5, 125, 160, 198–9, 303, 305, 341; *Bristol Royal Infirmary reports*, I: 1878–9, Bristol 1879, 246.

[67] Robert Pinker, *English hospital statistics, 1861–1938*, London 1966, ch. xiii.

[68] BI *State*, passim.

[69] S. Cherry, 'The role of the provincial hospital: the Norfolk and Norwich Hospital, 1771–1880', *Population Studies* xxvi (1972); Guenter B. Risse, *Hospital life in Enlightenment Scotland: care and teaching at the Royal Infirmary of Edinburgh*, Cambridge 1986, epilogue; Boss, 'Bristol Infirmary'; Mary Fissell, 'The "sick and drooping poor" in eighteenth-century Bristol and its region', *Social History of Medicine* ii (1989), 35–58; *BRI Reports*, i. 245–308; BI *State*, passim.

Table 30

Illiteracy, school attendance and population growth in selected large towns

	% Illiterate		% of scholars to total population, 1851							Growth rate of population	
				By category of school:							
	1850	1866	Total	Public	Private	Endowed	Voluntary	Other	Sunday	1801-51	1851-81
Brighton	21	12	13.55	7.31	6.24	0.07	5.49	1.47	4	943	164
Bath	23	17	13.87	10.26	3.61	0.36	8.72	0.65	7	164	96
Hull	27	21	12.05	6.01	6.04	0.29	4.91	0.38	6	283	181
Plymouth	30	21	9.23	5.21	4.03	0.42	2.41	2.13	6	225	137
Newcastle-upon-Tyne	33	23	10.35	6.07	4.28	1.46	3.71	0.54	5	267	165
Bristol	29	23	13.27	8.65	4.62	1.00	5.91	1.74	9	225	151
Norwich	31	24	11.38	7.64	3.74	0.78	6.27	0.52	7	189	129
Leicester	39	26	9.23	6.14	3.09	0.17	4.89	0.95	10	359	200
Nottingham	40	26	10.32	5.80	4.52	0.63	4.61	0.37	9	197	328
Leeds	40	29	12.67	7.65	5.03	0.51	5.65	1.21	10	325	180
Manchester	46	31	8.65	5.34	3.31	0.16	4.95	0.20	11	404	113
Birmingham	40	32	9.53	5.60	3.93	0.71	4.27	0.50	7	328	172
Liverpool	41	33	12.07	9.36	2.71	0.34	6.91	0.88	4	459	147
Sunderland	35	33	11.81	5.43	6.38	1.27	3.72	0.38	8	267	183
Sheffield	43	34	11.54	6.90	4.64	1.04	5.56	0.21	8	293	211
Salford	31	38	8.21	5.25	2.96	0.00	5.25	0.00	10	457	275
Bradford	59	38	9.23	5.73	3.50	0.12	4.29	1.32	14	800	176
Bolton	62	41	9.78	6.40	3.39	0.65	5.41	0.33	18	339	172
Oldham	65	41	7.64	3.77	3.88	0.52	2.64	0.46	16	442	209
Stockport	53	43	8.44	2.12	6.32	0.00	0.25	1.70	17	318	111
Preston	57	46	11.04	7.64	3.40	0.21	7.13	0.03	12	583	139

Sources: *Census of Great Britain 1851: education,* report and tables; Stephens, *Education, literacy and society*, appendix k

played a part in public health initiatives, and the public profile of their doctors helped erode the cultural barriers of distrust of official intervention- ism by local Medical Officers of Health.[70]

The statistics of the Registrar of Births, Marriages and Deaths can also offer an indication of the efficacy of educational charity through the informa- tion they yield on literacy rates, measured by the annual percentage of brides and grooms able to sign the marriage register.[71] Here the relationship between the goals of the charity and the measurable outcome is clearer than in the case of the hospital and mortality, even if the motivation was not to cultivate literacy *per se* as much as 'an intimate acquaintance with the Scrip- tures'.[72] In England and Wales the level of illiteracy fell from 41 per cent in 1840–1, to 24 per cent in 1870, to 8 per cent in 1890, while Bristol's experi- ence was rather better than the nation as a whole: 34 per cent in 1840–1, 19 per cent in 1870, and 7 per cent in 1890.[73] Given the city's impressive number of educational foundations in the nineteenth century, does this con- stitute a vindication of charity? Table 30 sets Bristol's experience against that of twenty-one large English towns for which schooling data was recorded in the 1851 education census. The literacy levels in 1850 and 1866 are shown, the first date coinciding with the census, and the second to show the situa- tion some fifteen years after, when the cohort at school at the time of the enumeration was appearing in the marriage registers.[74] This is also put in the context of longer-term population movements, with growth rates shown for the early and mid-century. The remaining columns compare levels of atten- dance, showing the percentage of scholars recorded in the census as a propor- tion of the town's population, broken first into total day schools, then public and private schools. The next three columns disaggregate the public schools into endowed and voluntary establishments, while the 'other' category takes in ragged schools, orphan asylums, institutions for the disabled, and so on; Sunday scholars are shown in the final column.

Bristol was one of the more literate towns, amongst which there is a strong showing of England's old established urban centres, while the least literate places are those northern industrial towns whose rapid growth took off only in the eighteenth and nineteenth centuries. Rate of population growth

---

[70] John Woodward, 'Medicine and the city: the nineteenth-century experience', in Woods and Woodward, *Urban disease*, 65–78 at p. 77; Hardy, *Epidemic streets*, conclusion.
[71] Sanderson, *Education, economic change and society*, ch. i; Lawrence Stone, 'Literacy and education in England, 1640–1900', *P&P* xlii (1969), 69–139, David Vincent, *Literacy and popular culture in England, 1750–1914*, Cambridge 1989, 73–94; R. S. Schofield, 'Dimen- sions of illiteracy, 1750–1850', *Explorations in Economic History* x (1973), 437–57; W. B. Stephens, *Education, literacy and society, 1830–70*, Manchester 1987.
[72] *Bristol Gazette*, 30 June 1836, Diocesan school report.
[73] *Annual report of the Registrar-General*, passim. Bristol includes Clifton and Bedminster.
[74] School-age: Beryl Madoc Jones, 'Patterns of attendance and their social significance: Mitcham National School 1830–1839', in McCann, *Popular education*, 41–66 at 50–1; N. L. Tranter, *Population and society, 1750–1940*, London 1985, 52.

appears to be an important factor in the success or failure of urban educational efforts, with slower growth rates before 1851 shown by those towns
where literacy was greater. There are anomalies such as Brighton, with an
illiteracy level almost half the national average alongside substantial population increase, and Nottingham whose expansion was more moderate before
the mid-century, but whose illiteracy rates just exceeded those of the country
as a whole. Slowing rates of population increase after 1851 might coincide
with rising literacy between 1851 and 1866 (Manchester), or relative stagna-
tion (Liverpool), or a failure to improve ranking against other towns with
increased growth (Stockport, Preston); rising population rates after 1851
might correspond with a slip in literacy ranking (Salford), but also might not
(Newcastle). Bristol was one of those towns, like Bath, Leeds, Plymouth, Birmingham and Manchester, whose success in educating its citizens seems
likely to have been related in part to its demographic experience. It ranked
fourth on the literacy scale in 1850, having enjoyed the fourth lowest rate of
population growth up to 1851; by 1866 it had slipped back one place in the
ranking, as it numbers started to increase at a faster pace.

Illiteracy was also influenced by the extent of day school provision. Three
of the four most literate towns in 1850, one of which was Bristol, were
amongst the four towns with the best ratios of scholars to population, while
the most illiterate town of the sample, Oldham, also had the lowest number
of day scholars. Again, anomalies abound, such as those with good ratios of
scholars to population (Leeds and Liverpool) hampered by their rates of
demographic increase from translating provision into literacy ranking. The
relative importance of public and private education does not appear to have
been an important issue. High levels of public schooling might coincide with
high literacy rankings (Bristol, Bath and Norwich), or they might not (Liverpool). Lower levels of public provision (Hull, Plymouth) could co-exist with
lower illiteracy. By the same token, private schooling appears to have been
significant to achievement in some areas (Brighton, Hull), but not in others
(Stockport, Sheffield), although since this category embraced everything
from expensive academies to dame schools it is difficult to assess in detail.
Again, Bristol was comparatively well-served by its private sector.

Breaking down the public schools into their constituent categories isolates
the voluntary schools as a contributary force to literacy. The rankings reveal
no consistent correlation between high levels of denominational schooling
and high levels of literacy. Charity schools could be important (Bath, Bristol,
Norwich), but other areas which were well-served by the voluntary sector
(Preston, Liverpool) were lower on the literacy scale: in Preston, for example,
illiteracy levels ran at 57 per cent in 1850 and 46 per cent in 1866, more than
15 per cent above the national average. Nor did the more literate towns necessarily have a high level of scholars in voluntary schools, as Plymouth and
Newcastle-upon-Tyne demonstrate. Cities with more substantial proportions
of endowed scholars (Bristol and Newcastle) enjoyed an additional benefit
in the combination of factors contributing to literacy, but as Sheffield's

226

experience shows, the numbers were too small to be instrumental. A similar verdict must be reached for 'others', although it is interesting that three of the five most literate towns were well-provided in this respect – Brighton, like Bristol, was well-served with ragged schools, and Plymouth had two large non-religious subscription schools. Finally, there was a close inverse relationship between numbers of Sunday scholars and literacy ranking, to the extent that the six towns with the highest illiteracy were also the six with the highest Sunday school ratios. This suggests the importance of regional variations in work, and the influence of child labour and occupational concerns on the aspiration to literacy. In the textile towns, where industrialisation had increased the opportunities for children to contribute a wage to the family budget, the thirst for education during leisure time was slaked by the Sunday schools, yet they were unable to raise literacy levels significantly.[75] The inverse relationship between day and Sunday scholars seen elsewhere was less pronounced in Bristol, perhaps reflecting the strength of nonconformity and the nature of the child labour market. A comparison between selected large English towns therefore shows that the extent of voluntary schooling available was not the key determinant of a town's success in educating its citizens. The overall proportion of day scholars appears to have been of greater significance to literacy than the proportion in public schools, and the extent of child labour (indicated by Sunday school attendance) more important than rates of population growth. Other salient forces not captured here were migration patterns, the age structure of the town, popular perceptions of the utility of literacy for work, political awareness and leisure, and differing attitudes to girls' and boys' schooling.[76]

In Bristol then, charity was just one of several favourable agents contributing to effective education. Relatively slow population growth allowed day-school provision to keep pace with demand, older endowed schools supported the contribution of the newer charities, and there was also a strong private sector role. Anecdotal evidence points to the strong popular aspirations to literacy for work and leisure among Bristol artisans, and a study linking literacy with occupation has confirmed this.[77] Campbell's analysis of St Philip and St Jacob's marriage registers between 1840 and 1890 demonstrates that literacy was higher in occupations like trades and services, woodwork and engineering, where education had a functional utility. By contrast, masons and unskilled workers, who lacked either functional or cultural motivation

---

[75] Stephens, Education, literacy and society, 26–7, 38–9.

[76] Idem, 'Literacy studies: a survey', in W. B. Stephens (ed.), Studies in the history of literacy: England and North America, Leeds 1983, 2–3.

[77] Newcastle Commission: Reports of the Royal Commisson of Popular Education, PP 1861 xxi II p. 21; John Bennet, untitled manuscript, 2, 11; Revd Edmund Butcher, An excursion from Sidmouth to Chester, London 1805, 72–3; LMDMS, 12th annual report, 1851, 14–15.

were only pushed towards full literacy by the compulsory trends in local schooling at the end of the century.[78]

Does this artisan approval of education provide qualitative evidence for the success of Bristol charity schooling which the quantitative method cannot catch? Not necessarily, for as Philip Gardner has persuasively argued in a study based on Bristol, the extent and efficacy of working-class private schools has been under-estimated by historians swayed by the writings of Victorian officials intent on denigrating the reputation of 'dame-schooling'.[79] The expansion of charity schooling in the city occurred at the expense of cheap private venture schools and this may even have had a detrimental effect.[80] In the suburb of Bedminster, where, by contrast, the proportion of private scholars had increased in the 1850s, literacy rose faster than in both the city and Clifton.[81] This hints, in line with Gardner's claims, that the teaching in the more intimate dame schools was equally effective.[82] Lastly there was a substantial number of children of school age (5–15 years) who did not attend any establishment, the proportion falling from 40 per cent in 1841, to 34 per cent in 1851, to 19 per cent in 1871.[83] And, as shown in the discussion of funding, the charity schools' heyday as providers was brief; they were soon superseded by board schools and only then were regional and occupational pockets of illiteracy eradicated.[84]

The limitations of philanthropy were plain enough to its practitioners. As Bristol's Unitarian domestic missionary observed in 1841: 'Until (employment) is secured, and that too in a way which does not imply social degradation, every other means will be proportionately ineffectual.'[85] Inevitably then the contribution of the voluntary sector towards social improvement was as one of a range of factors – among them regional economic variation, demographic change, the standard of living and the intervention of local or national government. Its achievement was its ability to develop new forms of social intervention and to win them public support. However voluntary societies and institutions faced difficulties in securing reliable funding sources, due to such problems as the free rider tendency and the faddishness of subscribers. Long-term survival might be achieved by various different

---

[78] John Campbell, 'Occupation and literacy in Bristol and Gloucestershire, 1755–1870', in Stephens, Studies in the history of literacy.

[79] Gardner, Lost elementary schools.

[80] Gorsky, 'Charity', 326.

[81] Ibid. 260 n. 92; Newcastle Commission, iii. 82, cited in Stephens, Education, literacy and society, 255.

[82] Gardner, Lost elementary schools, ch. v.

[83] 1841: 'Statistics of education in Bristol', 256; 1851: 1851 Census: population, education; 1871: BRO, Bristol School Board, minute book no. 1, Bristol School Board Educational Census, 56.

[84] Stephens, Education, literacy and society, conclusion.

[85] LMDMS, 2nd annual report, 1841, p. 5.

means depending on the nature of the charity. Missions and proselytising groups existed in alliance with the congregations from which they sprang. Savings banks and building societies extended their facilities to a broader range of people than the humble labourers at whom they had nominally been aimed.[86] Schools and other institutions for the young enjoyed great support from public and government and hence moved rapidly to a situation of mixed voluntary, private and statutory funding, and then towards state predominance as desire to universalise the service grew. Voluntary hospitals also had wide public approval, but the state remained uninvolved since public payments were already directed towards care of the chronically ill and aged through the poor law. They remained well-supported by the benevolent through legacies, but for consistency of funding they increasingly turned from the support of private individuals towards subscriptions organised around the workplace and other institutions, and thus altered their character. Philanthropic insufficiency was therefore successfully tackled in Bristol's hospitals, although provision was developing unevenly in the country at large, a situation which would have long-term implications for hospital care under the welfare state.[87]

[86] Gorsky, 'Charity', 184–91.
[87] DHSS, *Sharing resources for health in England*, London 1976, 7.

Conclusion

This study began by identifying a renewed interest in the history of voluntary provision and the light it shed on the mixed economy of welfare. Indeed an accurate historical understanding has become more important at a time when political scientists turn increasingly to once neglected theories of civil society as a panacea for the perceived ills of the late twentieth-century welfare state. Such theories reassert Tocquevillian claims for the importance of a vigorous associational life, claiming the active citizenship which this promotes also sustains participatory democracy and ensures responsive government.[1] There are also practical proposals to devolve authority from the state back to the users of public institutions; thus, for example, greater parental power in schools, community involvement in hospital governorship, 'stakeholder' pensions and so on.[2] Since historical precedent is frequently adduced to justify such shifts it is surely incumbent upon historians to present a critical judgement on the voluntary past.[3] In general, though, the entangling of histories of charity with histories of class, and the lingering distaste for 'philanthropic paternalism', has obscured its virtues. By contrast, the concern of revisionists to avoid teleological fallacy risks idealising voluntarism and disregarding the dissatisfaction with its effectiveness felt by contemporaries. This study has documented the transformation of charitable organisation in the eighteenth and nineteenth centuries, with the rejection of endowed charities and the rise of new institutions and societies. What broader conclusions about voluntary provision may be drawn?

At the heart of the transition from traditional to new associational forms lay the the issue of public trust which the latter embodied. Certainly the context for the eclipse of endowed charity was the stress which rapid urban growth had placed on existing infrastructure, and it was argued that donor disenchantment with parochial charities arose because the vestry was regarded as too limited and selective to address the changing scale of need. However, this does not fully explain why an increasingly efficient and reliable means of guaranteeing income in perpetuity lost popularity, especially since

---

[1]   R. D. Putnam, *Making democracy work: civic traditions in modern Italy*, Princeton 1993, and 'The prosperous community: social capital and public life', *The American Prospect*, Spring 1993, 35–42; R. Bellah and others, *Habits of the heart: individualism and commitment in American life*, San Francisco 1985.

[2]   E. Meehan, *Civil society*, Swindon 1995; C. Ham, *Public, private or community: what next for the NHS?*, London 1996.

[3]   Ibid. 37–51; P. Hirst, *Associative democracy: new forms of economic and social governance*, Oxford 1994, 212–13; Frank Field, *Making welfare work: reconstructing welfare for the millenium*, London 1995, 124–6.

the chronology of change and the evidence of trusteeship suggests that corruption and maladministration existed more in the rhetoric of reform than in the practice of charity management. However much perceptions were at odds with reality, the key concern was trust – the confidence that a prospective donor might feel that the object of the gift would not be distorted at some time in the future.

Public accountability then, was the hallmark of the new voluntary forms. But in addition, societies and subscriber institutions provided a means of addressing social problems which neither market nor state could tackle, the former because the private purchase of social insurance, good education and health care was beyond the means of many, and the latter because the broad consensus for social spending obtained only for the extremes of disadvantage: lunacy, the destitute, the aged and infirm. They represented the efforts of a plural society, sometimes under the leadership of political and social elites, and often guided by the churches and chapels, to experiment with new forms of intervention and to support hitherto marginal and perhaps unpopular groups, such as prostitutes, 'delinquent' children and American slaves.

However they were not socially heterogenous. Despite a small but indeterminate working-class presence as contributors and activists, the early nineteenth century saw increasing class differentiation in the voluntary world, represented not only by the profusion of new societies run by the middle class, but also by the latter's withdrawal from mutualist association and their changing use of public space. The influence of voluntarism on the formation of a middle-class consciousness is difficult to gauge. Certainly there were common themes, of which many, perhaps most, approved: organisational transparency, the meliorative power of the Bible, the capacity of institutions predicated upon work and discipline to re-establish societal norms, the appropriateness of female visiting in support of the family and the importance of more extensive schooling and hospitals staffed by regular practitioners. But because voluntarism was characterised by plurality and localist innovation it continued to represent difference, both in respect of the religious and political bases of membership and of attitudes to recipients. Nor is it certain that participation was sufficiently far-reaching to privilege voluntary associations as the instrument of class formation rather than work, domesticity, and patterns of consumption and leisure.[4] What is more clear is that nineteenth-century philanthropy was a relationship between have and have-not, and that reciprocity was characterised by a range of responses, from deferential gratitude to pragmatic acceptance to outright resentment.

What can the events in Bristol reveal of the national scene? The city was unusual in the numbers of its endowed charities and hence their prominence in the debate over local government reform has not hitherto been demonstrated elsewhere. At the level of national politics it is assumed that cabinet

---

4 For example, BRL, B3951, BABS, *11th report*, 1821, for the reluctance of merchants to subscribe.

approval of the Charity Commission indicates bipartisan support for charity reform, yet this is at odds with the combative tactics used by Brougham to advance the issue.[5] This raises the future research question of whether the crisis of trust was articulated politically in other towns, and if so how? In respect of its numerous subscriber charities Bristol has a better claim to be representative, though idiosyncratic factors determined the configuration of voluntary activity in different places. For example, in the eighteenth century only Bristol, Glasgow and London had county societies,[6] while in the nineteenth the city was distinguished by the initiatives of individuals such as Muller and Carpenter, by the emphasis placed on the needs of a youthful, mobile population, and by the distinctive energy and concerns of female nonconformists. The situation in different towns then might depend on the nature of the local economy, demographic structure, religious and cultural tradition, the longevity of philanthropic infrastructure and the contingent impact of individuals. The case of Bristol, an old provincial capital with a long history of charitable activity, therefore directs attention to issues which may be less apparent in the 'shock cities' of the industrial revolution. For example, the importance of political partisanship in earlier times sits uneasily with an exclusively social explanation of nineteenth-century voluntarism. The emphasis on the Napoleonic era as a watershed also becomes less emphatic; as Barry has observed, charitable activity was in some respects a cyclical process 'in which voluntary associations took on a key role at times when other forms of community organisation were incapable of sustaining their traditional tasks'.[7] However, perhaps the most valuable evidence from Bristol of the broader development of voluntarism is that provided by the internal economic histories of the various charities surveyed and the external perceptions of their functions.

Where charities strove for permanence they confronted the recurring difficulties of inadequacy and unpredictability of income. Donations and legacies could not be relied upon, while subscription was vulnerable to the mobility and mortality of contributors, to the novelty of other causes, and to the free rider effect. Charitable provision was also marked by inefficiency and lack of co-ordination, owing to the unplanned development and multiple sectarian bases of voluntary associations. Local efforts to organise and rationalise were made first by the Samaritan Society from 1807, and later by the Charity Organisation Society, with a good deal of attendant publicity, but little success.[8] Duplication of effort kept costs high: the hospitals, for example, did not attempt joint purchase of food or drugs, nor joint fundraising until the merger of the Infirmary and the General in 1937. There was also the concern

---

5 *Edinburgh Review,* Sept. 1818, 487–93; Mar. 1819, 497–535; *Quarterly Review,* July 1818, 493–523, 538–50, 564.
6 I thank Peter Clark for this information.
7 Jonathan Barry, 'Review article', 200.
8 *Charity Organisation Reporter,* 12 June 1872; *Condition of the poor,* 213–14.

with the contradiction between the indiscriminate nature of religious charity, whose main aim was to proselytise, and the interrogative approach of scientific charity whose goal was moral reform.[9] Prochaska's observation that 'philanthropists were their own worst enemies' therefore contains an important truth.[10] As popular approval of voluntary sector services grew in recognition of their achievement, so the struggle for financial viability became more urgent, and the debate they provoked about social policy became more intense.

While in the long run this tension was resolved by the replacement of voluntary provision with that of the state, it is possible to observe in the period surveyed here the transition of organisations which were essentially autonomous and private, into public institutions. This was first discernible in the case of the endowed charities. Gilbert's Enquiry marked the beginning of a process which culminated in the Endowed Schools Act, a process by which the perception of an endowment as essentially the private property of its trustees, shifted to one in which it was regarded as a public benefit. Indeed, by 1869 one pole of opinion in the national debate held that successful application of endowed charity could only be achieved 'in accordance with the supreme intelligence and will of the nation, as represented in Parliament'.[11] True, the powers of the Charity Commission were to remain limited, and drastic alterations to testators' wishes did not extend much beyond the Endowed Schools Act (1869) and the City Parochial Charities Act (1883). However, Bristol's experience of the politicisation of charity exemplifies at local level this notion of charity as public good.

In the subscriber charities both internal funding problems and external public pressures drove the transition. The unpredictability of voluntary income necessitated a diversification of funding sources away from the reliance on the private lay subscriber, and this altered the character of institutions. In the Infirmary for instance the growing importance of contributions from firms and workmen blurred the boundary between charity and insurance, while the hospital's role as site for the professional activities of doctors distanced it further from its original charitable nature. This was a slow and gradual process, but by the end of the century Charles Booth's comment on the London hospitals was equally applicable in Bristol: 'It is not as charities but as public institutions that the hospitals make their appeals.'[12] Elsewhere, as in the Muller Homes and the Children's Hospital, the paternalist intercession of the named subscriber gave way after 1850 before the authority of the charity administrators and doctors. In the schools the rapidity with which

9 Charles Booth, *Life and labour of the people in London*, III: *Religious influences*, vii: *Summary*, London 1902–4, 406–13.
10 Prochaska, *Voluntary impulse*, 69.
11 Joshua Fitch, *Fraser's Magazine*, Jan. 1869, cited in Beveridge, *Voluntary action*, 196; Sir Arthur Hobhouse, *The dead hand: addresses on endowments*, London 1880, 46, 121, 237–9.
12 Charles Booth, *Life and labour, final volume*, London 1902, 151–3.

philanthropy was augmented by private and statutory funding demonstrates how broad approval for a service could undermine the leading role of hierarchical charity after a short time.

It was not until the post-war period though, that the role of charity in core services came to be considered inappropriate. Thus in its final annual report before nationalisation, the Bristol Royal Infirmary made the following observation on the renaming of its Almoner's Department, henceforth to be known as the Welfare Department:

> Originally the name was considered appropriate when hospital treatment itself was looked upon as a medical charity. The Almoner was a person who dispensed it in the sense of deciding whether an individual was eligible for this help or not. The community no longer regards hospital care as charity and the Almoner, in her capacity as assessor of patients' payments no longer dispenses but collects.[13]

The comment reflects on two themes of this book, the success of voluntary organisations in pioneering forms of social provision that won popular acceptance, and the difficulties faced by philanthropy in sustaining the desired level of service. Change in the 'community's' attitude to charity was not a necessary outcome of this contradictory tendency, but came in the wake of political and social developments of the twentieth century.

[13] Bristol Royal Infirmary, *Annual report*, 1946.

Endowed Charities in Bristol: Statistical Note

In addition to the general comments in the text of chapter 2 on the reliability of the information submitted to the Charity Commissioners, there were problems in handling the data to arrive at the statistical presentation.

Dating

In some cases the commissioners were unable to date the establishment of the trust, and it has been impossible to find a date through cross-referencing the reports, or to infer an approximate date from the names of trustees or particular targets mentioned in a dated trust. In the Brougham Report there are fourteen such undated entries. Most were for small amounts, though three were over £2: one at £18 7s. 6d., one at £5 and one at £6. Together the undated entries total £43 1s. 6d., and this could distort, in a minor way, some of the figures and the conclusions drawn, should they by chance all fall in the same decade, or two decades. This is highly improbable, given that the enquiry listed charities over a 300-year timespan, the earliest being 1492 (Foster's Almshouse). Also, the reason for charities being entered undated is presumably because their founding records were lost, and it is plausible to assume that this is because their inception was before the 1660 starting point used here.

Valuation

There are two problems here. Should annual income be chosen as the indicator of value, or the capital sum donated, and how should adjustment be introduced to account for price fluctuations over the period? Income has been chosen in preference to the capital sum bequeathed, since a number of gifts took the form of property, generating an annual rent for the charity, hence no capital value is recorded. This is not an ideal approach, but the alternative, estimating capital values from descriptions such as 'two houses', is clearly not viable. One drawback of basing the table on income rather than capital values is that deliberately interest-free loan monies are lost; during the period covered these amount to the Quaker loan fund in the 1730s (£100), and the fund spread between four parishes by Orchard in the 1800s (£334). I have been content to omit these on the grounds that they will show up in figure 2 and table 7, but if a theoretical interest rate of 5 per cent is posited for them, this would add £5 to the 1730s and £16 18s. 0d. to the 1800s. The first would not distort the conclusions drawn for the 1730s and the second would only accentuate the argument for a revival of beneficence in the early nineteenth century. Finally, annual income calculated this way represents the nearest possible indicator of the actual amounts that were, theoretically, at the disposal of the spending authorities.

All property endowments are seen in terms of 1822 rental values, rather than the actual rentals in the decade of the gift. All trust income from the two later enquiries has been adjusted to 1822 values, using the Rousseaux Overall Price Index. In figure 4, where the overall value of endowments to the poor is contrasted with the poor rates and Infirmary income, all figures are again adjusted to 1820s values, by means of the Schumpeter-Gilboy Consumer Goods, and the Rousseaux Overall Price Indices. The 1820s are the base decade because this was when the Brougham Commission reported for Bristol, and therefore the first point at which there is an accurate record of charity income.

Volume

In order to catch the full range of targets, gifts divided by the testator between several specified objectives have been treated throughout as distinct endowments. This has meant that the number of trusts displayed in figure 2 and table 7 slightly exceeds the number of actual donors.

APPENDIX 2

Bristol Infirmary, 1742–1870:
income composition, numbers of patients and subscribers

Bristol Infirmary, 1742-1870: income composition, numbers of patients and subscribers

Year	Subscription	Interest on securities	Legacies	Donations/ sundries	Workmens' subscriptions	Congregational collections	Miscellaneous	Patients: In	Out	Subscribers	Year
	£	£	£	£	£	£	£	no.	no.	no.	
1742	588	133	5,000	34				349	581	209	1742
1743	738	178	0	266							1743
1744	744	196	181	183							1744
1745	741	196	341	639							1745
1746	708	217	0	165							1746
1747	724	217	440	277				593	1,117	285	1747
1748	773	217	190	160							1748
1749	768	217	250	134							1749
1750	779	217	200	80							1750
mean 1742-50	729	199	734	215				471	849	247	
1751	909	209	70	4,227		375					1751
1752	921	297		574				693	1,642	378	1752
1753	925	298		233							1753
1754	930	298		750							1754
1755	926	280		653							1755
1756	972	280	200	294		266		1,214	2,658	425	1756
1757	989	290	859	327		662					1757
1758	1,066	267	250	234		9					1758
1759	1,159	257	300	225		566					1759
1760	1,126	257	370	157		188		954	2,150	402	1760
mean 1751-60	992	273	205	767							
1761	1,113	270	791	120				1,157	2,633	466	1761
1762	1,098	270	1,041	77		356					1762
1763	1,137	270	651	244			532				1763
1764	1,109	270	600	113			57				1764
1765	1,095	270	700	182			208				1765

Year										Year
1766	1,112	270	810	403						1766
1767	1,226	278	773	289			1,206	3,464	514	1767
1768	1,186	288	857	107	192					1768
1769	1,193	290	503	205	220	31				1769
1770	n/a									1770
mean 1761-70	1,141	275	747	193	85	92	1,182	3,049	490	mean 1761-70
1771	1,251	290	1,690	337	181					1771
1772	1,317	315	150	687	263		1,224	3,026	562	1772
1773	1,288	315	350	290	176					1773
1774	1,283	360	1,425	474	250					1774
1775	1,286	390	325	109	215					1775
1776	1,335	390	700	69	236					1776
1777	1,338	405	400	272	263		1,507	2,618	579	1777
1778	1,280	526	470	222	167					1778
1779	1,235	562	5,720	101	70					1779
1780	1,172	686	350	126	122					1780
mean 1771-80	1,162	385	1,053	244	177		910	1,881	380	mean 1771-80
1781	1,259	686	575	574	91					1781
1782	1,274	686	677	101			1,410	2,616	539	1782
1783	1,153	734	252	498	3					1783
1784	1,134	734	80	204	16	1,440				1784
1785	1,079	659	125	309						1785
1786	1,108	584	1,130	106	221	327				1786
1787	1,100	629	191	138	109	207	1,392	3,216	486	1787
1788	1,051	614	454	1,672	113	1,609				1788
1789	1,067	614	1,200	213	128	3,603				1789
1790	1,157	247	2,633	328	148					1790
mean 1781-90	1,138	619	732	414	83	719	1,401	2,916	513	mean 1781-90
1791	1,194	637	47	879	87					1791
1792	1,297	369	370	639	129		1,445	3,145	570	1792
1793	1,289	344	150	1,798	247	1,250				1793

Year	Subscription £	Interest on securities £	Legacies £	Donations/sundries £	Workmens' subscriptions £	Congregational collections £	Miscellaneous £	Patients: In no.	Patients: Out no.	Subscribers no.
1794	1,442	344	700	1,017		210	188			
1795	1,521	344	775	219		138				
1796	1,567	344	191	3,262		151				
1797	2,054	363	612	10,208		202		1,315	2,607	918
1798	2,189	700	243	321		146				
1799	2,094	566	566	322		132				
1800	2,283	783	994	642		432				
mean 1791-1800	1,693	479	465	1,931		187	144	1,380	2,876	744
1801	2,075	868	1,921	612		204				
1802	2,035	960	617	705		467		1,290	2,830	915
1803	1,913	1,007	667	843		161				
1804	1,968	1,057	1,268	783		221				
1805	2,051	1,421	462	9,326		752				
1806	2,763	870	730	382		234	1,092			
1807	2,790	1,003	376	288		206	2,405	1,219	2,593	1,062
1808	2,849	1,023	541	790		260	2,561			
1809	2,478	2,326	322	420		273	1,787			
1810	2,690	3,914	522	1,025		202	1,237	1,255	2,712	989
mean 1801-10	2,361	1,445	743	1,517		298	908			
1811	2,739	1,299	1,210	526		239	250			
1812	2,749	1,712	1,365	313		409	1,126	1,303	2,520	1,092
1813	3,237	1,638	648	960		313	526			
1814	3,407	1,615	335	1,789		289	455			
1815	3,118	1,656	1,090	248		190	40			
1816	3,015	1,888	728	586		37	360			
1817	3,351	4,446	532	604			103	1,608	3,955	1,250
1818	2,636	1,968	682	27			80			
1819	3,029	1,966	1,099	82			100			

Year									
1820	1,171	3,238	1,456	87	148	366	790	2,019	2,520
mean 1811–20				313		550	848	2,021	2,980
1821				87		662	370	1,924	2,785
1822	1,004	3,865	1,720	80		275	551	1,958	1,694
1823				68		94	212	1,947	3,167
1824				98		611	1,085	1,980	2,384
1825				72		38	2,397	1,939	2,368
1826				132		83	135	1,970	2,365
1827	979	4,635	1,934	27	278	281	494	1,879	2,335
1828				40	37	108	2,287	1,883	2,628
1829				33		127	402	1,918	2,452
1830				46		61	1,114	1,918	2,426
mean 1821–30	992	4,250	1,827	68	32	234	905	1,932	2,460
1831				47		265	1,273	1,921	2,329
1832	954	5,461	1,814	35		115	296	1,869	2,326
1833				41		170	2,064	1,784	2,141
1834				26		193	1,392	1,826	2,093
1835				27		53	1,185	1,841	2,114
1836				32		10	1,007	1,841	1,999
1837	820	5,077	1,544	33		139	1,369	1,841	1,868
1838				51		128	2,094	1,858	1,893
1839				44	343	361	1,011	1,879	2,203
1840				31		1,049	309	1,883	2,174
mean 1831–40	887	5,269	1,679	37	34	248	1,200	1,854	2,114
1841				37		271	525	1,883	2,257
1842	1,041	5,730	2,189	43		405	1,316	1,855	2,244
1843				42		348	503	1,882	2,317
1844				32		1,080	542	1,753	2,288
1845				31	27	130	1,556	1,888	2,404
1846				39	116	1,281	923	1,806	2,353

Year	Subscription	Interest on securities	Legacies	Donations/ sundries	Workmens' subscriptions	Congregational collections	Miscellaneous	Patients: In	Patients: Out	Subscribers
	£	£	£	£	£	£	£	no.	no.	no.
1847	2,260	1,822	155	415		7	35	2,062	9,750	1,089
1848	2,294	1,900	1,561	564		280	30			
1849	3,287	1,861	863	1,009		120	29			
1850	2,701	1,861	550	508			29			
mean 1841-50	2,441	1,851	849	601		61	35	2,126	7,740	1,065
1851	2,451	1,861	998	1,094			36			
1852	2,570	1,861	2,187	1,470	291	744	45	2,699	17,161	1,181
1853	2,631	1,837	1,149	774			47			
1854	2,816	1,654	874	664		233	67			
1855	2,939	1,472	830	165	389	9	31			
1856	2,086	1,560	2,150	179	448	182	81			
1857	2,905	2,393	425	1,073		61	117	2,490	19,166	1,266
1858	2,838	2,283	169	572		295	84			
1859	2,810	1,824	95	910		195	75			
1860	2,917	1,817	2,226	671	449	143	57	2,595	18,164	1,224
mean 1851-60	2,696	1,856	1,110	757	158	186	64			
1861	2,926	1,842	795	2,216	684	675	47			
1862	2,942	1,835	2,184	451	617	409	43	2,945	16,254	1,209
1863	2,908	1,820	1,100	434	656	459	40			
1864	2,884	1,821	1,288	369	633	536	92			
1865	2,918	1,823	1,241	436	724	495	67			
1866	2,935	2,136	3,268	1,336	732	770	65			
1867	2,825	1,903	3,554	265	786	610	65	2,572	21,033	1,166
1868	2,811	926	3,661	652	759	569	59			
1869	2,846	927	1,827	165	766	624	72			
1870	2,862	930	2,572	680	814	595	49			
mean 1861-70	2,886	1,596	2,149	700	717	574	60	2,759	18,644	1,188

Bibliography

Unpublished primary sources

Bristol, Ancient Order of Foresters Friendly Society
Foresters' directory
Formularies and lectures of the Ancient Order of Foresters Friendly Society
(n.d., based on the 1857 Formularies)
Ancient Order of Foresters, City of Bristol, minute book of court

Bristol Municipal Charities
BMC, MB Bristol Charity Trustees, minute book, vol. i
BMC, NC Scrapbooks of newspaper cuttings, memorabilia, vols i, 1867–1870; ii,
1870–3; iii, 1873–81
BMC, YB Year book and notes on Bristol Municipal Charities and Endowed
Schools 1987

Bristol Record Office

Bristol Infirmary records
FCH/BRI/3k, o, t Admissions registers, 1814, 1836, 1854
35893/2/e Weekly committee minute book
35893 21a–e *The state of the Bristol Infirmary*, 1742–1873
35893 36n, Richard Smith Collection, Bristol Lying-In Institution, annual
reports, vol. xiv

Parish records
P/St Aug/V St Augustine's vestry, minutes, 1803–31
P/St Aug/Soc/1a, b Clifton Loan Blanket Society, minute books, 1555–70
P/St J/Ch/3 Fund to relieve poor unemployed, abstract of returns, minute book
P/St J/Ch/8 Signed recommendations for relief, 1814–15
P/StJ/Ch/11/6 Records of distribution of charities, 1825, 1832–3, 1845
P/St J/Ch/92 St James's vestry, list of charities, 1915
P/St J/ChW 36 Articles of agreement for repairs, 1802
P/StJ/V/6 St James's vestry, minutes, 1802–24
P/St J/V/7 St James's vestry, minutes, 1824–1868
P/St P/Ch/1 Index of charities/notes on St Paul's parish charities
P/St P/V/1a St Paul's vestry, minutes, 1794–1839
P/St T/V/1 St Thomas's vestry, minutes, 1824–78
P/Tm/Kb 1 Temple Blue Girls' School, minutes and accounts
P/Tm/ La 3 Temple vestry minutes, 1811–35
P/St BM/X/1 Bristol Lying-In Institution, minute book

Voluntary associations/institutions

Quarter sessions papers, friendly society papers

8029/11 Friendly Society of the Exercisers of Arms, articles and orders

9492/17 b; 4492 17h Bristol Savings Bank, savings books, 1885–8

24759 (1) *Preliminary prospectus of the Bristol and District Permanent Economic Benefit Building and Investment Society*

24759 53, *Rules for the management of the Bristol Savings Bank*, Bristol 1857

35722/4/b, c, Bristol Female Penitentiary, minute books

35893 36n Bristol Lying-In Institution, annual report

38463 Minute book of Female Misericordia

38603/Z/S/1 Zion Chapel Dorcas Society, records

39204/M/1a Bristol and District Permanent Economic Benefit Building Society, minute book

39399/CD/S/3d Bristol Dorcas Society, *Annual reports*, 1841–70

39461/F/4b Unitarian subscription book

40145/P/24 *Bristol Old Park Lock Hospital, annual report*, 1878

Craft gilds

9748 Company of Bakers, ordinances, 1623

08155 Company of Bakers, minute book

01244 Company of Drapers, ordinances, 1654

08156 2, Company of Feltmakers and Haberdashers, minute book

35684 15 Company of Merchant Taylors, memorandum and account book, 1707–1818

08019 Company of Whitawers, Pointmakers, Glovers, Pursers and Pointers, account book

043691 Company of Joiners, 1606

Society of Friends archive

SF/A1/15 Mens Monthly Meeting

SF/2/A2/2–7 Women's Monthly Meeting, minutes, 1781–1873

SF/A9/3 Rice Committee

SF/A9/4a, 4b Navvies Committee, 1860

SF/A9/5 New St Mission Committee report

SF/FD/AR/1a Friends' First Day School, annual reports

SF/F1/1 Collection lists for miscellaneous purposes

SF/MM/6 Bristol Men's Monthly Meeting, minutes

SF/R3/3 Bristol Society of Friends Monthly Meeting, membership list

Miscellaneous

Acts, orders and proceedings of the Commissioners of Pitching and Paving, no. 1, minute book, 1806–7

Bristol School Board, minute book no. 1

Bristol Dock Company, accounts

Bristol pamphlets

Common Council proceedings

DC/E/40/39/7 Bristol diocese, property valuation book.

P/A/43/4 List of meeting houses, 1762–1808, Registry of the Episcopal Consistory Court of Diocese of Bristol

4965 34g Conveyance of two tenements

00568, Folder 3 Correspondence concerning transference and miscellaneous charity deeds and papers

06527 James Kerle Haberfield, memorial scrapbook

34908 16a, *Bristol police instruction book*, Bristol 1836

36097b John Bennet, untitled manuscript, typescript copy, Portishead 1858

36771/73 Livock papers

40301 Diary, author unknown, presumed to be a journalist (1878)

S. R. Woods, 'Westbury-on-Trym, V: Friendly societies', unpubl. MS 1975

Bristol Reference Library

931 John Camplin, *The duty of providing for a family recommended and enforced in a sermon preached before the Society of Captains belonging to the port of Bristol*, Bristol 1789

3217 *Proceedings of the anti-slavery meeting held at the Guildhall Bristol on February 2nd. 1826*

3218 Bristol Auxiliary Anti-Slavery Society, *Report of proceedings from the formation of the institution to the 31st. December, 1830*, Bristol 1831

3745 *Report of the Bristol General Hospital for the year ending 1843*

4593 *Report of the 2nd AGM of the Bristol Statistical Society*, Bristol 1838

5860 John Price, *The advantages of unity considered, sermon preached before the antient and honourable society of free and accepted Masons*, Bristol 1747

7952 Jeffries collection

9180–1 *State of the Prudent Man's Friend Society for the year 1814*, Bristol 1814; *3rd. annual report of the Prudent Man's Friend Society*, Bristol 1815

9351 *Eighth report of the Bristol Auxiliary Bible Society*, Bristol 1817

9354 *Fourteenth annual report of the Bristol Auxiliary Bible Society*, Bristol 1824

9356 *Eighteenth annual report of the Bristol Auxiliary Bible Society*, Bristol 1828

9628 John Price, *The antiquity of the festival of St David asserted: a sermon preached before the Society of Antient Britons*, Bristol 1754

10103 Collection of broadsides, addresses, notices etc., relating to the election of 1841

10109 Collection of broadsides, addresses, notices etc., relating to the election of 1847

20095 William Dyer's diary

24078 Bristol Temperance Society declaration by doctors and surgeons against 'ardent spirits'

B1533 *Address delivered at the Broadmead Room Tuesday, June 14th, 1853 at the inaugural gathering of the Young Men's Christian Association*, Bristol 1853

B1534 National Benevolent Institution

B3951 *8th. Report of the Bristol Auxiliary Bible Society*, Bristol 1817

B4048 *Report of the Strangers Friend Society*, Bristol 1826

B4620 *Bristol Samaritan Society, its rules and an address to the public*, Bristol 1807

B4621–44 *Reports of the Samaritan Society*, Bristol 1807–14, 1816–17, 1819–26, 1828–31, 1833, 1835, 1840

B7054–9 *Lewin's Mead Chapel Working and Visiting Society annual reports*, Bristol 1835–50

B7060–8 *Lewin's Mead Domestic Mission Society, annual reports*, Bristol 1841–58

B7435 *South Gloucestershire Friendly Society: tract explanatory of the nature and benefits of this society*, Bristol 1825

B7437 *South Gloucestershire Friendly Society, 5th report of the Stapleton, Winterbourne etc association*

B7891 *State of Bristol Dispensary for the year ending . . .*, annual reports 1791–1855

B8213 *The Bristolian*

B8214 *The Discoverer*

B9780–1 *State of the Orphan Asylum for the year . . .*, 1821, 1826

B15136 Handbill, Friendly Union Society

B16885 *15th annual report of the Bristol City Mission Society*, Bristol 1842.

B16888 *Proceedings of the fourteenth annual meeting of the Bristol Baptist Itinerant Society*, Bristol 1838

Microfiche 97290/1, 3, 6, 8, 10, 12, Bristol presentments, 1801, 1811, 1821, 1831, 1841, 1851

Microfilm Estlin papers, reel 5, Bristol and Clifton Auxiliary Ladies Anti-Slavery Society, minute book, 1840–61

RLSA B32045 Papers of J. B. and Mary Estlin: correspondence of Mary Estlin; letter-book from eye-patients; *Dispensary for the Cure of Complaints in the Eyes: twenty-eighth annual report, for the year 1840*

Bristol, St Mary Redcliffe Vestry Archive

Soup Society minutes, 1854–61

St Mary Redcliffe vestry minutes, 1822–45

St Mary Redcliffe gift books, 1797–1822, 1822–47

St Mary Redcliffe lease/land grant book

London, Public Record Office, Kew

HO 41/223 Home Office, Disturbance entry book

HO 42/155 Home Office, Domestic correspondence

Published primary sources

Official documents and publications

Reports from the committees of the House of Commons, X: Provisions; Poor; 1774–1802: Further appendix to the report from the committee on certain returns relative to the state of the poor, and to charitable donations, & c. 1787

Abstract of answers and returns pursuant to: 'An act for procuring returns relative to the expence and maintenance of the poor in England', PP 1803–4 xiii

Abstract of returns of charitable donations for benefit of poor persons: – 26 Geo. III, 1786, PP 1816 xvia

Minutes of evidence before Select Committee on Select and Other Vestries, PP 1830 iv

Appendix to the first report from the Commissioners on the Poor Laws: answers to town queries, 1832

Appendix to the first report from the Commissioners on the Poor Laws, PP 1834 xxviii

Census of Great Britain: population (England and Wales), 1841

Minutes of evidence taken before the Select Committee on Bribery at Elections, 1835

English Municipal Commission: report on the city and council of Bristol, PP 1835 xxiv

Analytical digest of the reports made by the Commissioners of Inquiry into Charities, PP 1843 xvi, xvii

Summary of the reports made by the Commissioners of Inquiry into charities, PP 1845 xvii

A return of the total amount of assessed taxes for each of the years ending 5th. April 1845, 1846, and 1847, PP 1847–8 xxxix

Schools aided by parliamentary grants, school building grants, grants for fittings apparatus books and maps, annual grants payable from the parliamentary fund, PP 1850 xliii

Census of Great Britain: population (England and Wales), 1851

Census of Great Britain: religious worship (England and Wales), 1851

Census of Great Britain: education report (England and Wales), 1851

Comparative statement of the amount of poor rates levied and expended during the year ended at Lady-day, 1859 . . . . . . 1870, PP 1859 xxiv; 1860 lviii; 1861 liii; 1862 xlviii; 1863 li; 1864 li; 1865 xlviii; 1866 lxii; 1867 lx; 1868 lx; 1869 liii; 1870 lviii

Reports of the Royal Commisson of Popular Education (Newcastle Commission), PP 1861 xxi/II

Return of the amount of education grants paid to each parish or place in the year 1860, PP 1862 xliii

Copies of the general digest of endowed charities for the counties and cities mentioned in the fourteenth report of the Charity Commissioners, &c, PP 1873 li

Friendly and Benefit Building Societies Commission: reports of the assistant commissioners, southern and eastern counties, by Sir George Young, Bart, PP 1874 xxiii, pt 2

General digest of endowed charities in England and Wales, PP 1877 lxvi

Return of the digest of endowed charities in the county of Gloucester including Bristol . . ., PP 1893–4 lxvii

Return for each public school examined etc. for the year ended 31st. August 1893, PP 1894 lxv

Hansard, 1812

House of Commons Journal, 1813, 1828

House of Lords Journal, 1835

Supplement to the twenty-fifth annual report of the Registrar-General of Births, Deaths and Marriages in England, London 1864

Supplement to the thirty-fifth annual report of the Registrar-General of Births, Deaths and Marriages in England, London 1875

Supplement to the forty-fifth annual report of the Registrar-General of Births, Deaths and Marriages in England, London 1885

Annual report of the Registrar-General, 1840–1, 1845, 1850, 1866, 1870, 1890

Newspapers and periodicals

Bristol Gazette
The Bristolian
Bristol Journal
Bristol Mercury
Bristol Mirror

Bristol Oracle
Bristol Temperance Herald
Charity Organisation Reporter
Felix Farley's Bristol Journal
Oracle and County Advertiser
Political Register
The Trades' Newspaper and Mechanics Weekly Journal

Trade directories

Matthews, W., *The new history, survey and description of the city and suburbs of Bristol*, Bristol 1794

Matthews's annual Bristol directory and almanack

Matthews' Bristol directory with adjacent villages: re-modelled by J. Wright & co (after 1870)

J. Wright & co's Matthew's Bristol and Clifton directory (after 1880)

Pre-1900 books and articles

A committee of the Statistical Society, Bristol, 'Statistics of education in Bristol', *Journal of the Statistical Society of London* iv (1841), 250–63

Anon., *An account of the Bristol Infirmary from the first institution to this time*, Bristol 1738

Anon., *An account of hospitals, alms-houses and public schools in Bristol*, Bristol 1775

Anon., *Rights of the poor, charities of Bristol*, London 1827

Anon., *The Bristol municipal annual for 1838*, Bristol 1838

Anon., *Report of the Committee to Inquire into the Condition of the Bristol Poor*, Bristol 1884

Bacon, Francis, 'Of riches', in *Essays*, London 1625

Beaven, A. B., *Bristol lists municipal and miscellaneous*, Bristol 1899

Beddoes, Thomas, *Hints to husbandmen on intemperate drinking at harvest-time*, Dublin 1813

Bristol poll books, 1781–1832

Bristol Poor Act, Bristol 1823

Bristol Royal Infirmary reports, I: 1878–9, Bristol 1879

Broad, John S., *A history of the origins and progress of the Sunday schools in the city of Bristol and its vicinity under the patronage of the Methodist Sunday School Society*, Bristol 1816 (also at BRL, B10398)

Brodrick, George C., *English land and English landlords*, London 1881

Brougham, Henry, *Lord Brougham's speeches*, iii, Edinburgh 1838

Burdett, Henry C., *Burdett's hospitals and charities: the yearbook of philanthropy and hospital annual 1893*, London 1893

Butcher, Revd Edmund, *An excursion from Sidmouth to Chester*, London 1805

Carpenter, J. Estlin, *The life and work of Mary Carpenter*, London 1879

Cave, C., *A history of banking in Bristol*, Bristol 1899

Cobbett, William, *History of the Protestant Reformation in England and Wales*, London 1824–7, repr. London 1896

Cranidge, J., *A mirror for the burgesses and commonalty of the city of Bristol*, Bristol 1818

Davies, William, *Sermons on religious and moral subjects*, Bristol 1754

Defoe, Daniel, 'Essays on projects' (1697), in *The works of Daniel Defoe*, London 1843

De La Beche, Sir H. T. and Dr Lyon Playfair, *Report on the sanatory* [sic] *condition of Bristol*, Bristol 1845

Eden, Frederick Morton, *The state of the poor*, London 1797, repr. London, 1928

Encyclopédie ou dictionnaire raisonné des sciences, des arts et des métiers: tome douzième, Paris 1765

Fox, F. F., *Some account of the Merchant Taylors of Bristol*, Bristol 1880

───── and J. Taylor, *Some account of the weavers in Bristol*, Bristol 1889

Hobhouse, Sir Arthur, *The dead hand: addresses on endowments*, London 1880

Hunt, Henry, *A letter from Mr Hunt to the freemen of Bristol*, London 1812

───── *Memoirs of Henry Hunt*, ii, iii, London 1821, repr. New York 1970

Johnson, J., *Transactions of the Corporation of the Poor*, Bristol 1826

Johnson, Samuel, *Dictionary of the English language*, London 1831

Kington, J. B., 'A burgess's' *letters*, Bristol 1836

Manchee, Thomas John (ed.), *The Bristol charities, being the report of the commissioners for inquiring concerning charities in England and Wales so far as relates to the charitable institutions in Bristol*, i, ii, Bristol 1831

More, Martha, *Mendip annals*, ed. with additional material by Arthur Roberts, London 1859

Naish, A., J. S. Fry and W. Sturge, *Some particulars concerning the establishment and early history of the first-day schools conducted by the Society of Friends in Bristol*, Bristol 1860

Nicholls, J. F., *Bristol biographies: life of George Thomas*, Bristol 1870

───── and John Taylor, *Bristol: past and present*, II: *Ecclesiastical history*, Bristol 1881

───── and John Taylor, *Bristol: past and present*, III: *Civil and modern history*, Bristol 1882

Nightingale, Florence, *Notes on lying-in institutions*, London 1871

Pole, Thomas, *A history of the origin and progress of adult schools*, Bristol 1816, repr. London 1968

Pryce, George, *A popular history of Bristol*, Bristol 1861

Reynell, Carew, *A sermon preached before the contributors to the Bristol Infirmary*, Bristol 1738

Seyer, Samuel, *Memoirs historical and topographical of Bristol and its neighbourhood*, i, Bristol 1821

Taunton, W., *Account of Anthony Edmond's Charity*, Bristol 1834

Tucker, Josiah, *A sermon preach'd in the parish church of St James in Bristol*, London 1746

Tuke, Samuel, *Description of the Retreat*, York 1813

Wilkinson, John Frome, *The friendly society movement*, London 1886

Secondary Sources
Post-1900: Bristol

Alford, B. W. E., 'The flint and bottle glass industry in the early nineteenth century: a case study of a Bristol firm', *Business History* x (1968), 12–21

───── *W. D. & H. O. Wills and the development of the UK tobacco industry, 1786–1965*, London 1973

——— 'The economic development of Bristol in the nineteenth century: an enigma?', in P. McGrath and J. Cannon (eds), *Essays in Bristol and Gloucestershire history*, Bristol 1976, 252–83

Archer, Ian, Spencer Jordan and Keith Ramsay, *Abstract of Bristol historical statistics*, I: *Poor law statistics, 1835–1948*, Bristol 1997

Arrowsmith, J. W., *Dictionary of Bristol*, Bristol 1906

Atkinson, B. J., 'An early example of the decline of the industrial spirit?: Bristol "enterprise" in the first half of the nineteenth century', *Southern History* ix (1987), 69–89

Baigent, E., 'Economy and society in eighteenth-century English towns: Bristol in the 1770s', in Dietrich Denecke and Gareth Shaw (eds), *Urban historical geography: recent progress in Britain and Germany*, Cambridge 1988, 109–24

Barot, Rohit, *Bristol and the Indian independence movement*, Bristol 1988

Barry, Jonathan, 'Piety and the patient: medicine and religion in eighteenth century Bristol', in Roy Porter (ed.), *Patients and practitioners: lay perceptions of medicine in pre-industrial society*, Cambridge 1985, 145–75

——— 'The parish in civic life: Bristol and its churches 1640–1750', in Wright, *Parish, church and people*, 153–78

——— 'The politics of religion in Restoration Bristol', in Tim Harris, Paul Seaward and Mark Goldie (eds), *The politics of religion in restoration England*, Oxford 1990, 163–89

——— 'The press and the politics of culture in Bristol 1660–1775', in J. Black and J. Gregory (eds), *Culture, politics and society in Britain, 1660–1800*, Manchester 1991, 49–81

——— 'Bristol charities in the eighteenth century' (Bristol Record Society lecture, 27 Feb. 1993)

——— and Kenneth Morgan (eds), *Reformation and revival in eighteenth century Bristol* (Bristol Record Society xlv, 1994)

Bergin, G. Frederick (ed.), *Autobiography of George Muller, or a million and a half in answer to prayer*, Bristol 1906

Bickley, F. (ed.), *The little red book of Bristol*, i, Bristol 1900

Bowen, F. W. E., *Queen Elizabeth's Hospital, Bristol*, Clevedon 1971

Bruce-Perry, C., *The Bristol Medical School*, Bristol 1984

——— *The voluntary medical institutions of Bristol*, Bristol 1984

Burrows, Jean, 'The Finzels of Counterslip and Clevedon', *The Bristol Templar 1992: Bristol faces and places*, Bristol 1992, 7–17

Bush, Graham, *Bristol and its municipal government, 1820–1851* (Bristol Record Society xxix, 1976)

Butcher, E. E., *Bristol Corporation of the Poor, 1696–1898*, Bristol 1932

——— (ed.), *Bristol Corporation of the Poor: selected records, 1696–1834* (Bristol Record Society iii, 1932)

Campbell, John, 'Occupation and literacy in Bristol and Gloucestershire, 1755–1870', in Stephens, *History of literacy*, 20–36

Cannon, J., *The Chartists in Bristol*, Bristol 1964

Cleeves, Ronald, *Mission of mercy*, Bristol 1979

Diaper, S. J., 'Christopher Thomas and Brothers Ltd: the last Bristol soapmakers: an aspect of Bristol's economic development in the nineteenth century', *Transactions of the Bristol and Gloucestershire Archaeological Society* cv (1987), 223–32

———— 'J. S. Fry & Sons: growth and decline in the chocolate industry, 1753–1918', in Harvey and Press, *Business history of Bristol*, 33–54

Dresser, Madge, 'Protestants, Catholics and Jews: religious difference and political status in Bristol, 1750–1850', in Dresser and Ollerenshaw, *Making of modern Bristol*, 96–123

———— and Philip Ollerenshaw (eds), *The making of modern Bristol*, Tiverton 1996

Farr, G., *Shipbuilding in the port of Bristol*, London 1977

Fissell, Mary E., 'The "sick and drooping poor" in eighteenth-century Bristol and its region', *Social History of Medicine* ii (1989), 35–58

———— *Patients, power, and the poor in eighteenth-century Bristol*, Cambridge 1991

———— 'Charity universal?: institutions and moral reform in eighteenth- century Bristol', in Lee Davison, Tim Hitchcock, Tim Keirn and Robert B. Shoemaker (eds), *Stilling the grumbling hive: the response to social and economic problems in England, 1689–1750*, Stroud 1992, 121–64

Garton, Nancy, *George Muller and his orphans*, London 1963

Gorsky, Martin, 'James Tuckfield's ride: combination and social drama in early nineteenth-century Bristol', *Social History* xix (1994), 319–38

———— 'Experiments in poor relief: Bristol, 1816–1817', *The Local Historian* xxv (1995), 17–30

———— 'Mutual aid and civil society: friendly societies in nineteenth-century Bristol', *Urban History* 25 (1998), 302–22

Greenacre, F. and S. Stoddard, *W. J. Muller*, Bristol 1991

Hannam, June, ' "An enlarged sphere of usefulness": the Bristol women's movement, c. 1860–1914', in Dresser and Ollerenshaw, *Making of modern Bristol*, 184–209

Harrison, Mark, *Crowds and history: mass phenomena in English towns, 1790–1835*, Cambridge 1988

Harvey, Charles, 'Old traditions, new departures: the later history of the Bristol & West Building Society', in Harvey and Press, *Business history of Bristol*, 239–72

———— and Jon Press, 'Industrial change and the economic life of Bristol', in Harvey and Press, *Business history of Bristol*, 1–32

———— and Jon Press (eds), *Studies in the business history of Bristol*, Bristol 1988

Hill, C., *The history of the Bristol Grammar School*, Bath 1951

Hopkins, Mary Alden, *Hannah More and her circle*, New York 1947

Humphries, S., 'Schooling and the working class in Bristol, 1870–1914', *Southern History* i (1979), 171–207

Ison, Walter, *The Georgian buildings of Bristol*, London 1952

Jackson, E., *A study in democracy: being an account of the rise and progress of industrial co-operation in Bristol*, Manchester 1911

Large, D., *Radicalism in Bristol in the nineteenth century* Bristol 1981

———— (ed.), *The port of Bristol, 1848–84* (Bristol Record Society xxxvi, 1984)

———— and Frances Round, *Public health in mid-Victorian Bristol*, Bristol 1974

Latimer, John, *Annals of Bristol in the nineteenth century*, Bristol 1887

———— *Annals of Bristol in the eighteenth century*, Bristol 1893

———— *Annals of Bristol in the seventeenth century*, Bristol 1900

Little, B., *The city and county of Bristol*, London 1954

———— *The history of Barley Wood*, Bristol 1978

McGrath, P., *The Merchant Venturers of Bristol*, Bristol 1975

Mackeson, John F., *Bristol transported*, Bristol 1987

Malos, Ellen, 'Bristol women in action, 1839–1919: the right to vote and the need to earn a living', in Ian Bild (ed.), *Bristol's other history*, Bristol 1983, 97–128

Manton, Jo, *Mary Carpenter and the children of the streets*, London 1976

Marshall, Peter, *The anti-slave trade movement in Bristol*, Bristol 1968

────── *Bristol and the abolition of slavery: the politics of emancipation*, Bristol 1975

Meakin, Annette M. B., *Hannah More: a biographical study*, London 1911

Meller, H. E., *Leisure and the changing city, 1870–1914*, London 1976

Minchinton, W. E., 'Bristol: metropolis of the west in the eighteenth century', *Transactions of the Royal Historical Society* 5th ser. iv (1954), 69–89

────── 'The port of Bristol in the eighteenth century', in P. McGrath (ed.), *Bristol in the eighteenth century*, Newton Abbot 1972, 128–60

Morgan, Kenneth, 'Bristol and the Atlantic trade in the eighteenth century', *EHR* cvii (1992), 626–50

────── *Bristol and the Atlantic trade in the eighteenth century*, Cambridge 1993

Munro Smith, G., *A history of the Bristol Royal Infirmary*, Bristol 1917

Neve, Michael, 'Science in a commercial city: Bristol, 1820–60', in Ian Inkster and Jack Morrell (eds), *Metropolis and province: science in British culture, 1780–1850*, London 1983, 179–204

Ollerenshaw, P., 'The development of banking in the Bristol region', in Harvey and Press, *Business history of Bristol*, Bristol 1988, 55–82

Orme, Nicholas, 'The Guild of Kalendars, Bristol', *Transactions of the Bristol and Gloucestershire Archaeological Society* xcvi (1978), 32–52

Pierson, Arthur T., *George Muller of Bristol*, London 1912

Powell, Arthur and Joseph Littleton, *A history of Freemasonry in Bristol*, Bristol 1910

Roslyn, H. E., *History of the Ancient Society of St Stephen's Ringers*, Bristol 1928

Ross, C., 'Bristol in the Middle Ages', in C. Macinnes and W. Whittard (eds), *Bristol and its adjoining counties*, Bristol 1955, 179–92

Sacks, David Harris, 'The demise of the martyrs: the feasts of St Clement and St Katherine in Bristol, 1400–1600', *Social History* xi (1986), 141–69

────── *The widening gate: Bristol and the Atlantic economy, 1450–1700*, London 1991

Saunders, Charles J. G., *The Bristol Eye Hospital*, Bristol 1960

────── *The Bristol Royal Hospital for Sick Children*, Bristol 1960

Saywell, Ruby J., *Mary Carpenter of Bristol*, Bristol 1964

Selleck, R. J. W., 'Mary Carpenter: a confident and contradictory reformer', *History of Education* xiv (1985), 101–13

Shannon, H. A. and E. Grebenick, *The population of Bristol*, Cambridge 1943

Symes, J. O., *A short history of the Bristol General Hospital*, Bristol 1932

Tanner, S. J., *Suffrage movement in Bristol: how the women's suffrage movement began in Bristol fifty years ago*, Bristol 1918

Thomas, Susan, *The Bristol riots*, Bristol 1974

Unwin, F. M., *Ada Vachell of Bristol*, Bristol 1928

Vanes, J., *Apparrelled in red*, Gloucester 1984

Veale, E. W. W. (ed.), *The great red book of Bristol: pt I* (Bristol Record Society iv, 1933): *pt III* (Bristol Record Society xvi, 1951).

Walters, Roderick, *The establishment of the Bristol police force*, Bristol 1975

Ward, J., 'Speculative building at Bristol and Clifton, 1783–1793', *Business History* xx (1978), 3–18

Winstone, Reece, *Bristol suburbs long ago*, Bristol 1985

Post-1900: Philanthropy, voluntary associations, health, education, poverty

Abel-Smith, Brian, *The hospitals 1800–1948: a study in social administration in England and Wales*, London, 1964

Andrew, Donna T., *Philanthropy and police: London charity in the eighteenth century*, Princeton 1989

Barry, Jonathan and Colin Jones (eds), *Medicine and charity before the welfare state*, London 1991

Bellah, R. and others, *Habits of the heart: individualism and commitment in American life*, San Francisco 1985

Bennett, Judith, 'Conviviality and charity in medieval and early modern England', *P&P* cxxxiv (1992), 19–41

Beveridge, William, *Voluntary action: a report on methods of social advance*, London 1948

Bittle, W. and R. Todd Lane, 'Inflation and philanthropy in England: a reassessment of W. K. Jordan's data', *EcHR* 2nd ser. xxix (1976), 203–10

Booth, Charles, *Life and labour of the people in London*, III: *Religious influences*, vii: *Summary*, London 1902–4

——— *Life and labour of the people in London: final volume*, London 1902

Borsay, Anne, ' "Persons of honour and reputation": the voluntary hospital in an age of corruption', *Medical History* xxxv (1991), 281–94

Boylan, Anne M., 'Women in groups: an analysis of women's benevolent organisations in New York and Boston, 1797–1840', *Journal of American History* lxxi (1984), 497–519

Brand, Jeanne L., *Doctors and the state: the British medical profession and government action in public health, 1870–1912*, Baltimore 1965

Brigden, Susan, 'Religion and social obligation in early sixteenth-century London', *P&P* ciii (1984), 67–112

Brown, Ford K., *Fathers of the Victorians: the age of Wilberforce*, Cambridge 1961

Cale, Michelle, 'Girls and the perception of sexual danger in the Victorian reformatory system', *History* lxxviii (1993), 201–17

Carrier, James G., 'The rituals of Christmas giving', in Daniel Miller (ed.), *Unwrapping Christmas*, Oxford 1993, 55–74

Cavallo, Sandra, 'The motivations of benefactors: an overview of approaches to the study of charity', in Barry and Jones, *Medicine and charity*, 46–62

Checkland, Olive, *Philanthropy in Victorian Scotland*, Edinburgh 1980

Cherry, S., 'The role of the provincial hospital: the Norfolk and Norwich Hospital, 1771–1880', *Population Studies* xxvi (1972)

——— 'The hospitals and population growth: the voluntary general hospitals, mortality and local populations in the English provinces in the eighteenth and nineteenth centuries: pt I', *Population Studies* xxxiv (1980), 59–75; 'part II', xxxv (1980), 251–65.

——— 'Beyond National Health Insurance: the voluntary hospitals and hospital contributory schemes: a regional study', *Social History of Medicine* v (1992), 455–82

Clark, Peter, *Sociability and urbanity: clubs and societies in the eighteenth-century city*, Leicester 1986

Clarke, W. K. Lowther, *A history of the SPCK*, London 1959

Clarkson, Kenneth W., 'Some implications of property rights in hospital management', *Journal of Law and Economics* xv (1972), 363–84

Constantelos, D., *Byzantine philanthropy and social welfare*, New Jersey 1968

Cooper, Walter G., *The Ancient Order of Foresters Friendly Society: 150 Years, 1834–1984*, Southampton 1984

Cope, Zachary, 'The history of the dispensary movement', in F. N. L. Poynter (ed.), *The evolution of hospitals in Britain*, London 1964, 73–6

Crowther, M.A., 'Family responsibility and state responsibility in Britain before the welfare state', *HJ* xxv (1982), 131–45

Cunnington, Phillis and Catherine Lucas, *Charity costumes of children, scholars, almsfolk, pensioners*, London 1978

Curtis, T. C. and W. A. Speck, 'The Societies of the Reformation of Manners: a case study in the theory and practice of moral reform', *Literature and History* iii (1976), 45–64

Daunton, Martin, 'Introduction', in Daunton, *Charity, self-interest and welfare*, 1–22

——— (ed.), *Charity, self-interest and welfare in the English past*, London 1996

DHSS, *Sharing resources for health in England*, London 1976

Deutsch, Albert 'Historical inter-relationships between medicine and social welfare', *Bulletin of the History of Medicine* xi (1942), 485–502

Dick, Malcolm, 'The myth of the working-class Sunday school', *History of Education* ix (1980), 27–41

Digby, Anne, *British welfare policy*, London 1989

——— *Making a medical living: doctors and patients in the English market for medicine, 1720–1911*, Cambridge 1994

Donnison, Jean, *Midwives and medical men: a history of the struggle for the control of childbirth*, London 1977, 2nd edn, London 1988

Duthie, John L., 'Philanthropy and evangelism among Aberdeen seamen, 1814–1924', *Scottish Historical Review* lxiii (1984), 155–73

Evans, Neil, 'Urbanisation, elite attitudes and philanthropy: Cardiff, 1850–1914', *International Review of Social History* xxvii (1982), 290–323

Finlayson, Geoffrey, 'A moving frontier: voluntarism and the state in British social welfare, 1911–49', *Twentieth-Century British History* i (1990), 183–206

——— *Citizen, state and social welfare in Britain, 1830–1990*, Oxford 1994

Foucault, Michel, *Madness and civilisation*, Paris 1961, repr. London 1993

Fraser, Derek, *The evolution of the British welfare state*, London 1973

Fuller, Margaret D., *West country friendly societies*, Reading 1964

Gardner, Philip W., *The lost elementary schools of Victorian England*, London 1984

Gilman, Amy, 'From widowhood to wickedness: the politics of class and gender in New York City private charity', *History of Education Quarterly* (1984), 59–74

Gorsky, Martin, 'The growth and distribution of English friendly societies in the early nineteenth century', *EcHR* li (1998), 489–511

Gosden, P. H. J. H., *The friendly societies in England, 1815–1875*, Manchester 1961

——— Self-help: voluntary associations in the nineteenth century, London 1973

Grace, Mary, Records of the Gild of St George in Norwich, Norwich 1937

Grady, Kevin, 'The records of the Charity Commissions as a source for urban history', Urban History Yearbook (1982), 31–7

Granshaw, Lindsay, ' "Fame and fortune by means of bricks and mortar": the medical profession and specialist hospitals in Britain, 1800–1948', in Granshaw and Porter, The hospital in history, 199–220

——— and Roy Porter (eds), The hospital in history, London 1989

Green, D. G., Re-inventing civil society: the rediscovery of welfare without politics, London 1993

Gray, B. Kirkman, A history of English philanthropy, London 1905

Hadwin, J. F., 'Deflating philanthropy', EcHR 2nd ser. xxxi (1978), 105–20

Hall, Peter Dobkin, The organisation of American culture, 1700–1900: private institutions, elites and the origins of American nationality, New York 1982

Hansmann, Henry B., 'The role of nonprofit enterprise', Yale Law Journal lxxxix (1980), 835–901

Hardy, Anne, The epidemic streets: infectious diseases and the rise of preventive medicine, 1856–1900, Oxford 1993

——— ' "Death is the cure of all diseases": using the General Register Office cause of death statistics for 1837–1920', Social History of Medicine vii (1994), 477–80.

Harris, Bernard, 'Responding to adversity: government-charity relations and the relief of unemployment in interwar Britain', Contemporary Record ix (1995), 529–61

Harrison, Brian, 'Philanthropy and the Victorians', Victorian Studies ix (1966), 353–74, rev. in Harrison, Peacable kingdom, 217–59

——— Drink and the Victorians, London 1971

Harrison, J. F. C., Learning and living, 1790–1960: a study of the English adult education movement, London 1961

Hartwell, R. M. et al., The long debate on poverty, London 1972

Heal, Felicity, 'The idea of hospitality in early modern England', P&P cii (1984), 66–93

——— Hospitality in early modern England, Oxford 1990

Hellmuth, Eckhart (ed.), The transformation of political culture: England and Germany in the late eighteenth century, Oxford 1990

Henriques, Ursula, Before the welfare state, London 1979

Himmelfarb, Gertrude, The demoralisation of society: from Victorian virtues to modern values, London 1995

Hodgkinson, Ruth G., The origins of the National Health Service: the medical services of the New Poor Law, 1834–1871, London 1967

Hopkins, Eric, Working-class self-help in nineteenth-century England, London 1995

Humphreys, Robert, Bygone charity: myths and realities (LSE Working Paper no. 23/94, 1994)

Jones, Beryl Madoc, 'Patterns of attendance and their social significance: Mitcham National School, 1830–1839', in McCann (ed.), Popular education, 41–66

Jones, Colin, 'Some recent trends in the history of charity', in Daunton Charity, self-interest and welfare, 51–63

Jones, Dot, 'Did friendly societies matter?: a study of friendly societies in Glamorgan, 1794–1910', *Welsh History Review* cccxxiv (1985), 324–49

Jones, Gareth, *History of the law of charity, 1532–1827*, Cambridge 1969

Jones, Kathleen, *Lunacy, law, and conscience, 1744–1845: the social history of the care of the insane*, London 1955

Jones, M. G., *The charity school movement in the XVIII century*, Cambridge 1938

Jordan, W. K., *Philanthropy in England, 1480–1660*, London 1959

—— *The forming of the charitable institutions of the west of England* (Transactions of the American Philosophical Society i, 1960)

Kidd, Alan J., ' "Outcast Manchester": voluntary charity, poor relief and the casual poor, 1860–1905', in A. J. Kidd and K. W. Roberts (eds), *City, class and culture: studies of cultural production and social policy in Victorian Manchester*, Manchester 1985, 48–73

Kiernan, V., 'Evangelicalism and the French Revolution', *P&P* i (1952), 44–56

Koven, Seth, 'Borderlands: women, voluntary action, and child welfare in Britain, 1840 to 1914', in Seth Koven and Sonya Michel (eds), *Mothers of a new world: maternalist politics and the origin of welfare states*, London 1993, 94–135

—— 'Remembering and dismemberment: crippled children, wounded soldiers, and the Great War in Great Britain', *American Historical Review* xcix (1994), 1167–202

Laqueur, Thomas W., *Religion and respectability: Sunday schools and working-class culture*, London 1976

Laslett, Peter, 'Preface', in Pelling and Smith, *Life, death and the elderly*, pp. xiii–xvi

Levi-Strauss, Claude, 'The principle of reciprocity', in L. Coser and B. Rosenberg (eds), *Sociological theory*, New York 1965, 61–9

Lewis, Jane, 'Gender, the family and women's agency in the building of welfare states: the British case', *Social History* xix (1994), 37–55

Little, Kenneth, *Urbanisation as a social process: an essay on movement and change in contemporary Africa*, London 1974

Loudon, Irvine, *Medical care and the general practitioner, 1750–1850*, Oxford 1986

Marland, Hilary, *Medicine and society in Wakefield and Huddersfield, 1780–1870*, Cambridge 1987

Martin, Mary Clare, 'Women and philanthropy in Walthamstow and Leyton, 1740–1870', *London Journal* xix (1994), 119–50

Mauss, Marcel, *The gift*, Paris 1925, trans. I. Cunnison, repr. London 1967,

McCann, Phillip, 'Popular education, socialisation and social control: Spitalfields, 1812–1824', in McCann, *Popular education*, 1–40

—— (ed.), *Popular education and socialisation in the nineteenth century*, London 1977

McCord, N., 'Aspects of the relief of poverty in early nineteenth-century Britain', in Hartwell et al., *Long debate on poverty*, 91–109

McIntosh, Marjorie K., 'Local responses to the poor in late medieval and Tudor England', *Continuity and Change* iii (1988), 209–45

McRee, Ben R., 'Charity and gild solidarity in late medieval England', *Journal of British Studies* xxxii (1993), 195–225

Melling, J., 'Welfare capitalism and the origins of the welfare states', *Social History* xvii (1992), 453–78

Midgley, Clare, *Women against slavery: the British campaigns, 1780–1860*, London 1992

——— 'Anti-slavery and feminism in nineteenth-century Britain', *Gender and History* v (1993), 343–62

Moffrey, R. W., *A century of Oddfellowship*, Manchester 1910

Money, John, 'Freemasonry and the fabric of loyalism in Hanoverian England', in Hellmuth, *Transformation of political culture*, 235–71

Morris, R. J., 'Voluntary societies and British urban elites, 1780–1850: an analysis', *HJ* xxvi (1983), 95–118

——— 'Clubs, societies and associations', in Thompson, *Cambridge social history of Britain*, iii. 395–443

Moscucci, Ornella, *The science of woman: gynaecology and gender in England, 1800–1929*, Cambridge 1990

Newby, Howard, 'The deferential dialectic', *Comparative Studies in Society and History* xvii (1975), 139–64

Owen, David, *English philanthropy, 1660–1960*, London 1964

Parker, Julia, *Women and welfare*, London 1989

Parry-Jones, William, *The trade in lunacy: a study of private madhouses in England in the eighteenth and nineteenth centuries*, London 1972

Pelling, Margaret and Richard M. Smith (eds), *Life, death and the elderly: historical perspectives*, London 1991

Pickstone, John V., *Medicine and industrial society*, Manchester 1985

Pinker, Robert, *English hospital statistics, 1861–1938*, London 1966

Pooley, Marilyn E. and Colin G. Pooley, 'Health, society and environment in Victorian Manchester', in Robert Woods and John Woodward (eds), *Urban disease and mortality in nineteenth century England*, London 1984, 148–75

Porter, Roy, *Mind forg'd manacles: a history of madness in England from the Restoration to the Regency*, London 1987

——— 'The gift relation: philanthropy and provincial hospitals in eighteenth-century England', in Granshaw and Porter, *The hospital in history*, 149–78

Porter, Roy, *Disease, medicine and society in England, 1550–1860*, London 1993

Prochaska, Frank, *Women and philanthropy in nineteenth-century England*, Oxford 1980

——— *The voluntary impulse*, London 1988

——— 'Philanthropy', in Thompson, *Cambridge social history of Britain*, iii. 357–93

——— *Philanthropy and the hospitals of London: the King's fund, 1897–1990*, Oxford 1992

Risse, Guenter B., *Hospital life in Enlightenment Scotland: care and teaching at the Royal Infirmary of Edinburgh*, Cambridge 1986

Roberts, M. J. D., 'Reshaping the gift relationship: the London Mendicity Society and the suppression of begging in England, 1818–1869', *International Review of Social History* xxxvi (1991), 201–31

Robson, Derek, *Some aspects of education in Cheshire in the eighteenth century* (Chetham Society 3rd ser. xiii, 1966)

Roe, James Moulton, *The British and Foreign Bible Society, 1905–1954*, London 1965

Rose, Craig, 'London's charity schools, 1690–1730', *History Today* xl (1990), 17–23

——— ' "Seminaries of faction and rebellion": Jacobites, Whigs and the London charity schools, 1716–1724', *HJ* xxxiv (1991), 831–55

Ross, Ellen, 'Survival networks: women's neighbourhood sharing in London before World War I', *History Workshop Journal* xv (1983), 4–27

——— 'Hungry children: housewives and London charity, 1870–1918', in Peter Mandler (ed.), *The uses of charity: the poor on relief in the nineteenth-century metropolis*, Philadelphia 1990, 161–96

Ross, Jack C., 'Toward a reconstruction of voluntary association theory', *British Journal of Sociology* xxiii (1972), 20–30

Rubin, Miri, *Charity and community in medieval Cambridge*, Cambridge 1987

——— 'Development and change in English hospitals, 1100–1500', in Granshaw and Porter, *Hospital in history*, 41–59

Ryan, Mary P., *Cradle of the middle class: the family in Oneida County, New York*, Cambridge 1981

Salamon, Lester M., *Partners in public service: government-nonprofit relations in the modern welfare state*, London 1995

Sanderson, Michael, *Education, economic change and society in England, 1780–1870*, London 1983

Schofield, R. S., 'Dimensions of illiteracy, 1750–1850', *Explorations in Economic History* x (1973), 437–57

Schwartz, B., 'The social psychology of the gift', *American Journal of Sociology* lxxiii (1967), 1–11

Scull, Andrew T., *Museums of madness: the social organisation of insanity in nineteenth-century England*, London 1979

Searby, P., 'The relief of the poor in Coventry, 1830–63', *HJ* xx (1977), 345–61

Seed, John, 'Unitarianism, political economy and the antinomies of liberal culture in Manchester, 1830–50', *Social History* vii (1982), 1–25

Seldon, Arthur (ed.), *Re-privatising welfare: after the lost century*, London 1996

Showalter, Elaine, *The female malady: women, madness and English culture, 1830–1980*, London 1987

Simmel, Georg, 'The poor', and 'Faithfulness and gratitude', in K. Wolff (ed.), *The sociology of Georg Simmel*, trans. C. Jacobson, Glencoe, Ill. 1950, repr. New York 1964

Simon, Brian, *Studies in the history of education, 1780–1870*, London 1960

Simon, Joan, 'Was there a charity school movement?: the Leicestershire evidence', in Brian Simon (ed.), *Education in Leicestershire, 1640–1940*, Leicester 1968, 55–100

Simey, Margaret, *Charity rediscovered: a study of philanthropic effort in nineteenth-century Liverpool*, Liverpool 1992, first publ. as *Charitable effort in Liverpool in the nineteenth century*, Liverpool 1951

Slack, Paul, *Poverty and policy in Tudor and Stuart England*, London 1988

Smelser, Neil J. *Social paralysis and social change: British working-class education in the nineteenth century*, Oxford 1991

Smith, F. B., *The people's health, 1830–1910*, London 1979

Smith, Richard M., 'The manorial court and the elderly tenant in late medieval England', in Pelling and Smith, *Life, death and the elderly*, 39–61

Stephens, W. B., 'Literacy studies: a survey', in Stephens, *History of literacy*, 1–6

——— *Education, literacy and society, 1830–70*, Manchester 1987

———— (ed.), *Studies in the history of literacy: England and North America*, Leeds 1983

Stone, Lawrence, 'Literacy and education in England 1640–1900', *P&P* xlii (1969), 69–139

Sturt, Mary, *The education of the people*, London 1967

Summers, Ann, 'A home from home: women's philanthropic work in the nineteenth century', in Sandra Burman (ed.), *Fit work for women*, London 1979, 33–63

Supple, Barry, 'Legislation and virtue: an essay on working-class self-help and the state in the early nineteenth century', in N. McKendrick (ed.), *Historical perspectives: studies in English thought and society, in honour of J. H. Plumb*, London 1974, 211–54

Szreter, Simon, 'The importance of social intervention in Britain's mortality decline, c. 1850–1914: a re-interpretation of the role of public health', *Social History of Medicine* i (1988), 1–37

Taylor, Clare, *British and American abolitionists: an episode in transatlantic understanding*, Edinburgh 1974

Temperley, Howard, *British anti-slavery, 1833–70*, London 1972

Thane, Pat, *Foundations of the welfare state*, 2nd edn, Harlow 1996

Thomson, David, 'Welfare and the historians', in Lloyd Bonfield, Richard M. Smith and Keith Wrightson (eds), *The world we have gained: histories of population and social structure*, Oxford 1980, 355–78

———— ' "I am not my father's keeper": families and the elderly in nineteenth century England', *Law and History Review* ii (1984), 267–86

———— 'The decline of social welfare: falling state support for the elderly since early Victorian times', *Ageing and Society* iv (1984), 451–82

Titmuss, R. M., *The gift relationship*, London 1970

Tompson, R., *The Charity Commission and the age of reform*, London 1979

Vincent, David, *Literacy and popular culture in England, 1750–1914*, Cambridge 1989

Waddington, Keir, ' "Grasping gratitude": charity and hospital finance in late-Victorian London', in Daunton *Charity, self-interest and welfare*

Wagg, H. J. and M. Thomas, *A chronological survey of work for the blind*, London 1932

Walter, John, 'The social economy of dearth in early modern England', in John Walter and Roger Schofield (eds), *Famine, disease and the social order in early modern society*, Cambridge 1989, 75–128

Walton, John K., 'Lunacy in the industrial revolution: a study of asylum admissions in Lancashire, 1848–1850', *Journal of Social History* xiii (1979), 1–22

Weisbrod, Burton A., 'Toward a theory of the voluntary non-profit sector in a three-sector economy', in Edmund S. Phelps (ed.), *Altruism, morality and economic theory*, New York 1975, 171–95

Weisser, Michael R., *A brotherhood of memory: Jewish Landmanschaften in the New World*, New York 1985

West, E. G., 'Resource allocation and growth in early nineteenth-century British education', *EcHR* 2nd ser. xxxiii (1970), 68–95

Whelan, Robert, *The corrosion of charity: from moral renewal to contract culture*, London 1996

Williams, Karel, *From pauperism to poverty*, London 1981

Wilson, Kathleen, 'Urban culture and political activism in Hanoverian England: an example of voluntary hospitals', in Hellmuth, *Transformation of political culture*, 165–84

Wohl, Anthony S., *Endangered lives*, London 1983

Woodroofe, Kathleen, *From charity to social work in England and the United States*, London 1962

Woods, Robert, 'Mortality and sanitary conditions in late nineteenth-century Birmingham', in Woods and Woodward, *Urban disease and mortality*, 176–202

———— and John Woodward (eds), *Urban disease and mortality in nineteenth-century England*, London 1984

Woodward, John, *To do the sick no harm: a study of the British voluntary hospital system to 1875*, London 1974

———— 'Medicine and the city: the nineteenth-century experience', in Woods and Woodward, *Urban disease and mortality*, 65–78

Woolf, Stuart, 'The Société de Charité Maternelle, 1788–1815', in Barry and Jones, *Medicine and charity*, 98–112

Wuthnow, Robert, 'The voluntary sector: legacy of the past, hope for the future?', in Robert Wuthnow (ed.), *The voluntary sector in comparative perspective*, Princeton 1991, 3–29

Post-1900: General works

Anderson, Michael, *Family structure in nineteenth-century Lancashire*, Cambridge 1971

———— 'The social implications of demographic change', in Thompson, *Cambridge social history of Britain 1750–1950*, ii. 1–70

Aries, Phillippe and George Duby (eds), *The history of private life*, iv, Cambridge, Mass. 1990

Armstrong, Alan, *Stability and change in an English county town: a social study of York, 1801–51*, Cambridge 1974

Aspinall, Arthur, *Lord Brougham and the Whig party*, Manchester 1927

Bailey, Peter, ' "Will the real Bill Banks please stand up?": towards a role analysis of mid-Victorian working-class respectability', *Journal of Social History* xiii (1979), 336–53

Banks, Olive, *Becoming a feminist: the social origins of first wave feminism*, Brighton 1986

Barnett, S. A., *Canon Barnett, his life, work and friends*, iii, London 1918

Barry, Jonathan, 'Provincial town culture, 1640–1780: urbane or civic?', in A. Wear and J. H. Pittock (eds), *Interpretation and cultural history*, Basingstoke 1991, 193–234

———— 'Introduction' and 'Bourgeois collectivism?: urban association and the middling sort', in Jonathan Barry and Christopher Brooks (eds), *The middling sort of people: culture, society and politics in England, 1550–1800*, London 1994, 1–27, 84–112

———— 'Review article: the making of the middle class?', *P&P* cxlv (1995), 194–208

Bebbington, D. W., *Evangelicalism in modern Britain: a history from the 1730s to the 1980s*, London 1989

Belchem, John, *'Orator' Hunt: Henry Hunt and English working-class radicalism*, Oxford 1985

Borsay, P., *The English urban renaissance: culture and society in the provincial town, 1660–1770*, Oxford 1989

Bradley, Ian, *The call to seriousness: the evangelical impact on the Victorians*, London 1976

Bradley, James, *Religion, revolution and English radicalism: nonconformity in eighteenth-century politics and society*, Cambridge 1990

Bramwell, Bill, 'Public space and local communities: the example of Birmingham, 1840–1880', in Gerry Kearns and Charles J. Withers (eds), *Urbanising Britain: essays on class and community in the nineteenth century*, Cambridge 1991, 31–54

Brewer, John, *The sinews of power*, London 1989

Brewer, N. J., 'Commercialisation and politics', in N. J. McKendrick, J. Brewer and J. H. Plumb, *The birth of a consumer society: the commercialisation of eighteenth-century England*, London 1982

Brown, Ford K., *Fathers of the Victorian: the age of Wilberforce*, Cambridge 1961

Burgess, Clive, ' "A fond thing vainly invented": an essay on purgatory and pious motive in later medieval England', in Wright, *Parish, church and people*, 56–83

Bushaway, Bob, *By rite: custom, ceremony and community in England, 1700–1880*, London 1982

Cain, P. J. and A. G. Hopkins, *British imperialism: innovation and expansion, 1688–1914*, London 1993

Cannadine, David, *Lords and landlords: the aristocracy and the towns, 1774–1967*, Leicester 1980

Carr-Saunders, A. M. and P. A. Wilson, *The professions*, Oxford 1933

Clark, Peter, *The English alehouse: a social history, 1200–1830*, London 1983

Cole, G. D. H. and Raymond Postgate, *The common people, 1746–1938*, London 1938

Colley, Linda, 'Whose nation?: Class and national consciousness in Britain, 1750–1830', *P&P* cxiii (1986), 97–117

—— *Britons: forging the nation, 1707–1837*, Yale 1992

Corfield, P. J., 'Class by name and number in eighteenth-century Britain', in P. J. Corfield (ed.), *Language, history and class*, Oxford 1991, 101–30

—— *Power and the professions in Britain, 1700–1850*, London 1995

—— and Serena Kelly, ' "Giving directions to the town": the early town directories', *Urban History Yearbook* (1984), 22–35

Cott, Nancy F., *Bonds of womanhood: 'woman's sphere' in New England, 1780–1835*, London 1977

Crafts, N. F. R., *British economic growth during the industrial revolution*, Oxford 1985

Crossick, Geoffrey and Heinz-Gerhard Haupt, *The petite bourgeoisie in Europe, 1780–1914: enterprise, family and independence*, London 1995

Cunningham, Hugh, 'Leisure and culture' in Thompson, *Cambridge social history of Britain*, ii. 279–339

—— *The children of the poor: representations of childhood since the seventeenth century*, Oxford 1991

Davidoff, Leonore and Catherine Hall, *Family fortunes: men and women of the English middle class, 1780–1850*, London 1987

Dickson, P., *The financial revolution in England*, London 1967

Dictionary of National Biography

Earle, Peter, *The making of the English middle class: business, society and family life in London, 1660–1730*, London 1989

Eastwood, David, *Governing rural England: tradition and transformation in local government, 1780–1840*, Oxford 1994

Engels, Frederick, *The condition of the working class in England*, London 1882

English, Barbara, *The great landowners of East Yorkshire, 1530–1910*, London 1990

Field, Frank, *Making welfare work: reconstructing welfare for the millenium*, London 1995

Filler, Louis, *The crusade against slavery, 1830–1860*, London 1960

Finlayson, G. B. A. M., 'The politics of municipal reform, 1835', *EHR* lxxxi (1966), 673–92

Flinn, M., *The history of the British coal industry*, iii, Oxford 1984

Foster, John, *Class struggle in the industrial revolution: early industrial capitalism in three English towns*, London 1974

Fraser, Derek, *Urban politics in Victorian England: the structure of politics in Victorian cities*, Leicester, 1976

—————— *Power and authority in the Victorian city*, Oxford 1979

Gash, Norman, *Politics in the age of Peel*, London 1952

Gleadle, Kathryn, *The early feminists: radical Unitarians and the emergence of the women's rights movement*, London 1995

Gunn, S., 'The "failure" of the Victorian middle class: a critique', in J. Wolff and J. Seed (eds), *The culture of capital*, Manchester 1988, 17–43

Hall, Catherine, *White, male and middle-class: explorations in feminism and history*, Cambridge 1992

—————— 'From Greenland's icy mountains . . . to Afric's golden sand': ethnicity, race and nation in mid nineteenth-century England', *Gender and History* v (1993), 212–30

Hall, Donald E. (ed.), *Muscular Christianity: embodying the Victorian age*, Cambridge 1994

Ham, C., *Public, private or community: what next for the NHS?*, London 1996

Hannam, June, *Isabella Ford*, Oxford 1989

Hardy, Thomas, *Tess of the D'Urbevilles*, London 1891

Hargreaves, E., *The national debt*, London 1930

Harris, José, *Private lives, public spirit: Britain, 1870–1914*, Oxford 1993, repr. Harmondsworth 1994

Harrison, Brian, *Peacable kingdom: stability and change in modern Britain*, Oxford 1983

Harvey, Barbara, *Living and dying in England, 1100–1540*, Oxford 1993

Hennock, E. P., *Fit and proper persons: ideal and reality in nineteenth-century urban government*, London 1973

Hills, Philip, 'Division and cohesion in the nineteenth-century middle class: the case of Ipswich, 1830–70' *Urban History Yearbook* (1987), 42–50

Hilton, Boyd, *The age of atonement*, Oxford 1988

Hirst, Paul, *Associative democracy: new forms of economic and social governance*, Oxford 1994

Hobsbawm, E. J., *Labouring men: studies in the history of labour*, London 1964

Hollis, Patricia, *Women in public: the women's movement, 1850–1900*, London 1979

Hoskins, W. G., *Local history in England*, London 1959, 3rd edn, London 1984

Howkins, Alun, 'The taming of Whitsun in nineteenth-century Oxfordshire', in Eileen Yeo and Stephen Yeo (eds), *Popular culture and class conflict, 1590–1914: explorations in the history of labour and leisure*, London 1981, 187–208

Ignatieff, Michael, *A just measure of pain: the penitentiary in the industrial revolution, 1750–1850*, London 1978

Inglis, K. S., 'Patterns of religious worship in 1851', *Journal of Ecclesiastical History* xi (1960), 74–86

Jones, Gareth Stedman, *Outcast London: a study in the relationship between classes in Victorian society*, Oxford 1971

—— *Languages of class: studies in English working-class history, 1832–1982*, Cambridge 1983

Joyce, Patrick, *Visions of the people: industrial England and the question of class, 1848–1914*, Cambridge 1991

Kent, John, 'The role of religion in the cultural structure of the later Victorian city', *Transactions of the Royal Historical Society* 5th ser. xxiii (1972), 153–73

Koditschek, Theodore, *Class formation and urban-industrial society: Bradford, 1750–1850*, Cambridge 1990

Lambert, W. R., *Drink and society in Victorian Wales, c. 1820–c. 1895*, Cardiff 1983

Landes, Joan B., *Women and the public sphere in the age of the French Revolution*, Ithaca 1988, 117–21

Langford, Paul, *A polite and commercial people: England, 1727–83*, Oxford 1989

Law, C. M., 'Some notes on the urban population of England and Wales in the eighteenth century', *The Local Historian* x (1972), 13–26

Lee, C. H., *The British economy since 1700: a macro-economic perspective*, Cambridge 1986

Leeson, R. A., *Travelling brothers: the six centuries' road from craft fellowship to trade unionism*, London 1979

Lewis, Jane, 'Gender, the family and women's agency in the building of welfare states: the British case', *Social History* xix (1994), 37–55.

Lis, Catharina and Hugo Soly, 'Neighbourhood social change in West European cities, sixteenth to nineteenth centuries', *International Review of Social History* xxxviii (1993), 1–30

McClelland, Keith, 'Masculinity and the "representative artisan" in Britain, 1850–80', in Tosh and Roper, *Manful assertions*, 74–91

McKendrick, N., J. Brewer and J. H. Plumb, *The birth of a consumer society: the commercialisation of eighteenth-century England*, London 1982

McKeown, Thomas, *The modern rise of population*, London 1976

Magarey, Susan, 'The invention of juvenile delinquency in early nineteenth-century England', *Labour History* xxxiv (1978), 11–27

Mangan, J. A. and James Walvin (eds), *Manliness and morality*, Manchester 1987

'Mass Observation', *The pub and the people, a Worktown study*, London 1943

Matthias, Peter, *The brewing industry in England, 1700–1830*, Cambridge 1959

Meehan, E., *Civil society*, Swindon 1995

Meller, H. E., *Leisure and the changing city, 1870–1914*, London 1976

Mitchell, B. R., *British historical statistics*, Cambridge 1988

Morris, R. J., 'The middle class and the property cycle during the industrial revolution', in T. C. Smout (ed.), *The search for wealth and stability*, London 1979, 91–113

────── *Class, sect and party: the making of the British middle class, Leeds, 1820–1850*, Manchester 1990

Mort, Frank, *Dangerous sexualities: medico-moral politics in England since 1830*, London 1987

Neal, Frank, *Sectarian violence: the Liverpool experience, 1819–1914*, Manchester 1988

Neuburg, V. E., *Popular literature*, London 1977

New, Chester, *The life of Henry Brougham to 1830*, Oxford 1961

Norton, Jane E., *Guide to the national and provincial directories of England and Wales, excluding London, published before 1856* (Royal Historical Society Guides and Handbooks v, 1950)

O'Gorman, Frank, 'Campaign rituals and ceremonies: the social meaning of elections in England 1780–1860', *P&P* cxxxv (1992), 79–105

Pareto, V., *The mind and society: a treatise on general sociology*, trans. Andrea Bongiorno and Arthur Livingstone, London 1935

Pearson, Geoffrey, *Hooligan: a history of respectable fears*, London 1983

Perkin, Harold, *Origins of modern English society*, London 1969

────── *The rise of professional society: England since 1880*, London 1989

Phillips, J. A., *Electoral behaviour in unreformed England: plumpers, splitters and straights*, Princeton 1982

────── *The Great Reform Bill in the boroughs: English electoral behaviour, 1818–41*, Oxford 1992

Pigott, Stuart, *The Druids*, London 1968

Poynter, J. R., *Society and pauperism: English ideas on poor relief, 1795–1834*, London 1969

Prothero, I., *Artisans and politics in early nineteenth-century London*, Chatham 1979

Pryce, W. T. R., 'Towns and their regional settings', in W. T. R. Pryce (ed.), *From family history to community history*, Cambridge 1994, 131–8

Putnam, R. D., *Making democracy work: civic traditions in modern Italy*, Princeton 1993

────── 'The prosperous community: social capital and public life', *The American Prospect*, Spring 1993, 35–42

Reid, Alistair, 'Intelligent artisans and aristocrats of labour: the essays of Thomas Wright', in J. Winter (ed.), *The working class in modern British history: essays in honour of Henry Pelling*, Cambridge 1983, 171–86

Reid, Caroline, 'Middle-class values and working-class culture in nineteenth-century Sheffield: the pursuit of respectability', in S. Pollard and C. Holmes (eds), *Essays in the economic and social history of South Yorkshire*, Sheffield 1976, 275–95

Richardson, Ruth, *Death, dissection and the destitute*, London 1987

Roe, James Moulton, *The British and Foreign Bible Society, 1905–1954*, London 1965

Rogers, Nicholas, *Whigs and cities: popular politics in the age of Walpole and Pitt*, Oxford 1989

Rostow, W. W., 'Cycles in the British economy: 1790–1914', in Derek Aldcroft and Peter Fearon (eds), *British economic fluctuations, 1790–1939*, London 1972, 74–96

Rubinstein, W. D., 'Wealth elites and class structure in Britain', *P&P* lxxvi (1977), 99–126

———— 'The end of "Old Corruption" in Britain, 1780–1860', *P&P* ci (1983), 55–86

———— 'The size and distribution of the English middle classes in 1860', *Historical Research* lxi (1988), 65–89

———— (ed.), *Elites and the wealthy in modern British history*, Brighton 1987

Scarisbrick, J. J., *The Reformation and the English people*, Oxford 1984

Scott, Joan Wallach, *Gender and the politics of history*, New York 1988

Seed, John, 'Theologies of power: Unitarians and the social relations of religious discourse, 1800–50', in R. J. Morris (ed.), *Class, power and social structure in British nineteenth-century towns*, Leicester 1986, 107–56

———— 'From 'middling sort' to middle class in late eighteenth- and early nineteenth-century England', in M. L. Bush (ed.), *Social orders and social classes in Europe since 1500*, London 1992, 114–35

Segal, Lynne, *Slow motion: changing masculinities, changing men*, London 1990

Semmel, Bernard, *The Methodist revolution*, London 1974

Shanley, Mary Lyndon, *Feminism, marriage and the law in Victorian England, 1850–1895*, London 1989

Shaw, Gareth, 'The content and reliability of nineteenth-century trade directories', *The Local Historian* xiii (1978), 205–9

Staves, Susan, *Married women's separate property in England, 1660–1833*, London 1990

Summers, Anne, 'Edwardian militarism', in Raphael Samuel (ed.), *Patriotism: the making and unmaking of British identity*, I: *History and politics*, London 1989, 236–56

Supple, Barry, *The Royal Exchange Assurance: a history of British insurance, 1720–1970*, Cambridge 1970

Tanner, N. P., *The Church in late medieval Norwich*, Toronto 1984

Tate, W., *The parish chest*, Cambridge 1946

Taylor, Barbara, *Eve and the New Jerusalem*, London 1983

———— and F. Moghaddam, *Theories of inter-group relations: international social psychological perspectives*, New York 1987

Tholfsen, Trygve R., *Working-class radicalism in mid-Victorian England*, London 1976

Thompson, E. P., *The making of the English working class*, London 1963

———— *Customs in common*, London 1991

Thompson, F. M. L., *English landed society in the nineteenth century*, London 1963

———— 'Social control in Victorian Britain', *EcHR* xxxiv (1981), 189–208.

———— 'Town and city', in Thompson, *Cambridge social history*, i. 1–86

———— (ed.), *The Cambridge social history of Britain, 1750–1950*, I: *Regions and communities*; II: *People and their environment*; III: *Social agencies and institutions*, Cambridge 1990

Torrance, John, 'Social class and bureaucratic innovation: the commissioners for examining the public accounts, 1780–1781', *P&P* lxxviii (1978), 56–81

Tosh, John and Michael Roper (eds), *Manful assertions: masculinities in Britain since 1800*, London 1991

Trainor, Richard H., *Black Country elites: the exercise of authority in an industrial area, 1830–1900*, Oxford 1993

Tranter, N. L., *Population and society, 1750–1940*, London 1985

Trebilcock, Clive, *Phoenix Assurance and the development of British insurance*, I: *1782–1870*, Cambridge 1985

Trevelyan, G. M., *English social history*, London 1942, rev. edn Harmondsworth 1967

Trudgill, Eric, *Madonnas and magdalens: the origin and development of Victorian sexual attitudes*, London 1976

Vance, Norman, *The sinews of the spirit*, Cambridge 1985

Vickery, Amanda, 'Golden age to separate spheres?: a review of the categories and chronology of English women's history', *HJ* xxxvi (1993), 383–414

Vincent, John, *The formation of the Liberal Party*, London 1966

———— *Pollbooks: how Victorians voted*, Cambridge 1967

Wahrman, Dror, 'National society, communal culture: an argument about the recent historiography of eighteenth-century Britain', *Social History* xvii (1992), 43–72

———— 'Virtual representation: parliamentary reporting and languages of class in the 1790s', *P&P* cxxxvi (1992), 83–113

Walkowitz, Judith R., *Prostitution and Victorian society: women, class and the state*, Cambridge 1980

Walsh, John, 'Origins of the Evangelical revival', in G. V. Bennett and J. D. Walsh (eds), *Essays in modern church history*, London 1966, 136–62

Webb, Sidney and Beatrice Webb, *The parish and the county*, first publ. London 1906, London 1963

———— *English local government: statutory authorities for special purposes*, London 1922

Westlake, H. F., *The parish gilds of mediaeval England*, London 1919

Williams, Raymond, *Keywords*, Glasgow 1976, 45–6.

Wilson, Adrian, 'A critical portrait of social history', in Adrian Wilson (ed.), *Rethinking social history: English society, 1570–1920, and its interpretation*, Manchester 1993, 9–58

Woodward, E. L., *The age of reform, 1815–1870*, Oxford 1938

Wrigley, E. A., *Continuity, chance and change: the character of the industrial revolution in England*, Cambridge 1988

———— 'Urban growth and agricultural change: England and the continent in the early modern period', in P. Borsay (ed.), *The eighteenth-century town: a reader in English urban history*, London 1990, 39–82

———— and R. S. Schofield, *The population history of England, 1541–1871: a reconstruction*, Cambridge 1981

Wright, S. J. (ed.), *Parish, church and people*, London 1988

Zegger, Robert E., *John Cam Hobhouse: a political life, 1819–1852*, Columbia 1973

Unpublished works

Baigent, E., 'Bristol society in the later eighteenth century with special reference to the handling by computer of fragmentary historical sources', unpubl. DPhil. diss. Oxford 1985

Barry, Jonathan, 'The cultural life of Bristol, 1640–1775', unpubl. DPhil. diss. Oxford 1985

Berry, Amanda, 'Patronage, funding and the hospital patient, c. 1750–1815: three English regional case studies', unpubl. DPhil. diss. Oxford 1995

Boss, Bernice, 'The Bristol Infirmary, 1761–2, and the "laborious-industrious poor" ', unpubl. PhD diss. Bristol 1995

Brett, Peter, 'The Liberal middle classes and politics in three provincial towns – Newcastle, Bristol and York – c. 1812–1841', unpubl. PhD diss. Durham 1991

Campbell, M. J., 'The development of literacy in Bristol and Gloucester, 1755–1870', unpubl. PhD diss. Bath 1980

Carter, D. J., 'Social and political influence of Bristol churches, 1830–1914', unpubl. MLitt diss. Bristol 1971

Fissell, Mary E., 'The physic of charity: health and welfare in the West Country, 1690–1834', unpubl. PhD diss. Pennsylvania 1988

Gorsky, Martin, 'Charity, mutuality and philanthropy: voluntary provision in Bristol, 1800–70', unpubl. PhD diss. Bristol 1995

Neve, M., 'Natural philosophy, medicine and the culture of science in provincial England: the cases of Bristol and Bath, 1790–1850, and Bath, 1750–1820', unpubl. PhD diss. London 1984

Rogers, F. H., 'The Bristol craft gilds during the sixteenth and seventeenth centuries', unpubl. MA diss. Bristol 1949

Walker, M. J., 'The extent of guild control of trades in England, c. 1660–1820', unpubl. PhD diss. Cambridge 1986

Whittle, Meg, 'Philanthropy in Preston: the changing face of charity in a nineteenth-century provincial town', unpubl. PhD diss. Lancaster 1990

Index